REAL WORLD

MACRO

TWENTY-THIRD EDITION

edited by

**Daniel Fireside,
John Miller, and the
Dollars & Sense
Collective**

REAL WORLD MACRO
TWENTY-THIRD EDITION

ISBN: 1-878585-59-2

Published by:
Economic Affairs Bureau, Inc.
Dollars and Sense
29 Winter Street
Boston, MA 02108
tel: 617-447-2177
dollars@dollarsandsense.org
www.dollarsandsense.org

Real World Macro is edited by the *Dollars & Sense* collective, publishers of *Dollars & Sense* magazine and *Real World Micro*, *Real World Globalization*, *Current Economic Issues*, *Real World Banking*, *The Environment in Crisis*, *Grassroots Journalism*, *Introduction to Political Economy*, *Striking a Balance*, *Unlevel Playing Fields*, and *The Wealth Inequality Reader*.

The 2006 Collective: Beth Burgess, Esther Cervantes, Grace Chang, Faisal Chaudhry, Chuck Collins, Arthur Conquest, Daniel Fireside, Ellen Frank, Amy Gluckman, Tyler Hauck, Mary Jirmanus, Toussaint Losier, James McBride, John Miller, Laura Orlando, Alejandro Reuss, Brian Riley, Chris Sturr, Chris Tilly, Ramaa Vasudevan, Jeanne Winner, and James Woolman.

Production: Alyssa Hassan

Manufactured by Vision Lithographics
Printed in U.S.A.

CONTENTS

Introduction 1

CHAPTER 1: MEASURING ECONOMIC PERFORMANCE
Introduction   3
1.1   High and Dry: The Economic Recovery Fails to Deliver   *John Miller*   5
1.2   The Growth Consensus Unravels   *Jonathan Rowe*   10
1.3   Wages for Housework: The Movement and the Numbers   *John Miller and Lena Graber*   14
1.4   Unemployment Rate Deception   *Eoghan Stafford*   16
1.5   Ruling the Empire   *Alejandro Reuss*   17
1.6   Tax Cuts for the Rich or Public Programs for Everyone?   *Michelle Sheehan*   19

CHAPTER 2: WEALTH, INEQUALITY AND POVERTY
Introduction   20
2.1   Wealth Inequality by the Numbers   *Dollars & Sense and United for a Fair Economy*   21
2.2   Slow Wage Growth but Soaring Profits in the Economic Recovery   *John Miller*   23
2.3   Measures of Poverty   *Ellen Frank*   24
2.4   The Death of Horatio Alger   *Paul Krugman*   25
2.5   Geese, Golden Eggs, and Traps: Why Inequality Is Bad for the Economy   *Chris Tilly*   27
2.6   Transforming the Engines of Inequality   *William Greider*   30
2.7   Rich and Poor in the Global Economy   *Interview with Bob Sutcliffe*   32

CHAPTER 3: SAVINGS AND INVESTMENT
Introduction   36
3.1   Boosting Investment: The Overrated Influence of Interest Rates   *Gretchen McClain and Randy Albelda*   37
3.2   Who Decides Stock Prices?   *Ellen Frank*   39
3.3   No More Savings: The Case for Social Wealth   *Ellen Frank*   40
3.4   Bubble Trouble   *Dean Baker*   43
3.5   Burlington Busts the Affordable Housing Debate   *Daniel Fireside*   44
3.6   Labor's Capital: Putting Pension Wealth to Work for Workers   *Adria Scharf*   46

CHAPTER 4: FISCAL POLICY, DEFICITS, AND DEBT
Introduction   49
4.1   What Spending Boom?   *John Miller*   50
4.2   Tax Cut Time Bomb   *Adria Scharf*   52
4.3 $262 Billion: Case Closed?   *John Miller*   53
4.4   Don't the Rich Pay a Lot of Taxes?   *Ellen Frank*   55
4.5   The Tax Cut Con   *Paul Krugman*   56
4.6   Social Security Isn't Broken   *Doug Orr*   59
4.7   The Social Security Administration's Cracked Crystal Ball   *John Miller*   62
4.8   African Americans and Social Security   *William Spriggs*   64
4.9   Bush Strikes Out on Health Care   *Elise Gould*   67
4.10   The Case Against Privatizing National Security   *Ann Markusen*   69

CHAPTER 5: MONETARY POLICY AND FINANCIAL MARKETS
Introduction   73
5.1   What Is Money?   *Doug Orr*   74
5.2   The Decline of the Dollar System   *James K. Galbraith*   76

5.3   Focus on the Fed   *Doug Orr and Ellen Frank*   77

5.4   How Do Fiscal and Monetary Policy Compare?   *Arthur MacEwan*   81

5.5   The Discount Rate   *Ellen Frank*   82

5.6   Bernanke's Dilemma   *William Greider*   83

5.7   Transforming the Fed   *Robert Pollin*   84

CHAPTER 6: UNEMPLOYMENT AND INFLATION

Introduction   87

6.1   The "Natural Rate" of Unemployment: It's All About Class Conflict   *Robert Pollin*   88

6.2   Raw Deal for Workers   *Chris Tilly*   91

6.3   Missing Jobs Still Lost   *John Miller*   94

6.4   Offshoring by the Numbers   *Angel Chen and Adria Scharf*   96

6.5   Black Workers Need More than an Economic Boom   *William M. Rodgers III*   97

6.6   Where is the North of Today?   *Attieno Davis*   99

6.7   What Are the Real Costs of Inflation—and to Whom?   *Bryan Snyder*   100

CHAPTER 7: PERSPECTIVES ON MACROECONOMIC POLICY

Introduction   102

7.1   The Revenge of the Classics   *John Miller and Gina Neff*   103

7.2   What's Wrong with Neoliberalism? The Marx, Keynes, and Polanyi Problems   *Robert Pollin*   106

7.3   Life After Keynes   *Ellen Frank*   109

7.4   Opening Pandora's Box: The Basics of Marxist Economics   *Alejandro Reuss*   112

7.5   Under the Margins: Feminist Economists Look at Gender and Poverty   *Randy Albelda*   115

7.6   Marxian Class Analysis and Economics   *Richard Wolff*   120

CHAPTER 8: INTERNATIONAL TRADE AND FINANCE

Introduction   123

8.1   What is Globalization   *Arthur MacEwan*   125

8.2   The Gospel of Free Trade: The New Evangelists   *Arthur MacEwan*   129

8.3   Falling Off a Cliff   *Keith Yearman and Amy Gluckman*   132

8.4   Understanding the Trade Deficit   *Arthur MacEwan*   135

8.5   Free, Free at Last   *John Miller*   136

8.6   Dollar Anxiety   *John Miller*   138

8.7   Will the WTO Strike Out in Hong Kong?   *Deborah James*   141

8.8   CAFTA's Debt Trap   *Aldo Caliari*   143

8.9   China and the Global Economy   *Thomas I. Palley*   146

8.10   Sweatshops 101   *Dara O'Rourke*   150

8.11   Is It Oil?   *Arthur MacEwan*   153

8.12   Fair Trade and Farm Subsidies: How Big a Deal? Two Views   156
        Make Trade Fair   *Gawain Kripke* / False Promises on Trade   *Dean Baker and Mark Weisbrot*

Contributors   161

INTRODUCTION

THE TWO ECONOMIES

It sometimes seems that the United States has not one, but two economies. The first economy exists in economics textbooks and in the minds of many elected officials. It is an economy in which no one goes for long without work, families are rewarded with an ever-improving standard of living, and anyone who works hard can live the American Dream. In this economy, people are free and roughly equal, and each individual carefully looks after him- or herself, making uncoerced choices to advance their own economic interests. Government has some limited roles in this world, but it is increasingly marginal, since the macroeconomy is a self-regulating system of wealth generation.

The second economy is described in the writings of progressives, environmentalists, union supporters, and consumer advocates—as well as honest business writers who recognize that the real world does not always conform to textbook models. This second economy features vast disparities of income, wealth, and power. It is an economy where economic instability and downward mobility are facts of life. Jobs disappear, workers suffer long spells of unemployment, and new jobs seldom afford the same standard of living as those lost. As for the government, it sometimes adopts policies that ameliorate the abuses of capitalism, and other times does just the opposite, but it is always an active and essential participant in economic life.

If you are reading this introduction, you are probably a student in an introductory college course in macroeconomics. Your textbook will introduce you to the first economy, the harmonious world of self-regulating stability. *Real World Macro* will introduce you to the second.

WHY "REAL WORLD" MACRO?

A standard economics textbook is full of powerful concepts. It is also, by its nature, a limited window on the economy. What is taught in most introductory macroeconomics courses today is a relatively narrow set of concepts. Inspired by classical economic theory, most textbooks depict an inherently stable economy in little need of government intervention. But fifty years ago, textbooks were very different. Keynesian economic theory, which holds that government action can and must stabilize modern monetized economies, occupied a central place in introductory textbooks. Even Marxist economics, with its piercing analysis of class structure and instability in capitalism, appeared regularly on the pages of those textbooks. The contraction of economics education has turned some introductory courses into little more than celebrations of today's economy as "the best of all possible worlds."

Real World Macro, designed as a supplement to a standard macroeconomics textbook, is dedicated to widening the scope of economic inquiry. Its articles rub mainstream theory up against reality by providing vivid, real-world illustrations of economic concepts. And where most texts uncritically present the key assumptions and propositions of traditional macroeconomic theory, *Real World Macro* asks provocative questions: What are alternative propositions about how the economy operates and who it serves? What difference do such propositions make? What might actually constitute the best of all possible macroeconomic worlds?

For instance, *Real World Macro* questions the conventional wisdom about economic problems such as inflation, asking who is hurt and who benefits. While mainstream textbooks readily allow that inflation favors debtors over creditors, they create the impression that inflation is equally bad for workers, employers, and investors. But a fast-growing economy that pushes up prices also tightens labor markets, strengthening the economic position of workers and threatening investors, whose asset values are eroded by rising prices.

Similarly, when the Fed prioritizes price stability over employment, monetary policy does not serve us all, as most textbooks suggest, but puts the interests of owners and bondholders ahead of the interests of workers and job-seekers. Those policies come at a considerable human cost. Researchers have found that with every one percentage point increase in the U.S. unemployment rate, 920 more people commit suicide, 650 commit homicide, 20,000 suffer heart attacks, 500 die from heart and kidney disease and cirrhosis of the liver, 4,000 are admitted to state mental hospitals, and 3,300 are sent to state prisons.

William Vickery, the Nobel-prize winning economist, used his 1993 presidential address to the American Economics Association to advocate macroeconomic policies that would lower the unemployment rate to roughly 2%. Genuine full employment, Vickery argued, would bring about "a major reduction in the incidence of poverty, homelessness, sickness, and crime." We think that policies like this, and the alternative propositions that lie behind them, are worth debating—and that requires hearing a range of views.

WHAT'S IN THIS BOOK

Real World Macro is organized to follow the outline of a standard economics text. We have specifically keyed our table of contents to David Colander's *Economics* (6th edition) and its *Macroeconomics* "split," but since the topics covered by all major texts are similar, this reader is a good fit with other textbooks as well. Each chapter leads off with a brief introduction, including study questions for the entire chapter, and then provides several short articles from *Dollars & Sense* magazine that illustrate the chapter's key concepts—60 articles in all. In many cases, the articles have been updated or otherwise edited to heighten their relevance.

Here is a quick walk through the chapters.

Chapter 1, Measuring Economic Performance, starts off the volume by taking a critical look at the standard measures of economic activity. What do those measures actually tell us about the quality of life in today's economy, and what crucial aspects of economic life do they leave uncounted? This chapter also examines the current economic recovery and asks why it has created so few jobs and made so few people better off.

Chapter 2, Wealth, Inequality, and Poverty examines these two end products of today's economic growth. *Dollars & Sense* authors show who is accumulating wealth and who isn't, and argue that inequality is not a prerequisite to economic growth.

Chapter 3, Savings and Investment, peers inside the pump house of economic growth and comes up with some provocative questions. How are stock prices determined? What constitutes savings? What public policies have proven track record of promoting investment? And what role can pension funds play in promoting investment?

Chapter 4, Fiscal Policy, Deficits, and Debt, assesses current government spending and taxing policies. The chapter's authors argue that tax cuts for the rich, the new military buildup, a failed health care policy, and this year's proposals to privatize Social Security won't stimulate economic growth, but have already squandered budget surpluses that could have provided for social needs.

Chapter 5, Monetary Policy and Financial Markets, explains how the Fed conducts monetary policy. It asks whose interests the Fed serves: those who hold financial assets, or the rest of us, and how it can be transformed to better serve our needs.

Chapter 6, Unemployment and Inflation, reveals how macroeconomic policy that prioritizes price stability over employment puts the interests of owners and bondholders ahead of the interests of workers. The chapter begins with a critique of the "natural rate" of unemployment. It also looks at the effects of unemployment, inflation, and productivity growth on workers' bargaining power and living standards. It closes with a discussion of black unemployment rates, the jobless economic recovery, and outsourcing.

Chapter 7, Perspectives on Macroeconomic Policy, introduces alternatives to classical-inspired macroeconomic theory. It begins with a critical analysis of the New Classical economics claim that the macroeconomy is inherently stable and moves on to discuss Keynesian, Marxist, and feminist perspectives on macroeconomic theory and policy, and neoliberal economic policymaking.

Chapter 8, International Trade and Finance, critically assesses the prevailing neoliberal policy prescriptions for the global economy. The articles criticize globalization based on "free trade" and financial liberalization. They also look at the role of China in today's global economy and oil in the war in Iraq. Finally, the articles assess proposals to reform international financial institutions, eliminate sweatshop conditions, and bring about fair trade between developed countries and the developing world. Finally, the chapter considers the impact that the decline of the dollar will have on the global economy.

KEY TO COLANDER

In each chapter introduction, we provide a key that links our text to David Colander's *Economics*, 6th edition, and its macroeconomics "split," *Macroeconomics*, 6th edition. Professors and students using other textbooks should, of course, feel free to ignore these keys. Here is the summary key for the entire table of contents.

Here and in the individual chapter keys, *Economics* Chapter 1 is abbreviated "E1," and *Macroeconomics* Chapter 1 is abbreviated "M1."

Chapter 1—Colander chapters E2, E22, E23; or M2, M6, M7.

Chapter 2—Colander chapters E22-E26; or M6-M10.

Chapter 3—Colander chapters E24-E26, M34; or M8-M10, M19.

Chapter 4—Colander chapters E25-E26, E30-E31, E34; or M9-M10, M14-M15, M19.

Chapter 5—Colander chapters E27-E28, E34; or M11-M12, M19.

Chapter 6—Colander chapter E29; or M13.

Chapter 7—Colander chapters E22, E25-E26; or M6, M9-M10.

Chapter 8—Colander chapters E21 and E32-E33; or M16-M18.

CHAPTER 1

MEASURING ECONOMIC PERFORMANCE

INTRODUCTION

Most macroeconomics textbooks begin with a snapshot of today's economy as seen through the lens of the standard measures of economic performance. This chapter provides a different view of today's economy, one far more critical of current economic policy and performance that asks what the standard measures of economic performance really tell us.

In "High and Dry: The Economic Recovery Fails to Deliver," John Miller tracks the current economic recovery that began in November 2001. Despite its length and a heavy dose of economic stimulants—everything from tax cuts, record low interest rates, and massive military and prison spending—job creation in this recovery remains the worst on record. Miller argues that the recent growth spurt has done little to resolve the underlying problems of the post-bubble U.S. economy and is unlikely to create self-sustaining growth that will better the lives of most workers (Article 1.1).

Real GDP, or Gross Domestic Product adjusted for inflation, is the economist's measure of the value of economic output. Increases in real GDP define economic growth, and for economists, rising real GDP per capita shows that a nation is enjoying an improving standard of living. Our authors are not convinced. Jonathan Rowe argues that GDP actually counts environmental destruction, worsening health, and ruinous overconsumption as contributions to economic growth and national well-being (Article 1.2). While Rowe worries that GDP includes the wrong things, Lena Graber and John Miller discuss what it excludes: work in the home that is essential to economic well-being. They report that counting home-based work—from cleaning to child care—would add 33% to 112% to the GDP of industrialized economies and even more to the GDP of developing economies (Graber and Miller, Article 1.3). Finally, in "Unemployment Rate Deception," Eoghan Stafford argues that the official unemployment rate is artificially low and that a more accurate measure would increase the July 2003 rate by more than half (Article 1.4).

Of course, macroeconomics textbooks examine not only the ups and downs of the business cycle, but also trade-offs in economies whose resources are fully employed. Many present the famed trade-off between "guns" and "butter." Economists use a *production possibilities curve* to demonstrate the *opportunity cost* of devoting economic resources to certain kinds of production. For example, the opportunity cost of producing arms ("guns") is the set of social goods ("butter") that society must forego. That trade-off is being made today in the United States, and Alejandro Reuss presents a vivid depiction of its staggering social cost, as well as its global

political significance (Article 1.5). Michele Sheehan wraps up the chapter by weighing the opportunity cost of the Bush Administration's tax cuts for the rich in terms of public programs that might have been enacted instead (Article 1.6).

DISCUSSION QUESTIONS

1) (Article 1.1) How has the current economic expansion of the U.S. economy done when it comes to economic growth and creating jobs? Compare the outlook for the U.S. economy in "High and Dry" with the predictions for the U.S. economy of the most recent *Wall Street Journal* survey of blue-chip economists (published in the beginning of January and July of every year in the *Wall Street Journal*).

2) (Article 1.1) In what ways have the post-bubble U.S. economy and policy responses been similar to or different from those in Japan after that country's economic boom ended? Have U.S. policymakers been effective in counteracting the threat of economic stagnation and in improving the economic prospects of most people?

3) (Article 1.2) How is GDP is measured, and what does it represent? What are Rowe's criticisms of GDP? Do you find them convincing?

4) (Article 1.2) Rowe discusses the Genuine Progress Indicator (GPI) as an alternative measure of economic progress. What are the differences between GDP per capita and the GPI? Which do you think provides a better measure of economic progress, and why?

5) (Article 1.3) Wages for housework might sound outlandish, but what are the economic justifications for valuing work in the home? Do you find them persuasive?

6) (Article 1.3) Suppose we decided that home-based work

KEY TO COLANDER

E = Economics   M = Macroeconomics

This chapter is designed to be used with chapters E2 and E22-E23, or M2 and M6-M7.

Chapter E22 or M6 contains sections on dating business cycles and economic performance (the topic of Article 1.1) and measuring unemployment rates (the topic of Article 1.4).

Article 1.2 and 1.3 complement the section "Some Limitations of National Income Accounting" in chapter E23 or M7. Both Rowe and Colander discuess the Genuine Progress Incdicator.

Articles 1.5 and 1.6 go with the discussion of production possibilities curves in E2 and M2.

should be included in macroeconomic measures. That still leaves some practical questions. How should it be counted? And should work in the home be paid? If so, by whom?

7) (Article 1.4) Calculate the traditional Bureau of Labor Statistics (BLS) unemployment rate and describe how this measure treats involuntary part-time workers and people who want work but aren't actively looking. Show how the BLS unemployment rate can be adjusted to account for workers marginally attached to the labor force and for part-time workers who would prefer full-time work. Which unemployment rate do you think better represents the extent of unemployment, and why?

8) (Article 1.5) Since 2001 federal government spending has changed dramatically. A military buildup accelerated by the Bush Administration's invasion and occupation of Iraq pushed up military related spending (including homeland security and foreign aid) from 3.2% of GDP to 4.4% of GDP in 2004. At the same time, domestic discretionary spending remained unchanged at 3.2% of GDP, although a few education programs, airline relief, and the National Institute of Health programs enjoyed substantial increases, while spending on the environment, housing assistance, and job training lost out. Entitlement expenditures (mostly social security and Medicare), the third major spending category, grew from 10.1% of GDP to 10.9% of GDP over the three years. What has been the opportunity cost of this military buildup? And where is the U.S. economy today in a production possibilities diagram?

9) (Article 1.6) Review the list of 2001-2003 tax cuts Sheehan presents in her article and their costs in social programs. Assess in each case if the benefits of the tax cut matched its opportunity cost.

GRADING THE ECONOMY
Bush's recovery comes up short.

When George W. Bush was in college, students who were not serious about their studies would walk into a final exam pretending to walk a dog, to make it clear to everyone that they would be happy to pass the course with a D. George W. Bush undoubtedly walked the dog a few times during his college days at Yale.

Now it is time for the final exam for today's dismal economic expansion, already four years old. As president and steward of our economy, George W. Bush should be walking the dog again. But this time he insists he deserves an A—for overseeing an economic recovery that has underperformed every other economic recovery since World War II. Now that's grade inflation.

The table below compares how the U.S. economy has fared three to four years into the current recovery to the average of the nine other postwar recoveries at the same point.

—*James McBride and John Miller*

COMPARING POST-WAR RECOVERIES		
	Average of Previous Postwar Recoveries	Current Recovery
Average Quarterly GDP Growth[a]	4.48%	3.32%
Average Quarterly Gain in Corporate Profits[a]	7.83%	11.13%
Private Sector Employment Growth[a]	2.29%	0.6%
Average Quarterly Rise In Wages & Salaries[a]	3.97%	1.62%
Months to regain jobs lost to recession[a]	21	46
Poverty Rate[b]	-1.20%	1.00%

a - Average over period of 15 quarters (45 months)
b - After 3 years from start of recovery
Sources: Center for Budget & Policy Priorities <http://www.cbpp.org/8-9-05bud.pdf>; US Census Bureau <www.census.gov>; Economic Policy Institute <http://www.epinet.org>; Bureau of Economic Analysis <http://www.bea.gov>

HIGH AND DRY

THE ECONOMIC RECOVERY FAILS TO DELIVER

BY JOHN MILLER

This economy is pumped. Boosted by economic stimulants—military spending, tax rebates, interest rate cuts, and a spate of mortgage refinancing—the U.S. economy expanded at an 8.2% annual rate in the third quarter of 2003, its fastest pace in nearly two decades, and at a respectable 4% rate in the fourth quarter. The Dow is back over 10,000. Corporate profits are up. Business investment is improving, and consumer confidence is holding.

Predictably, the *Wall Street Journal's* editors spent the winter holidays chortling about "the merry economy." The 55 blue-chip economists the Journal surveyed predict that economic growth will exceed 4% and that the economy will create 1.5 million jobs this year, just in time for George W. Bush's election campaign.

But despite this ginned-up sense of economic well-being, the specter of stagnation—that the United States could go the way of Japan and sink into a decade-long economic funk—continues to haunt the U.S. economy.

The current wave of frenetic economic activity has done nothing to solve the underlying flaws of the post-bubble economy. Overcapacity, especially the hangover from the collapse of manufacturing and the dot-coms, oppressive consumer debt burdens, an ever-widening trade deficit, burgeoning budget deficits, and unprecedented inequality—all are still with us. And even after a heavy dose of economic stimulants, job creation in this recovery remains the worst on record.

The Bush administration has expended a lot of fiscal firepower to stimulate this recovery. But the administration's stimulants of choice are not generating a cumulative and self-sustaining economic expansion. What's more, the prescription on many of them is about to expire. Future tax cuts will go ever more exclusively to the well-to-do, resulting in less new consumer spending. The Fed has little room left to cut short-term interest rates further. Higher long-term rates have already slowed mortgage refinancing. And that is to say nothing of the toxic side effects of the Bush team's economic antidepressants: they gut public-sector social spending and support an economic growth that does surprisingly little to improve the living standard of most people.

EIGHT MONTHS DOWN, THREE YEARS SIDEWAYS

Last July, the National Bureau of Economic Research (NBER)—the nation's official arbiter of the business cycle—declared that the recession that began in March 2001 had ended way back in November of that year, only eight months later. The 2001 recession was neither long nor deep. The average duration of post-World War II recessions is 11 months. And the output lost in the 2001 recession, measured by the decline in real Gross Domestic Product (GDP, the broadest single measure of economic output), was less than a third of the drop-off during the 1990-91 recession.

Why did it take the NBER's economists 20 months to recognize a recovery that was already underway? Because this recovery has been so weak that the NBER hesitated to declare the recession over. The economy fell for just eight months but it has crawled sideways for nearly three years. Real personal income (income of households adjusted for inflation) has grown much more slowly than in past recoveries, and the economy has continued to lose jobs long after a typical recovery would have returned to pre-recession job numbers.

Instead of a robust recovery, the economy has entered "a twilight zone—growing fast enough to avoid an official recession but not fast enough to create jobs," according to Paul Krugman, economist and *New York Times* columnist. Economic growth averaged just 2.6% from the official end of the recession in November 2001 through the second quarter of 2003. Economic journalist William Greider warned the U.S. economy was flirting with something far worse, "a low-grade depression." (See "The Japan Syndrome," page 7.)

RUNNING ON FUMES

At this January's World Economic Summit in Davos, Switzerland, Stephen Roach, chief economist at Morgan Stanley investment bank in New York, warned business leaders that "the main engine of the global economy, the ... U.S., is right now running on fumes." Tax cuts, home sales and mortgage refinancing fueled by low interest rates, and Iraq-driven military spending—not self-sustaining job and wage growth—fueled the 2003 growth spurt. Each of those additives to the economic fuel tank will be less able to power future economic growth, either because it's now in short supply or because it has gummed up the economic engine.

Take monetary policy. Interest rate cuts were key to keeping the weak, post-bubble economy out of a deep recession:

---

*Dates denote when the article appeared in *Dollars & Sense* magazine.

they helped underwrite last year's surge in consumer spending on durable goods, especially housing and automobiles.

But the Fed will be hard pressed to coax more spending out of the economy. With the federal funds rate at 1%, there is not much room left for further rate cuts. In addition, interest rates on home mortgages are already rising. This will slow the spate of mortgage refinancing that put money in consumers' pockets in 2002 and 2003: over the last two years, half of all U.S. homeowners refinanced $4.5 trillion in mortgage debt.

On top of that, consumers are up to their eyeballs in debt. Debt service now claims a record 13% of disposable income, despite the interest rate cuts. Three years of a bear market has put a real dent in people's net worth, and less mortgage refinancing will do nothing good for the value of their homes. With employment lower than three years ago and wages stagnant, consumers sooner or later will stop spending, as Roach warns. In fact, by the end of last year the surge in consumer spending, especially for automobiles, had already cooled.

Fed interest rate cuts never bolstered investment spending as much as consumer spending. Lingering excess productive capacity across the economy left businesses reluctant to make new investments. During much of the recovery, corporations have used the lower interest rates to pay down short-term debt and to buy back their own stock, not to add to capital spending.

> DURING THE RED-HOT THIRD QUARTER OF 2003, REAL BUSINESS INVESTMENT WAS STILL 7% LOWER THAN IT WAS IN 2000 AND EVEN BELOW ITS AVERAGE LEVEL DURING THE 2001 RECESSION.

Business investment did pick up considerably in the second half of 2003, posting its strongest gains since the first quarter of 2000. Robert Shapiro, economist with the centrist Progressive Policy Institute, says that "with consumer spending slowing, improved business fixed investment is now the strongest private sector support for the expansion in 2004." But even with the recent upswing in corporate spending, investment levels are quite modest. During the red-hot third quarter of last year, real business investment, as Shapiro himself emphasizes, was still 7% lower than it was in 2000 and even below its average level during the 2001 recession.

Fed interest-rate cuts were also supposed to fix another obstacle to sustained economic growth and job creation: the gaping U.S. trade deficit. But the fix hasn't worked too well. (See "That Pesky Trade Deficit," page 10.)

FISCAL POLICY MISSES THE MARK

Fiscal policy, the manipulation of government spending and taxing policies, is just as problematic for sustaining economic growth as monetary policy. For the Bush administration, fiscal policy usually means just one thing: cutting taxes for the well-to-do. Three rounds of tax cuts for the rich, combined with last year's military spending for the Iraq war and its aftermath, have indeed shifted the government's fiscal status in a big way: the federal budget went from a $236 billion surplus in fiscal year 2000 to a $521 billion projected deficit in fiscal year 2004.

Such a powerful fiscal swing, the equivalent of about 7% of GDP, was sure to lift economic growth over the short term, almost regardless of the particulars. And Bush fiscal policy did goose economic growth rates in 2003. When the invasion of Iraq gave rise to the biggest quarterly increase in military spending since the Korean War, GDP growth rates during the second quarter picked up from 2.0% to 3.1%, with economic analysts attributing three-quarters of the spike to government spending. Similarly, tax rebates over the summer added to the consumer spending that drove the third quarter GDP growth spurt.

But the limitations of the Bush team's attempt to punch up a sluggish economy for the election year have already begun to show. First off, future tax cuts will do less to add to consumer spending because they go ever more exclusively to the well-to-do, who spend a smaller share of their income than other taxpayers. Even in 2003, nearly one-half of taxpayers (49%) got $100 or less back in lower taxes, reports Citizens for Tax Justice. In 2005, that number rises to three-quarters of taxpayers, and it continues up from there. At the same time, nearly two-fifths of the Bush tax cut goes the richest 1%.

Second, the Bush stimulus package has done little or nothing to relieve the pressure on state and local budgets. With 30 states still facing between $39 and $41 billion in budget shortfalls in fiscal year 2005—the equivalent of 8% of their expenditures—more cutbacks in state spending are inevitable. Those state budget cuts are sapping the stimulative effect of any federal deficit spending. Nicholas Johnson, director of the State Fiscal Project at the Center on Budget and Policy Priorities, estimates that the state fiscal crisis is "taking at least half a percentage point out of the growth rate of the national economy."

The administration's failure to address the budget crisis in the states is not only trimming economic growth, it's also destroying critical programs. State budget cuts have hit working people and the poor especially hard. The federal government has shifted responsibility for social spending onto the states, and that is what's being cut. California, for instance, cut spending by $12 billion in the two years prior to last fall's recall election; schools there now go without computers, and public libraries are unable to purchase books. Nationwide, 34 states have cut programs such as Medicaid and the Children's Health Insurance Program that provide health care to low- and moderate-income families.

And while fiscal stimulus might be pumping up measured growth rates, the Bush administration is running large deficits likely to be sustained even if investment spending continues to improve and labor markets eventually tighten. Those long-term structural deficits, as economists call them,

THE JAPAN SYNDROME: COULD IT HAPPEN HERE?

It isn't only left-leaning journalists sounding the alarm bells. Even the *Wall Street Journal* asked, "Is the U.S. economy at risk of emulating Japan's long swoon?"

During the 1980s, Japan enjoyed an economic boom as heady as the one the United States saw in the 1990s, complete with a soaring stock market and a red-hot housing market. But when the bubble burst, the Japanese economy sank into a decade-long economic slump. Japanese income growth slowed, falling behind the United States'. The Nikkei, Japan's major stock market index, lost three-quarters of its value from its peak in 1989. The Japanese real estate boom collapsed in 1991; in 2003 a house in Tokyo cost less than half of what it did in 1991. A tanking real estate sector and a slowing economy saddled Japanese banks with bad loans. Excess capacity, especially high for Japanese automakers, discouraged new investment and ensured that the slowdown would persist.

The 1990s boom in the United States came to a similar if less severe end. By 2000, the U.S. stock market bubble had burst. Broad measures of stock values lost about one-third of their peak values over the next two years. Manufacturing had already hit the skids. Industrial production fell steadily, contributing to a general excess of industrial capacity. Today, capacity utilization rates still hover at about 75%, and the manufacturing sector has shed jobs for some 42 straight months. The new economy fared no better. The NASDAQ, the high-tech stock index, melted down, losing nearly three-quarters of its value from March 2000 to July 2002, and gaggles of dot-com firms folded, putting plenty of white-collar workers out of work.

Only the continued strength of the U.S. real estate market, along with the willingness of debt-strapped U.S. consumers to spend, seemed to stand between the U.S. economy and Japan's fate. The Fed would add one more factor that insulated the U.S. economy against a Japan-style economic collapse: monetary policy. Ironically, it was the Fed's own repeated interest rate hikes in the second half of 1999 and the first half of 2000, along with the Clinton administration's downsizing of the federal government, that contributed mightily to bringing on the economic slowdown in the first place.

In the summer of 2002, the Fed devoted its annual retreat in Jackson Hole, Wyoming, to the threat of Japanese-style stagnation. Fed members and their boosters ended up assuring themselves that they had averted the threat by acting more quickly than Japanese central bankers had. While the Japanese central bank (CBJ) had waited nearly two years after the bubble burst to act, it then set about furiously cutting short-term interest rates, from 6% in 1991 to under 1% in 1995. The Fed did act more quickly than its Japanese counterpart, dropping the federal funds rate on overnight loans to commercial banks from 6.25% to 1.25% in just two years.

Has the Fed saved the day? That the U.S economy has muddled through the last three years with slow growth and is now in the midst of a growth spurt is enough for many to conclude that the threat of stagnation is behind us. But that would be a mistake. Japan's economy did not collapse into stagnation but slid gradually, as the Japanese bankers attending the Jackson Hole retreat emphasized. At the same time, economic forecasters repeatedly predicted that Japanese economic growth rates would soon pick up. Most ominously, Japan's real estate bubble burst a couple of years after its stock market bubble. If the housing market does fall apart, U.S. banks could end up in critical condition much as they did during the mid-1980s banking crisis that gripped much of the nation. And with U.S interest rates already close to zero, Pam Woodall, economics editor of the conservative British weekly the *Economist*, worries that "a housing bust might therefore nudge the economy into deflation."

could provide the political justification for further cutbacks in social and infrastructure spending necessary to put economic growth on a more solid footing. In fact, if the Bush tax cuts are made permanent, there would be no room in the federal budget for any domestic discretionary spending in just eight years, according to a recent study by Eugene Steuerle, a senior fellow at the Urban Institute. By 2012, entitlements (Social Security, Medicare, and Medicaid), military spending, and interest on the growing government debt would have absorbed all remaining federal revenues, leaving not a dollar for education, job training, housing, environment, community development, energy, public infrastructure, or other domestic programs. That would be a disaster not only for working families and children, as the Urban Institute emphasizes, but for the productivity of the U.S. economy as well.

JOBLESS RECOVERY TO JOB-LOSS RECOVERY

Whatever administration and Fed policies have done to produce an uptick in measured economic growth, they have done little to create jobs—the key to sustaining wage growth and a self-perpetuating economic expansion. And the Bush administration sure did promise new jobs. With the 2003 tax cut in place, the president's Council of Economic Advisors insisted, the economy would create 306,000 jobs a month from July 2003 to December 2004.

Hardly. When economic growth picked up in the final five months of 2003, the recovery finally stopped losing jobs. But the economy added a total of just 278,000 new jobs in those five months, with 80% of those job gains concentrated in temporary staffing, education, health care, and government. That is fewer jobs than the Bush team's promised monthly total.

Job creation in this recovery does not fall short just with respect to the administration's inflated promises, but by any reasonable measure. Even with those new jobs in the last five months of the year, the economy lost a net 331,000 jobs for 2003, on top of 1.5 million lost in 2002. The last time payroll employment declined for two consecutive years was in 1944 and 1945, as war production wound down. And that is a far cry from the average 300,000 new jobs per month the U.S. economy posted from 1995 to 2000.

Since the recession began 33 months ago, 2.4 million U.S. jobs have disappeared. Following every other post-World War II recession, jobs had fully recovered to their pre-recession levels within 31 months of the start of the recession. Worse yet, as a recent study by economists at the New York Federal Reserve Bank shows, a far larger share of recent layoffs have been permanent, rather than the temporary cyclical layoffs dominant in most previous recessions.

The current recovery can't even stack up to the only other "jobless" recovery on record, the 1991-92 recovery that cost Bush's father re-election. *Business Week* calculates that to equal the job creation record of the early 1990s rebound, the economy would need to have added 3 million more private sector jobs by now, including 1,547,000 more manufacturing jobs and 707,000 more information technology jobs.

Jesse Jackson warned the 2000 Democratic Convention to "Stay out of the Bushes"—advice that should be taken seriously by anyone concerned with holding onto a job or finding a new one. We have gone from a jobless recovery under the elder Bush to a job-loss recovery under the younger Bush.

Employers are unwilling to add new jobs because they remain unconvinced that the economic recovery is sustainable. Instead of hiring new workers, bosses are squeezing more out of the old ones. This, along with corporate restructuring and layoffs, has produced rapid increases in productivity—the economy's output per hour of labor input. For instance, during the last two years, the hourly output of U.S. workers has gone up at a 5.3% pace, exceeding the "new economy" productivity growth rate of 2.6% from 1996 to 2001. For the first time in a postwar recovery, productivity is growing far faster than the economy.

Manufacturing has been especially devastated. Factory productivity has gone up by 15%, versus a 9% rise in the comparable period in the early 1990s. That has helped produce the longest string of manufacturing layoffs since the Great Depression. Ohio, Michigan, and Pennsylvania have each lost 200,000 or more manufacturing jobs since January 2001.

Another drain on U.S. job creation is the increasing number of jobs lost to global outsourcing. Not only manufacturing jobs are going abroad, but also white collar work, from backroom office operations (bookkeeping, customer service, and marketing) to engineering and computer software design. Increased competition engendered by the Internet has allowed formerly non-tradable jobs to escape abroad, in this latest bout of corporate cost-cutting. How many jobs are being lost to this global arbitrage, as economists call it, is a matter of dispute. There are no official data, but estimates range from 500,000 to 995,000 jobs since March 2001, or somewhere between 15% and 35% of the total decline in employment. Gregory Mankiw, the politically tone-deaf chair of Bush's Council of Economic Advisors, recently assured Americans that outsourcing is "a plus for the economy in the long run"—cold comfort for those who have seen their jobs move offshore.

Stephen Roach puts IT-enabled "offshoring" at the top of his list of possible explanations for the inability of this recovery to create jobs. "In my discussions with a broad cross-section of business executives," reports Roach, "I was hard-pressed to find any who weren't contemplating white-collar offshoring."

Typically, economic stimulus policies activate "multiplier effects" that sustain economic growth over time. Higher government spending calls forth more output. Employers in turn hire more workers. New jobs put money in workers' pockets and empower workers who already have jobs to press for higher wages. And that fuels consumption. But without new jobs, that internally generated fuel is all but absent in the current upturn. Outsourcing and other trends are eroding the bargaining position of U.S. workers; predictably, wage and salary disbursements are currently running some $350 billion below the path of previous upturns. With cost-saving productivity gains and the offshoring of jobs showing no sign of abating, there is little reason to believe that this recovery will soon be able to run on its own steam. More likely, the economy will continue to grow slowly but create few new jobs.

FACING UP TO OUR ECONOMIC PROBLEMS

This is no time to balance the budget. Dimitri Papadimitriou, president of the Levy Institute, a progressive economics think tank, estimates that the government sector as a whole (federal, state, and local) will have to run a deficit of 7% to 8% of GDP to keep the economy growing.

The public sector must both provide immediate economic stimulus and move to correct the economy's underlying problems through policies that will counteract economic stagnation and spread the benefits of economic growth more widely. Economic stimulus need not be toxic. Alternative policies are fully capable of jogging the economy back to life and at the same time creating jobs and making the economy stronger rather than weaker over the long haul.

Here is some of what has to happen. First, the Bush administration's pro-rich tax cuts, which provide less bang for the buck than more broad-based tax cuts, have to go. With 80% of taxpayers now paying more in payroll taxes than in income taxes, lowering payroll taxes would do more to boost consumer spending than cutting income taxes. But even payroll tax cuts, dollar for dollar, do less to stimulate economic growth than government spending. A one-dollar payroll tax cut adds just 90 cents to output in the following year, while a hike in unemployment benefits would generate $1 in output for each dollar the government spends, and one dollar in federal government spending to build up infrastructure would add an additional $1.80 in output over the next year, estimates David Wyss, chief economist at Standard & Poors.

There is still room for additional government outlays, especially if the Bush tax cuts for the super-rich are repealed. Relative to the size of the economy, the federal government is still no larger than its postwar average. And there is much to be done. To begin with, temporary federal unemploy-ment benefits that were allowed to expire in December 2003 must be reinstated. Otherwise, by the middle of this year, an estimated two million unemployed people will see their benefits expire. The Bush budget proposal for FY2005 will cut another $6 billion in support for the states, but as much as an additional $100 billion in federal aid is needed to support cash-strapped states in the coming years.

Public investment, which has fallen to about one-half its levels during the 1960s and 1970s relative to the size of the economy, must be restored to maintain the nation's economic competitiveness. That means increased public investments in education, job training, and child care as well as in basic infrastructure, the environment, energy, and research and development. Many of these programs, especially spending on the environment and natural resources and on job training and employment services, have suffered deep cuts since 2000.

"In the end," as economist Anwar Shaikh points out, "government expenditures need to provide not only demand stimulus but also social stimulus." Otherwise, while GDP growth may be momentarily high(er), the well of sustained expansion and broad-based economic gains will stay dry.

Sources: "Jobless Recovery? Not in 2004, Economists Say," *WSJ*, 1/2/03; Jacob M. Schlesinger and Peter Landers, "Parallel Woes: Is the US Economy At Risk of Emulating Japan's Long Swoon?" *WSJ*, 11/07/01; Pam Woodall, "House of Cards," *The Economist*, 5/29/03; Nicholas Johnson and Bob Zahradnik, "State Budget Deficits Projected For FY2005," Center on Budget and Policy Priorities, 1/30/04; Louis Uchitelle, "Red Ink in States Beginning to Hurt Economic Recovery," *NYT*, 7/28/03; "The Hurting Heartland," Business Week, 12/15/03; "JobWatch," Economic Policy Institute, 1/04; Louis Uchitelle, "A Statistic That's Missing: Jobs That Moved Overseas," *NYT*, 10/5//03; James C. Cooper and Michael J. Mandel, "So Where Are The Jobs?" *Business Week*, 1/26/04; Jacob Schlesinger, "Bush's Early Electoral Edge: It's Not His Father's Economy," *WSJ*, 1/12/04; Stephen Roach, "False Recovery," Morgan Stanley Global Economic Forum, 1/12/04; Anwar Shaikh et al., "Deficits, Debts, and Growth: A Reprieve But Not a Pardon," Levy Economics Institute, 10/03; Randall Wray and Dimitri Papadimitriou, "Understanding Deflation: Treating The Disease, Not the Symphthoms," Levy Economics Institute, Winter 2004; Robert J. Shapiro, "Economic Recovery Remains Vulnerable to Setbacks," Center for American Progress, 12/22/03.

THE GROWTH CONSENSUS UNRAVELS

BY JONATHAN ROWE

Economics has been called the dismal science, but beneath its gray exterior is a system of belief worthy of Pollyanna.

Yes, economists manage to see a dark cloud in every silver lining. Downturn follows uptick, and inflation rears its ugly head. But there's a story within that story—a gauzy romance, a lyric ode to Stuff. It's built into the language. A thing produced is called a "good," for example, no questions asked. The word is more than just a term of art. It suggests the automatic benediction which economics bestows upon commodities of any kind.

By the same token, an activity for sale is called a "service." In conventional economics there are no "dis-services," no actions that might be better left undone. The bank that gouges you with ATM fees, the lawyer who runs up the bill—such things are "services" so long as someone pays. If a friend or neighbor fixes your plumbing for free, it's not a "service" and so it doesn't count.

The sum total of these products and activities is called the Gross Domestic Product, or GDP. If the GDP is greater this year than last, then the result is called "growth." There is no bad GDP and no bad growth; economics does not even have a word for such a thing. It does have a word for less growth. In such a case, economists say growth is "sluggish" and the economy is in "recession." No matter what is growing—more payments to doctors because of worsening health, more toxic cleanup—so long as there is more of it, then the economic mind declares it "good."

This purports to be "objective science." In reality it is a rhetorical construct with the value judgments built in, and this rhetoric has been the basis of economic debate in the United States for the last half century at least. True, people have disagreed over how best to promote a rising GDP. Liberals generally wanted to use government more, conservatives less. But regarding the beneficence of a rising GDP, there has been little debate at all.

If anything, the Left traditionally has believed in growth with even greater fervor than the Right. It was John Maynard Keynes, after all, who devised the growth-boosting mechanisms of macroeconomic policy to combat the Depression of the 1930s; it was Keynesians who embraced these strategies after the War and turned the GDP into a totem. There's no point in seeking a bigger pie to redistribute to the poor, if you don't believe the expanding pie is desirable in the first place.

Today, however, the growth consensus is starting to unravel across the political spectrum and in ways that are both obvious and subtle. The issue is no longer just the impact of growth upon the environment—the toxic impacts of industry and the like. It now goes deeper, to what growth actually consists of and what it means in people's lives. The things economists call "goods" and "services" increasingly don't strike people as such. There is a growing disconnect between the way people experience growth and the way the policy establishment talks about it, and this gap is becoming an unspoken subtext to much of American political life.

The group most commonly associated with an antigrowth stance is environmentalists, of course. To be sure, one faction, the environmental economists, is trying to put green new wine into the old bottles of economic thought. If we would just make people pay the "true" cost of, say, the gasoline they burn, through the tax system for example, then the market would do the rest. We'd have benign, less-polluting growth, they say, perhaps even more than now. But the core of the environmental movement remains deeply suspicious of the growth ethos, and probably would be even if the environmental impacts somehow could be lessened.

In the middle are suburbanites who applaud growth in the abstract, but oppose the particular manifestations they see around them—the traffic, sprawl and crowded schools. On the Right, meanwhile, an anti-growth politics is arising practically unnoticed. When social conservatives denounce gambling, pornography, or sex and violence in the media, they are talking about specific instances of the growth that their political leaders rhapsodize on other days.

Environmentalists have been like social conservatives in one key respect. They have been moralistic regarding growth, often scolding people for enjoying themselves at the expense of future generations and the earth. Their concern is valid, up to a point—the consumer culture does promote the time horizon of a five year old. But politically it is not the most promising line of attack, and conceptually it concedes too much ground. To moralize about consumption as they do is to accept the conventional premise that it really is something chosen—an enjoyable form of self-indulgence that has unfortunate consequences for the earth.

That's "consumption" in the common parlance—the sport utility vehicle loading up at Wal-Mart, the stuff piling up in the basement and garage. But increasingly that's not what people actually experience, nor is it what the term really means. In economics, consumption means everything people spend money on, pleasurable or not. Wal-Mart is just one dimension of a much larger and increasingly unpleasant whole. The lawyers' fees for the house settlement or divorce; the repair work on the car after it was rear-ended; the cancer treatments for the uncle who was a three-pack-a-day smoker; the stress medications and weight loss regimens—all these and more are "consumption." They all go into the GDP.

Cancer treatments and lawyer's fees are not what come to mind when environmentalists lament the nation's excess consumption, or for that matter when economists applaud America's "consumers" for keeping the world economy afloat. Yet increasingly such things are what consumption actually consists of in the economy today. More and more, it consists not of pleasurable things that people choose, but rather of things that most people would gladly do without.

Much consumption today is addictive, for example. Millions of Americans are engaged in a grim daily struggle with themselves to do less of it. They want to eat less, drink less, smoke less, gamble less, talk less on the telephone—do less buying, period. Yet economic reasoning declares as growth and progress, that which people themselves regard as a tyrannical affliction.

Economists resist this reality of a divided self, because it would complicate their models beyond repair. They cling instead to an 18th century model of human psychology—the "rational" and self-interested man—which assumes those complexities away. As David McClelland, the Harvard psychologist, once put it, economists "haven't even discovered Freud, let alone Abraham Maslow." (They also haven't discovered the Apostle Paul, who lamented that "the good that I would I do not, but the evil that I would not, that I do.")

Then too there's the mounting expenditure that sellers foist upon people through machination and deceit. People don't choose to pay for the corrupt campaign finance system or for bloated executive pay packages. The cost of these is hidden in the prices that we pay at the store. As I write this, the *Washington Post* is reporting that Microsoft has hired Ralph Reed, former head of the Christian Coalition, and Grover Norquist, a right-wing polemicist, as lobbyists in Washington. When I bought this computer with Windows 95, Bill Gates never asked me whether I wanted to help support a bunch of Beltway operators like these.

This is compulsory consumption, not choice, and the economy is rife with it today. People don't choose to pay some $40 billion a year in telemarketing fraud. They don't choose to pay 32% more for prescription drugs than do people in Canada. ("Free trade" means that corporations are free to buy their labor and materials in other countries, but ordinary Americans aren't equally free to do their shopping there.) For that matter, people don't choose to spend $25 and up for inkjet printer cartridges. The manufacturers design the printers to make money on the cartridges because, as the *Wall Street Journal* put it, that's "where the big profit margins are."

Yet another category of consumption that most people would gladly do without arises from the need to deal with the offshoots and implications of growth. Bottled water has become a multibillion dollar business in the United States because people don't trust what comes from the tap. There's a growing market for sound insulation and double-pane windows because the economy produces so much noise. A wide array of physical and social stresses arise from the activities that get lumped into the euphemistic term "growth."

The economy in such cases doesn't solve problems so much as create new problems that require more expenditure to solve. Food is supposed to sustain people, for example. But today the dis-economies of eating sustain the GDP instead. The food industry spends some $21 billion a year on advertising to entice people to eat food they don't need. Not coincidentally there's now a $32 billion diet and weight loss industry to help people take off the pounds that inevitably result. When that doesn't work, which is often, there is always the vacuum pump or knife. There were some 110,000 liposuctions in the United States last year; at five pounds each that's some 275 tons of flab up the tube.

It is a grueling cycle of indulgence and repentance, binge and purge. Yet each stage of this miserable experience, viewed through the pollyanic lens of economics, becomes growth and therefore good. The problem here goes far beyond the old critique of how the consumer culture cultivates feelings of inadequacy, lack and need so people will buy and buy again. Now this culture actually makes life worse, in order to sell solutions that purport to make it better.

Traffic shows this syndrome in a finely developed form. First we build sprawling suburbs so people need a car to go almost anywhere. The resulting long commutes are daily torture but help build up the GDP. Americans spend some $5 billion a year in gasoline alone while they sit in traffic and go nowhere. As the price of gas increases this growth sector will expand.

THERE IS A GROWING DISCONNECT BETWEEN THE WAY PEOPLE EXPERIENCE GROWTH AND THE WAY THE POLICY ESTABLISHMENT TALKS ABOUT IT.

Commerce deplores a vacuum, and the exasperating hours in the car have spawned a booming subeconomy of relaxation tapes, cell phones, even special bibs. Billboards have 1-800 numbers so commuters can shop while they stew. Talk radio thrives on traffic-bound commuters, which accounts for some of the contentious, get-out-of-my-face tone. The traffic also helps sustain a $130 billion a year car wreck industry; and if Gates succeeds in getting computers into cars, that sector should get a major boost.

The health implications also are good for growth. Los Angeles, which has the worst traffic in the nation, also leads—if that's the word—in hospital admissions due to respiratory ailments. The resulting medical bills go into the GDP. And while Americans sit in traffic they aren't walking or getting exercise. More likely they are entertaining themselves orally with a glazed donut or a Big Mac, which helps explain why the portion of middle-aged Americans who are clinically obese has doubled since the 1960s.

C. Everett Koop, the former Surgeon General, estimates that some 70% of the nation's medical expenses are lifestyle induced. Yet the same lifestyle that promotes disease also produces a rising GDP. (Keynes observed that traditional virtues like thrift are bad for growth; now it appears that health is bad for growth too.) We literally are growing ourselves sick, and this puts a grim new twist on the economic doctrine of "complementary goods," which describes the way new products tend to spawn a host of others. The automobile gave rise to car wash franchises, drive-in restaurants, fuzz busters, tire dumps, and so forth. Television produced an antenna industry, VCRs, soap magazines, ad infinitum. The texts present this phenomenon as the wondrous perpetual motion machine of the market—goods beget more goods. But now the machine is producing complementary ills and collateral damages instead.

Suggestive of this new dynamic is a pesticide plant in Richmond, California, which is owned by a transnational corporation that also makes the breast cancer drug tamoxifen. Many researchers believe that pesticides, and the toxins created in the production of them, play a role in breast cancer. "It's a pretty good deal," a local physician told the *East Bay Express*, a Bay Area weekly. "First you cause the cancer, then you profit from curing it." Both the alleged cause and cure make the GDP go up, and this syndrome has become a central dynamic of growth in the U.S. today.

Mainstream economists would argue that this is all beside the point. If people didn't have to spend money on such things as commuting or medical costs, they'd simply spend it on something else, they say. Growth would be the same or even greater, so the actual content of growth should be of little concern to those who promote it. That view holds sway in the nation's policy councils; as a result we try continually to grow our way out of problems, when increasingly we are growing our way in.

To the extent conventional economics has raised an eyebrow at growth, it has done so mainly through the concept of "externalities". These are negative side effects suffered by those not party to a transaction between a buyer and a seller. Man buys car, car pollutes air, others suffer that "externality." As the language implies, anything outside the original transaction is deemed secondary, a subordinate reality, and therefore easily overlooked. More, the effects upon buyer and seller—the "internalities" one might say—are assumed to be good.

Today, however, that mental schema is collapsing. Externalities are starting to overwhelm internalities. A single jet ski can cause more misery for the people who reside by a lake, than it gives pleasure to the person riding it.

More importantly, and as just discussed, internalities themselves are coming into question, and with them the assumption of choice, which is the moral linchpin of market thought.

If people choose what they buy, as market theory posits, then—externalities aside—the sum total of all their buying must be the greatest good of all. That's the ideology behind the GDP. But if people don't always choose, then the model starts to fall apart, which is what is happening today. The practical implications are obvious. If growth consists increasingly of problems rather than solutions, then scolding people for consuming too much is barking up the wrong tree. It is possible to talk instead about ridding our lives of what we don't want as well as forsaking what we do want—or think we want.

Politically this is a more promising path. But to where? The economy may be turning into a kind of round robin of difficulty and affliction, but we are all tied to the game. The sickness industry employs a lot of people, as do ad agencies and trash haulers. The fastest-growing occupations in the country include debt collectors and prison guards. What would we do without our problems and dysfunctions?

The problem is especially acute for those at the bottom of the income scale who have not shared much in the apparent prosperity. For them, a bigger piece of a bad pie might be better than none.

This is the economic conundrum of our age. No one has more than pieces of an answer, but it helps to see that much growth today is really an optical illusion created by accounting tricks. The official tally ignores totally the cost side of the growth ledger—the toll of traffic upon our time and health for example. In fact, it actually counts such costs as growth and gain. By the same token, the official tally ignores the economic contributions of the natural environment and the social structure; so that the more the economy destroys these, and puts commoditized substitutes in their places, the more the experts say the economy has "grown." Pollute the lakes and oceans so that people have to join private swim clubs and the economy grows. Erode the social infrastructure of community so people have to buy services from the market instead of getting help from their neighbors, and it grows some more. The real economy—the one that sustains us—has diminished. All that has grown is the need to buy commoditized substitutes for things we used to have for free.

So one might rephrase the question thus: how do we achieve real growth, as opposed to the statistical illusion that passes for growth today? Four decades ago, John Kenneth Galbraith argued in *The Affluent Society* that conventional economic reasoning is rapidly becoming obsolete. An economics based upon scarcity simply doesn't work in an economy of hyper-abundance, he said. If it takes a $200 billion (today) advertising industry to maintain what economists quaintly call "demand," then perhaps that demand isn't as urgent as conventional theory posits. Perhaps it's not even demand in any sane meaning of the word.

Galbraith argued that genuine economy called for shifting some resources from consumption that needs to be prodded, to needs which are indisputably great: schools, parks, older people, the inner cities and the like. For this he was skewered as a proto-socialist. Yet today the case is even stronger, as advertisers worm into virtually every waking moment in a desperate effort to keep the growth machine on track.

Galbraith was arguing for a larger public sector. But that brings dysfunctions of its own, such as bureaucracy; and it depends upon an enlarging private sector as a fiscal base to begin with. Today we need to go further, and establish new ground rules for the economy, so that it produces more genuine growth on its own. We also need to find ways to revive the nonmarket economy of informal community exchange, so that people do not need money to meet every single life need.

In the first category, environmental fiscal policy can help. While the corporate world has flogged workers to be more productive, resources such as petroleum have been in effect loafing on the job. If we used these more efficiently the result could be jobs and growth, even in conventional terms, with less environmental pollution. If we used land more efficiently—that is, reduced urban sprawl—the social and environmental gains would be great.

Another ground rule is the corporate charter laws. We need to restore these to their original purpose: to keep large business organizations within the compass of the common good. But such shifts can do only so much. More efficient cars might simply encourage more traffic, for example. Cheap renewable power for electronic devices could encourage more noise. In other words, the answer won't just be a more efficient version of what we do now. Sooner or later we'll need different ways of thinking about work and growth and how we allocate the means of life.

This is where the social economy comes in, the informal exchange between neighbors and friends. There are some promising trends. One is the return to the traditional village model in housing. Structure does affect content. When houses are close together, and people can walk to stores and work, it encourages the spontaneous social interaction that nurtures real community. New local currencies, such as Time Dollars, provide a kind of lattice work upon which informal nonmarket exchange can take root and grow.

Changes like these are off the grid of economics as conventionally defined. It took centuries for the market to emerge from the stagnation of feudalism. The next organizing principle, whatever it is, most likely will emerge slowly as well. This much we can say with certainty. As the market hurdles towards multiple implosions, social and environmental as well as financial, it is just possible that the economics profession is going to have to do what it constantly lectures the rest of us to do: adjust to new realities and show a willingness to change.

WAGES FOR HOUSEWORK

THE MOVEMENT AND THE NUMBERS

BY LENA GRABER AND JOHN MILLER

The International Wages for Housework Campaign (WFH), a network of women in Third World and industrialized countries, began organizing in the early 1970s. WFH's demands are ambitious—"for the unwaged work that women do to be recognized as work in official government statistics, and for this work to be paid."

Housewives paid wages? By the government? That may seem outlandish to some, but consider the staggering amount of unpaid work carried out by women. In 1990, the International Labor Organization (ILO) estimated that women do two-thirds of the world's work for 5% of the income. In 1995, the UN Development Programme's (UNDP) Human Development Report announced that women's unpaid and underpaid labor was worth $11 trillion worldwide, and $1.4 trillion in the United States alone. Paying women the wages they "are owed" for unwaged work, as WFN puts it, would go a long way toward undoing these inequities and reducing women's economic dependence on men.

Publicizing information like this, WFH—whose International Women Count Network now includes more than 2,000 non-governmental organizations (NGOs) from the North and South—and other groups have been remarkably successful in persuading governments to count unwaged work. In 1995, the UN Fourth World Conference on Women, held in Beijing, developed a Platform for Action that called on governments to calculate the value of women's unpaid work and include it in conventional measures of national output, such as Gross Domestic Product (GDP).

So far, only Trinidad & Tobago and Spain have passed legislation mandating the new accounting, but other countries—including numerous European countries, Australia, Canada, Japan, and New Zealand in the industrialized world, and Bangladesh, the Dominican Republic, India, Nepal, Tanzania, and Venezuela in the developing world—have undertaken extensive surveys to determine how much time is spent on unpaid household work.

THE VALUE OF HOUSEWORK

Producing credible numbers for the value of women's work in the home is no easy task. Calculating how many hours women spend performing housework—from cleaning to childcare to cooking to shopping—is just the first step. The hours are considerable in both developing and industrialized economies. (See Table 1.)

What value to place on that work, and what would constitute fair remuneration—or wages for housework—is even more difficult to assess. Feminist economists dedicated to making the value of housework visible have taken different approaches to answering the question. One approach, favored by the UN's International Research and Training Institute for the Advancement of Women (INSTRAW), bases the market value of work done at home on the price of market goods and services that are similar to those produced in the home (such as meals served in restaurants or cleaning done by professional firms). These output-based evaluations estimate that counting unpaid household production would add 30-60% to the GDP of industrialized countries, and far more for developing countries. (See Table 2.)

A second approach evaluates the inputs of household production—principally the labor that goes into cooking, cleaning, childcare, and other services performed in the home, overwhelmingly by women. Advocates of this approach use one of three methods. Some base their calculations on what economists call opportunity cost—the wages women might have earned if they had worked a similar number of hours in the market economy. Others ask what it would cost to hire

	TABLE 1					
	WOMEN'S TIME SPENT PER DAY PERFORMING HOUSEHOLD LABOR, BY ACTIVITY, IN HOURS:MINUTES					
	Childcare Time	Cleaning Time	Food Prep Time	Shopping Time	Water/Fuel Collection	Total Country Time[a]
Australia (1997[b])	2:27	1:17	1:29	0:58	n.a.	3:39
Japan (1999)	0:24	2:37	n.a.	0:33	n.a.	3:34
Norway (2000)	0:42	1:16	0:49	0:26	0:01	3:56
U.K. (2000)	1:26	1:35	1:08	0:33	n.a.	4:55
Nepal (1996)	1:28	2:00	5:30	0:13	1:10	11:58

Note: Some activities, especially childcare, may overlap with other tasks
[a] Totals may include activities other than those listed.
[b] Only some percentage of the population recorded doing these activities. Averages are for that portion of the population. Generally, figures represent a greater number of women than men involved. *Sources:* Australia: <www.abs.gov.au/ausstats>; Japan: <www.unescap.org/stat>; Norway: <www.ssb.no/tidsbruk_en>; United Kingdom: <www.statistics.gov.uk/themes/social_finances/TimeUseSurvey>; Nepal: INSTRAW, *Valuation of Household Production and the Satellite Accounts* (Santo Domingo: 1996), 34-35; <www.cbs.nl/isi/iass>.

someone to do the work—either a general laborer such as a domestic servant (the generalist-replacement method) or a specialist such as a chef (the specialist-replacement method)—and then assign those wages to household labor. Ann Chadeau, a researcher with the Organization for Economic Cooperation and Development, has found the specialist-replacement method to be "the most plausible and at the same time feasible approach" for valuing unpaid household labor.

These techniques produce quite different results, all of which are substantial in relation to GDP. With that in mind, let's look at how some countries calculated the monetary value of unpaid work.

UNPAID WORK IN CANADA, GREAT BRITAIN, AND JAPAN

In Canada, a government survey documented the time men and women spent on unpaid work in 1992. Canadian women performed 65% of all unpaid work, shouldering an especially large share of household labor devoted to preparing meals, maintaining clothing, and caring for children. (Men's unpaid hours exceeded women's only for outdoor cleaning.)

The value of unpaid labor varied substantially, depending on the method used to estimate its appropriate wage. (See Table 3.) The opportunity-cost method, which uses the average market wage (weighted for the greater proportion of unpaid work done by women), assigned the highest value to unpaid labor, 54.2% of Canadian GDP. The two replacement methods produced lower estimates, because the wages they assigned fell below those of other jobs. The specialist-replacement method, which paired unpaid activities with the average wages of corresponding occupations—such as cooking with junior chefs, and childcare with kindergarten teachers—put the value of Canadian unpaid labor at 43% of GDP. The generalist-replacement method, by assigning the wages of household servants to unpaid labor, produced the lowest estimate of the value of unpaid work: 34% of Canadian GDP. INSTRAW's output-based measure, which matched hours of unpaid labor to a household's average expenditures on the same activities, calculated the value of Canada's unpaid work as 47.4% of GDP.

In Great Britain, where unpaid labor hours are high for an industrialized country (see Table 1), the value of unpaid labor was far greater relative to GDP. The British Office for National Statistics found that, when valued using the opportunity cost method, unpaid work was 112% of Britain's GDP in 1995! With the specialist-replacement method, British unpaid labor was still 56% of GDP—greater than the output of the United Kingdom's entire manufacturing sector for the year.

In Japan—where unpaid labor hours are more limited (see Table 1), paid workers put in longer hours, and women perform over 80% of unpaid work—the value of unpaid labor is significantly smaller relative to GDP. The Japanese Economic Planning Agency calculated that counting unpaid work in 1996 would add between 15.2% (generalist-replacement method) and 23% (opportunity-cost method) to GDP. Even at those levels, the value of unpaid labor still equaled at least half of Japanese women's market wages.

HOUSEWORK NOT BOMBS

While estimates vary by country and evaluation method, all of these calculations make clear that recognizing the value of unpaid household labor profoundly alters our perception of economic activity and women's contributions to production. "Had household production been included in the system of macro-economic accounts," notes Ann Chadeau, "governments may well have implemented quite different economic and social policies."

For example, according to the UNDP, "The inescapable implication [of recognizing women's unpaid labor] is that the fruits of society's total labor should be shared more equally." For the UNDP, this would mean radically altering property and inheritance rights; access to credit; entitlement to social security benefits, tax incentives, and child care; and terms of divorce settlements.

For WFH advocates, the implications are inescapable as well: women's unpaid labor should be paid—and "the money," WFH insists, "must come first of all from military spending."

Here in the United States, an unneeded and dangerous military buildup begun last year has already pushed up military spending from 3% to 4% of GDP. Devoting just the additional 1% of GDP gobbled up by the military budget to wages for housework—far from being outlandish—would

TABLE 2 VALUE OF UNPAID HOUSEHOLD LABOR AS % OF GDP, USING OUTPUT-BASED EVALUATION METHOD	
Country	*% of GDP*
Canada (1992)	47.4%
Finland (1990)	49.1%
Nepal (1991)	170.7%

Source: INSTRAW, *Valuation of Household Production and the Satellite Accounts* (Santo Domingo, 1996), 62, 229.

TABLE 3 VALUE OF UNPAID HOUSEHOLD LABOR IN CANADA AS % OF GDP, 1992	
Evaluation Method	*% of GDP*
Opportunity Cost (before taxes)	54.2 %
Specialist-Replacement	43.0%
Generalist-Replacement	34.0%
Output-Based	47.4%

Source: INSTRAW, *Valuation of Household Production and the Satellite Accounts* (Santo Domingo: 1996), 229.

be an important first step toward fairly remunerating women who perform much-needed and life-sustaining household work.

Resources: Ann Chadeau, "What is Households' Non-Market Production Worth?" *OECD Economic Studies* No. 18 (Spring 1992); Economic Planning Unit, Department of National Accounts, Japan, "Monetary Valuation of Unpaid Work in 1996" <unstats.un.org/unsd/methods/timeuse/tusresource_papers/japanunpaid.htm>; INSTRAW, *Measurement and Valuation of Unpaid Contribution: Accounting Through Time and Output* (Santo Domingo: 1995); INSTRAW, *Valuation of Household Production and the Satellite Accounts* (Santo Domingo: 1996); Office of National Statistics, United Kingdom, "A Household Satellite Account for the UK," by Linda Murgatroyd and Henry Neuberger, *Economic Trends* (October 1997) <www.statistics.gov.uk/hhsa/hhsa/Index.html>; Hilkka Pietilä, "The Triangle of the Human Ecology: Household-Cultivation-Industrial Production," *Ecological Economics Journal* 20 (1997); UN Development Programme, Human Development Report (New York: Oxford University Press, 1995); Wages For Housework <ourworld.compuserve.com/homepages/crossroadswomenscentre/WFH.html>

ARTICLE 1.4

September/October 2004

UNEMPLOYMENT RATE DECEPTION

BY EOGHAN STAFFORD

When June's dismal unemployment data came out (at 6.4%, the official unemployment rate hit its highest level in nine years), the administration was quick to put a positive spin on the news. "While the unemployment rate is disappointing," Labor Secretary Elaine Chao reassured us, "it can be viewed as an indication of renewed confidence in the economy with the increased labor-force participation rate." In other words, the jump in unemployment reflects renewed optimism among the jobless—or so the administration would have the country believe.

The key to understanding Secretary Chao's statement lies in the way unemployment is figured. The official unemployment rate, as calculated by the Bureau of Labor Statistics (BLS), includes only jobless people who have looked for work in the previous four weeks—the unemployed who are "in the labor force." The BLS considers people who want jobs but don't have them and who have sought work in the past year but not in the past month to be "marginally attached" to the labor force, whatever their reason for not looking. Those who give an economic reason (for example, they were previously unable to find work in their field, they feel they need more training, or they suffered discrimination in hiring) are considered "discouraged workers," a subset of the marginally attached.

Secretary Chao suggests that official unemployment increased because the labor force increased; some of the marginally attached felt optimistic enough about their prospects to take up new job searches. But this would be cause for optimism only if the increase in the labor force (up 611,000) coincided with a decline in the number of the marginally attached. In actuality, the ranks of the marginally attached increased by about 40,000 between May and June. In addition, during that same period, another 444,000 people began working part-time despite wanting full-time work.

The secretary's attempt to spin the news inadvertently points to a yet larger issue: The official unemployment rate actually understates the the extent of unemployment. A more realistic unemployment rate—one that includes the marginally attached—is shown in Table 1. Counting all marginally attached individuals (discouraged workers plus the rest of the marginally attached) as unemployed brings June's unemployment rate up to 7.3%. If those working part-time involuntarily are added (by counting them as unemployed—the BLS considers them employed), the figure climbs to 10.5%. In total, the government's official measure of unemployment disregards nearly 7 million people who are unemployed or underemployed. (The tables are based on July 2003 BLS data.)

TABLE 1 ALTERNATIVE UNEMPLOYMENT RATE, JULY 2003*		
	Rate	*Thousands***
Unemployed (official)	6.3%	9,313
+ discouraged workers	6.6%	9,788
+ other marginally attached	7.3%	10,907
+ involuntarily part-time	10.5%	16,250

*Not seasonally adjusted

**Cumulative total

TABLE 2 LABOR FORCE BY RACE (IN THOUSANDS)			
	May	*June*	*Change*
White	120,420	120,881	+0.38%
African-American	16,618	16,717	+0.59%

The administration's downplaying of the scale of unemployment is matched by its silence about the effects of the economic downturn on workers of color. Although both white and black workers entered the labor force in June, white workers gained jobs overall, while black workers lost jobs (despite searching for positions in growing numbers). (See Tables 2 and 3.) Racial inequity in the job market is nothing new. Over the past decade, the unemployment rate among African Americans was always more than double that of Whites. (See Table 4.) In the boom year of 1998, African-American unemployment was worse than white unemployment in the recessionary year of 2003. Today African-American unemployment has reached crisis proportions at 10.8%—and that's just the *official* rate.

Common sense might tell you that the millions of jobless and underemployed workers, huge gaps in the employment prospects of different races, and a swelling pool of jobless, disenfranchised youth call for urgent reform. But judging by its complete silence on these issues, the administration appears not to think so—or not to care.

Resources: Bureau of Labor Statistics <www.bls.gov>; "Unemployment Rate Jumps, While Payrolls Decline," Economic Policy Institute (July 3, 2003).

TABLE 3 EMPLOYED PERSONS BY RACE (IN THOUSANDS)			
	May	*June*	*Change*
White	113,882	114,203	+0.28%
African-American	14,819	14,746	−0.49%

TABLE 4 ANNUAL AVERAGE OF MONTHLY UNEMPLOYMENT RATES BY ETHNICITY			
	1993	*1998*	*2003**
White	6.1%	3.9%	5.3%
Hispanics	10.7%	7.2%	7.8%
African-American	11.5%	8.9%	10.8%
*January through July			

ARTICLE 1.5

November/December 2002, revised April 2006

RULING THE EMPIRE

BY ALEJANDRO REUSS

Every few years, the President issues a document called the "National Security Strategy of the United States." Always eagerly awaited, the document is often described as the administration's "blueprint" for U.S. foreign policy. But it's really more like a press release, designed to give the U.S. government's global aims a noble-sounding spin.

The Bush administration's most recent "National Security Strategy," issued September 2002, abounds with pious lip service: On the subject of democracy, it applauds the "elected leaders replac[ing] generals in Latin America" without mentioning who put the generals in power in the first place. On the environment, it calls for "global efforts to stabilize greenhouse gas concentrations" without mentioning that the U.S. government had scuttled the Kyoto Protocol. On the global economy, it decries as "neither just nor stable" a state of affairs "where some live in comfort and plenty, while half of the human race lives on less than $2 a day," yet it offers no solution other than more "free markets and free trade."

The document's crowning hypocrisy, however, is its repeated use of the buzz-phrase "a balance of power that favors freedom," as if that were what the U.S. government was really after. You get the distinct feeling that the drafters don't believe in it for a minute. By its final and most important section, on the country's "National Security Institu-

tions," the document abandons all pretext. The "unparalleled strength of the United States armed forces, and their forward presence, have maintained the peace," it declares. The United States must "reaffirm the essential role of American military strength" and "build and maintain our defenses beyond challenge." It must maintain forces "strong enough to dissuade potential adversaries" from the dream of ever "surpassing, or equaling, the power of the United States."

Well, if those are the real aims of U.S. ruling elites, they're easily succeeding. In 2004, U.S. military spending—the highest, by far, of any country in the world—exceeded the combined spending of the next nine countries—the United Kingdom, France, Japan, China, Germany, Italy, Russia, Saudi Arabia, and South Korea—by over $160 billion (see Graph 1). In fact, U.S. military spending represented nearly half of the total of the *entire world*. This grotesquely overgrown war machine comes at no little cost. In 2004, total federal defense spending devoured more than half of the discretionary spending budget (the part of the federal budget that Congress debates and decides every year), dwarfing spending on education, science, international affairs, and health (see Graph 2). US military spending shows no sign of slowing either; since 2001, spending has increased by a massive $120 billion.

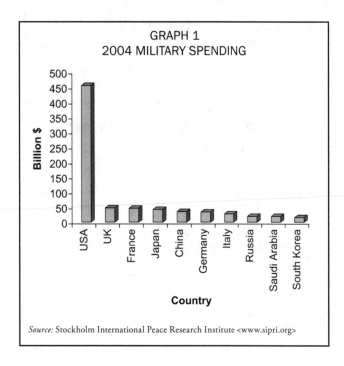

GRAPH 1
2004 MILITARY SPENDING

Source: Stockholm International Peace Research Institute <www.sipri.org>

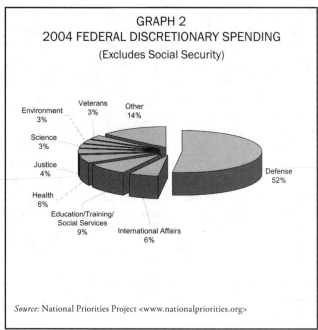

GRAPH 2
2004 FEDERAL DISCRETIONARY SPENDING
(Excludes Social Security)

Source: National Priorities Project <www.nationalpriorities.org>

In light of these realities, the "balance of power" rhetoric isn't really fooling anybody. Writing in the mainstream *Christian Science Monitor*, Gail Russell Chaddock argues that the document "asserts American dominance as the lone superpower—a status no rival power will be allowed to challenge." It is a vision, she says, of a "Pax Americana" (the modern-day equivalent of Roman imperial power). Even the senior defense policy analyst at the right-wing Cato Institute, Charles V. Peña, writes that "although it's all dressed up with the rationale of extending liberty, democracy, and freedom around the globe (except, of course, in Saudi Arabia and Pakistan)" the document really envisions a "Pax Americana enforced by dominant military power and … U.S. forces deployed around the globe."

None of this is exactly news. The United States, after all, has been a major imperial power in the Western Hemisphere for over a century. And it has been the single dominant capitalist power for more than half that period. The truth, however, should be clearer than ever. As the title of Peña's article puts it: "The New National Security Strategy Is American Empire."

TAX BREAKS FOR THE RICH
OR PUBLIC PROGRAMS FOR EVERYONE?

BY MICHELLE SHEEHAN

Who is benefiting from the massive 2001 and 2003 tax cuts? Not the working families President Bush talked about when he pushed the cuts, but the wealthy. The 2001 tax cut was the largest income tax rollback in two decades; it lowered tax rates on the top four income brackets and gave small advance refunds to those less well-off. The 2003 tax cut—the third largest in U.S. history—slashed dividend and capital gains taxes, and accelerated the 2001 rate cut for the top income brackets. Finally, the 2001 estate tax cut reduced the top tax rate each year, meaning that the top 2% of taxpayers will pay progressively fewer taxes on wealth that they leave to heirs.

The figures on the next page represent just a sliver of what the rich will get from the 2001–2003 cuts. The largest tax breaks, and those most geared toward the wealthy, were designed to kick in later. According to Citizens for Tax Justice, the cumulative costs of the 2001–2003 tax cuts will be $824.1 billion in 2010. If the cuts are made permanent beyond 2010, as Bush's 2005 budget proposes, they will cost $5.9 trillion over the next 75 years, and could force massive cuts to already strapped social welfare programs. The right-hand column of the table shows some of the things that the 2001–2003 tax cuts could have paid for in 2004.

TAX CUTS VS. SOCIAL PROGRAMS		
2001–2003 Tax Cuts	*Cost of Tax Cuts in 2004*	*Cost in Social Programs**
Estate tax break for top 1%	$7 billion	Provide Section 8 housing subsidies for 1 million families
Dividends and capital gains tax cut for top 1%	$15 billion	Insure 11 million children under Medicaid (2000)
Benefits to top 1% from cuts in corporate taxes	$25 billion	Fund 2 million Americorps members
Personal income tax cut for top 1%	$32 billion	Bridge "No Child Left Behind" budget gap (excluding dividends and capital gains)
Total tax cuts for top 1%	$79 billion	Bridge the Head Start funding gap 18 times over
Dividends and capital gains tax cut for top 5%	$20 billion	Clean up 143 Superfund "megasites"
Benefits to top 5% from cuts in corporate taxes	$36 billion	Fund Amtrak 20 times over (FY 2005)
Total dividends and capital gains tax cut	$28 billion	Provide WIC nutrition subsidies to 47 million parents and children
Total corporate tax cut	$61 billion	Build 871,000 new units of affordable housing
Total tax cut on personal income (excluding dividends and capital gains)	$169 billion	Pay salary and benefits for 3.1 million elementary school teachers (2001)
TOTAL TAX CUTS IN 2004	$266 billion	Pay four years' tuition at public universities for 13 million students *or* more than half of all Social Security benefits

* Numbers for 2003 unless otherwise noted.

Sources: Tax cuts: Citizens for Tax Justice <www.ctj.org>. *Social spending figures:* Center for Budget and Policy Priorities <www.cbpp.org>; Center for Medicare and Medicaid Services <www.cms.hhs.gov>; Americorps <www.americorps.org>; National Education Association <www.nea.org/esea>; U.S. Department of Health and Human Services, Administration for Children and Families <www.acf.hhs.gov> and United Way <national.unitedway.org>; *Environmental Health Perspectives,* March 2003 <ehp.niehs.nih.gov>; Amtrak <www.amtrak.com>; USDA Food and Nutrition Service <www.fns.usda.gov>; National Priorities Project <www.nationalpriorities.org>; Bureau of Labor Statistics, Occupational Employment Statistics <www.bls.gov/oes>; Social Security 2004 Trustees Report <www.ssa.gov>; College Board <www.collegeboard.com>.

CHAPTER 2

WEALTH, INEQUALITY AND POVERTY

INTRODUCTION

Wealth and inequality are both end products of today's economic growth. But while all macroeconomics textbooks investigate wealth *accumulation*, most give less attention to wealth *disparities*. The authors in this chapter fill in the gap by looking at who makes out, and who doesn't, with the accumulation of wealth.

"Wealth Inequality by the Numbers" (Article 2.1) starts the discussion by providing hard numbers on income and wealth gaps. Inequality in the United States has reached levels unseen since the Great Depression. That is true for income (how much you or your family makes in a year) and wealth (the assets you or your family own minus your debts). Today, the top 1% of households own nearly two-fifths of the nation's wealth; the richest 20% get one-half of our national income.

All told, greater wealth hasn't made for greater equality or social mobility. As Paul Krugman reports, it is not just left critics who say so, but the business press as well. The number of people who go from rags to riches—while always so few as to be near-mythical—has become even smaller since 1980 (Article 2.4). And, as John Miller documents, the current economic recovery has done less to improve wages than any other recovery since World War II (Article 2.2). Finally, poverty rates, which, according to most experts, badly underestimate the extent of poverty in the U.S. economy, continue to rise in the current economic recovery (Article 2.3)

It didn't have to be this way. Chris Tilly debunks the myth that inequality is necessary for economic growth, showing that among both developing and industrial economies and across regions within countries, there is no correlation between higher inequality and faster economic growth. He argues that greater equality actually supports economic growth by bolstering spending, promoting agricultural and industrial productivity, and lessening social conflict (Article 2.5). William Greider provides a blueprint for how the engines of inequality of today's economy can be transformed through workplace democracy, strategic investment of public and union-managed pension funds, and shareholder activism (Article 2.6).

What has happened to world income inequality is a matter of sharp dispute. Many analysts claim that world incomes have converged, leading to a sharp reduction in world inequality in the second half of the twentieth century. Many others report that the gaps between the poorest and the richest people and between countries have continued to widen over the last two decades. Economist Bob Sutcliffe has taken a close look at these studies. In his *Dollars & Sense* interview, Sutcliffe reports that "the wide range of different results of respected studies of world inequality in the last two decades casts doubt on the idea that world inequality has sharply and unambiguously declined or increased during the epoch of neoliberalism" (Article 2.7).

DISCUSSION QUESTIONS

1) (General) The authors in this chapter believe that the distribution of wealth is as important as wealth itself, and consider greater economic equality an important macroeconomic goal. What are some arguments for and against this position? Where do you come down in the debate?

2) (Articles 2.1, 2.2, 2.4) Who benefited from the wealth accumulation of the 1990s? How did stockholders fare versus wage earners? How did the concentration of wealth-holding by income group and by race change during the decade?

3) (Articles 2.1, 2.2, 2.4) "A rising tide lifts all boats," proclaimed John F. Kennedy as he lobbied for pro-business tax cuts in the early 1960s. Did the 1990s boom and the current economic recovery lift all boats? What do the changes in income, wealth, and poverty suggest?

4) (Article 2.3) What are the shortcomings of the federal poverty threshold? How should the United States change the way it calculates the poverty threshold to get a more accurate measure of the incidence of poverty?

5) (Article 2.4) The "New Economy" fed the myth that anyone can get rich quick in this country, but Paul Krugman says it just ain't so. What evidence does he present to argue that social mobility is declining? Do you find his evidence persuasive?

6) (Article 2.5) Why do conservatives argue that inequality is good for economic growth? What counterarguments does Tilly use to challenge this traditional view of the

---

> ### KEY TO COLANDER
>
> E = *Economics*   M = *Macroeconomics*
>
> This chapter fits with chapters E22-E23 or M6-M7; and informs chapters E24-E26 or M8-M10. Inequality and wealth accumulation are also important topics in chapters on monetary policy (E27-E28; M11-M12), inflation, unemployment, and growth (E29; M13) and the section "Policy Issues In Depth" (E30-E31; M14-M15).
>
> Articles 2.1, 2.2, 2.4, and 2.6 fit with chapter E22 or M6, and the discussion of who benefits from the "New Economy" in chapter E29 or M13.
>
> Article 2.5 fits with any discussion of the requisites for growth, such as chapter E24 or M8.
>
> Article 2.7 goes with the discussion of the convergence debate in E24 or M8.

tradeoff between inequality and growth? What evidence convinces Tilly that equality is good for economic growth? Does that evidence convince you?

7) (Article 2.6) Why, in Greider's opinion, is transforming the workplace the key to making the U.S. economy more egalitarian and democratic?

8) (Article 2.7) If Sutcliffe is right that world inequality has neither sharply declined or increased during the epoch of neoliberalism, what does his reading of the world inequality data suggest about the convergence hypothesis—the hypothesis that per capita income in countries with similar institutional structures will converge to the higher level?

ARTICLE 2.1

January/February 2004, revised October 2004

WEALTH INEQUALITY BY THE NUMBERS

BY DOLLARS & SENSE AND UNITED FOR A FAIR ECONOMY

INCOME INEQUALITY IN 1970, 1980, 1990, AND 2003

Household	Mean Income (in 2003)	Share of Aggregate Income			
		1970	1980	1990	2003
Lowest Fifth	$9,996	4.1%	4.3%	3.9%	3.4%
Second Fifth	$25,678	10.8%	10.3%	9.6%	8.7%
Third Fifth	$43,588	17.4%	16.9%	15.9%	14.8%
Fourth Fifth	$68,994	24.5%	24.9%	24.0%	23.4%
Highest Fifth	$147,078	43.0%	43.7%	46.6%	49.8%
Top 5%	$253,239	16.6%	15.8%	18.6%	21.4%

Source: U.S. Bureau of the Census, Historical Tables H-1 and H-2.

INCOME INEQUALITY

Income has never been distributed equally in the United States, but over the past 30 years the gap has been widening. The top 20% now gets half of all the national income, up from 43% in 1970. The top 5% claims over a fifth. The mean income for the top fifth of households is nearly 15 times more than that of the bottom fifth.

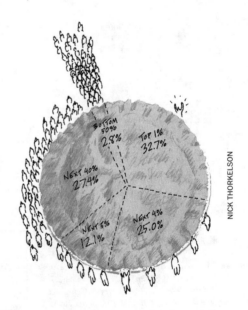

THE WEALTH PIE

The wealthiest 1% of households owns almost a third of the nation household wealth. The next tier, those in the 95th through 98th percentiles, claims another 25%. While the top 5% holds well over half of the wealth pie, the bottom 50% makes do with the crumbs—holding a meager 2.8% of total net worth.

Source: Arthur B. Kennickell, "A Rolling Tide."

HOUSEHOLDS WITH LITTLE OR NO NET WORTH, 1983–2001

	Percentage of households with zero or negative net worth*	Percentage of households with net worth less than $5,000*
1983	15.5%	25.4%
1989	17.9%	27.6%
1992	18.0%	27.2%
1995	18.5%	27.8%
1998	18.0%	27.7%
2001	17.6%	26.6%

* Constant 1995 dollars. Excluding the value of automobiles.

Source: Edward N. Wolff, "Changes in Household Wealth." Studies of wealth ownership define wealth differently. Because Wolff subtracts the value of automobiles, his figures show a higher percentage of the population with little or no wealth than studies that include cars as wealth.

THE WEALTHLESS

The 1980s and 1990s were supposed to be economic good times, but the share of Americans with no wealth at all was larger in 2001 than it had been in 1983. The late-1990s economy gave a small boost to those at the bottom, but it didn't make up for the losses of the previous 15 years. The result: even after the 1990s—the most fabulous decade of economic growth in recent U.S. history—over a quarter of American households had less than $5,000 in assets.

THE SUPER-RICH

Over a 30-year period beginning in 1970, the richest 1% (as ranked by income) accrued a mounting share of the nation's private wealth. Throughout the 1990s, the top percentile held a larger concentration of total household wealth than at any time since the 1920s. Its wealth share declined somewhat during the 2001 recession, thanks to falling corporate share prices, but remained above 33%.

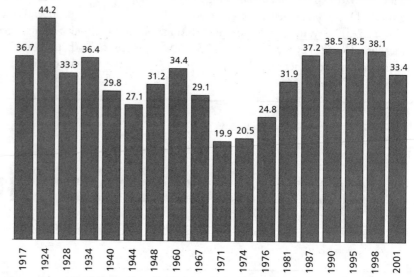

PERCENTAGE SHARE OF HOUSEHOLD WEALTH HELD BY THE TOP 1%, 1917–2001

Sources: Edward N. Wolff, *Top Heavy,* The New Press, 2002 (for 1917-1989) and Wolff, "Recent Trends in Wealth Ownership 1983-1998," Jerome Levy Economics Institute, April 2000 (for 1992-1998).

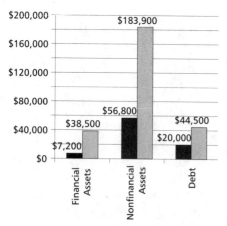

MEDIAN FINANCIAL ASSETS, NON FINANCIAL ASSETS, AND DEBT BY RACE, 2001

■ Families of color   ■ White families

Source: Ana M. Aizcorbe, Arthur B. Kennickell, and Kevin B. Moore, "Recent Changes in U.S. Family Finances: Evidence from the 1998 and 2001 Survey of Consumer Finances," *Federal Reserve Bulletin,* vol. 89 (January 2003). Also see "African Americans Have Less Wealth and More Debt than White Americans," <www.faireconomy.org>.

THE RACIAL WEALTH GAP

The United States has a racial wealth gap that far exceeds its racial income gap. This wealth gap persists even during periods of economic growth. Over the course of the 1990s boom, the wealth of families of color (nonwhite and Latinos of all races) actually fell. This intransigent wealth gap is the product of a long history of discrimination in the United States, and it's perpetuated by family inheritance patterns that pass accumulated racial advantages and disadvantages from one generation to the next. The median net worth of families of color is just a fraction of that of white families'. White families not only have more financial assets (e.g. savings, bonds, stocks, pensions, etc.) and nonfinancial assets (e.g. homes and other property, vehicles, privately held businesses, etc.) than families of color, but also have an easier time securing credit through debt (e.g. mortgages, credit card balances, and other loans).

		1995	1998	2001	$ change	% change
WEALTH VS. INCOME BY RACE, 1995–2001						
Median Net Worth	Families of color	$18,300	$17,900	$17,100	– $1,200	– 7%
	White families	$88,500	$103,400	$120,900	$32,400	3
Median Income	Families of color	$23,000	$25,400	$25,700	$2,700	12%
	White families	$38,200	$41,100	$45,200	$7,100	18%

Source: Ana M. Aizcorbe, Arthur B. Kennickell, and Kevin B. Moore, "Recent Changes in U.S. Family Finances: Evidence from the 1998 and 2001 Survey of Consumer Finances," *Federal Reserve Bulletin,* vol. 89 (January 2003), pp. 1-32, <www.federalreserve.gov>. Also see "African Americans Have Less Wealth and More Debt than White Americans," <www.FairEconomy.org>.

SLOW WAGE GROWTH BUT SOARING PROFITS IN THE CURRENT RECOVERY

BY JOHN MILLER

The current economic recovery has done less to raise wages and more to pump up profits than any of the eight other recoveries since World War II. No wonder inequality continues to worsen, and most people still doubt that the economic turnaround will ever benefit them.

A recent study conducted the Economic Policy Institute, a labor-funded think tank, reports the alarming details. Over the three-year period beginning in early 2001, when the last economic expansion peaked and the recession began, corporate profits rose 62.2%, compared to an average growth of 13.9% by the same point in the other postwar recoveries that lasted that long. Total labor compensation (the sum of all paychecks and employee benefits), on the other hand, grew only 2.8%, well under the historical average of 9.9%. (See Figure 1.) What's more, most of labor's gains came in the form of higher benefits payments to cover the increasing cost of health care and pensions, not higher wages. In fact, in 2003 median weekly wages corrected for inflation declined, for the first time since 1996.

The extreme imbalance between wage and profit growth in this recovery is hardly surprising. Corporate cost-cutting has been the hallmark of this recovery; instead of hiring new workers, bosses have squeezed more out of the old ones. Corporate restructuring, layoffs, and the global outsourcing of both white-collar and manufacturing jobs have all made new jobs scarce. This recovery is still a long way from even replacing the jobs lost since the recession began in March 2001. As of June 2004, some 39 months after the recession began—and 31 months after it officially ended—total employment was still down 1.2 million jobs. Every other economic recovery, even the jobless recovery of the early 1990s, had restored job losses and added a large number of new jobs to the economy by the 39-month mark.

Poor jobs growth has left workers in no position to push for higher wages. Only the jobless recovery of the early 1990s did as poorly as the current job-loss recovery at improving workers' wages and salaries. After adjusting for inflation, wages and salaries increased just 1.1% during the first two years of each of these two recoveries, reports economist Christian Weller of the Cen-

ter for American Progress. Wages and salaries in all other postwar recoveries, on the other hand, rose an average of 12.1% in the same period, or about 11 times more quickly. (See Figure 2.)

At the same time, corporate cost-cutting measures have made for rapid increases in productivity—how much a worker can produce per hour. For instance, in 2002 and 2003, the hourly output of U.S. workers went up at a 5.3% pace, exceeding the "new economy" productivity growth rate of 2.6% from 1996 to 2001. For the first time in a postwar recovery, productivity is growing far faster than the economy.

With little wage growth, the gains from improved productivity have gone nearly exclusively to corporate profits. But few of those profits are getting reinvested. Relative to the size of the economy, real investment at the end of 2003, some 10.3% of GDP, remained well below its pre-recession level of 12.6% of GDP at the end of 2000. Weller estimates that nonfinancial corporations are investing fewer of their resources than at any time since the 1950s. And with little investment, soaring profits have not translated into a hiring boom.

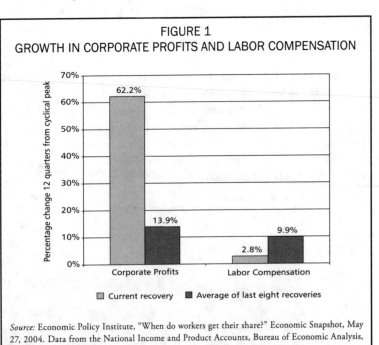

FIGURE 1
GROWTH IN CORPORATE PROFITS AND LABOR COMPENSATION

Percentage change 12 quarters from cyclical peak

62.2%
13.9%
2.8%
9.9%

Corporate Profits   Labor Compensation

■ Current recovery   ■ Average of last eight recoveries

Source: Economic Policy Institute, "When do workers get their share?" Economic Snapshot, May 27, 2004. Data from the National Income and Product Accounts, Bureau of Economic Analysis, U.S. Dept. of Commerce.

Only when labor markets genuinely tighten will workers be able to press for wage gains that match those of workers in earlier economic expansions. Until then, the benefits of this economic expansion, for as long as it can continue without the self-sustaining fuel of wage growth, will continue to go overwhelmingly to profits, exacerbating an economic inequality that is already unprecedented by postwar standards.

Sources: Economic Policy Institute, Job Watch Bulletin, July 2, 2004; Economic Policy Institute, "When do workers get their share?" *Economic Snapshot*, May 27, 2004; Christian Weller, "Reversing the 'Upside-Down' Economy: Faster Income Growth Necessary for Strong and Durable Growth," Center for American Progress, May 24, 2004.

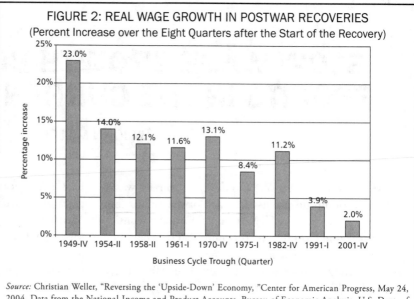

FIGURE 2: REAL WAGE GROWTH IN POSTWAR RECOVERIES
(Percent Increase over the Eight Quarters after the Start of the Recovery)

Source: Christian Weller, "Reversing the 'Upside-Down' Economy, "Center for American Progress, May 24, 2004. Data from the National Income and Product Accounts, Bureau of Economic Analysis, U.S. Dept. of Commerce.

January/February 2006

MEASURES OF POVERTY

ELLEN FRANK

Dear Dr. Dollar:

Can you explain how poverty is defined in government statistics? Is this a realistic definition?

—*Susan Balok, Savannah, Ga.*

Each February, the Census Bureau publishes the federal poverty thresholds—the income levels for different sized households below which a household is defined as living "in poverty." Each August, the bureau reports how many families, children, adults, and senior citizens fell below the poverty threshold in the prior year. As of 2004, the federal poverty thresholds were as follows:

Household Size	Federal Poverty Threshold
1 person	$ 9,310
2 people	12,490
3 people	15,670
4 people	18,850
5 or more	Add $3,180 per person

Using these income levels, the Census Bureau reported that 12.7% percent of U.S. residents and 17.8% of U.S. children lived in poverty in 2004. Black Americans experience

poverty at nearly double these rates: 24.9% of all Blacks and 33.3% of Black children live in households with incomes below the poverty line.

The poverty threshold concept was originally devised by Social Security analyst Mollie Orshansky in 1963. Orshansky estimated the cost of an "economy food plan" designed by the Department of Agriculture for "emergency use when funds are low." Working from 1955 data showing that families of three or more spent one-third of their income on food, Orshansky multiplied the food budget by three to calculate the poverty line. Since the early 1960s, the Census Bureau has simply recalculated Orshansky's original figures to account for inflation.

The poverty line is widely regarded as far too low for a household to survive on in most parts of the United States. For one thing, as antipoverty advocates point out, since 1955 the proportion of family budgets devoted to food has fallen from one-third to one-fifth. Families expend far more on nonfood necessities such as child care, health care, transportation, and utilities today than they did 50 years ago, for obvious reasons: mothers entering the work force, suburbanization and greater dependence on the auto, and soaring health care costs, for example. Were Orshansky formulating a poverty threshold more recently, then, she would likely have multiplied a basic food budget by five rather than by three.

Furthermore, costs—particularly for housing and energy—vary widely across the country, so that an income that might be barely adequate in Mississippi is wholly inadequate in Massachusetts. Yet federal poverty figures make no adjustment for regional differences in costs.

A number of state-level organizations now publish their own estimates of what it takes to support a family in their area, in conjunction with the national training and advocacy group Wider Opportunities for Women. Using local data on housing costs, health care premiums, taxes, and child care costs as well as food, transportation and other necessities, these "self-sufficiency standards" estimate that a two-parent two-child family needs between $40,000 and $50,000 a year, depending on the region, to cover basic needs.

State and federal officials often implicitly recognize that official poverty thresholds are unrealistically low by setting income eligibility criteria for antipoverty programs higher than the poverty level. Households with incomes of 125%, 150%, or even 185% of the federal poverty line are eligible for a number of federal and state programs. In addition, the Census Bureau publishes figures on the number of households with incomes below 200% of the federal poverty line—a level many social scientists call "near poor" or "working poor."

Poverty calculations also have critics on the right. Conservative critics contend that the official poverty rate *overstates* poverty in the United States. While the Census Bureau's poverty-rate calculations include Social Security benefits, public assistance, unemployment and workers' compensation, SSI (disability) payments, and other forms of cash income, they exclude noncash benefits from state and federal antipoverty programs like Food Stamps, Medicaid, and housing subsidies. If the market value of these benefits were counted in family income, fewer families would count as "poor." On the other hand, by not counting such benefits, policy makers have a better grasp of the numbers of Americans in need of such transfer programs.

Resources: For background information on poverty thresholds and poverty rate calculations, see <aspe.hhs.gov/poverty/papers/hptgssiv.htm>. Self-sufficiency standards for different states can be found at <www.sixstrategies.org/states/states.cfm>. In addition, the Economic Policy Institute has calculated family budgets for the 435 metropolitan areas: <www.epi.org/content.cfm/datazone_fambud_budget>.

ARTICLE 2.4

THE DEATH OF HORATIO ALGER

BY PAUL KRUGMAN

The other day I found myself reading a leftist rag that made outrageous claims about America. It said that we are becoming a society in which the poor tend to stay poor, no matter how hard they work; in which sons are much more likely to inherit the socioeconomic status of their fathers than they were a generation ago.

The name of the leftist rag? *Business Week*, which published an article titled "Waking Up From the American Dream." The article summarizes recent research showing that social mobility in the United States (which was never as high as legend had it) has declined considerably over the past few decades. If you put that research together with other research that shows a drastic increase in income and wealth inequality, you reach an uncomfortable conclusion: America looks more and more like a class-ridden society.

And guess what? Our political leaders are doing everything they can to fortify class inequality, while denouncing anyone who complains—or even points out what is happening—as a practitioner of "class warfare."

Let's talk first about the facts on income distribution. Thirty years ago we were a relatively middle-class nation. It had not always been thus: Gilded Age America was a highly unequal society, and it stayed that way through the 1920s. During the 1930s and '40s, however, America experienced what the economic historians Claudia Goldin and Robert Margo have dubbed the Great Compression: a drastic narrowing of income gaps, probably as a result of New Deal policies. And the new economic order persisted for more than a generation. Strong unions, taxes on inherited wealth, corporate profits and high incomes, and close public scrutiny of corporate management all helped to keep income gaps relatively small. The economy was hardly egalitarian, but a generation ago the gross inequalities of the 1920s seemed very distant.

Now they're back. According to estimates by the economists Thomas Piketty and Emmanuel Saez—confirmed by data from the Congressional Budget Office—between 1973 and 2000 the average real income of the bottom 90% of American taxpayers actually fell by 7%. Meanwhile, the income of the top

1% rose by 148%, the income of the top 0.1% rose by 343% and the income of the top 0.01% rose 599%. (Those numbers exclude capital gains, so they're not an artifact of the stock-market bubble.) The distribution of income in the United States has gone right back to Gilded Age levels of inequality.

Never mind, say the apologists, who churn out papers with titles like that of a 2001 Heritage Foundation piece, "Income Mobility and the Fallacy of Class-Warfare Arguments." America, they say, isn't a caste society—people with high incomes this year may have low incomes next year and vice versa, and the route to wealth is open to all. That's where those commies at *Business Week* come in. As they point out (and as economists and sociologists have been pointing out for some time), America actually is more of a caste society than we like to think. And the caste lines have lately become a lot more rigid.

The myth of income mobility has always exceeded the reality. As a general rule, once they've reached their 30s, people don't move up and down the income ladder very much. Conservatives often cite studies like a 1992 report by Glenn Hubbard, a Treasury official under the elder Bush who later became chief economic adviser to the younger Bush, that purport to show large numbers of Americans moving from low-wage to high-wage jobs during their working lives. But what these studies measure, as the economist Kevin Murphy put it, is mainly "the guy who works in the college bookstore and has a real job by his early 30s." Serious studies that exclude this sort of pseudo-mobility show that inequality in average incomes over long periods isn't much smaller than inequality in annual incomes.

It is true, however, that America was once a place of substantial intergenerational mobility—sons often did much better than their fathers. A classic 1978 survey found that among adult men whose fathers were in the bottom 25% of the population as ranked by social and economic status, 23% had made it into the top 25%. In other words, during the first thirty years or so after World War II, the American dream of upward mobility was a real experience for many people.

Now for the shocker: The *Business Week* piece cites a new survey of today's adult men, which finds that this number has dropped to only 10%. That is, over the past generation upward mobility has fallen drastically. Very few children of the lower class are making their way to even moderate affluence. This goes along with other studies indicating that rags-to-riches stories have become vanishingly rare, and that the correlation between fathers' and sons' incomes has risen in recent decades. In modern America, it seems, you're quite likely to stay in the social and economic class into which you were born.

Business Week attributes this to the "Wal-Martization" of the economy, the proliferation of dead-end, low-wage jobs and the disappearance of jobs that provide entry to the middle class. That's surely part of the explanation. But public policy plays a role—and will, if present trends continue, play an even bigger role in the future.

Put it this way: Suppose that you actually liked a caste society, and you were seeking ways to use your control of the government to further entrench the advantages of the haves against the have-nots. What would you do?

One thing you would definitely do is get rid of the estate tax, so that large fortunes can be passed on to the next generation. More broadly, you would seek to reduce tax rates both on corporate profits and on unearned income such as dividends and capital gains, so that those with large accumulated or inherited wealth could more easily accumulate even more. You'd also try to create tax shelters mainly useful for the rich. And more broadly still, you'd try to reduce tax rates on people with high incomes, shifting the burden to the payroll tax and other revenue sources that bear most heavily on people with lower incomes.

Meanwhile, on the spending side, you'd cut back on healthcare for the poor, on the quality of public education and on state aid for higher education. This would make it more difficult for people with low incomes to climb out of their difficulties and acquire the education essential to upward mobility in the modern economy.

And just to close off as many routes to upward mobility as possible, you'd do everything possible to break the power of unions, and you'd privatize government functions so that well-paid civil servants could be replaced with poorly paid private employees.

It all sounds sort of familiar, doesn't it?

Where is this taking us? Thomas Piketty, whose work with Saez has transformed our understanding of income distribution, warns that current policies will eventually create "a class of rentiers in the U.S., whereby a small group of wealthy but untalented children controls vast segments of the US economy and penniless, talented children simply can't compete." If he's right—and I fear that he is—we will end up suffering not only from injustice, but from a vast waste of human potential.

Goodbye, Horatio Alger. And goodbye, American Dream.

Reprinted with permission from the January 5, 2004 issue of *The Nation*. For subscription information call 1-800-333-8536. Portions of each week's *Nation* magazine can be accessed at <www.thenation.com>.

GEESE, GOLDEN EGGS, AND TRAPS

WHY INEQUALITY IS BAD FOR THE ECONOMY

BY CHRIS TILLY

Whenever progressives propose ways to redistribute wealth from the rich to those with low and moderate incomes, conservative politicians and economists accuse them of trying to kill the goose that lays the golden egg. The advocates of unfettered capitalism proclaim that inequality is good for the economy because it promotes economic growth. Unequal incomes, they say, provide the incentives necessary to guide productive economic decisions by businesses and individuals. Try to reduce inequality, and you'll sap growth. Furthermore, the conservatives argue, growth actually promotes equality by boosting the have-nots more than the haves. So instead of fiddling with who gets how much, the best way to help those at the bottom is to pump up growth.

But these conservative prescriptions are absolutely, dangerously wrong. Instead of the goose-killer, equality turns out to be the goose. Inequality stifles growth; equality gooses it up. Moreover, economic expansion does not necessarily promote equality—instead, it is the types of jobs and the rules of the economic game that matter most.

INEQUALITY: GOOSE OR GOOSE-KILLER?

The conservative argument may be wrong, but it's straightforward. Inequality is good for the economy, conservatives say, because it provides the right incentives for innovation and economic growth. First of all, people will only have the motivation to work hard, innovate, and invest wisely if the economic system rewards them for good economic choices and penalizes bad ones. Robin Hood-style policies that collect from the wealthy and help those who are worse off violate this principle. They reduce the payoff to smart decisions and lessen the sting of dumb ones. The result: people and companies are bound to make less efficient decisions. "We must allow [individuals] to fail, as well as succeed, and we must replace the nanny state with a regime of self-reliance and self-respect," writes conservative lawyer Stephen Kinsella in The Freeman: Ideas on Liberty (not clear how the free woman fits in). To prove their point, conservatives point to the former state socialist countries, whose economies had become stagnant and inefficient by the time they fell at the end of the 1980s.

If you don't buy this incentive story, there's always the well-worn trickle-down theory. To grow, the economy needs productive investments: new offices, factories, computers, and machines. To finance such investments takes a pool of savings. The rich save a larger fraction of their incomes than those less well-off. So to spur growth, give more to the well-heeled (or at least take less away from them in the form of taxes), and give less to the down-and-out. The rich will save their money and then invest it, promoting growth that's good for everyone.

Unfortunately for trickle-down, the brilliant economist John Maynard Keynes debunked the theory in his *General Theory of Employment, Interest, and Money* in 1936. Keynes, whose precepts guided liberal U.S. economic policy from the 1940s through the 1970s, agreed that investments must be financed out of savings. But he showed that most often it's changes in investment that drive savings, rather than the other way around. When businesses are optimistic about the future and invest in building and retooling, the economy booms, all of us make more money, and we put some of it in banks, 401(k)s, stocks, and so on. That is, saving grows to match investment. When companies are glum, the process runs in reverse, and savings shrink to equal investment. This leads to the "paradox of thrift": if people try to save too much, businesses will see less consumer spending, will invest less, and total savings will end up diminishing rather than growing as the economy spirals downward. A number of Keynes's followers added the next logical step: shifting money from the high-saving rich to the high-spending rest of us, and not the other way around, will spur investment and growth.

Of the two conservative arguments in favor of inequality, the incentive argument is a little weightier. Keynes himself agreed that people needed financial consequences to steer their actions, but questioned whether the differences in payoffs needed to be so huge. Certainly state socialist countries' attempts to replace material incentives with moral exhortation have often fallen short. In 1970, the Cuban government launched the Gran Zafra (Great Harvest), an attempt to reap 10 million tons of sugar cane with (strongly encouraged) volunteer labor. Originally inspired by Che Guevara's ideal of the New Socialist Man (not clear how the New Socialist Woman fit in), the effort ended with Fidel Castro tearfully apologizing to the Cuban people in a nationally broadcast speech for letting wishful thinking guide economic policy.

But before conceding this point to the conservatives, let's look at the evidence about the connection between equality and growth. Economists William Easterly of New York University and Gary Fields of Cornell University have recently summarized this evidence:

- Countries, and regions within countries, with more equal incomes grow faster. (These growth figures do not include environmental destruction or improvement. If they knocked off points for environmental destruction and added points for environmental improvement, the correlation between equality and growth would be even stronger, since desperation drives poor people to adopt environmentally destructive practices such as rapid deforestation.)
- Countries with more equally distributed land grow faster.
- Somewhat disturbingly, more ethnically homogeneous countries and regions grow faster—presumably because there are fewer ethnically based inequalities.

In addition, more worker rights are associated with higher rates of economic growth, according to Josh Bivens and Christian Weller, economists at two Washington think tanks, the Economic Policy Institute and the Center for American Progress.

These patterns recommend a second look at the incentive question. In fact, more equality can actually *strengthen* incentives and opportunities to produce.

EQUALITY AS THE GOOSE

Equality can boost growth in several ways. Perhaps the simplest is that study after study has shown that farmland is more productive when cultivated in small plots. So organizations promoting more equal distribution of land, like Brazil's Landless Workers' Movement, are not just helping the landless poor—they're contributing to agricultural productivity!

Another reason for the link between equality and growth is what Easterly calls "match effects," which have been highlighted in research by Stanford's Paul Roemer and others in recent years. One example of a match effect is the fact that well-educated people are most productive when working with others who have lots of schooling. Likewise, people working with computers are more productive when many others have computers (so that, for example, e-mail communication is widespread, and know-how about computer repair and software is easy to come by). In very unequal societies, highly educated, computer-using elites are surrounded by majorities with little education and no computer access, dragging down their productivity. This decreases young people's incentive to get more education and businesses' incentive to invest in computers, since the payoff will be smaller.

Match effects can even matter at the level of a metropolitan area. Urban economist Larry Ledebur looked at income and employment growth in 85 U.S. cities and their neighboring suburbs. He found that where the income gap between those in the suburbs and those in the city was largest, income and job growth was slower for everyone.

"Pressure effects" also help explain why equality sparks growth. Policies that close off the low-road strategy of exploiting poor and working people create pressure effects, driving economic elites to search for investment opportunities that pay off by boosting productivity rather than squeezing the have-nots harder. For example, where workers have more rights, they will place greater demands on businesses. Business owners will respond by trying to increase productivity, both to remain profitable even after paying higher wages, and to find ways to produce with fewer workers. The CIO union drives in U.S. mass production industries in the 1930s and 1940s provide much of the explanation for the superb productivity growth of the 1950s and 1960s. (The absence of pressure effects may help explain why many past and present state socialist countries have seen slow growth, since they tend to offer numerous protections for workers but no right to organize independent unions.) Similarly, if a government buys out large land-holdings in order to break them up, wealthy families who simply kept their fortunes tied up in land for generations will look for new, productive investments. Industrialization in Asian "tigers" South Korea and Taiwan took off in the 1950s on the wings of funds freed up in exactly this way.

INEQUALITY, CONFLICT, AND GROWTH

Inequality hinders growth in another important way: it fuels social conflict. Stark inequality in countries such as Bolivia and Haiti has led to chronic conflict that hobbles economic growth. Moreover, inequality ties up resources in unproductive uses such as paying for large numbers of police and security guards—attempts to prevent individuals from redistributing resources through theft.

Ethnic variety is connected to slower growth because, on the average, more ethnically diverse countries are also more likely to be ethnically divided. In other words, the problem isn't ethnic variety itself, but racism and ethnic conflict that can exist among diverse populations. In nations like Guatemala, Congo, and Nigeria, ethnic strife has crippled growth—a problem alien to ethnically uniform Japan and South Korea. The reasons are similar to some of the reasons that large class divides hurt growth. Where ethnic divisions (which can take tribal, language, religious, racial, or regional forms) loom large, dominant ethnic groups seek to use government power to better themselves at the expense of other groups, rather than making broad-based investments in education and infrastructure. This can involve keeping down the underdogs—slower growth in the U.S. South for much of the country's history was linked to the Southern system of white supremacy. Or it can involve seizing the surplus of ethnic groups perceived as better off—in the extreme, Nazi Germany's expropriation and genocide of the Jews, who often held professional and commercial jobs.

Of course, the solution to such divisions is not "ethnic cleansing" so that each country has only one ethnic group—in addition to being morally abhorrent, this is simply impossible in a world with 191 countries and 5,000 ethnic groups. Rather, the solution is to diminish ethnic inequalities. Once the 1964 Civil Rights Act forced the South to drop racist laws, the New South's economic growth spurt began. Easterly reports that in countries with strong rule of law, professional bureaucracies, protection of contracts, and freedom from expropriation—all rules that make it harder for one ethnic group to economically oppress another—ethnic diversity has no negative impact on growth.

If more equality leads to faster growth so everybody benefits, why do the rich typically resist redistribution? Looking at the ways that equity seeds growth helps us understand why. The importance of pressure effects tells us that the wealthy often don't think about more productive ways to invest or reorganize their businesses until they are forced to. But also, if a country becomes very unequal, it can get stuck in an "inequality trap." Any redistribution involves a tradeoff for the rich. They lose by giving up part of their wealth, but they gain a share in increased economic growth. The bigger the disparity between the rich and the rest, the more the rich have to lose, and the less likely that the equal share of boosted growth they'll get will make up for their loss. Once the gap goes beyond a certain point, the wealthy have a strong incentive to restrict democracy, and to block spending on education which might lead the poor to challenge economic injustice—making reform that much harder.

DOES ECONOMIC GROWTH REDUCE INEQUALITY?

If inequality isn't actually good for the economy, what about the second part of the conservatives' argument—that growth itself promotes equality? According to the conservatives, those who care about equality should simply pursue growth and wait for equality to follow.

"A rising tide lifts all boats," President John F. Kennedy famously declared. But he said nothing about which boats will rise fastest when the economic tide comes in. Growth does typically reduce poverty, according to studies reviewed by economist Gary Fields, though some "boats"—especially families with strong barriers to participating in the labor force—stay "stuck in the mud." But inequality can increase at the same time that poverty falls, if the rich gain even faster than the poor do. True, sustained periods of low unemployment, like that in the late 1990s United States, do tend to raise wages at the bottom even faster than salaries at the top. But growth after the recessions of 1991 and 2001 began with years of "jobless recoveries"—growth with inequality.

For decades the prevailing view about growth and inequality within countries was that expressed by Simon Kuznets in his 1955 presidential address to the American Economic Association. Kuznets argued that as countries grew, inequality would first increase, then decrease. The reason is that people will gradually move from the low-income agricultural sector to higher-income industrial jobs—with inequality peaking when the workforce is equally divided between low- and high-income sectors. For mature industrial economies, Kuznets's proposition counsels focusing on growth, assuming that it will bring equity. In developing countries, it calls for enduring current inequality for the sake of future equity and prosperity.

But economic growth doesn't automatically fuel equal-

ity. In 1998, economists Klaus Deininger and Lyn Squire traced inequality and growth over time in 48 countries. Five followed the Kuznets pattern, four followed the reverse pattern (decreasing inequality followed by an increase), and the rest showed no systematic pattern. In the United States, for example:

- incomes became more equal during the 1930s through 1940s New Deal period (a time that included economic decline followed by growth)
- from the 1950s through the 1970s, income gaps lessened during booms and expanded during slumps
- from the late 1970s forward, income inequality worsened fairly consistently, whether the economy was stagnating or growing.

The reasons are not hard to guess. The New Deal introduced widespread unionization, a minimum wage, social security, unemployment insurance, and welfare. Since the late 1970s, unions have declined, the inflation-adjusted value of the minimum wage has fallen, and the social safety net has been shredded. In the United States, as elsewhere, growth only promotes equality if policies and institutions to support equity are in place.

UNION DRIVES IN U.S. MASS PRODUCTION INDUSTRIES IN THE 1930S AND 1940S PROVIDE MUCH OF THE EXPLANATION FOR THE SUPERB PRODUCTIVITY GROWTH OF THE 1950S AND 1960S.

TRAPPED?

Let's revisit the idea of an inequality trap. The notion is that as the gap between the rich and everybody else grows wider, the wealthy become more willing to give up overall growth in return for the larger share they're getting for themselves. The "haves" back policies to control the "have-nots," instead of devoting social resources to educating the poor so they'll be more productive.

Sound familiar? It should. After two decades of widening inequality, the last few years have brought us massive tax cuts that primarily benefit the wealthiest, at the expense of investment in infrastructure and the education, child care, and income supports that would help raise less well-off kids to be productive adults. Federal and state governments have cranked up expenditures on prisons, police, and "homeland security," and Republican campaign organizations have devoted major resources to keeping blacks and the poor away from the polls. If the economic patterns of the past are any indication, we're going to pay for these policies in slower growth and stagnation unless we can find our way out of this inequality trap.

TRANSFORMING THE ENGINES OF INEQUALITY

BY WILLIAM GREIDER

American politics has always involved a struggle between "organized money" and "organized people." It's a neglected truth that has resurfaced with ironic vengeance in our own time—ironic because the 20th century produced so much progress toward political equality among citizens, and because the emergence of a prosperous and well-educated middle class was expected to neutralize the overbearing political power of concentrated wealth. Instead, Americans are reminded, almost any time they read a newspaper, that the rich do indeed get richer and that our political system is, as Greg Palast put it, "the best democracy money can buy."

What should we make of this retrogressive turn—a nation of considerable abundance still ruled by gilded-age privilege? A cynic would say it was ever thus, end of story. Political commentators argue it's a sign of the country's maturation that its citizens now accept what they once resisted—gross and growing inequalities of wealth. And many economists simply avert their gaze from the troubling consequences of maldistribution for economic progress and the well-being of society.

I stake out a contrary claim: The United States remains an unfinished nation—stunted in its proclaimed values—so long as it fails to confront the enduring contradictions between wealth and democracy. That is not a utopian lament for radical change, but simply an observation of what our own era has taught us.

Inequality retains its crippling force over society and politics and the lives of citizens, despite the broader distribution of material comforts. We are not the nation of 80 or 100 years ago, when most Americans struggled in very modest circumstances, often severe deprivation. Yet, despite the nation's wealth (perhaps also because of it), the influence of concentrated economic power has grown stronger and more intimate in our lives. Today the social contract is determined more by the needs and demands of corporations and finance than by government or the consensual will of the people.

The federal government and several generations of liberal and labor reformers did achieve great, life-improving gains during the last century. But those reforms and redistributive programs did not succeed in altering the root sources of economic inequality, much less taming them. On the contrary, the U.S. economic system recreates and even expands the maldistribution of incomes and wealth in each new generation.

The root sources of inequality are located within the institutions of advanced capitalism—in the corporation and financial system—with their narrow operating values and the peculiar arrangements that consign enormous decision-making power to a remarkably small number of people. The problem of inequality is essentially a problem of malformed power relationships: Advanced capitalism deprives most people of voice and influence, while it concentrates top-down authority among the insiders of finance and business. Ameliorative interventions by government (for example, through regulation, taxation, and reform) have never succeeded in overcoming the tendency within capitalism toward increased concentrations of economic power.

The drive for greater equality must involve governmental actions, of course, but it cannot succeed unless it also confronts the engines of inequality within the private realm and forces deep changes in how American capitalism functions. The challenge is nothing less than to rearrange power relationships within the corporation and finance capital.

Who has the power to restructure capitalist institutions? In my view, ordinary people do—at least potentially—acting collectively as workers, investors, consumers, managers or owners and, above all, as citizens, to force change. Many are, in small and different ways, already at work on the task of reinventing capitalism.

TRANSFORMING THE WORKPLACE

The workplace is perhaps the most effective engine of inequality, since it teaches citizens resignation and subservience, while it also maldistributes the returns of enterprise. For most Americans, the employment system functions on the archaic terms of the master-servant relationship inherited from feudalism. The feudal lord commanded the lives and livelihoods of serfs on his land and expelled those who disobeyed. The corporate employer has remarkably similar powers, restrained only by the limited prohibitions in law or perhaps by the terms of a union contract. Elaine Bernard, director of Harvard's trade union studies program, described the blunt reality:

> As power is presently distributed, workplaces are factories of authoritarianism polluting our democracy. Citizens cannot spend eight hours a day obeying orders and being shut out of important decisions affecting them, and then

be expected to engage in a robust, critical dialogue about the structure of our society.

Where did people learn to accept their powerlessness? They learned it at work. Nor is this stunted condition confined to assembly lines and working-class occupations. The degradation of work now extends very far up the job ladder, including even well-educated professionals whose expert judgments have been usurped by distant management systems.

In most firms, only the insiders at the top of a very steep command-and-control pyramid will determine how the economic returns are distributed among the participants. Not surprisingly, the executives value their own work quite generously while regarding most of the employees below as mere commodities or easily interchangeable parts. More importantly, these insiders will harvest the new wealth generated by an enterprise, while most workers will not. In the long run, this arrangement of power guarantees the permanence of wealth inequalities.

Joseph Cabral, CEO of Chatsworth Products Inc., a successful employee-owned computer systems manufacturer in California, is an accountant, not a political philosopher, but he understands the wealth effects of closely held control in private businesses. "The wealth that's created ends up in too few hands," he said. "The entrepreneur who's fortunate enough to be there at the start ends up really receiving a disproportionate amount of wealth. And the working folks who enabled that success to take place share in little of that wealth. At some point, capitalism is going to burst because we haven't done right for the folks who have actually created that wealth."

But there are other, more democratic, ways to structure the work environment. At Chatsworth, where the workers collectively purchased the enterprise, "Everyone is sharing in the wealth they're creating. … We're not just doing this for some outside shareholder. We're doing it because we are the shareholders."

Employee ownership, worker-management, and other systems of worker self-organization provide a plausible route toward reforming workplace power relations and spreading financial wealth among the many instead of the few.

TRANSFORMING FINANCE CAPITAL

The top-down structure of how Wall Street manages "other people's money" ensures the maldistribution of financial returns. As wealthy people know, those who bring major money to the table are given direct influence over their investments and a greater return on their risk-taking. The rank-and-file investors—because their savings are modest and they lack trustworthy intermediaries to speak for them—are regarded as passive and uninformed, treated more or less like "widows and orphans," and blocked from exerting any influence over how their wealth is invested. To put the point more crudely, the stock market is a casino, and the herd of hapless investors is always the "mark."

Nevertheless, finance capital is, I predict, the realm of capitalism most vulnerable to reform pressures. That's mainly because it operates with other people's money, and most of that money belongs not to the wealthiest families but to the broad ranks of ordinary working people. A historic shift in the center of gravity has occurred in U.S. finance over the past decade: Fiduciary institutions like pension funds and mutual funds have eclipsed individual wealth as the largest owner of financial assets. Their collectivized assets now include 60% of the largest 1,000 corporations. Because these funds invest across the broad stock market, they literally own the economy.

Public pension funds, union-managed pension funds, and shareholder activists are already working to forge an engaged voice for the individuals whose wealth is in play, and to force the fiduciary institutions to take responsibility for the social and environmental effects of how these trillions in savings are invested. The collapse of the stock-market bubble and subsequent corporate scandals have accelerated these reform efforts.

Some of the largest public-employee pension funds including the California Public Employees' Retirement System and the New York State public employees fund, joined by state officials who sit on supervisory boards, are aggressively leading the fight for corporate-governance reform and for stricter social accountability on urgent matters like workers' rights and global warming. The labor movement is organizing proxy battles to press for corporate reforms at individual companies including the Disney Corporation and Royal Dutch Shell, while the AFL's Office of Investment won a victory for mutual-fund investors in early 2003 when it persuaded the Securities and Exchange Commission to require mutual funds to disclose their proxy votes in corporate-governance shareholder fights. (The mutual fund industry is working to resist the measure, and for good reason. Investment firms regularly vote against the interests of their own rank-and-file investors in order to curry favor with the corporations that hire them to manage corporate-run pension funds and 401(k) plans.)

The major banks and brokerages cannot brush aside these new critics as easily as corporate directors often do. Wall Street will respond to fiduciary concerns because it must. It needs the rank-and-file's capital to operate. When six or seven major funds, collectively holding nearly $1 trillion, speak to Wall Street, things do change. Their unspoken threat to scorn companies or financial firms that ignore

THE DRIVE FOR GREATER EQUALITY MUST INVOLVE GOVERNMENTAL ACTIONS, BUT IT CANNOT SUCCEED UNLESS IT ALSO CONFRONTS THE ENGINES OF INEQUALITY WITHIN THE PRIVATE REALM.

larger social obligations and shift their money elsewhere sends broad shockwaves across both financial markets and corporate boardrooms.

The more profound tasks are to challenge fraudulent economic valuations (think Enron) and to account for (and internalize) the true costs of products and production processes. Both steps would refocus capital investing toward creating real, long-term value and away from the transient thrill of quarterly returns. The fiduciary funds have the potential power to enforce this new economic perspective, though it is not yet widely understood or accepted by them. As universal owners of the economy, their own portfolios are the losers when individual corporations throw off externalities in order to boost their bottom lines. The costs will be borne by every other firm, by the economy as a whole, or by taxpayers who have to clean up the mess. The compelling logic of this new economic argument is this: what is bad for society cannot be good for future retirees or for their communities and their families.

Citizens, in other words, have more power than they imagine. If they assert influence over these intermediaries, they have the power to punish rogue corporations for antisocial behavior and block the low-road practices that have become so popular in business circles. In coalition with organized labor, environmentalists, and other engaged citizens, they have the capacity to design—and enforce—a new social contract that encourages, among other things, participatory management systems and worker ownership, loyalty to community, and respect for our deeper social values.

While none of this promises a utopian outcome of perfect equality, the redistribution of power within capitalism is certainly a predicate for the creation of a more equitable society.

My conviction is that we are on the brink of a broad new reform era, in which reorganizing capitalism becomes the principal objective. What I foresee is a long, steady mobilization of people attempting to do things differently, often in small and local settings, trying out new arrangements, sometimes failing, then trying again. As these inventive departures succeed, others will emulate them. In time, an alternative social reality will emerge with different values, alongside the archaic and destructive system that now exists. When that begins to happen and gains sufficient visibility, the politics is sure to follow. If all this sounds too remote to the present facts, too patient for our frenetic age, remember that this is how deep change has always occurred across American history.

This article is adapted from *The Soul of Capitalism* (Simon & Schuster, 2003).

ARTICLE 2.7   *March/April 2005*

RICH AND POOR IN THE GLOBAL ECONOMY

INTERVIEW WITH BOB SUTCLIFFE

Whether economic inequality is rising or falling globally is a matter of intense debate, a key question in the larger dispute over how three decades of intensified economic globalization have affected the world's poor. Bob Sutcliffe is an economist at the University of the Basque Country in Bilbao, Spain, and the author of 100 Ways of Seeing an Unequal World. *He has been analyzing both the statistical details and the broader political-economic import of the debate and shared some of his insights in a recent interview with* Dollars & Sense.

DOLLARS & SENSE: If someone asked you whether global inequality has grown over the past 25 years, I assume you'd say, "It depends—on how inequality is defined, on what data is used, on how that data is analyzed." Is that fair?

BOB SUTCLIFFE: Yes, it's fair, but it's not enough. First, the most basic fact about world inequality is that it is monstrously large; that result is inescapable, whatever the method or definition. As to its direction of change in the last 25 years, to some extent there are different answers. But also there are different questions. Inequality is not a simple one-dimensional concept that can be reduced to a single number. Single overall measures of world inequality (where all incomes are taken into account) give a different result from measures of the relation of the extremes (the richest compared with the poorest). Over the last 25 years, you find that the bottom half of world income earners seems to have gained something in relation to the top half (so, in this sense, there is less inequality), but the bottom 10% have lost seriously in comparison with the top 10% (thus, more inequality), and the bottom 1% have lost enormously in relation to the top 1% (much more inequality). None of these measures is a single true measure of inequality; they are all part of a complex structure of inequalities, some of which can lessen as part of the same overall process in which others increase.

We do have to be clear about one data-related question

that has caused huge confusion. To look at the distribution of income in the world, you have to reduce incomes of different countries to one standard. Traditionally it has been done by using exchange rates; this makes inequality appear to change when exchange rates change, which is misleading. But now we have data based on "purchasing power parity" (the comparative buying power, or real equivalence, of currencies). Using PPP values achieves for comparisons over space what inflation-adjusted index numbers have achieved for comparisons over time. Although many problems remain with PPP values, they are the only way to make coherent comparisons of incomes between countries. But they produce estimates that are astonishingly different from exchange rate-based calculations. For instance, U.S. income per head is 34 times Chinese income per head using exchange rates, but only 8 times as great using PPP values. (And, incidentally, on PPP estimates the total size of the U.S. economy is now only 1.7 times that of China, and is likely to be overtaken by it by 2011.) So when you make this apparently technical choice between two methods of converting one currency to another, you come up not only with different figures on income distribution but also with two totally different world economic, and thus political, perspectives.

D&S: So even if some consensus were reached on the choices of definition, data, and method, you're urging a complex, nuanced portrait of what is happening to global inequality, rather than a yes or no answer. Could you give a brief outline of what you think that portrait looks like?

BS: Most integral measures—integral meaning including the entire population rather than comparing the extremes—that use PPP figures suggest that overall income distribution at the global level during the last 25 years has shown a slight decline in inequality, though there is some dissent on this. In any event this conclusion is tremendously affected by China, a country with a fifth of world population which has been growing economically at an unprecedented rate. Second, there seems to me little room for debate over the fact that the relative difference between the very rich and the very poor has gotten worse. And the smaller the extreme proportions you compare, the greater the gap. So the immensely rich have done especially well in the last 25 years, while the extremely poor have done very badly. The top one-tenth of U.S. citizens now receive a total income equal to that of the poorest 2.2 billion people in the rest of the world.

There have also been clear trends within some countries. Some of the fastest growing countries have become considerably more unequal. China is an example, along with some other industrializing countries like Thailand. The most economically liberal of the developed countries have also become much more unequal—for instance, the United States, the United Kingdom, and Australia—and so have the post-communist countries. The most extreme figures for inequality are found in a group of poor countries including

Namibia and Botswana in southern Africa and Paraguay and Panama in Latin America.

Finally, the overall index of world inequality (measured by the Gini coefficient, a measure of income distribution) is about the same as that for two infamously unequal countries, South Africa and Brazil. And in the last few years it has shown no signs of improvement whatsoever.

D&S: People use the terms "unimodal" and "bimodal" to describe the global distribution of income. Can you explain what these mean? Also, you have referred elsewhere to a possible trimodal distribution—what does that refer to?

BS: The mode of a distribution is its most common value. In many countries there is one level of income around which a large proportion of the population clusters; at higher or lower levels of income there are progressively fewer people, so the distribution curve rises to a peak and then falls off. That is a unimodal distribution. But in South Africa, for example, due to the continued existence of entrenched ethnic division and economic inequality, the curve of distribution has two peaks—a low one, the most common income received by black citizens, and another, higher one, the the most common received by whites. This is a bimodal distribution because there are two values that are relatively more common than those above or below them. Because of its origins you could call it the "Apartheid distribution." The world distribution is in many respects uncannily like that of South Africa. It could be becoming trimodal in the sense that the frequency distribution of income has three peaks—one including those in very poor countries which have not been growing economically (e.g., parts of Africa), one in those developing countries which really have been developing (e.g., in South and East Asia), and one in the high-income industrialized countries. It's a kind of "apartheid plus" form of distribution.

D&S: In 2002, you wrote that many institutions, like the United Nations and the World Bank, were not being exactly honest in this debate—for example, emphasizing results based on data or methods that they elsewhere acknowledged to be poor. Has this changed over the past few years? Has the quality of the debate over trends in global income inequality improved?

BS: The most egregious pieces of statistical opportunism have declined. But I think there is a strong tendency in general for institutions to seize on optimistic conclusions regarding distribution in order to placate critics of the present world order. This increasingly takes the form of putting too much weight on measures of welfare other than income, for instance, life expectancy, for which there has been more international convergence than in the case of income. But there has been very little discussion of the philosophical basis for using life expectancy instead of or combined with income to measure inequality. If poor people live longer but in income terms remain as relatively poor as ever, has the world become less unequal?

The problem of statistical opportunism is not confined to those who are defending the world economic order; it also exists on the left. So, on the question of inequality, there is a tendency to accept whatever numerical estimate shows greatest inequality on the false assumption that this confirms the wickedness of capitalism. But capitalist inequality is so great that the willful exaggeration of it is not needed as the basis of anti-capitalist propaganda. It is more important for the left to look at the best indicators of the changing state of capitalism, including indicators of inequality, in order to intervene more effectively.

Finally, the quality of the debate, regardless of the intentions of the participants, is still greatly restricted by the shortage of available statistics about inequalities. That has improved somewhat in recent years although there are many things about past and present inequalities which we shall probably never know.

D&S: Do you see any contexts in which it's more important to focus on absolute poverty levels and trends in those levels rather than on inequality?

BS: The short answer is no, I do not. Plans for minimum income guarantees or for reducing the number of people lacking basic necessities can be important. But poverty always has a relative as well as an absolute component. It is a major weakness of the Millenium Development Goals, for example, that they talk about halving the number of people in absolute extreme poverty without a single mention of inequality. [The Millenium Development Goals is a U.N. program aimed at eliminating extreme poverty and achieving certain other development goals worldwide by 2015. —*Eds.*] And there is now a very active campaign on the part of anti-egalitarian, pro-capitalist ideologues in favor of the complete separation of the two. That is wrong not only because inequality is what partly defines poverty but more importantly because inequality and poverty reduction are inseparable. To separate them is to say that redistribution should not form part of the solution to poverty. Everyone is prepared in some sense to regard poverty as undesirable. But egalitarians see riches as pathological too. The objective of reducing poverty is integrally linked to the objective of greater equality and social justice.

D&S: Can you explain the paradox that China's economic liberalization since the late 1970s has increased inequality within China and at the same time reduced global inequality? Some researchers and policymakers interpret China's experience over this period as teaching us that it may be necessary for poor countries to sacrifice some equality in order to fight poverty. Do you agree with this—if not, how would you respond?

BS: When you measure *global* inequality, you are not just totalling the levels of inequality in individual countries. In theory all individual countries could become more unequal and yet the world as a whole become more equal, or vice versa. In China, a very poor country in 1980, average incomes have risen much faster than the world average and this has reduced world inequality. But different sections of the population have done much better than others so that inequality within China has grown. If and when China becomes on average a richer country than it is now, further unequal growth there may contribute to increasing rather than decreasing world inequality.

China's growth has been very inegalitarian, but it has been very fast. And the proportion of the population in poverty seems to have been reduced. But it is possible to envisage a more egalitarian growth path which would have been slower in aggregate but which would have reduced the number of poor people at least as much if not more than China's actual record. So I do not think it is right to say that higher inequality is the cause of reduced poverty, though it may for a time be a feature of the rapid growth which in turn creates employment and reduces poverty.

This does not mean that all increases in inequality are necessarily pathological. The famous Kuznets curve sees inequality first rising and then falling during economic growth as an initially poor population moves by stages from low-income, low-productivity work into high-income, high-productivity work, until at the end of the process 100% of the population is in the second group. If you measure inequality during such a process, it does in fact rise and then fall again to its original level—in this example at the start everyone is equally poor, at the end everyone is equally richer. That might be called transitional inequality; many growth processes may include an element of it. In that case equality is not really being "sacrificed" to reduce poverty— poverty is reduced by a process which increases inequality and then eliminates it again. But at the same time inequality may be growing for many other reasons which are not, like the Kuznets effect, self-eliminating, but rather cumulative. When inequality grows, this malign variety tends to be more important than the self-eliminating variety. But many economists are far too ready to see growing inequality as the more benign, self-eliminating variety.

D&S: Where do you think the question of what is happening to global income inequality fits into the broader debate over neoliberalism and globalization?

BS: Many people say that since some measures of inequality started to improve in about 1980 and that is also when neoliberalism and globalization accelerated, it is those processes which have produced greater equality. There are many problems with this argument, among them the fact that at least on some measures global inequality has grown since 1980. In any case, measures which show global inequality falling in this period are, as we have seen, very strongly influenced by China. China's extraordinary growth has, of course, in part been expressed in and permitted by greater globalization (its internationalization has grown faster than its production), and it is also clear that liberalization of economic policy has played a role, though China hardly has a neoliberal economy. But to permit is not to cause. The real cause is surely to be found not so much in economic policy as in a profound social movement in which a new and highly dynamic capitalist class (combined with a supportive authoritarian state) has once again become an agent of massive capitalist accumulation, as seen before in Japan, the United States, and Western Europe. So, an important part of what we are observing in figures which show declining world inequality is not any growth of egalitarianism, but the dynamic ascent of Chinese and other Asian capitalisms.

This interview also appears on the website of the Political Economy Research Institute at the University of Massachusetts-Amherst, along with Bob Sutcliffe's working paper "A More or Less Unequal World? World Income Distribution in the 20th Century." See <www.umass. edu/peri>.

CHAPTER 3

SAVINGS AND INVESTMENT

INTRODUCTION

Never a slip from the savings cup to the investment lip. That is the orderly world of classical macroeconomics, where every cent of household savings is neatly transferred to corporate investment. In the classical world, savings markets—governed by all-powerful interest rates—work seamlessly to assure that savings are matched by investments, fueling growth in the private economy, which in turn guarantees full employment. Should the flow of savings exceed the uptake of corporate investment, falling interest rates automatically solve the problem.

In the real world, macroeconomies are far messier than classical macroeconomics suggests. Keynes argued that there is no neat connection, or nexus, between savings and investment in a modern financial economy. Savings often sit, hoarded and uninvested. And interest rates, no matter how low, seldom coax balky investors to lay out their money in a weak economy. In the Keynesian world, economies regularly suffer from investment shortfalls that lead to recessions and cost workers their jobs.

In this chapter, Gretchen McClain and Randy Albelda report on one critical test of the classical and Keynesian visions, conducted by economist Steven Fazzari. In a massive study of 5,000 manufacturing firms, Fazzari rated the influence of interest rates, business cycle conditions, and firms' financial conditions on their investment in plant and equipment. He concluded that the influence of interest rates is overrated, putting him squarely in the Keynesian camp (McClain and Albelda, article 3.1).

Dean Baker adds that historically low interest rates have fueled an outburst of speculative investment that has driven up housing prices, saddling the economy with a housing bubble that may well leave the economy in another recession when it bursts (Article 3.4). Ellen Frank explains why there is no logical connection between rising stock prices and rising investment. Stock prices are based on traders' guesses about which stocks are likely to catch the eye of other traders–guesses that can have little to do with actual economic conditions (Article 3.2).

With economic advancement more limited than any time in the last three decades, Ellen Frank (Article 3.3) argues that increasing social wealth–through improved social insurance programs from social security, unemployment insurance, better public education and public financed higher education, and health care—will do more to enrich most people than any attempt to restore private savings. Daniel Fireside reports on how one Vermont city managed to provide affordable housing despite skyrocketing housing prices through a community land trust (Article 3.5). Finally, Adria Scharf describes how pension wealth, labor's capital, can be used to fund investments that generate good jobs and empower workers (Article 3.6).

DISCUSSION QUESTIONS

1) (Articles 3.1) Keynes argued that savings and investment were not balanced by the interest rate but by changes in the level of aggregate output. How does the essay by McClain and Albelda support Keynes's claim about investment?

2) (Article 3.1) According to McClain and Albelda, how did Fazzari rate the influence of interest rates, business cycle conditions, and firms' financial conditions on corporate investment? What do his findings suggest about Keynesian and classical theories of investment? Based on his findings, what stabilization policies might be appropriate to promote investment?

3) (Article 3.2) During the 1930s, Keynes compared the stock market to a newspaper beauty contest that asked readers to pick the photo of the contestant that other readers would pick as the prettiest. Frank suggests that Keynes's analogy still holds for today's stock market. How does Frank's explanation of stock prices compare with those in your textbook? Do you find it convincing?

4) (Article 3.3) How would the improved social insurance programs that Ellen Frank advocates resolve the paradox of thrift and enhance social mobility and wealth accumulation for most people? Does Frank's approach to augmenting social wealth make good economic sense?

5) (Article 3.4) Baker warns of the threat of a recession. Others including Pam Woodall, economics editor of the *Econ-*

KEY TO COLANDER

E = *Economics*   M = *Macroeconomics*

This chapter takes up topics in chapters E24-E26 or M8-M10; and prefigures the policy debates in chapters E28 and E34, or M12 and M19.

Article 3.1 discusses investment, the subject of chapter E24 or M8; the macro models in chapters E25-E26 or M9-M10; and the effectiveness of lowering interest rates to encourage investment, the topic of chapter E29 or M13.

Articles 3.2 and 3.3 fit with the discussion of growth in chapter E24 or M8, and the box on the stock boom in chapter E34 or M19.

Articles 3.4, 3.5, and 3.6 fit with chapters E24-E26 or M8-M10, which rely on an understanding of household savings.

---

omist, have worried that "a housing bust" would push the U.S. economy into deflation. How real of a threat is this?

6) (Article 3.5) How did the Burlington Community Land Trust (BCLT) allow the city to increase the supply of affordable housing? Can the BCLT model be applied successfully to housing markets in other cities?

7) (Article 3.6) What is the legal space that would allow the custodians of workers' pensions to invest them in a way that creates good jobs and empowers them? Give examples of pension investments that have benefited workers. How effective do you think pension fund investing can be at making the U.S. economy more worker-friendly?

ARTICLE 3.1   *July 1993, revised April 2001*

BOOSTING INVESTMENT

THE OVERRATED INFLUENCE OF INTEREST RATES

BY GRETCHEN McCLAIN AND RANDY ALBELDA

Few economists or politicians would disagree that an economy's prospects for long-term growth depend on the productive capacity of its people and its physical equipment. But what to invest in—and how to get the appropriate economic actors to invest—is a matter of much debate.

All economies face a choice between using their productive resources to produce goods and services to be consumed now, and forsaking today's consumption to produce more goods for the future. While catering to consumption today may be more satisfying for wealthier countries and absolutely vital for poor countries, it fails to provide for future growth.

Investing in new plant and equipment can stimulate growth over time, as it provides the physical capacity for new production. Moreover, new plant and equipment tend to be better designed than the existing capital stock, and the improvement usually helps to boost output per worker. If this new productivity translates into higher wages, investment can also increase a country's standard of living and improve employment possibilities. In turn, improving human productive capacity—through training and education—can lead to growth and increased productivity in the long run.

Investment, and the consequent increase in productivity, is critical for international economic success. The more efficiently a country can produce a product, the more competitive that country will be in the world market. Since international markets provide an avenue of demand for our goods, the more domestically produced products and services we can sell abroad, the more jobs we can support here.

Investment can also help stimulate the economy in the short run. During an economic downturn, increased investment will yield more jobs and income for workers who would otherwise be unemployed. They will then return their income to the market when they purchase goods and services, which will boost demand for those products. Economists call this the "multiplier effect." The increase in demand in turn encourag-

es firms to invest more so that they can meet that demand—known to economists as the "accelerator effect." All in all, such a cycle creates more jobs, income, and spending.

While few economists dispute the importance of investment, many disagree on what type is needed, which sectors of the economy are best able to provide it, and what are the best ways to encourage investment. Typically, these debates have revolved around the government's role in encouraging private investment in new plant and equipment. But the role that public investment in infrastructure and education plays in promoting not only our economic well-being and growth, but also in encouraging private investment, could and should widen the terms of the debate.

THE BACKDROP

The traditional economic argument about investment—and the prevailing conservative line espoused by elected officials at the federal and state levels—has been that the most important fiscal policies to encourage privately owned firms to invest are those which boost profits. If the government helps provide the conditions for profitability, the argument goes, firms will be encouraged to make the right types of investment.

Government tax-and-spend policies during the 1980s and 1990s have often tried to promote investment by reducing corporate taxes, in order to boost profits and stimulate savings. Such measures were supposed to leave firms with a bigger bottom line, in the hope that they would turn profits into new plant and equipment. Cuts in personal income tax rates—especially for the wealthiest—were intended to leave people with more after-tax income that they could save. Higher savings, according to this logic, translates into lower interest rates which in turn lead to more investment. While such policies have been very effective in redistributing money from the poor to the wealthy, they did not do much for investment. For example, the amount of new fixed investment (i.e., new plant and equipment) relative to the total amount of plant and equipment actually sank to its lowest post-World War II mark between 1989 and 1991.

Merely providing the conditions for profit-making does not mean that private firms will plow those profits back into new plant and equipment. Speculation on real-estate markets, the value of foreign currencies, or the price of silver and gold could easily eat up new profits. Much of the money generated for investment in the 1980s financed mergers and acquisitions, which generally resulted in less employment and little new physical productive capacity. And, perhaps even more important, new investment by U.S. firms may not take place in the United States. Investing abroad has been the trend since the 1970s. Finally, even if there is domestic investment and it increases productivity, unless workers share in those gains it may not promote robust growth or increase the standard of living of the country as a whole.

In the face of the failure of the 1980s policies to promote investment, conservatives came up with a new explanation of why the economy was so sluggish: the deficit. Ironically, the conservative policies mentioned above were largely responsible for the public debt, but nonetheless Republicans, along with many Democrats galvanized by billionaire Ross Perot, latched onto deficit reduction as the most important fiscal policy of the 1990s.

The deficit, they argued, kept long-term interest rates high because it created competition for precious funds. The result was that federal borrowing, necessitated by debt-financed government spending and tax cuts, "crowded out" private investment. The best solution, they said, was to reduce the deficit and bring down long-term interest rates so that private investment would thrive.

IDENTIFYING INFLUENCE

Economist Steven Fazzari tackled these assumptions in a study of the influence of the federal government's taxing and spending policies on private investment. Using a large data base from Standard and Poor on over 5,000 manufacturing firms from 1971 to 1990, Fazzari tested three different factors for their effects on levels of investment in plant and equipment: interest rates, the business cycle, and the financial conditions of the firms.

According to Fazzari, these three "channels of influence" shape patterns of investment. First, he takes on the traditionalists, by addressing the costs associated with investment: the price of borrowing money (i.e., interest rates), depreciation (how fast the new piece of equipment or building will lose its value), and taxes affecting both corporate profits and dividends. To measure this channel, Fazzari employs the interest rate on one type of corporate bond.

Next, he considers the influence of the business cycle by looking at sales growth. Traditional economic theory tends to assume a ready market, but Fazzari suggests instead that firms make investment decisions based on their perception of their ability to sell their products. The more robust current

sales are and are expected to be, the more likely firms will be willing to risk new investment—regardless of the interest rate. Since the general condition of the economy influences sales levels, it also has an impact on investment.

In Fazzari's examination of the third channel of influence—the financial condition of firms—he again questions conventional wisdom, this time about the supply and demand for loans. Most economists assume that if the expected return on an investment exceeds the interest rate, then the project is profitable and will be undertaken. This is most likely to be true when the firm in question has enough cash on hand from prior profits to make the investment without asking a bank for a loan. Many firms, though, need to borrow money, and some are unable to persuade banks to loan it to them. Banks often refuse loan applications from new businesses with few assets, or charge them prohibitively high interest rates. Even if a young firm finds a potentially profitable investment, severe constraints on raising capital may prevent the firm from pursuing it. A firm's financial condition—not the projected rate of return on the new investment—can thus end up determining whether or not investment takes place.

PERFECTING POLICY

After looking at the importance of interest rates, the business cycle, and the financial conditions of firms in determining investment, Fazzari found that interest rates exert the weakest influence of the three factors. He concludes that there is no evidence that interest rates significantly affect investment for the fastest growing firms in his sample. Based on these findings, Fazzari claims that "it would be speculative to base policy on the assumption that interest rates drive investment to an important extent, especially for growing firms."

So, what kinds of fiscal policies should we adopt? If we believe Fazzari's results, we should be looking for those that attend to the financial conditions of firms and stimulate demand for products.

A tax cut targeted not at the very rich but at the "middle class" would probably give investment at least a temporary boost by generating increased consumption. Increased sales from a temporary tax cut create the illusion of a permanent increase in demand, and the multiplier and accelerator effects discussed earlier come into play. In order to meet what firms believe is a permanent increase in demand for their goods, they make investments in more equipment, more factories, and more employees.

Another means of encouraging investment that Fazzari evaluates is cutting corporate income taxes. Such cuts increase firms' after-tax profits, leaving them with a larger pool of funds to invest if they so choose. Since there is no guarantee that they will invest the savings from reduced taxes, though, Fazzari prefers investment tax credits (ITCs) to cuts in taxes for all firms. Only if firms invested would they be able to reduce their corporate tax bills. In Fazzari's view, ITCs will effectively encourage investment whether it is sensitive to interest rates or not.

The most important lesson from Fazzari's analysis is that concerns about investment should not stand in the way of policy initiatives that are important for society, such as spending on education and job training, simply because they may increase the federal budget deficit and cause interest rates to rise. Government investments in public works and education will likely increase productivity in the long run, and this can only be good for investment. Moreover, if investment is not sensitive to interest rates, then the much-discussed "crowding out" effect of deficit spending on private business is bound to be very small. And as Fazzari points out, when unemployment is high, the stimulative effects of deficit spending on sales may far outweigh the impacts of increased interest rates.

The focus on balanced budgets should be tempered by a thorough analysis of what this policy implies for society's immediate and long-term welfare. When we underinvest in the economy during a recession by eliminating educational and social investments, the foregone technical innovation resulting from this underinvestment may lead to less efficient workers, and lower productivity, for many years.

Fazzari's results not only repudiate the traditional answer to lagging investment—tax cuts for the wealthy and the lowering of interest rates. Instead, the government should be trying to stimulate the economy through improved physical and social infrastructure, which will boost not only sales but investment and incomes.

May/June 2002

WHO DECIDES STOCK PRICES?

BY ELLEN FRANK

Dear Dr. Dollar:

During the course of a single day, a stock can go up and down frequently. These changes supposedly reflect the changing demand for that stock (and its potential resale value) or changing expectations of a company's profitability. But this seems too vague to me. How can these factors be so volatile? Who actually decides, or what is the mechanism for deciding, when a stock price should go up or down and by how much?

—*Joseph Balszak, Muskegon, Michigan*

Let's start with your last question first—how are stock prices determined? Shares in most large established corporations are listed on organized exchanges like the New York or American Stock Exchanges. Shares in most smaller or newer firms are listed on the NASDAQ—an electronic system that tracks stock prices.

Every time a stock is sold, the exchange records the price at which it changes hands. If, a few seconds or minutes later, another trade takes place, the price at which that trade is made becomes the new market price, and so on. Organized exchanges like the New York Stock Exchange will occasionally suspend trading in a stock if the price is excessively volatile, if there is a severe mismatch between supply and demand (many people wanting to sell, no one wanting to buy) or if they suspect that insiders are deliberately manipulating a stock's price. But in normal circumstances, there is no official arbiter of stock prices, no person or institution that "decides" a price. The market price of a stock is simply the price at which a willing buyer and seller agree to trade.

Why then do prices fluctuate so much? The vast bulk of stock trades are made by professional traders who buy and sell shares all day long, hoping to profit from small changes in share prices. Since these traders do not hold stocks over the long haul, they are not terribly interested in such long-term considerations as a company's profitability or the value of its assets. Or rather, they are interested in such factors mostly insofar as news that would affect a company's long-term prospects might cause *other traders* to buy the stock, causing its price to rise. If a trader believes that others will buy shares (in the expectation that prices will rise), then she will buy as well, hoping to sell when the price rises. If others believe the same thing, then the wave of buying pressure will, in fact, *cause* the price to rise.

Back in the 1930s, economist John Maynard Keynes compared the stock market to a contest then popular in British tabloids, in which contestants had to look at photos and choose the faces that *other contestants* would pick as the prettiest. Each contestant had to look for photos "likeliest to catch the fancy of the other competitors, all of whom are looking at the problem from the same point of view." Similarly, stock traders try to guess which stocks other traders will buy. The successful trader is the one who anticipates and outfoxes the market, buying before a stock's price rises and selling before it falls.

Financial firms employ thousands of market strategists and technical analysts who spend hours poring over historical stock data, trying to divine the logic behind these price changes. If they could unlock the secret of stock prices, they could arm their traders with the ability to always buy low and sell high. So far, no one has found this particular holy grail. And by continuing to guess and gamble, traders send prices gyrating.

For small investors, who do hold stock for the long term and will need to cash in their stocks at some point to finance their retirements, the volatility of the market can be a source of constant anxiety. Every time a share in, say, General Electric is traded, the new price is used to revalue *all* outstanding shares—just as the value of your home appreciates when the house down the block sells for more than a similar house sold

last week. But the value of your home wouldn't be so high if every house on your block were suddenly put up for sale. Similarly, if all ten billion outstanding shares of General Electric—or even a small fraction of them—were put up for sale, they wouldn't fetch anywhere near the current market price. Small investors need to keep in mind that the gains and losses on their 401(k) statements are just hypothetical paper gains and losses. You won't know the true value of your stocks until you actually try to sell them.

ARTICLE 3.3

May/June 2004

NO MORE SAVINGS!
THE CASE FOR SOCIAL WEALTH

BY ELLEN FRANK

Pundits from the political left and right don't agree about war in Iraq, gay marriage, national energy policy, tax breaks, free trade, or much else. But they do agree on one thing: Americans don't save enough. The reasons are hotly disputed. Right-wingers contend that the tax code rewards spenders and punishes savers. Liberals argue that working families earn too little to save. Environmentalists complain of a work-spend rat race fueled by relentless advertising. But the bottom line seems beyond dispute.

Data on wealth-holding reveal that few Americans possess adequate wealth to finance a comfortable retirement. Virtually none have cash sufficient to survive an extended bout of unemployment. Only a handful of very affluent households could pay for health care if their insurance lapsed, cover nursing costs if they became disabled, or see their children through college without piling up student loans. Wealth is so heavily concentrated at the very top of the income distribution that even upper-middle class households are dangerously exposed to the vagaries of life and the economy.

With low savings and inadequate personal wealth identified as the problem, the solutions seem so clear as to rally wide bipartisan support: Provide tax credits for savings. Encourage employers to establish workplace savings plans. Educate people about family budgeting and financial investing. Promote home ownership so people can build home equity. Develop tax-favored plans to pay for college, retirement, and medical needs. More leftist proposals urge the government to redistribute wealth through federally sponsored "children's development accounts" or "American stakeholder accounts," so that Americans at all income levels can, as the Demos-USA website puts it, "enjoy the security and

benefits that come with owning assets."

But such policies fail to address the paradoxical role savings play in market economies. Furthermore, looking at economic security solely through the lens of personal finance deflects focus away from a better, more direct, and far more reliable way to ensure Americans' well-being: promoting social wealth.

THE PARADOX OF THRIFT

Savings is most usefully envisaged as a physical concept. Each year businesses turn out automobiles, computers, lumber, and steel. Households (or consumers) buy much, but not all, of this output. The goods and services they leave behind represent the economy's savings.

Economics students are encouraged to visualize the economy as a metaphorical plumbing system through which goods and money flow. Firms produce goods, which flow through the marketplace and are sold for money. The money flows into peoples' pockets as income, which flows back into the marketplace as demand for goods. Savings represent a leak in the economic plumbing. If other purchasers don't step up and buy the output that thrifty consumers shun, firms lay off workers and curb production, for there is no profit in making goods that people don't want to buy.

On the other hand, whatever consumers don't buy is available for businesses to purchase in order to expand their capacity. When banks buy computers or developers buy lumber and steel, then the excess goods find a market and production continues apace. Economists refer to business purchases of new plant and equipment as "investment." In the plumbing metaphor, investment is an injection—an additional flow of spending into the economy to offset the leaks caused by household saving.

During the industrial revolution, intense competition meant that whatever goods households did not buy or could not afford would be snatched up by emerging businesses, at least much of the time. By the turn of the 20th century, however, low-paid consumers had become a drag on economic growth. Small entrepreneurial businesses gave way to immense monopolistic firms like U.S. Steel and Standard Oil whose profits vastly exceeded what they could spend on expansion. Indeed expansion often looked pointless since, given the low level of household spending, the only buyers for their output were other businesses, who themselves faced the same dilemma.

As market economies matured, savings became a source of economic stagnation. Even the conspicuous consumption of Gilded Age business owners couldn't provide enough demand for the goods churned out of large industrial factories. Henry Ford was the first American corporate leader to deliberately pay his workers above-market wages, reasoning correctly that a better-paid work force would provide the only reliable market for his automobiles.

Today, thanks to democratic suffrage, labor unions, social welfare programs, and a generally more egalitarian culture, wages are far higher in industrialized economies than they were a century ago; wage and salary earners now secure nearly four-fifths of national income. And thrift seems a quaint virtue of our benighted grandparents. In the United States, the personal savings rate—the percentage of income flowing to households that they did not spend—fell to 1% in the late 1990s. Today, with a stagnant economy making consumers more cautious, the personal savings rate has risen—but only to around 4%.

Because working households consume virtually every penny they earn, goods and services produced are very likely to find buyers and continue to be produced. This is an important reason why the United States and Europe no longer experience the devastating depressions that beset industrialized countries prior to World War II.

Yet there is a surprisingly broad consensus that these low savings are a bad thing. Americans are often chastised for their lack of thrift, their failure to provide for themselves financially, their rash and excessive borrowing. Politicians and economists constantly exhort Americans to save more and devise endless schemes to induce them to do so.

At the same time, Americans also face relentless pressure to spend. After September 11, President Bush told the public they could best serve their country by continuing to shop. In the media, economic experts bemoan declines in "consumer confidence" and applaud reports of buoyant retail or auto sales. The U.S. economy, we are told, is a consumer economy—our spendthrift ways and shop-til-you-drop culture the motor that propels it. Free-spending consumers armed with multiple credit cards keep the stores hopping, the restaurants full, and the factories humming.

Our schizophrenic outlook on saving and spending has two roots. First, the idea of saving meshes seamlessly with a conservative ideological outlook. In what author George Lakoff calls the "strict-father morality" that informs conservative Republican politics, abstinence, thrift, self-reliance, and competitive individualism are moral virtues. Institutions that discourage saving—like Social Security, unemployment insurance, government health programs, state-funded student aid—are by definition socialistic and result in an immoral reliance on others. Former Treasury Secretary Paul O'Neill bluntly expressed this idea to a reporter for the *Financial Times* in 2001. "Able-bodied adults," O'Neill opined, "should save enough on a regular basis so that they can provide for their own retirement and for that matter for their health and medical needs." Otherwise, he continued, elderly people are just "dumping their problems on the broader society."

This ideological position, which is widely but not deeply shared among U.S. voters, receives financial and political support from the finance industry. Financial firms have funded most of the research, lobbying, and public relations for the campaign to "privatize" Social Security, replacing the current system of guaranteed, publicly-funded pensions with individual investment accounts. The finance industry and its wealthy clients also advocate "consumption taxes"—levying taxes on income spent, but not on income saved—so as to "encourage saving" and "reward thrift." Not coincidentally, the finance industry specializes in committing accumulated pools of money to the purchase of stocks, bonds and other paper assets, for which it receives generous fees and commissions.

SOCIAL SECURITY BENEFITS REPLACE, ON AVERAGE, ONLY ONE-THIRD OF PRIOR EARNINGS IN EUROPE, PUBLIC PENSIONS REPLACE FROM 50% TO 70% OF PRIOR EARNINGS.

Our entire economic system requires that people spend freely. Yet political rhetoric combined with pressure from the financial services industry urges individuals to save, or at least to try to save. This rhetoric finds a receptive audience in ordinary households anxious over their own finances and among many progressive public-interest groups alarmed by the threadbare balance sheets of so many American households.

So here is the paradox. People need protection against adversity, and an ample savings account provides such protection. But if ordinary households try to save and protect themselves against hard times, the unused factories, barren malls, and empty restaurants would bring those hard times upon them.

SOCIAL WEALTH

The only way to address the paradox is to reconcile individuals' need for economic security with the public need for a stable economy. The solution therefore lies not in personal thrift or individual wealth, but in social insurance and public wealth.

When a country promotes economic security with dependable public investments and insurance programs, individuals have less need to amass private savings. Social Security, for example, provides the elderly with a direct claim on the nation's economic output after they retire. This guarantees that retirees keep spending and reduces the incentive for working adults to save. By restraining personal savings, Social Security improves the chances that income earned will translate into income spent, making the overall economy more stable.

> INDIVIDUALS AND HOUSEHOLDS FARE BETTER WHEN THEY ARE ASSURED SOME SECURE POLITICAL CLAIM ON THE ECONOMY'S OUTPUT ... BECAUSE SOCIAL CLAIMS ON THE ECONOMY RENDER THE ECONOMY ITSELF MORE STABLE.

Of course, Americans still need to save up for old age; Social Security benefits replace, on average, only one-third of prior earnings. This argues not for more saving, however, but for more generous Social Security benefits. In Europe, public pensions replace from 50% to 70% of prior earnings.

Programs like Social Security and unemployment insurance align private motivation with the public interest in a high level of economic activity. Moreover, social insurance programs reduce people's exposure to volatile financial markets. Proponents of private asset building seem to overlook the lesson of the late 1990s stock market boom: that the personal wealth of small-scale savers is perilously vulnerable to stock market downswings, price manipulation, and fraud by corporate insiders.

It is commonplace to disparage social insurance programs as "big government" intrusions that burden the public with onerous taxes. But the case for a robust public sector is at least as much an economic as a moral one. Ordinary individuals and households fare better when they are assured some secure political claim on the economy's output, not only because of the payouts they receive as individuals, but because social claims on the economy render the economy itself more stable.

Well-funded public programs, for one thing, create reliable income streams and employment. Universal public schooling, for example, means that a sizable portion of our nation's income is devoted to building, equipping, staffing, and maintaining schools. This spending is less susceptible than private-sector spending to business cycles, price fluctuations, and job losses.

Programs that build social wealth also substantially ameliorate the sting of joblessness and minimize the broader economic fallout of unemployment when downturns do occur. Public schools, colleges, parks, libraries, hospitals, and transportation systems, as well as social insurance programs like unemployment compensation and disability coverage, all ensure that the unemployed continue to consume at least a minimal level of goods and services. Their children can still attend school and visit the playground. If there were no social supports, the unemployed would be forced to withdraw altogether from the economy, dragging wages down and setting off destabilizing depressions.

In a series of articles on the first Bush tax cut in 2001, the *New York Times* profiled Dr. Robert Cline, an Austin, Texas, surgeon whose $300,000 annual income still left him worried about financing college educations for his six children. Dr. Cline himself attended the University of Texas, at a cost of $250 per semester ($650 for medical school), but figured that "his own children's education will likely cost tens of thousands of dollars each." Dr. Cline supported the 2001 tax cut, the *Times* reported. Ironically, though, that cut contributed to an environment in which institutions like the University of Texas raise tuitions, restrict enrollments, and drive Dr. Cline and others to attempt to amass enough personal wealth to pay for their children's education.

Unlike Dr. Cline, most people will never accumulate sufficient hoards of wealth to afford expensive high-quality services like education or to indemnify themselves against the myriad risks of old age, poor health, and unemployment. Even when middle-income households do manage to stockpile savings, they have little control over the rate at which their assets can be converted to cash.

Virtually all people—certainly the 93% of U.S. households earning less than $150,000—would fare better collectively than they could individually. Programs that provide direct access to important goods and services— publicly financed education, recreation, health care, and pensions— reduce the inequities that follow inevitably from an entirely individualized economy. The vast majority of people are better off with the high probability of a secure income and guaranteed access to key services such as health care than with the low-probability prospect of becoming rich.

The next time a political candidate recommends some tax-exempt individual asset building scheme, progressively minded people should ask her these questions. If consumers indeed save more and the government thus collects less tax revenue, who will buy the goods these thrifty consumers now forgo? Who will employ the workers who used to manufacture those goods? Who will build the public assets that lower tax revenues render unaffordable? And how exactly does creating millions of little pots of gold substitute for a collective commitment to social welfare?

BUBBLE TROUBLE

BY DEAN BAKER

As lukewarm as the economic recovery has been, it would have been far chillier if not for the housing market. Throughout the recession and recovery, overheated housing prices have kept the economy simmering.

Since late 1995, housing prices have risen nationwide by almost 35% after adjusting for inflation. In some regions, real home prices have risen by more than 50% (see table). Such a steep run-up is abnormal. Prior to 1995, home prices had closely tracked the inflation rate.

By borrowing against the inflated values of their homes throughout the economic slowdown, families spurred consumption growth—despite the weak job market and stagnant wages—providing much of the lift for the current recovery. Since Bush took office in 2000, the amount of outstanding mortgage debt has risen a remarkable 50.4%. As a result, the ratio of mortgage debt to home equity hit a record high in 2003.

Some argue there's no need to worry; the rise in housing prices is not a bubble, but is founded on genuine factors such as scarce urban land, immigration, and income growth—but these explanations don't make sense. Vacant land in many urban areas has long been scarce, but this never before led to such a surge in prices. And most immigrants are not in the market for the half-million dollar homes that are driving the bubble in several regions. Income doesn't get us far in explaining the bubble, either; income growth during the late 1990s pales in comparison to the period between 1951 and 1973, when there was no bubble. Plus, the housing bubble has continued to grow over the past 3.5 years, when income growth was leveling off.

The housing bubble most likely has its origins in another bubble—the stock bubble of the late 1990s, when investors used their Wall Street returns to buy pricier homes. The increased demand began to drive up prices; soon, homebuyers came to expect continued price increases and based their purchase decisions on that expectation. Homebuyers who may otherwise have viewed a $200,000 home as too costly became willing to pay that much in the expectation that the

THE RUN-UP IN HOME PRICES	
Rise in Price of Single-Family Homes, 1995 (fourth quarter) to 2005 (fourth quarter)	
	Rate adjusted for inflation
United States	55.9%
Northeast	82.5%
Mid-Atlantic	62.7%
East South Central	20.1%
West South Central	20.8%
South Atlantic	62.5%
East North Central	28.9%
West North Central	39.8%
Mountain States	52.6%
Pacific	109.1%

Source: Housing Price Index, Office of Federal Housing Enterprise Oversight

home would sell for far more down the road. Expectations of ever-rising prices drive speculative bubbles.

Sound familiar? Indeed, the current housing bubble is not unlike the run-up in stock prices to which it owes its origins. If and when this bubble bursts, as the stock bubble did, the economy will likely find itself in another recession, and millions of families will see their net worth disappear as their homes, particularly those in over-inflated housing markets, plummet in value. With nearly 40% of new homebuyers choosing adjustable-rate mortgages, and interest rates on the rise, some homebuyers could face increased mortgage payments even as the values of their homes fall. Those with high debt-to-equity balances could face negative equity, or the prospect of owing more than they own.

The recent rise in mortgage rates has begun to slow the four-year refinancing frenzy, but the middle class is now so laden with mortgage debt that the damage when the bubble bursts will be widely felt.

BURLINGTON BUSTS THE AFFORDABLE HOUSING DEBATE

BY DANIEL FIRESIDE

"Housing used to be an opportunity ladder in our country. You started out in a rental and began to save. Then you bought a small home, and eventually you moved up. Today, housing prices are so high that if you're renting an apartment, you can't possibly save," says Brenda Torpy, executive director of the Burlington Community Land Trust.

With housing prices skyrocketing beyond the means of the average worker, rents eating up a greater share of household income, and HUD funding on the chopping block, local governments have few tools at their disposal to create affordable housing. Too often, mayors are reduced to offering tax breaks to big developers in exchange for a few token "below market rate" apartments. In the old debate between supply-siders and government interventionists, it's clear who has the momentum.

Undaunted by these grim trends, community leaders in Burlington, Vt., are continuing to carry out a 20-year experiment in affordable housing based on the radical precept that housing should not be treated as a market commodity. The Burlington Community Land Trust (BCLT) represents an altogether different approach to housing security—and one that holds important lessons for community organizers around the country.

BCLT IS BORN

In the early 1980s, wealthy out-of-town speculators began driving up the cost of housing in Burlington. Harried New York City yuppies saw the bucolic college town of 40,000 as an ideal place for their vacation homes, and longtime working class residents were being rapidly priced out of their own neighborhoods. Housing prices in Burlington were rising at twice the national rate.

Frustration over housing issues came to a boiling point when the political establishment cut a deal with big-time developers to put an upscale apartment complex on the city's scenic waterfront. Voter disgust with this plan to privatize public space led to an upset victory in the mayoral race by Socialist gadfly Bernie Sanders and his ragtag Progressive Coalition in 1981.

Sanders and the Progressive Coalition quickly sought to develop institutions and programs that would have a lasting impact on the community. The Progressives decided to make affordable housing a signature issue. Things got off to a rough start when their proposal for rent control was voted down after a coalition of property owners and establishment politicians hired a professional consultant to defeat it. With rent control off the table, and federal funding in short supply, the Progressives had to turn to more creative measures to address the housing crisis.

In 1983, they created the Community and Economic Development Office (CEDO), a permanent community-development office that would set development goals and initiate creative projects. CEDO initially focused on three areas of housing policy: protecting the vulnerable, preserving affordable housing, and producing affordable housing. While these goals sound typical of many municipal development authorities, CEDO's strategy was distinctive. It sought to decommodify residential property, ensure its housing projects would be permanently affordable, and actually empower residents. Its most important initiative, and the key to all of these goals, was the Burlington Community Land Trust.

RETHINKING PRIVATE PROPERTY

In the late 1970s, Vermont environmentalist Rick Carbin had formed the Vermont Land Trust (VLT) in an effort to preserve open space as developers bought up farms. Instead of buying and holding land, as some land trusts do, the VLT used its resources to buy undeveloped properties at the edge of urban areas and resell them, often at a profit, but with strict conservation easements that prohibited future development. (For more on easements, see "Land Trusts Ease Control of U.S. Farmland Away from Developers," p. 16.) The VLT's successful track record paved the way for Burlington's housing land trust program.

The Institute for Community Economics, a thinktank based in Springfield, Mass., approached CEDO planners with a proposal to use the land trust model as a tool to address Burlington's housing crisis. Much as the VLT program "unbundled" the ownership of property from its function in the future, the housing land trust separated the ownership of a house from the land it sits on. As Brenda Torpy summarizes, "Conservation land trusts take land out of the market to protect the natural environment. Community land trusts take land out of market to protect the urban environment including the people who live there."

CEDO established the Burlington Community Land Trust as an independent nonprofit corporation in 1984, with official backing from the Burlington City Council and $200,000 in seed money. The trust was viewed as an integral part of the city's affordable housing program. Even traditional politicians came to see the land trust model as an acceptable compromise between a flawed free market approach and heavy-handed government intervention, especially as it promoted the popular concept of home ownership. Democratic and Republican politicians have found it difficult to oppose a program that offered life-long renters a "piece of the American Dream."

At its founding, the BCLT was the first municipally funded community land trust in the country. Today it is the nation's largest community land trust, with over 2,500 members.

HOUSING TRUST 101

Buying land through a housing trust involves several steps. To start, the trust acquires a parcel of land through purchase, foreclosure, tax abatements, or donation, and then arranges for a housing unit to be built on the parcel if one does not yet exist. The trust sells the building but retains ownership of the land underneath. It leases the land to the homeowner for a nominal sum (e.g., $25 per month), generally for 99 years or until the house is sold again.

This model supports affordable housing in several ways. First, homebuyers have to meet low-income requirements. Second, the buying price of the home is reduced because it does not include the price of the land. Third, the trust works with lenders to reduce the cost of the mortgage by using the equity of the land as part of the mortgage calculation. This reduces the size of the down payment and other closing costs and eliminates the need for private mortgage insurance. In all, the trust can cut the cost of home ownership by at least 25%.

For longtime BCLT member Bob Robbins, purchasing a home through the trust "was the only affordable option. We did not have access to money for a down payment on a regular home, and at our income level, we wouldn't have qualified for a mortgage. Through the BCLT, we were able to purchase a $99,000 home with just $2,500 down."

Unlike federal programs that only help the initial buyer, the BCLT keeps the property affordable in perpetuity by imposing restrictions on the resale of the house. Specifically, the contract restricts the profit buyers are able to take when they later sell the house. According to the terms of the BCLT leases, homeowners get back all of their equity from their mortgage plus the market value of any capital improvements they made. However, they only get 25% of any increase in the value of the house (which constitutes 75% of the total value of the property), and none of the increase in the value of the land.

Since buyers keep a portion of the housing value appreciation, families do accumulate some wealth through BCLT homeownership. And as time passes, if the surrounding housing prices continue to rise, the trust prices become even more affordable relative to market housing, and the trust captures more wealth on behalf of the community.

When the homeowner sells, the new buyer must agree to the same terms. If no buyers are interested or the owners default on the mortgage, the BCLT retains the option to buy the property.

This model gives the buyer the benefits of homeownership (including the tax deduction for mortgage interest, wealth accumulation through equity, and stable housing costs) that would otherwise be beyond her means. In return, she gives up the potential of windfall profits if the market keeps rising. BCLT recently published a study of the first 100 trust homes that were sold to a second generation. "The implications were very powerful," says Brenda Torpy. "The initial homebuyers realized a net gain of 29% on the money they had invested. Our homeowners were taking an average of $6,000 with them. These aren't the sky-high returns that some people have come to expect from the housing market, but these were people who would never have entered it in the first place." That's because most BCLT homeowners "would never have been able to buy homes otherwise, even with existing federal and state programs," explains Torpy. "For many, we are a stepping stone between renting and homeownership."

Urban land is not a normal economic good because it exists in a fixed quantity. (They're not making any more of it, as realtors say.) Since the supply cannot rise to meet growing demand, the price is subject to speculative forces. The housing supply can be increased by building in greater density, but this does not happen quickly. When a normal home is offered for sale on the usual terms, it does virtually nothing to make the overall housing market more affordable. A land trust home, by contrast, creates a permanently affordable property because the land it sits on is removed from the speculative market. Most of the appreciation is retained by the housing trust (and by extension, the community), rather than the individual. In this way the trust model creates a bridge between purely public and purely private property. "We're trying to stop the concentration of land in the hands of a wealthy minority," says Torpy.

The land trust program was designed to outlast any change in city hall. This was an important strategy in the Progressive Coalition's early years. As it turned out, the Progressives hung on to control, with the exception of a single Republican administration in the mid-1990s. As a result, they have been able to expand on the aims of their original programs and establish a broad base of support for their housing agenda.

The BCLT has become an important force in Burlington's housing market. After 20 years, the trust controls almost 650 housing units, including over 270 rental apartments and 370 shared-appreciation single-family homes and condominiums—about 4% of Burlington's total housing stock. The process is "buyer initiated"; the buyer picks out the house and asks the trust to incorporate it. Therefore the units are dotted all over the city. The trust has also built a wide variety of homes in various styles to fit into particular neighborhoods.

"Most of them are modest," says Torpy. "We've found that condos are good starter homes. They're something new but are still affordable. But we're also building modular homes and 2- and 3-bedroom homes." The BCLT's programs also include tenant-owned cooperatives, a family shelter, a transitional shelter, and housing for homeless youth, the mentally ill, and people with HIV/AIDS.

The BCLT is remarkable not only for its size, but as an organizing structure that promotes community empowerment. Tenants and owners of BCLT units vote for and serve on its governing board, along with government officials and other residents with technical expertise, such as architects and urban planners. The system is designed so that the BCLT doesn't play the role of landlord to tenants and homeowners. Rather, all interested parties have a voice and a vote. In this way it's also an experiment in democratic self-governance.

By looking at housing as a fundamental human right rather than a market good that goes to the highest bidder, and with shrewd political organizing in a hostile environment, housing advocates in Burlington have created a sustainable model for affordable housing that deserves to be emulated across the country. Others are catching on. Since the BCLT published its study, the Fannie Mae Corporation, other city planning offices, and state financing offices have all contacted the BCLT for information about how to use housing trusts in an environment of shrinking funds. Today there are 130 community land trusts in more than 30 states, including in large cities like Atlanta and Cincinnati. The largest growth has been in California and the Pacific Northwest. BCLT itself is expanding into the surrounding counties.

BCLT homeowner Bob Robbins says, "I think every community should have a land trust—not just as a fringe option but as the dominant model to keep housing affordable."

ARTICLE 3.6 *September/October 2005*

LABOR'S CAPITAL

PUTTING PENSION WEALTH TO WORK FOR WORKERS

BY ADRIA SCHARF

Pension fund assets are the largest single source of investment capital in the country. Of the roughly $17 trillion in private equity in the U.S. economy, $6 to 7 trillion is held in employee pensions. About $1.3 trillion is in union pension plans (jointly trusteed labor-management plans or collectively bargained company-sponsored plans) and $2.1 trillion is in public employee pension plans. Several trillion more are in defined contribution plans and company-sponsored defined benefit plans with no union representation. These vast sums were generated by—and belong to—workers; they're really workers' deferred wages.

Workers' retirement dollars course through Wall Street, but most of the capital owned *by* working people is invested with no regard *for* working people or their communities. Pension dollars finance sweatshops overseas, hold shares of public companies that conduct mass layoffs, and underwrite myriad anti-union low-road corporate practices. In one emblematic example, the Florida public pension system bought out the Edison Corporation, the for-profit school operator, in November 2003, with the deferred wages of Florida government employees—including public school teachers. (With just three appointed trustees, one of whom is Governor Jeb Bush, Florida is one of the few states with no worker representation on the board of its state-employee retirement fund.)

The custodians of workers' pensions—plan trustees and investment managers—argue that they are bound by their "fiduciary responsibility" to consider only narrow financial factors when making investment decisions. They maintain they have a singular obligation to maximize financial returns and minimize financial risk for beneficiaries—with no regard for broader concerns. But from the perspective of the teachers whose dollars funded an enterprise that aims to privatize their jobs, investing in Edison, however promising the expected return (and given Edison's track record, it wasn't very promising!), makes no sense.

A legal concept enshrined in the 1974 Employee Retirement Income Security Act (ERISA) and other statutes, "fiduciary responsibility" does constrain the decision-making of those charged with taking care of other people's money. It obligates fiduciaries (e.g., trustees and fund managers) to invest retirement assets for the exclusive benefit of the pension beneficiaries. According to ERISA, fiduciaries must act with the care, skill, prudence, and diligence that a "prudent man" would use. Exactly what that means, though, is contested.

The law does *not* say that plan trustees must maximize short-term return. It does, in fact, give fiduciaries some leeway to direct pension assets to worker- and community-friendly projects. In 1994, the U.S. Department of Labor issued rule clarifications that expressly permit fiduciaries to make "economically targeted investments" (ETIs), or investments that take into account collateral benefits like good jobs, housing, improved social service facilities, alternative energy, strengthened infrastructure, and economic development. Trustees and fund managers are free to consider a double bottom line, prioritizing investments that have a social pay-off so long as their expected risk-adjusted financial returns are equal to other, similar, investments. Despite a backlash against ETIs from Newt Gingrich conservatives in the 1990s, Clinton's Labor Department rules still hold.

Nevertheless, the dominant mentality among the asset management professionals who make a living off what United Steelworkers president Leo Gerard calls "the deferred-wage food table" staunchly resists considering any factors apart from financial risk and return.

This is beginning to change in some corners of the pension fund world, principally (no surprise) where workers and beneficiaries have some control over their pension capital. In jointly managed union defined-benefit (known as "Taft-Hartley") plans and public-employee pension plans, the ETI movement is gaining ground. "Taft-Hartley pension trustees have grown more comfortable with economically targeted investments as a result of a variety of influences, one being the Labor Department itself," says Robert Pleasure of the Center for Working Capital, an independent capital stewardship-educational institute started by the AFL-CIO. Concurrently, more public pension fund trustees have begun adopting ETIs that promote housing and economic development within state borders. Most union and public pension trustees now understand that, as long as they follow a careful process and protect returns, ETIs do not breach their fiduciary duty, and may in certain cases actually be sounder investments than over-inflated Wall Street stocks.

SAVING JOBS: HEARTLAND LABOR CAPITAL NETWORK

During the run-up of Wall Street share prices in the 1990s, investment funds virtually redlined basic industries, preferring to direct dollars into hot public technology stocks and emerging foreign markets, which despite the rhetoric of fiduciary responsibility were often speculative, unsound, investments. Even most collectively bargained funds put their assets exclusively in Wall Street stocks, in part because some pension trustees feared that if they didn't, they could be held liable. (During an earlier period, the Labor Department aggressively pursued union pension trustees for breaches of fiduciary duty. In rare cases where trustees were found liable, their personal finances and possessions were at risk.) But in the past five years, more union pension funds and labor-friendly fund managers have begun directing assets into investments that bolster the "heartland" economy: worker-friendly private equity, and, wherever possible, unionized

industries and companies that offer "card-check" and "neutrality." ("Card-check" requires automatic union recognition if a majority of employees present signed authorization cards; "neutrality" means employers agree to remain neutral during organizing campaigns.)

The Heartland Labor Capital Network is at the center of this movement. The network's Tom Croft says he and his allies want to "make sure there's an economy still around in the future to which working people will be able to contribute." Croft estimates that about $3 to $4 billion in new dollars have been directed to worker-friendly private equity since 1999—including venture capital, buyout funds, and "special situations" funds that invest in financially distressed companies, saving jobs and preventing closures. Several work closely with unions to direct capital into labor-friendly investments.

One such fund, New York-based KPS Special Situations, has saved over 10,000 unionized manufacturing jobs through its two funds, KPS Special Situations I and II, according to a company representative. In 2003, St. Louis-based Wire Rope Corporation, the nation's leading producer of high carbon wire and wire rope products, was in bankruptcy with nearly 1,000 unionized steelworker jobs in jeopardy. KPS bought the company and restructured it in collaboration with the United Steelworkers International. Approximately 20% of KPS's committed capital is from Taft-Hartley pension dollars; as a result, the Wire Rope transaction included some union pension assets.

The Heartland Labor Capital Network and its union partners want to expand this sort of strategic deployment of capital by building a national capital pool of "Heartland Funds" financed by union pension assets and other sources. These funds have already begun to make direct investments in smaller worker-friendly manufacturing and related enterprises; labor representatives participate alongside investment experts on their advisory boards.

"It's simple. Workers' assets should be invested in enterprises and construction projects that will help to build their cities, rebuild their schools, and rebuild America's infrastructure," says Croft.

"CAPITAL STEWARDSHIP": THE AFL-CIO

For the AFL-CIO, ETIs are nothing new. Its Housing Investment Trust (HIT), formed in 1964, is the largest labor-sponsored investment vehicle in the country that produces collateral benefits for workers and their neighborhoods. Hundreds of union pension funds invest in the $2 billion trust, which leverages public financing to build housing, including low-income and affordable units, using union labor. HIT, together with its sister fund the Building Investment Trust (BIT), recently announced a new investment program that is expected to generate up to $1 billion in investment in apartment development and rehabilitation by 2005 in targeted cities including New York, Chicago, and Philadelphia. The initiative will finance thousands of units of housing and millions of hours of union construction work. HIT and BIT require owners of many of the projects they help finance to agree to card-check recognition and neutrality for their employees.

HIT and BIT are two examples of union-owned investment vehicles. There are many others—including the LongView ULTRA Construction Loan Fund, which finances projects that use 100% union labor; the Boilermakers' Co-Generation and Infrastructure Fund; and the United Food and Commercial Workers' Shopping Center Mortgage Loan Program—and their ranks are growing.

Since 1997, the AFL-CIO and its member unions have redoubled their efforts to increase labor's control over its capital through a variety of means. The AFL-CIO's Capital Stewardship Program promotes corporate governance reform, investment manager accountability, pro-worker investment strategies, international pension fund cooperation, and trustee education. It also evaluates worker-friendly pension funds on how well they actually advance workers' rights, among other criteria. The Center for Working Capital provides education and training to hundreds of union and public pension fund trustees each year, organizes conferences, and sponsors research on capital stewardship issues including ETIs.

PUBLIC PENSION PLANS JOIN IN

At least 29 states have ETI policies directing a portion of their funds, usually less than 5%, to economic development within state borders. The combined public pension assets in ETI programs amount to about $55 billion, according to a recent report commissioned by the Vermont state treasurer. The vast majority of these ETIs are in residential housing and other real estate.

The California Public Employees' Retirement System (CalPERS) is an ETI pioneer among state pension funds. The single largest pension fund in the country, it has $153.8 billion in assets and provides retirement benefits to over 1.4 million members. In the mid-1990s, when financing for housing construction dried up in California, CalPERS invested hundreds of millions of dollars to finance about 4% of the state's single-family housing market. Its ETI policy is expansive. While it requires economically targeted investments earn maximum returns for their level of risk and fall within geographic and asset-diversification guidelines, CalPERS also considers the investments' benefits to its members and to state residents, their job creation potential, and the economic and social needs of different groups in the state's population. CalPERS directs about 2% of its assets—about $20 billion as of May 2001—to investments that provide collateral social benefits. It also requires construction and maintenance contractors to provide decent wages and benefits.

Other state pension funds have followed CalPERs' lead. In 2003, the Massachusetts treasury expanded its ETI program, which is funded by the state's $32 billion pension. Treasurer Timothy Cahill expects to do "two dozen or more" ETI investments in 2004, up from the single investment made in 2003, according to the *Boston Business Journal*. "It doesn't hurt our bottom line, and it helps locally," Cahill explained. The immediate priority will be job creation. Washington, Wisconsin, and New York also have strong ETI programs.

In their current form and at their current scale, economically targeted investments in the United States are not a panacea. Pension law does impose constraints. Many consultants and lawyers admonish trustees to limit ETIs to a small portion of an overall pension investment portfolio. And union trustees must pursue ETIs carefully, following a checklist of "prudence" procedures, to protect themselves from liability. The most significant constraint is simply that these investments must generate risk-adjusted returns equal to alternative investments—this means that many deserving not-for-profit efforts and experiments in economic democracy are automatically ruled out. Still, there's more wiggle room in the law than has been broadly recognized. And when deployed strategically to bolster the labor movement, support employee buyouts, generate good jobs, or build affordable housing, economically targeted investments are a form of worker direction over capital whose potential has only begun to be realized. And (until the day that capital is abolished altogether) that represents an important foothold.

As early as the mid-1970s, business expert Peter Drucker warned in *Unseen Revolution* of a coming era of "pension-fund socialism" in which the ownership of massive amounts of capital by pension funds would bring about profound changes to the social and economic power structure. Today, workers' pensions prop up the U.S. economy. They're a point of leverage like no other. Union and public pension funds are the most promising means for working people to shape the deployment of capital on a large scale, while directing assets to investments with collateral benefits. If workers and the trustees of their pension wealth recognize the power they hold, they could alter the contours of capitalism.

CHAPTER 4

FISCAL POLICY, DEFICITS, AND DEBT

INTRODUCTION

Most textbooks depict a macroeconomy stabilized by government intervention. Reflecting the influence of Keynes, they look at ways that the government can use fiscal policy—government spending and taxation—to bolster a flagging economy. Despite its recent growth, the U.S. economy is still reeling from the collapse of the high-tech sector, a soggy stock market, and the job losses of the last four years (see Article 1.1). What is the role of fiscal policy in this context? How is the federal government, under an administration committed to shrinking the size of government, using fiscal tools?

Articles 4.1 and 4.2 look at the Bush administration's reversal of fiscal fortune. The Bush team turned unprecedented projected budget surpluses into deficits likely to persist until 2013. The causes of those deficits, as John Miller shows in Article 4.1, were the Bush tax cuts and the military buildup, not the boom in social spending the *Wall Street Journal* alleges. In Article 4.2, Adria Scharf documents the devastating fiscal effects of the Bush tax cuts—making those cuts permanent would cost more than the money necessary to keep Social Security solvent in the decades ahead.

Tax cuts for the rich are the hallmark of Bush's tax policy. John Miller responds to the administration's claims that cutting capital gains and dividend taxes has flooded, rather than drained, the government with tax revenues (Article 4.3). While the administration argues that the well-to-do pay more than their fair share of taxes, Ellen Frank shows that U.S. tax policy actually does little to redistribute income (Article 4.4). Finally, Paul Krugman's article explains that the 2001-2003 tax cuts can only be sustained by shredding the social safety net. Unfortunately, Krugman shows that that's exactly the point (Article 4.5).

One of the key debates in policy circles today is whether to privatize programs that have long been the responsibility of the government. The Bush administration's current proposal to privatize social security is the foremost example. Our authors take on that proposal. Doug Orr shows that left alone, Social Security is unlikely to suffer a shortfall in revenues, let alone a crisis. He shows that proposals to privatize social security are not designed to make the system solvent, but rather, are aimed at propping up the prices of financial assets (Article 4.6). William Spriggs debunks the myth that social security is a bad deal for African Americans, and shows how privatization would exacerbate racial differences in benefits of retirees and leave African-American retirees worse off than before (Article 4.7). Finally, John Miller takes a close-up look at the macroeconomic projections that underlie the Social Security Administration's claim that the system will suffer a shortfall of revenues. Miller argues that

even conservative estimates of future immigration, productivity, and economic growth would keep the system solvent (Article 4.8).

Other programs are also suffering under the slash-and-burn approach of privatization. Elise Gould shows that the 2003 Medicare Modernization Act fails to provide seniors with the universal health care insurance and prescription drug coverage promised by the Bush administration (Article 4.9). And even the military, despite a massive influx of funds, is feeling the negative effects of privatization. Ann Markusen takes a close look at the Pentagon's large-scale effort to outsource its operations to private corporations. Markusen argues that there is little evidence that the privatization of military contracts has generated efficiencies (Article 4.10).

DISCUSSION QUESTIONS

1) (Article 4.1) How have Bush administration policies affected non-defense discretionary spending?
2) (Article 4.2) What is the cost of making the Bush tax cuts permanent? What would be the likely impact on social spending if this were to happen?
3) (Article 4.3) Why is the $262 billion increase in federal tax revenues in Fiscal Year 2005 not enough to convince Miller that cutting dividend and capital gains taxes is benefiting economic growth? Who has benefited the most from the Bush tax cuts, according to Miller?
4) (Article 4.4) According to Frank, how significantly does the U.S. tax code redistribute income? What evidence does she consider that the Heritage Foundation does not, and how does it influence her conclusion?
5) (Article 4.5) What does Krugman think is the hidden agenda of those currently pushing for tax cuts? Do you agree with his analysis? Expalin why or why not.
6) (Article 4.6) What convinces Orr that the Social Security system is not suffering a crisis? What is the looming

---

KEY TO COLANDER

E = *Economics*   M = *Macroeconomics*

Articles 4.1 and 4.2 address topics from E31 or M15. Articles 4.3, 4.4, and 4.5 go with chapters E25-E26 or M9-M10, or the macro policy discussions in E30, E31, and E34, or M14, M15, and M19. Articles 4.6, 4.7, 4.8, and 4.9 add to the discussion of Social Security and social spending in E31 and M15. Article 4.10 also illustrates macroeconomic policy issues in chapters E30, E31, and E34, or M14, M15, and M19.

bond market crisis that Orr says is the real concern of those who want to privatize Social Security?

7) (Article 4.7) Spriggs identifies three myths used by those who claim that social security is bad for African Americans. How does he debunk them? Do you find his arguments convincing?

8) (Article 4.8) How do changes in immigration levels and productivity growth affect the production possibilities of the nation and the solvency of the Social Security system?

9) (Article 4.9) According to Gould, what are the "three strikes" against the Bush administration's health care reform proposals? Do you agree with Gould that we need "a whole new ball game" when it comes to providing health care insurance? If so, what might such a system look like?

10) (Article 4.10) What evidence does Markusen present to call into question the claim that privatizing military spending will create competition and improve the efficiency of military services?

ARTICLE 4.1

November/December 2003

WHAT SPENDING BOOM?

BY JOHN MILLER

THE SPENDING BOOM

If our politicians are shedding more than crocodile tears about the deficit, we have a suggestion. They could always slow the growth of their own spending. CBO points out that in fiscal 2003 non-defense discretionary spending will … increase to 3.9% [of GDP], 'its highest level since 1985.' Anyone who argues that the war on terror is crowding out domestic spending should be laughed out of the room.

The CBO report makes another useful point: Its deficit estimates … do not include the monumental increases in federal outlays that are certain to follow the passage of a new Medicare entitlement for prescription drugs for seniors. If someone wants to guarantee deficits as far as the eye can see, just pass that huge expansion of the entitlement state.

—The Wall Street Journal, *Aug. 27, 2003*

Next year's federal deficit will reach $480 billion, the federal government will not balance its budget again before fiscal year 2013, and the deficit could get yet worse in the decade ahead. Those are the projections the Congressional Budget Office (CBO) made in its August *Budget and Economic Outlook* update.

Bad news for the Bush administration and its tax-cutting agenda, right? Not so, say the editors of The Wall Street Journal. In an editorial the day after the CBO update was released, they blamed the budget deficit not on the Bush administration but on a congressional "spending boom." That might come as a surprise to anyone who's been watching with alarm as vital government programs, from environmental protection to job training, get slashed. The surprise is

warranted. As it turns out, while the Journal's editorial may quote the CBO numbers accurately, its analysis is grossly misleading and plainly illogical.

First, the title. There is no "spending boom." According to the CBO report, post-9/11 spending has merely arrested the shrinking of the federal government that Reagan initiated and Clinton carried out so effectively. Relative to the size of the economy, today's federal government is no larger than in the past. At 20.2% of GDP, federal budget outlays in 2003 are no greater than the average from 1962 to 2001, and lower than federal outlays relative to GDP in every year during the 1980s and the first half of the 1990s. They're particularly low for a period of high unemployment: In 1991 and 1992, during the last recession, federal government outlays averaged a considerably higher 22.3% of GDP.

Second, the Bush administration's war on terror has in fact crowded out much-needed domestic spending. True enough: in 2003 "non-defense discretionary spending" (more or less everything outside of Social Security, Medicare, and the military) will reach its highest levels since 1985, some 3.9% of GDP. But that number is deceptive. To begin with, it is well below the 5.2% of GDP that went to these expenditures in 1980, before the Reagan administration began gutting social spending. Beyond that, the 3.9% figure includes not only domestic but also international spending, primarily foreign military assistance. Subtracting that out leaves domestic non-defense discretionary spending at just 3.5% of GDP.

That 3.5% represents more domestic spending than when Bush took office. But when the Journal's editors claim that growing non-defense spending means that the war on terror is not crowding out domestic spending, they're just flat-out wrong—the bulk of the new spending is for the war on terror. Over three-quarters of the new domestic discretionary spending from January 2001 to April 2003 that the Journal complains about went to homeland security (49.2%), New York City relief and recovery (22.5%), and airline relief (4.4%). The rest of the additional spending went to fund educational initiatives (although Head Start and even the president's No Child Left Behind Act were never fully funded), to double the National Institutes of Health budget, to pay for voting reform, and to provide medical care for veterans.

Domestic discretionary spending in all other areas declined by $11 billion. Among the programs suffering deep budget cuts were housing assistance (down $2.9 billion or 9.1%), spending on the environment and natural resources (down $1.3 billion or 4.3%), and job training and employment services (down $675 million or 11.5%).

Third, the gaping budget deficits that the CBO forecasts are not the result of congressional overspending. Bush's pro-rich tax cuts, which will siphon off about $275 billion in 2004 alone, along with slower economic growth, have constricted the flow of revenues to the federal government, holding them well below historic levels. Government revenues will amount to just 17.9% of GDP in 2004, according to the report, the lowest figure in a decade. Those lost revenues have saddled the federal government with a whopping deficit, some 4.2% of GDP in 2003, more than twice the size of the average deficit from 1962 to 2001.

Finally, what about the *Journal*'s clincher: that additional entitlement spending, not the war on terror, threatens to create a genuine and sustained budget crisis? Even if Congress passes a new prescription drug benefit for seniors under Medicare, it will not push federal outlays beyond historic levels. For instance, according to budget analyst Richard Kogan with the Center on Budget and Policy Priorities, spending $700 billion over ten years, enough to cover half of the prescription drug costs of the entire Medicare population and far more than Congress is likely to allocate, would

still leave government outlays in 2012 at 20.1% of GDP—no higher than today.

If the *Wall Street Journal* editors were really worried about policies likely "to guarantee deficits as far as the eye can see," then they would drop their demand that the Bush tax cuts be made permanent, a staple of their editorial page. Permanently enacting Bush's 2001 and 2002 tax cuts, including the repeal of the estate tax, would drain over $1 trillion from federal revenues, according to the CBO update. Using the more realistic spending and taxing assumptions hidden in the footnotes of the CBO report, the federal government would be left with a $1.1 trillion deficit in fiscal year 2013.

THERE IS NO "SPENDING BOOM." RELATIVE TO THE SIZE OF THE ECONOMY, TODAY'S FEDERAL GOVERNMENT IS NO LARGER THAN IN THE PAST.

But then isn't that the goal of the Bush administration's anti-public sector agenda: to starve the government of tax revenues and open up large, sustained deficits that will make further entitlement spending—so loathed by the *Journal*'s editors—impossible?

Resources: "The Spending Boom," *The Wall Street Journal*, 8/27/03; "The Budget and Economic Outlook: An Update," Congressional Budget Office, August, 2003; "Bush's $10 Trillion Borrowing Binge," Citizens For Tax Justice, 9/11/03; "What Has Caused Growth in Discretionary Spending," Democratic Staff, Senate Budget Committee, 5/5/03; Isaac Shapiro and Richard Kogan, "OMB Figures Show Revenues—Due to Tax Cuts—At Exceptionally Low Levels, While Spending Levels Are Not Especially High," Center on Budget and Policy Priorities, 7/23/03; Richard Kogan, "Costs of the Tax Cut and a Medicare Prescription Drug Benefit," Center on Budget and Policy Priorities, 6/14/02.

TAX CUT TIME BOMB

BY ADRIA SCHARF

President George W. Bush and Congress planted a time bomb in the federal budget, and they're about to light the fuse. The largest parts of the tax cuts passed in 2001 and 2003 didn't activate immediately, but were designed to kick in later this decade. If they go forward, the cuts will likely cripple or destroy the social programs that form the cornerstone of the federal welfare state. Even worse, the Bush administration is now pushing to make permanent virtually all of the 2001 and 2003 tax cuts, which were originally set to expire by 2010.

In 2001, Bush sought and won the largest income tax rollback in two decades—it reduced tax rates on the top four income brackets and gave advance refunds of $300 to $600 to 94 million taxpayers. In 2003, despite the growing budget deficit, the administration secured a second tax cut—the third largest in U.S. history. The 2003 package shrank dividend and capital gains taxes and accelerated the 2001 rate cut for top income brackets. Combined, the 2001 and 2003 tax cuts will cost at least $824.1 billion between 2001 and 2010, even if Republicans don't succeed in renewing the provisions scheduled to expire, or "sunset," according to Citizens for Tax Justice (CTJ). If the cuts are extended, CTJ estimates they will cost more than $1 trillion between 2004 and 2014, with over 80% of the revenue loss hitting after 2009. (See Figure 1.)

Aside from their sheer size, the 2001 and 2003 packages were notable for a couple of reasons: First, their major provisions were deliberately scheduled to hit later in the decade. Republican congressional leaders delayed the largest cuts to protect the bills from filibuster and deflect attention from their long-term effects on the budget and inequality. Second, they were frontloaded with tiny morsels for the middle class and backloaded with enormous benefits for the top 1%. (See Figure 2 and Table 1, which are conservative in that they assume expiring provisions will in fact "sunset.")

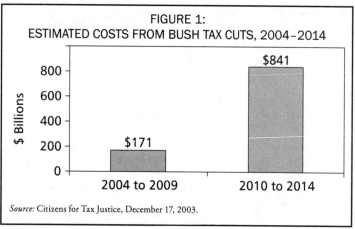

FIGURE 1:
ESTIMATED COSTS FROM BUSH TAX CUTS, 2004–2014

Source: Citizens for Tax Justice, December 17, 2003.

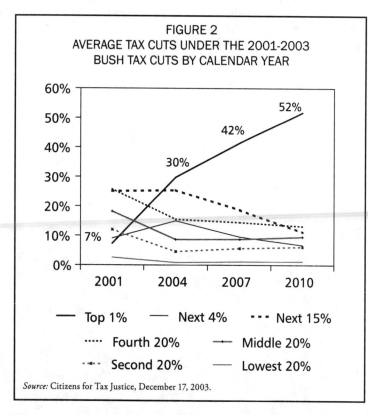

FIGURE 2
AVERAGE TAX CUTS UNDER THE 2001-2003 BUSH TAX CUTS BY CALENDAR YEAR

Source: Citizens for Tax Justice, December 17, 2003.

TABLE 1 AVERAGE TAX CUTS UNDER THE 2001-2003 BUSH TAX CUTS BY CALENDAR YEAR*			
	2001	2005	2010
Top 1%	$3,221	$41,264	$85,002
Next 4%	$1,015	$3,913	$2,780
Next 15%	$742	$2,015	$1,225
Fourth 20%	$572	$971	$1,081
Middle 20%	$403	$563	$791
Second 20%	$266	$371	$508
Lowest 20%	$57	$77	$98

*with sunsets

Source: Citizens for Tax Justice, December 17, 2003.

Over the next 75 years, the cost of extending the 2001 and 2003 tax cuts would amount to $5.9 trillion, or 1.1% of gross domestic product (GDP), according to William G. Gale and Peter R. Orszag of the Brookings Institution. To put that figure into perspective, the expected costs of funding Social Security during that same period are just $3.8 trillion (or 0.7% of GDP). Gale and Orszag warn the new Bush budget plan will necessitate one of the following changes, or a "change of a similar magnitude," within the decade, and argue that even deeper cuts may be required:

- A 29% cut in Social Security benefits;
- A 70% cut in federal Medicaid benefits;
- A 49% cut in all domestic discretionary spending, or
- A 21% increase in payroll taxes.

Resources: William G. Gale and Peter R. Orszag, "Should the President's Tax Cuts be Made Permanent?" Brookings, Washington, D.C., February 24, 2004; "The Bush Tax Cuts: The Most Recent CTJ Data," Citizens for Tax Justice, December 17, 2003, <www.ctj.org>; "Details of the Administration's Budget Proposals," Citizens for Tax Justice, February 3, 2004, <www.ctj.org>.

ARTICLE 4.3   *November/December 2005*

$262 BILLION: CASE CLOSED?

BY JOHN MILLER

$262 billion in additional federal tax revenues in fiscal year 2005 is the most ever, even after correcting for inflation. That should be enough to convince everyone, especially GOP senators, that the Bush tax cuts are working, and that now is the time to make those tax cuts permanent, hurricanes or no hurricanes.
—Wall Street Journal *editorials, August 17, September 6, and September 22, 2005 (paraphrase)*

I don't think so. The $262 billion figure might convince the *Wall Street Journal*'s editors—they've made the same point in *three* recent editorials—and other conservatives who already believed that the Bush tax cuts are working and that more tax cuts are the solution to any problem the earlier tax cuts haven't fixed. But if these folks were intellectually honest, they'd have to admit that the $262 billion figure shows no such thing.

To begin with, the fact that federal tax revenues are the most ever is far less impressive than the *Wall Street Journal* editors suggest. Yes, the $262 billion figure that the Congressional Budget Office reports is the biggest yearly increase in tax revenues on record. But setting a record for additional tax revenues is nothing unusual. As the economy expands over time, tax revenues increase along with it. Since 1901, additional tax revenues have exceeded the previous record for additional revenues in 19 fiscal years, or about once every five or six years. Prior to this year the previous high was the $197 billion increase in FY2000, five years ago. In addition, this year's turnaround in tax revenues comes after four straight years of declines in tax revenues—declines that have shrunk federal tax revenues to their lowest level relative to the size of the economy since the mid-1960s. And even

with the FY2005 burst in tax revenues, federal tax revenues are just 17.5% of GDP, well below the 17.9% average of the post-World War II period.

Now what does any of this have to do with the Bush tax cut? The answer is, not much.

First, half of this year's rise in tax revenues comes from a pick-up in corporate income tax revenues due mostly to a quirky tax-code provision—and have nothing to do with any real changes in economic performance, tax-cut induced or not. Changes in tax laws in 2002 and 2003 allowed corporations to deduct up to 50% of the amount they invest in equipment on top of their normal depreciation allowance. That "partial-expensing" provision enabled corporations to write off the cost of their capital expenditures more quickly. The additional write-offs lowered corporations' profits (on paper) and thus their tax bills in 2003 and 2004. In that way, corporations delayed their tax liability but did not reduce it, since the partial-expensing provisions expired at the end of 2004. Beginning with 2005, corporations can write off less of the value of their equipment; their profits on the books (not their actual profits) are thus higher, and their income tax liability greater.

That's why corporate profits for 2005 increased by 33% on paper, according to the CBO. This in turn swelled corporate income tax revenues to twice their 2003 level and added 0.6% of GDP to federal tax revenues. Even the CBO points out that these additional revenues had little to do with the Bush tax cuts. "Other recent tax-law changes, such as those in the American Jobs Creation Act of 2004, have had much smaller effects on corporate receipts in 2005," reads the agency's report.

Drop the largely accounting-induced increase in corpo-

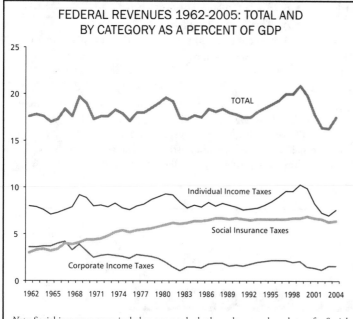

FEDERAL REVENUES 1962-2005: TOTAL AND BY CATEGORY AS A PERCENT OF GDP

TOTAL

Individual Income Taxes

Social Insurance Taxes

Corporate Income Taxes

Note: Social insurance taxes include payments by both employers and employees for Social Security, Medicare, Railroad Retirement, and unemployment insurance, as well as pension contributions by federal workers.

Source: Congressional Budget Office, "The Budget and Economic Outlook: Fiscal Years 2006 to 2015: Appendix F," January 2005.

rate income tax payments, and the FY2005 jump in federal tax revenues drops by half, to 0.6% of GDP. In fact, federal tax revenues increased by 0.6% of GDP in FY1994 as well, following the Clinton administration's *increase* in the top income tax rate. Would the *Journal*'s editors consider that proof positive that tax increases work?

The remainder of the additional tax revenue in FY2005 comes mostly from additional personal income tax collections. But that's not because wages are rising. As the CBO delicately put it, "strong growth in 2004 of personal income other than from wages and salaries" is a lot of what generated additional tax revenues in FY2005. Does that surge in tax revenues from capital income show that the Bush tax cuts, which reduced dividend and capital gains tax rates to 15% (from 20% and 35% respectively), are working?

Actually, the additional tax revenues are hardly surprising and say very little about any alleged benefits of slicing capital gains and dividend tax rates. Let's start with the capital gains tax cut. Economists readily allow that capital gains realizations (the profits from selling stocks or other capital assets for more than you bought them for) pick up when taxes on capital gains are lowered. But as the CBO pointed out in an earlier study, that response is "most likely to occur in the short run" and "may not be enough to produce additional receipts over the long period." And in the past, Congress's Joint Committee on Taxation has estimated that capital gains tax cuts of the magnitude of those passed two years ago would boost realizations sufficiently to increase revenues in the first year or two following the tax cut, but after that initial surge, revenues would decline.

What we have seen so far—income tax revenues from capital gains rising in the first two years following a capital gains tax cut—is therefore fully expected. This result does not suggest that lower capital gains tax rates will continue to add to tax revenues in the future. Furthermore, many tax analysts doubt that lower capital gains taxes will do much to promote economic growth. "I know of no evidence that establishes a connection between prosperity and at what rate we tax capital gains," reports Joel Slemrod, economist and director of the Office of Tax Policy Research at the University of Michigan.

Lower taxes on dividends are even less likely than lower taxes on capital gains to generate either economic growth or a sustained increase in tax revenues. Most of the increase in dividend income since the 2003 tax cut has come from special, one-time payouts, not from ongoing growth in dividends. In fact, most of that increase came from just *one* special dividend: the $32 billion, or $3 per share, that software giant Microsoft issued on December 3, 2004 (which falls in FY2005), unloading much of the pile of cash it had been sitting on for years. Microsoft's special dividend was one-and-a-half times the size of the other 272 dividend increases in 2004 combined. It paid off handsomely for company founder Bill Gates, the world's richest man, who owns more than 600 million of its shares.

Finally, even with the increase in revenues—an increase that's not likely to be sustained—from taxes on capital gains and dividends, income tax revenues will only reach a projected 7.6% of GDP in FY2005. This is well below the FY2001 level of 9.9% of GDP when Bush took office and lower than any year during the 1970s, 1980s, and 1990s except for two years, 1976 and 1992, when recession pushed income tax revenues down to 7.6% of GDP.

In the end, $262 billion is hardly proof positive that the Bush tax cuts are working. Trimmed of its accounting-induced jump in corporate income tax revenues, the increase in FY2005 tax revenues is mediocre by historical standards, unlikely to be sustained, and more likely to pay off CEOs than to pay off in more rapid economic growth. Maybe that is enough for the *Wall Street Journal*'s editors to celebrate, but don't let their merriment convince you that the Bush tax cuts are anything other than an ineffectual giveaway to the rich.

Resources: Joel Slemrod, "More Tax Cuts? The Truth About Taxes and Economic Growth," *Challenge*, Jan/Feb 2003; Joel Friedman, "Dividend and Capital Gains Tax Cuts Unlikely to Yield Touted Economic Gains," Center on Budget and Policy Priorities, March 2005; "The Budget and Economic Outlook: An Update," Congressional Budget Office, August 2005; "A GOP Tax Increase?" *Wall Street Journal*, 9/22/05; "Bush and Katrina," *WSJ*, 9/6/05; "Tax Cut Dividends," *WSJ*, 8/17/05.

DON'T THE RICH PAY A LOT OF TAXES?

BY ELLEN FRANK

Dear Dr. Dollar:

The Heritage Foundation, a conservative think tank, has a website that purports to present evidence that the wealthiest group of Americans historically pay more taxes than middle- or low-income folks. Their sources include the U.S. Treasury Department, the Office of Management and Budget, and the Census Bureau. The wealthiest 1% paid over a third of taxes, while those in the lower 50% paid only 4% of income taxes in 1999. How do those of us who criticize the tax system as inherently unfair to middle- and lower-income folks respond to this apparently progressive tax system?

—*Bruce Boccardy,*
Allston, Massachusetts

The most comprehensive source of information on "tax incidence"—who actually pays how much in taxes—is the Congressional Budget Office (CBO), which compiles data from the Internal Revenue Service every couple of years. The CBO's most recent report, entitled Effective Tax Rates, was released in March 2005 and is available online at <www.cbo.gov>. (The effective tax rate is the percentage of income actually paid in taxes—as opposed to the

tax bracket—after deductions and exemptions and loopholes and all the rest.)

The CBO divides families into five "quintiles"—from the lowest earning one-fifth of taxpayers (incomes ranging from $0 to $15,900 in 2002) to the highest paid fifth (incomes of $59,400 and up)—and further breaks down the top fifth into the top 10%, 5%, and 1%.

As the table shows, the top income groups do in fact pay income taxes at a greater rate than they earn. The poorest quintile gets 4.2% of income but pays −2.6% of federal income taxes—negative because most qualify for the Earned Income Tax Credit. The top fifth garners 51.5% of income but shells out 82.8% of the income tax. And the richest 1% of taxpayers (average income of $938,100) receives 13.4% of income but pays one-third of federal income taxes. After those taxes are collected, the wealthiest income groups end up with a slightly smaller share of the economic pie than they started out with, while the poorer groups end up with slightly more. So the folks at Heritage are not wrong. The federal income tax is indisputably progressive; it is intended to redistribute income, and that is what it does.

But the redistributive impact is mild—

and it's milder still since the Bush Administration's tax reforms. The top quintile starts out with slightly more than half of all pre-tax income generated by the U.S. economy, and ends up with a little less than half of all after-tax income. The poorest fifth begins the game with just 4.2% of income and ends up with 5.1%. The folks at Heritage, of course, oppose government redistribution schemes on principle. But redistributing income is the whole point of a progressive tax, and advocates of progressive taxation should not shy away from defending this. If one believes that Ken Lay deserved no less than the $100 million he collected from Enron in 2001, while the burger-flippers and office cleaners of America deserve no more that the $6.50 an hour they collect, then a progressive tax would seem immoral. But if one believes that incomes are determined by race, gender, connections, power, luck and (occasionally) fraud, then redistribution through the tax system is a moral imperative.

The Heritage study also conveniently overlooks the impact of levies other than the federal income tax. Social Security taxes, excise levies, tariffs, and other duties are regressive—their effective rates decline as income goes up. When these other federal taxes are added in, the tax burden on lower-income groups increases significantly. Social Security taxes take an especially large bite out of low-income workers' paychecks; the bite is even larger when we include payroll taxes paid by the employer. (Labor economists believe that the employer share of the Social Security tax functions, in practice, as a levy on wages, since employers reduce wages to compensate for the tax instead of paying for it out of profits). Further, because state and local governments collect regressive sales, excise, and property taxes, the lower four quintiles pay a larger share of their income in state and local taxes than the top quintile. If we were to add all of these taxes together, we would almost certainly find that the U.S. tax system, as a whole, is not progressive at all.

DISTRIBUTION OF INCOME AND TAXES BY INCOME GROUPS, 2002						
Income Group	1	2	3	4	5	6
Lowest 20%	$14,400	4.2%	−2.6%	5.1%	0.9%	9.3%
Second 20%	$33,600	9.3%	-0.2%	10.4%	4.8%	10.3%
Third 20%	$51,100	14.7%	5.3%	15.8%	10.2%	9.7%
Fourth 20%	$75,900	21.2%	14.8%	21.7%	19.1%	9.0%
Top 20%	$175,900	51.5%	82.8%	48.0%	64.8%	8.5%
Top 10%	$244,500	36.4%	67.4%	33.1%	49.0%	n.a.
Top 5%	$350,700	23.3%	54.5%	23.3%	37.3%	n.a.
Top 1%	$938,100	13.4%	33.0%	11.4%	21.1%	6.5%

1 = Average Household Income; 2 = Share of Pre-Tax Income; 3 = Share of Federal Income Taxes; 4 = Share of After-Tax Income; 5 = Share of All Federal Taxes; 6 = Effective State and Local Tax Rate (2002)

Sources: Congressional Budget Office, *Effective Tax Rates, 1979-2002*; Citizens for Tax Justice, *Who Pays? A Distributional Analysis of the Tax Systems in All 50 States*, 2002 (last column).

THE TAX-CUT CON

BY PAUL KRUGMAN

Bruce Tinsley's comic strip, "Mallard Fillmore," is, he says, "for the average person out there: the forgotten American taxpayer who's sick of the liberal media." In June 2003, that forgotten taxpayer made an appearance in the strip, attacking his TV set with a baseball bat and yelling: "I can't afford to send my kids to college, or even take 'em out of their substandard public school, because the federal, state and local governments take more than 50% of my income in taxes. And then the guy on the news asks with a straight face whether or not we can 'afford' tax cuts."

Nobody likes paying taxes, and no doubt some Americans are as angry about their taxes as Tinsley's imaginary character. But most Americans also care a lot about the things taxes pay for.

All politicians say they're for public education; almost all of them also say they support a strong national defense, maintaining Social Security and, if anything, expanding the coverage of Medicare. When the "guy on the news" asks whether we can afford a tax cut, he's asking whether, after yet another tax cut goes through, there will be enough money to pay for those things. And the answer is no.

But it's very difficult to get that answer across in modern American politics, which has been dominated for 25 years by a crusade against taxes.

I don't use the word "crusade" lightly. The advocates of tax cuts are relentless, even fanatical. An indication of the movement's fervor—and of its political power—came during the Iraq war. War is expensive and is almost always accompanied by tax increases. But not in 2003. "Nothing is more important in the face of a war," declared Tom DeLay, the House majority leader, "than cutting taxes." And sure enough, taxes were cut, not just in a time of war but also in the face of record budget deficits.

A result of the tax-cut crusade is that there is now a fundamental mismatch between the benefits Americans expect to receive from the government and the revenues government collect. This mismatch is already having profound effects at the state and local levels: teachers and policemen are being laid off and children are being denied health insurance. The federal government can mask its problems for a while by running huge budget deficits, but it, too, will eventually have to decide whether to cut services or raise taxes. And we are not talking about minor policy adjustments. If taxes stay as low as they are now, government as we know it cannot be maintained. In particular, Social Security will have to become far less generous; Medicare will no longer be able to guarantee comprehensive medical care to older Americans; Medicaid will no longer provide basic medical care to the poor.

How did we reach this point? What are the origins of the antitax crusade? And where is it taking us?

SUPPLY-SIDERS, STARVE-THE-BEASTERS, AND LUCKY DUCKIES

It is often hard to pin down what antitax crusaders are trying to achieve. The reason is not, or not only, that they are disingenuous about their motives—though as we will see, disingenuity has become a hallmark of the movement in recent years. Rather, the fuzziness comes from the fact that today's antitax movement moves back and forth between two doctrines. Both doctrines favor the same thing: big tax cuts for people with high incomes. But they favor it for different reasons.

One of those doctrines has become famous under the name "supply-side economics." It's the view that the government can cut taxes without severe cuts in public spending. The other doctrine is often referred to as "starving the beast," a phrase coined by David Stockman, Ronald Reagan's budget director. It's the view that taxes should be cut precisely in order to force severe cuts in public spending. Supply-side economics is the friendly, attractive face of the tax-cut movement. But starve-the-beast is where the power lies.

The starting point of supply-side economics is an assertion that no economist would dispute: taxes reduce the incentive to work, save and invest. A businessman who knows that 70 cents of every extra dollar he makes will go to the IRS is less willing to make the effort to earn that extra dollar than if he knows that the IRS will take only 35 cents. So reducing tax rates will, other things being the same, spur the economy.

This much isn't controversial. But the government must pay its bills. So the standard view of economists is that if you want to reduce the burden of taxes, you must explain what government programs you want to cut as part of the deal. There's no free lunch.

What the supply-siders argued, however, was that there was a free lunch. Cutting marginal rates, they insisted, would lead to such a large increase in gross domestic product that it wouldn't be necessary to come up with offsetting spending cuts. What supply-side economists say, in other words, is, "Don't worry, be happy and cut taxes." And when they say cut taxes, they mean taxes on the affluent: reducing the top marginal rate means that the biggest tax cuts go to people in the highest tax brackets.

The other camp in the tax-cut crusade actually welcomes the revenue losses from tax cuts. Its most visible spokesman today is Grover Norquist, president of Americans for Tax Reform, who once told National Public Radio: "I don't want to abolish government. I simply want to reduce it to the size where I can drag it into the bathroom and drown it in the bathtub." And the way to get it down to that size is to starve it of revenue. "The goal is reducing the size and scope of government by draining its lifeblood," Norquist told *U.S. News & World Report*.

What does "reducing the size and scope of government" mean? Tax-cut proponents are usually vague about the details. But the Heritage Foundation, ideological headquarters for the movement, has made it pretty clear. Edwin Feulner, the foundation's president, uses "New Deal" and "Great Society" as terms of abuse, implying that he and his organization want to do away with the institutions Franklin Roosevelt and Lyndon Johnson created. That means Social Security, Medicare, Medicaid—most of what gives citizens of the United States a safety net against economic misfortune.

The starve-the-beast doctrine is now firmly within the conservative mainstream. George W. Bush himself seemed to endorse the doctrine as the budget surplus evaporated: in August 2001 he called the disappearing surplus "incredibly positive news" because it would put Congress in a "fiscal straitjacket."

Like supply-siders, starve-the-beasters favor tax cuts mainly for people with high incomes. That is partly because, like supply-siders, they emphasize the incentive effects of cutting the top marginal rate; they just don't believe that those incentive effects are big enough that tax cuts pay for themselves. But they have another reason for cutting taxes mainly on the rich, which has become known as the "lucky ducky" argument.

Here's how the argument runs: to starve the beast, you must not only deny funds to the government; you must make voters hate the government. There's a danger that working-class families might see government as their friend: because their incomes are low, they don't pay much in taxes, while they benefit from public spending. So in starving the beast, you must take care not to cut taxes on these "lucky duckies." (Yes, that's what the *Wall Street Journal* called them in a famous editorial.) In fact, if possible, you must raise taxes on working-class Americans in order, as the *Journal* said, to get their "blood boiling with tax rage."

So the tax-cut crusade has two faces. Smiling supply-siders say that tax cuts are all gain, no pain; scowling starve-the-beasters believe that inflicting pain is not just necessary but also desirable. Is the alliance between these two groups a marriage of convenience? Not exactly. It would be more accurate to say that the starve-the-beasters hired the supply-siders—indeed, created them—because they found their naive optimism useful.

A look at who the supply-siders are and how they came to prominence tells the story. The supply-side movement likes to present itself as a school of economic thought like Keynesianism or monetarism—that is, as a set of scholarly ideas that made their way, as such ideas do, into political discussion. But the reality is quite different. Supply-side economics was a political doctrine from Day 1; it emerged in the pages of political magazines, not professional economics journals.

That is not to deny that many professional economists favor tax cuts. But they almost always turn out to be starve-the-beasters, not supply-siders. And they often secretly—or sometimes not so secretly—hold supply-siders in contempt. N. Gregory Mankiw, now chairman of George W. Bush's Council of Economic Advisers, is definitely a friend to tax cuts; but in the first edition of his economic-principles textbook, he described Ronald Reagan's supply-side advisers as "charlatans and cranks."

TO STARVE THE BEAST, YOU MUST MAKE VOTERS HATE THE GOVERNMENT.

It is not that the professionals refuse to consider supply-side ideas; rather, they have looked at them and found them wanting. A conspicuous example came earlier this year when the Congressional Budget Office tried to evaluate the growth effects of the Bush administration's proposed tax cuts. The budget office's new head, Douglas Holtz-Eakin, is a conservative economist who was handpicked for his job by the administration. But his conclusion was that unless the revenue losses from the proposed tax cuts were offset by spending cuts, the resulting deficits would be a drag on growth, quite likely to outweigh any supply-side effects.

But if the professionals regard the supply-siders with disdain, who employs these people? The answer is that since the 1970s almost all of the prominent supply-siders have been aides to conservative politicians, writers at conservative publications like *National Review*, fellows at conservative policy centers like Heritage or economists at private companies with strong Republican connections. Loosely speaking, that is, supply-siders work for the vast right-wing conspiracy. What gives supply-side economics influence is its connection with a powerful network of institutions that want to shrink the government and see tax cuts as a way to achieve that goal.

Supply-side economics is a feel-good cover story for a political movement with a much harder-nosed agenda.

A PLANNED CRISIS

Right now, much of the public discussion of the Bush tax cuts focuses on their short-run impact. Critics say that the 2.7 million jobs lost since March 2001 prove that the administration's policies have failed, while the administration says that things would have been even worse without the tax cuts and that a solid recovery is just around the corner.

But this is the wrong debate. Even in the short run, the right question to ask isn't whether the tax cuts were better than nothing; they probably were. The right question is whether some other economic-stimulus plan could have achieved better results at a lower budget cost. And it is hard to deny that, on a jobs-per-dollar basis, the Bush tax cuts have been extremely ineffective. According to the Congressional Budget Office, half of this year's $400 billion budget deficit is due to Bush tax cuts. Now $200 billion is a lot of money; it is equivalent to the salaries of four million average workers. Even the administration doesn't claim its policies have created four million jobs. Surely some other policy—aid to state and local governments, tax breaks for the poor and middle class rather than the rich, maybe even WPA-style public works—would have been more successful at getting the country back to work.

Meanwhile, the tax cuts are designed to remain in place even after the economy has recovered. Where will they leave us?

Here's the basic fact: partly, though not entirely, as a result of the tax cuts of the last three years, the government of the United States faces a fundamental fiscal shortfall. That is, the revenue it collects falls well short of the sums it needs to pay for existing programs. Even the U.S. government must, eventually, pay its bills, so something will have to give.

The numbers tell the tale. This year and next, the federal government will run budget deficits of more than $400 billion. Deficits may fall a bit, at least as a share of gross domestic product, when the economy recovers. But the relief will be modest and temporary. As Peter Fisher, undersecretary of the treasury for domestic finance, puts it, the federal government is "a gigantic insurance company with a sideline business in defense and homeland security." And about a decade from now, this insurance company's policyholders will begin making a lot of claims. As the baby boomers retire, spending on Social Security benefits and Medicare will steadily rise, as will spending on Medicaid (because of rising medical costs). Eventually, unless there are sharp cuts in benefits, these three programs alone will consume a larger share of GDP than the federal government currently collects in taxes.

THE LOOMING FISCAL CRISIS ISN'T A DEFEAT FOR THE LEADERS OF THE TAX-CUT CRUSADE. IT'S EXACTLY WHAT THEY HAD IN MIND.

Alan Auerbach, William Gale, and Peter Orszag, fiscal experts at the Brookings Institution, have estimated the size of the "fiscal gap"—the increase in revenues or reduction in spending that would be needed to make the nation's finances sustainable in the long run. If you define the long run as 75 years, this gap turns out to be 4.5% of GDP. Or to put it another way, the gap is equal to 30% of what the federal government spends on all domestic programs. Of that gap, about 60% is the result of the Bush tax cuts. We would have faced a serious fiscal problem even if those tax cuts had never happened. But we face a much nastier problem now

that they are in place.

And more broadly, the tax-cut crusade will make it very hard for any future politicians to raise taxes.

So how will this gap be closed? The crucial point is that it cannot be closed without either fundamentally redefining the role of government or sharply raising taxes.

Politicians will, of course, promise to eliminate wasteful spending. But take out Social Security, Medicare, defense, Medicaid, government pensions, homeland security, interest on the public debt and veterans' benefits—none of them what people who complain about waste usually have in mind—and you are left with spending equal to about 3% of gross domestic product. And most of that goes for courts, highways, education and other useful things. Any savings from elimination of waste and fraud will amount to little more than a rounding-off error.

So let's put a few things back on the table. Let's assume that interest on the public debt will be paid, that spending on defense and homeland security will not be compromised and that the regular operations of government will continue to be financed. What we are left with, then, are the New Deal and Great Society programs: Social Security, Medicare, Medicaid and unemployment insurance. And to close the fiscal gap, spending on these programs would have to be cut by around 40%.

It's impossible to know how such spending cuts might unfold, but cuts of that magnitude would require drastic changes in the system. It goes almost without saying that the age at which Americans become eligible for retirement benefits would rise, that Social Security payments would fall sharply compared with average incomes, that Medicare patients would be forced to pay much more of their expenses out of pocket—or do without. And that would be only a start.

All this sounds politically impossible. In fact, politicians of both parties have been scrambling to expand, not reduce, Medicare benefits by adding prescription drug coverage. It's hard to imagine a situation under which the entitlement programs would be rolled back sufficiently to close the fiscal gap.

Yet closing the fiscal gap by raising taxes would mean rolling back all of the Bush tax cuts, and then some. And that also sounds politically impossible.

For the time being, there is a third alternative: borrow the difference between what we insist on spending and what we're willing to collect in taxes. That works as long as lenders believe that someday, somehow, we're going to get our fiscal act together. But this can't go on indefinitely.

Eventually—I think within a decade, though not everyone agrees—the bond market will tell us that we have to make a choice.

In short, everything is going according to plan.

For the looming fiscal crisis doesn't represent a defeat for the leaders of the tax-cut crusade or a miscalculation on their part. Some supporters of President Bush may have really believed that his tax cuts were consistent with his promises to protect Social Security and expand Medicare; some people may still believe that the wondrous supply-side effects of tax cuts will make the budget deficit disappear. But for starve-the-beast tax-cutters, the coming crunch is exactly what they had in mind.

WHAT KIND OF COUNTRY?

The astonishing political success of the antitax crusade has, more or less deliberately, set the United States up for a fiscal crisis. How we respond to that crisis will determine what kind of country we become.

If Grover Norquist is right—and he has been right about a lot—the coming crisis will allow conservatives to move the nation a long way back toward the kind of limited government we had before Franklin Roosevelt. Lack of revenue, he says, will make it possible for conservative politicians—in the name of fiscal necessity—to dismantle immensely popular government programs that would otherwise have been untouchable.

In Norquist's vision, America a couple of decades from now will be a place in which elderly people make up a disproportionate share of the poor, as they did before Social Security. It will also be a country in which even middle-class elderly Americans are, in many cases, unable to afford expensive medical procedures or prescription drugs and in which poor Americans generally go without even basic health care. And it may well be a place in which only those who can afford expensive private schools can give their children a decent education.

But that's a choice, not a necessity. The tax-cut crusade has created a situation in which something must give. But what gives—whether we decide that the New Deal and the Great Society must go or that taxes aren't such a bad thing after all—is up to us. The American people must decide what kind of a country we want to be.

Excerpted from the *New York Times* Magazine, September 14, 2003

ARTICLE 4.6

SOCIAL SECURITY ISN'T BROKEN

SO WHY THE RUSH TO "FIX" IT?

BY DOUG ORR

Federal Reserve Chairman Alan Greenspan told Congress earlier this year that everyone knows there's a Social Security crisis. That's like saying "everyone knows the earth is flat."

Starting with a faulty premise guarantees reaching the wrong conclusion. The truth is there is no Social Security crisis, but there is a potential crisis in retirement income security and there may be a crisis in the future in U.S. financial markets. It's this latter crisis that Greenspan actually is worried about.

Social Security is the most successful insurance program ever created. It insures millions of workers against what economists call "longevity risk," the possibility they will live "too long" and not be able to work long enough, or save enough, to provide their own income. Today, about 10% of those over age 65 live in poverty. Without Social Security, that rate would be almost 50%.

Social Security was originally designed to supplement, and was structured to resemble, private-sector pensions. In the 1930s, all private pensions were defined-benefit plans. The retirement benefit was based on a worker's former wage and years of service. In most plans, after 35 years of service the monthly benefit, received for life, would be at least half of the income received in the final working year.

Congress expected that private-sector pensions eventually would cover most workers. But pension coverage peaked at 40% in the 1960s. Since then, corporations have systematically dismantled pension systems. Today, only 16% of private-sector workers are covered by defined-benefit pensions. Rather than supplementing private pensions, Social Security has become the primary source of retirement income for almost two-thirds of retirees. Thus, Congress was forced to raise benefit levels in 1972.

What has happened to private-sector defined benefit pensions? They've been replaced with defined-contribution (DC) savings plans such as 401(k)s and 403(b)s. These plans provide some retirement income but offer no real protection from longevity risk. Once a retiree depletes the amount saved in the plan, their retirement income is gone.

In a generous DC plan, a firm might match the worker's contribution up to 3% of his or her pay. With total contributions of 6%, average wage growth of 2% a year, and an average return on the investment portfolio of 5%, after 35 years of work, a retiree would exhaust the plan's savings in just 8.5 years even if her annual spending is only half of her final salary. If she restricts spending to just one-third of the final salary, the savings can stretch to 14 years.

At age 65, life expectancy for women today is about 20 years, and for men about 15 years, so DC savings plans will not protect the elderly from longevity risk. The conversion of defined-benefit pensions to defined-contribution plans is the source of the real potential crisis in retirement income. Yet Greenspan did not mention this in his testimony to Congress.

NO CRISIS

Opponents of Social Security have hated it since its creation in 1935. The first prediction of a Social Security crisis was published in 1936! The Heritage Foundation and Cato Institute are home to many of the program's opponents today, and they fixate on the concept of a "demographic imperative." In 1960, the United States had 5.1 workers per retiree, in 1998 we had 3.4, and by 2030 we will have only 2.1. Opponents claim that with these demographic changes, revenues will eventually be insufficient to pay Social Security retirement benefits.

The logic is appealingly simple, but wrong for two reasons. First, this "old-age dependency" ratio in itself is irrelevant. No amount of financial manipulation can change this fact: all current consumption must come from current physical output. The consumption of all dependents (non-workers) must come from the output produced by current workers. It's the overall dependency ratio—the number of workers relative to all non-workers, including the aged, the young, the disabled, and those choosing not to work—that determines whether society can "afford" the baby boomers' retirement years. In the 1960s we had only 0.62 workers for each dependent, and we were building new schools and the interstate highway system and getting ready to put a man on the moon. No one bemoaned a demographic crisis or looked for ways to cut the resources allocated to children; in fact, the living standards of most families rose rapidly. In 2030, we will have 0.98 workers per dependent. We'll have more workers per dependent in the future than we did in the past. While it is true a larger share of total output will be allocated to the aged, just as a larger share was allocated to children in the 1960s, society will easily produce adequate output to support all workers and dependents, and at a higher standard of living.

Second, the "demographic imperative" ignores productivity growth. Average worker productivity has grown by about 2% per year, adjusted for inflation, for the past half-century. That means real output per worker doubles every 36 years. This productivity growth is projected to continue, so by 2040, each worker will produce twice as much as today. Suppose each of three workers today produces $1,000 per week and one retiree is allocated $500 (half of his final salary)—then each worker gets $833. In 2040, two such workers will produce $2,000 per week each (after adjusting for inflation). If each retiree gets $1,000, each worker still gets

$1,500. The incomes of both workers and retirees go up. Thus, paying for the baby boomers' retirement need not decrease their children's standard of living. A larger share of output going to retirees does not imply that the standard of living of those still working will be lower. Those still working will have a slightly smaller share of a much larger pie.

So why the talk of a Social Security crisis? Social Security always has been a pay-as-you-go system. Current benefits are paid out of current tax revenues. But in the 1980s, a commission headed by Greenspan recommended raising payroll taxes to expand the trust fund in order to supplement tax revenues when the baby boom generation retires. Congress responded in 1984 by raising payroll taxes significantly. As a result, the Social Security trust fund, which holds government bonds as assets, has grown every year since. As the baby boom moves into retirement, these assets will be sold to help pay their retirement benefits.

Each year, Social Security's trustees must make projections of the system's status for the next 75 years. In 1996, they projected the trust fund balance would go to zero in 2030. In 2000, they projected a zero balance in 2036 and today they project a zero balance in 2042. The projection keeps changing because the trustees continue to make unrealistic assumptions about future economic conditions. The current projections are based on the assumption that annual GDP growth will average 1.8 % for the next 75 years. In no 20-year period, even including the Great Depression, has the U.S. economy grown that slowly. Each year the economy grows faster than 1.8%, the zero balance date moves further into the future. But the trustees continue to suggest that if we return to something like the Great Depression, the trust fund will go to zero.

Opponents of Social Security claim the system will then be "bankrupt." Bankruptcy implies ceasing to exist. But if the trust fund goes to zero, Social Security will not shut down and stop paying benefits. It will simply revert to the pure pay-as-you-go system that it was before 1984 and continue to pay current benefits using current tax revenues. Even if the trustees' worst-case assumptions come true, the payroll tax paid by workers would need to increase by only about 2% points, and only in 2042, not today.

If the economy grows at 2.4%—which is still slower than the stagnant growth of the 1980s—the trust fund never goes to zero. The increase in real output and real incomes will generate sufficient revenues to pay promised benefits. By 2042, we will need to lower payroll taxes or raise benefits to reduce the surplus.

The claim that benefits of future retirees must be reduced in order to not reduce the standard of living of future workers is simply wrong. It is being used to drive a wedge between generations and panic younger workers into supporting Bush's plan to destroy Social Security. Under the most likely version of his privatization proposal, according to Bush's own Social Security Commission, the guaranteed benefits from Social Security of a 20-year-old worker joining the

HOW DOES THE BOND MARKET WORK?

A bond is nothing more than an IOU. A company or government borrows money and promises to pay a certain amount of interest annually until it repays the loan. When you buy a newly issued bond, you are making a loan. The amount of the loan is the "face value" of the bond. The initial interest rate at which the bond is issued, the "face rate," multiplied by this face value determines the amount of interest paid each period. Until the debt is paid back, events in the financial markets affect the bond's value.

If market interest rates fall, prices of existing bonds rise. Why? Suppose you buy a bond with a face value of $100 that pays 10%. You then collect $10 per year. If the current interest rate falls to 5%, newly issued bonds will pay that new rate. Since your bond pays 10%, people would rather buy that one than one paying 5%. They are willing to pay more than the face value to get it, so the price will be bid up until interest rates equalize. The price at which you could sell your bond will rise to $200, since $10 is 5% of $200.

But changes in bond prices also affect interest rates. If more people are selling bonds than buying them, an excess supply exists, and prices will fall. If you need to sell your bond to get money to pay your rent, you might have to lower the price of the bond you hold to $50. Because the bond still pays $10 per year to the owner, the new owner gets a 20% return on the $50 purchase. Anyone trying to issue new bonds will have to match that return, so the new market interest rate becomes 20%.

labor force today would be reduced by 46%. That Commission also admitted that private accounts are unlikely to make up for this drop in benefits. An estimate made by the Goldman-Sacks brokerage firm suggests that even with private accounts, retirement income of younger workers would be reduced by 42% compared to what they would receive if nothing is done to change the Social Security system. Private accounts are a losing proposition for younger workers.

THE REAL FEAR: AN OVERSUPPLY OF BONDS

So why did Greenspan claim cutting benefits would become necessary? To understand the answer, we need to take a side trip to look at how bonds and the financial markets affect each other. It turns out that rising interest rates reduce the selling price of existing financial assets, and falling asset prices push up interest rates (see box "How Does the Bond Market Work?").

For example, in the 1980s, President Reagan cut taxes and created the largest government deficits in history up to that point. This meant the federal government had to sell lots of bonds to finance the soaring government debt; to attract enough buyers, the Treasury had to offer very high interest rates. During the 1980s, real interest rates (rates adjusted for inflation) were almost four times higher than the historic average. High interest rates slow economic growth by making it more expensive for consumers to buy homes or for businesses to invest in new infrastructure. The GDP growth rate in the 1980s was the slowest in U.S. history apart from the Great Depression.

But high interest rates also depress financial asset prices. A five percentage point rise in interest rates reduces the selling price of a bond (loan) that matures in 10 years by 50%. It was the impact of the record-high interest rates of the 1980s on the value of the loan portfolios of the savings and loan industry that caused the S&L crisis and the industry's collapse.

Greenspan is worried because he sees history repeating itself in the form of President Bush's tax cuts. In his testimony, Greenspan expressed concern over a potentially large rise in interest rates. This is his way of warning about an excess supply of bonds. Starting in 2020, Social Security will have to sell about $150 billion (in 2002 dollars) in trust fund bonds each year for 22 years. At the same time, private-sector pension funds will be selling $100 billion per year of financial assets to make their pension payments. State and local governments will be selling $75 billion per year to cover their former employees' pension expenses, and holdings in private mutual funds will fall by about $50 billion per year as individual retirees cash in their 401(k) assets. Private firms will still need to issue about $100 billion of new bonds a year to finance business expansion. Combined, these asset sales could total $475 billion per year.

This level of bond sales is more than double the record that was set in the 1980s following the Reagan tax cuts. But back then, the newly issued bonds were being purchased by "institutional investors" such as private-sector pension funds and insurance companies. After 2020, these groups will be net sellers of bonds. The financial markets will strain to absorb this level of asset sales. It's unlikely they will be able to also absorb the extra $400 billion per year of bond sales needed to cover the deficit spending that will occur if the new Bush tax cuts are made permanent. This oversupply of bonds will drive down the value of all financial assets.

In a 1994 paper, Sylvester Schieber, a current advisor to President Bush on pension and Social Security reform, predicted this potential drop in asset prices. After 2020, the value of assets held in 401(k) plans, already inadequate, will be reduced even more. More importantly, at least to Greenspan, the prices of assets held by corporations to fund their defined benefit pension promises will fall. Thus, pension payments will need to come out of current revenues, reducing corporate profits and, in turn, driving down stock prices.

It's this potential collapse in the prices of financial assets that worries Greenspan most. In order to reduce the run-up of long-term interest rates, some asset sales must be eliminated. Greenspan said, "You don't have the resources to do it all." But rather than rescinding Bush's tax cuts, Greenspan favors reducing bond sales by the Social Security trust fund. Doing that requires a reduction in benefits and raising payroll taxes even more.

Framing a question incorrectly makes it impossible to find a solution. The problem is not with Social Security, but rather with blind reliance on financial markets to solve all economic problems. If the financial markets are likely to fail us, what is the solution? The solution is simple once the question is framed correctly: where will the real output that baby boomers are going to consume in retirement come from?

The federal budget surplus President Bush inherited came entirely from Social Security surpluses resulting from the 1984 payroll tax increase. Bush gave away revenues meant to provide for workers' retirement as tax cuts for the wealthiest 10% of the population.

We should rescind Bush's tax cuts and use the Social Security surpluses to really prepare for the baby boom retirement. Public investment or targeted tax breaks could be used to encourage the building of the hospitals, nursing homes, and hospices that aging baby boomers will need. Such investment in public and private infrastructure would also stimulate the real economy and increase GDP growth.

Surpluses could be used to fund the training of doctors, nurses and others to staff these facilities, and of other high skilled workers more generally. The higher wages of skilled labor will help generate the payroll tax revenues needed to fund future benefits. If baby boomers help to fund this infrastructure expansion through their payroll taxes while they are still working, less output will need to be allocated when they retire. These expenditures will increase the productivity of the real economy, which will help keep the financial sector solvent to provide for retirees.

Destroying Social Security in order to "save" it is not a solution.

Sources: Dean Baker and Mark Weisbrot, *Social Security: The Phony Crises*, University of Chicago Press, 1999; William Wolman and Anne Colamosca, *The Great 401(k) Hoax*, Perseus Publishing, 2002; Sylvester J. Schieber and John B. Shoven, "The Consequences of Population Aging on Private Pension Fund Saving and Asset Markets," National Bureau of Economic Research, Working Paper No. 4665, 1994.

THE SOCIAL SECURITY ADMINISTRATION'S CRACKED CRYSTAL BALL

BY JOHN MILLER

2042. That's the year the Social Security Trust Fund will run out of money, according to the Social Security Administration (SSA). But its doomsday prophesy is based on overly pessimistic assumptions about our economic future: The SSA expects the U.S. economy to expand at an average annual rate of just 1.8% from 2015 to 2080—far slower than the 3.0% average growth rate the economy posted over the last 75 years.

What's behind the gloomy growth projections? Is there anything to them—or has the SSA's economic crystal ball malfunctioned?

FLAWED FORECAST

The Social Security Administration foresees a future of sluggish economic growth in which labor productivity, or output per worker, improves slowly; total employment barely grows; and workers put in no additional hours on the job. (It reasons that economic growth, or growth of national output, must equal the sum of labor productivity increases, increases in total employment, and increases in the average hours worked.)

In its widely cited "intermediate" 1.8% growth scenario, labor productivity improves by just 1.6% a year and work-

force growth slows almost to a standstill at 0.2% a year—rates well below their historical averages. (See Table 1.) Under these assumptions, and if average work time holds steady, Social Security exhausts its trust fund in the year 2042, at which point it faces an initial shortfall of 27% of its obligations. After that, Social Security would be able to pay out just 70% of the benefits it owes to retirees.

The problem is not with the logic of the method the Social Security Administration uses to make its projections, but rather with its demographic and economic assumptions. Its forecast of 1.6% annual labor productivity growth is especially suspect. When the nonpartisan Congressional Budget Office (CBO) assessed the financial health of Social Security earlier this year, it assumed that productivity would improve at a rate of 1.9% per year. In the CBO forecast, faster productivity growth, along with a lower unemployment rate, boosts wages—the tax base of the system—allowing Social Security to remain solvent until 2052, 10 years longer than the SSA had projected just a few months earlier.

One doesn't have to buy into the hype about the magic of the new economy to conclude that the CBO came closer

TABLE 1:
SOCIAL SECURITY ADMINISTRATION'S
PRINCIPAL ECONOMIC ASSUMPTIONS[a]

Annual Percentage Increase

Year	Real Gross Domestic Product[b]	Productivity (Total U.S. Economy)	Total Employment[c]	Average Hours Worked
2004	4.4%	2.7%	1.7%	0.0%
2005	3.6%	1.8%	1.7%	0.0%
2006	3.2%	1.9%	1.3%	0.0%
2007	3.0%	1.9%	1.1%	0.0%
2008	1.0%	1.8%	2.8%	0.0%
2009	2.7%	1.8%	0.9%	0.0%
2010	2.6%	1.7%	0.8%	0.0%
2011	2.4%	1.7%	0.8%	0.0%
2012	2.3%	1.6%	0.6%	0.0%
2013	2.2%	1.6%	0.6%	0.0%

Average Annual Percentage Increase

2010 to 2015	2.2%	1.6%	0.6%	0.0%
2015 to 2080	1.8%	1.6%	0.2%	0.0%

[a] These are the "intermediate economic assumptions" that the Social Security Administration regards as most plausible. The SSA also reports a "low cost" forecast that projects a 2.6% real growth rate from 2015 to 2080 and a "high cost" forecast that projects a 1.1% real growth rate from 2015 to 2080.

[b] Real Gross Domestic Product is calculated in constant 1996 dollars.

[c] Total employment is the total of civilian and military employment in the U.S. economy.

Source: Social Security Administration, 2004 Annual Report of the Board of Trustees (March 23, 2004), Table V.B.1 and Table V.B.2, pp. 89 and 94.

Social Security, helping to relieve the financial strain on the system created by the retirement of the baby-boom generation.

In its own optimistic or "low cost" scenario, the SSA erases the shortfall in the trust fund by assuming a faster productivity growth rate (of 1.9%), a lower unemployment rate (of 4.5% per year), and higher net immigration (of 1.3 million people per year). The still rather sluggish 2.6% average growth rate that results would wipe out the rest of the imbalance in the system and leave a sizeable surplus in the trust fund—0.15% of GDP over the next 75 years.

MAKING SHORT WORK OF THE SHORTFALL

Even in the unlikely event that the pessimistic predictions the SSA has conjured up actually do come to pass, the Social Security imbalance could be easily remedied.

The Social Security Trust Fund needs $3.7 trillion to meet its unfunded obligations over the next 75 years. That is a lot of money—about 1.89% of taxable payroll and about 0.7% of GDP over that period. But it's far less than the 2.0% of GDP the 2001 to 2003 tax cuts will cost over the next 75 years if they are made permanent. (Many of the tax cuts are currently scheduled to sunset in 2010.) The portion of the Bush tax cuts going to the richest 1% of taxpayers alone will cost 0.6% of GDP—more than the CBO projected shortfall of 0.4% of GDP.

Here are a few ways to make short work of any remaining shortfall without cutting retirement benefits or raising taxes for low- or middle-income workers. First, newly hired state and local government workers could be brought into the system. (About 3.5 million state and local government workers are not now covered by Social Security.) That move alone would eliminate about 30% of the projected deficit.

In addition, we could raise the cap on wages subject to payroll taxes. Under current law, Social Security is funded by a payroll tax on the first $87,900 of a person's income. As a result of this cap on covered income, the tax applies to just 84.5% of all wages today—but historically it applied to 90%. Increasing the cap for the next decade so that the payroll tax covers 87.3% of all wages, or halfway back to the 90% standard, would eliminate nearly one-third of the SSA's projected deficit.

Finally, stopping the repeal of the estate tax, a tax giveaway that benefits only the richest taxpayers, would go a long way toward closing the gap. Economists Peter Diamond and Peter Orszag, writing for The Century Fund, advocate dedicating the revenues generated by renewing the estate tax to the Social Security Trust Fund. They suggest an estate tax set

to getting the projected productivity growth rates right than the SSA did. The federal government's own Bureau of Labor Statistics estimates that productivity rates in the nonfarm sector improved at a 2.3% average pace from 1947 through 2003. Adjusting for the gap of 0.2 percentage points between the productivity growth of the nonfarm business sector and the economy as a whole still leaves productivity across the economy growing by a healthy 2.1% over the postwar period. That historical record convinces economist Dean Baker, from the Washington-based Center for Economic and Policy Research, that a productivity growth rate of 2.0% a year is a "very reasonable" assumption.

The drastic deceleration of employment growth, from its historic (1960 to 2000) average of 1.78% to 0.2% per year, is also overstated. As the trustees see it, employment will grow far more slowly as the baby-boomers leave the labor force. That is true as far as it goes. But if their projections are correct, the country will soon face a chronic labor shortage. And in that context, the immigration rate is unlikely to slow, as they assume, to 900,000 a year. Rather, future immigration rates would likely be at least as high as they were in the 1990s, when 1.3 million people entered the United States annually, and possibly even higher if immigration laws are relaxed in response to a labor shortage. Faster immigration would boost employment growth and add workers, who would pay into at its planned 2009 level, which would exempt $3.5 million of an individual's estate. The tax would fall exclusively on the wealthiest 0.3% of taxpayers. That alone would close another one-quarter of the SSA's projected shortfall. Returning the estate tax to its 2001 (pre-tax cut) level (with a $675,000 exemption for individuals) would do yet more to relieve any financial strain on Social Security.

Any way you look at it, Social Security can remain on sound financial footing even in the dreariest of economic futures, so long as alarmist reports like those of its trustees don't become an excuse to corrupt the system.

Sources: Congressional Budget Office, The Outlook for Social Security, June 2004; Social Security Administration, 2004 Annual Report of the Board of Trustees (March 23, 2004); "What the Trustees' Report Indicates About the Financial Status of Social Security," Robert Greenstein, Center on Budget and Policy Priorities (March 31, 2004); "The Implications of the Social Security Projections Issued By the Congressional Budget Office" Robert Greenstein, Peter Orszag, and Richard Kogan, Center on Budget and Policy Priorities (June 24, 2004); "Letter to Rudolph G. Penner" from Dean Baker, co-director of the Center For Economic and Policy Research (January 26, 2004); Countdown to Reform: The Great Social Security Debate, Henry Aaron and Robert Reischauer, The Century Foundation Press, 1998.

November/December 2004

AFRICAN AMERICANS AND SOCIAL SECURITY

WHY THE PRIVATIZATION ADVOCATES ARE WRONG

BY WILLIAM E. SPRIGGS

Proponents of Social Security privatization are trying to claim that the current program is unfair to African Americans and that a privatized program would serve African Americans better. This argument lends support to the privatization agenda while at the same time giving its advocates a compassionate gloss. But the claims about African Americans and Social Security are wrong.

The Old Age Survivors and Disability Insurance Program (OASDI), popularly known as Social Security, was put in place by Franklin Roosevelt to establish a solid bulwark of economic rights for the public—specifically, as he put it, "the right to adequate protection from the economic fears of old age, sickness, accident, and unemployment." Most Americans associate Social Security only with the retirement—or old age—benefit. Yet it was created to do much more, and it does.

As its original name suggests, Social Security is an insurance program that protects workers and their families against the income loss that occurs when a worker retires, becomes disabled, or dies. All workers will eventually either grow too old to compete in the labor market, become disabled, or die. OASDI insures all workers and their families against these universal risks, while spreading the costs and benefits of that insurance protection among the entire workforce. Currently, 70% of Social Security funds go to retirees, 15% to disabled workers, and 15% to survivors.

Social Security is a "pay as you go" system, which means the taxes paid by today's workers are not set aside to pay their own benefits down the road, but rather go to pay the benefits of current Social Security recipients. It's financed using the Federal Insurance Contribution Act (or FICA) payroll tax, paid by all working Americans on earnings of less than about $90,000 a year. While the payroll tax is not progressive, Social Security benefits are—that is, low-wage workers receive a greater percentage of pre-retirement earnings from the program than higher-wage workers.

In the 1980s, recognizing that the baby boom generation would strain this system, Congress passed reforms to raise extra tax revenues above and beyond the current need and set up a trust fund to hold the reserve. (See "Social Security Isn't Broken," p. 83) Trustees were appointed and charged with keeping Social Security solvent. Today's trustees warn that their projections, which are based on modest assumptions about the long-term growth of the U.S. economy, show the system could face a shortfall around 2042, when either benefits would have to be cut or the FICA tax raised.

Those who oppose the social nature of the program have pounced on its projected shortfall in revenues to argue that the program cannot—or ought not—be fixed, but should instead be fundamentally changed (see "Privatization Advocates.") Privatization proponents are seeking to frame the issue as a matter of social justice, as if Social Security "reform" would primarily benefit low-income workers, blue-collar workers, people of color, and women. Prompted by disparities in life expectancy between whites and African Americans and the racial wealth gap, a growing chorus within the privatization movement is claiming that privatizing Social Security would be beneficial to African Americans.

Opponents attack the program on the basis of an analogy to private retirement accounts. Early generations of Social Security beneficiaries received much more in benefits than they had paid into the system in taxes. Privatization proponents argue those early recipients received a "higher rate of return" on their "investment" while current and future generations are being "robbed" because they will see "lower rates of return." They argue the current system of social insurance—particularly the retirement program—should be privatized, switching from the current "pay-as-you-go" system to one in which individual workers claim their own contribution and decide where and how to invest it.

But this logic inverts the premise of social insurance. Rather than sharing risk across the entire workforce to ensure that all workers and their families are protected from the three inevitabilities of old age, disability, and death, privatizing Social Security retirement benefits would enable high-wage workers to reap gains from private retirement investment without having to help protect lower-wage workers from their (disproportionate) risks of disability and death. High-wage workers, who are more likely to live long enough to retire, could in fact do better on average if they opt out of the general risk pool and devote all their money to retirement without having to cover the risk of those who may become disabled or die, although they would of course be subjecting their retirement dollars to greater risk. But low-wage workers, who are far more likely to need disability or survivors' benefits to help their families and are less likely to live long enough to retire, would then be left with lower disability and survivors' benefits, and possibly no guaranteed benefits. This is what the Social Security privatization movement envisions. But you wouldn't know it from reading their literature.

And when the myths about Social Security's financial straits meet another American myth—race—even more confusion follows. Here is a look at three misleading claims by privatization proponents about African Americans and Social Security.

MYTH #1

Several conservative research groups argue that Social Security is a bad deal for African Americans because of their lower life expectancies. "Lifetime Social Security benefits depend, in large part, on longevity," writes the Cato Institute's Michael Tanner in his briefing paper "Disparate Impact: Social Security and African Americans." "At every age, African-American men and women both have shorter life expectancies than do their white counterparts. ... As a result, a black man or woman earning exactly the same lifetime wages, and paying exactly the same lifetime Social Security taxes, as his or her white counterpart will likely receive a far lower rate of return." Or as the Americans for Tax Reform web site puts it: "A black male born today has a life expectancy of 64.8 years. But the Social Security retirement age for that worker in the future will be 67 years. That means probably the majority of black males will never even receive Social Security retirement benefits."

The longevity myth is the foundation of all the race-based arguments for Social Security privatization. There are several problems with it.

First, the shorter life expectancy of African Americans compared to whites is the result of higher morbidity in mid-life, and is most acute for African-American men. The life expectancies of African-American women and white men are virtually equal. So the life expectancy argument can really only be made about African-American men.

Second, the claim that OASDI is unfair to African Americans because their expected benefits are less than their expected payments is usually raised and then answered from the perspective of the retirement (or "old age") benefit alone. That is an inaccurate way to look at the problem. Because OASDI also serves families of workers who become disabled or die, a correct measure would take into account the probability of all three risk factors—old age, disability, and death. Both survivor benefits and disability benefits, in fact, go disproportionately to African Americans.

While African Americans make up 12% of the U.S. population, 23% of children receiving Social Security survivor benefits are African American, as are about 17% of disability beneficiaries. On average, a worker who receives disability benefits or a family that receives survivor benefits gets far more in return than the worker paid in FICA taxes, notwithstanding privatizers' attempts to argue that Social Security is a bad deal.

PRIVATIZATION ADVOCATES

Powerful advocates for privatization include libertarian and conservative think tanks and advocacy groups such as the Cato Institute, the Heritage Foundation, Americans for Tax Reform, and Citizens for a Sound Economy, all driven by an ideological commitment to the abolition of federal social programs.

Wall Street too is thirsty for the $1.4 trillion that privatization would funnel into equities if the taxes collected to support the Social Security system were invested privately rather than reinvested in federal government bonds. That's not to mention the windfall of fees privatization would deliver for banks, brokerage houses, and investment firms.

Just after he took office, President Bush appointed a commission to examine privatizing the Social Security system. The commission could not figure out how to maintain payments to current recipients while diverting tax dollars to the savings of current workers, nor could it resolve how to cover the benefits of the disabled or resolve issues surrounding survivors' benefits. Although the president did not succeed in carrying out Social Security privatization in his first term, he has made the partial privatization of Social Security retirement accounts the top priority of his second-term domestic agenda.

Survivors' benefits also provide an important boost to poor families more generally. A recent study by the National Urban League Institute for Opportunity and Equality showed that the benefit lifted 1 million children out of poverty and helped another 1 million avoid extreme poverty (living below half the poverty line).

Finally, among workers who do live long enough to get the retirement benefit, life expectancies don't differ much by racial group. For example, at age 65, the life expectancies of African-American and white men are virtually the same.

President Bush's Social Security commission proposed the partial privatization of Social Security retirement accounts, but cautioned that it could not figure out how to maintain equal benefits for the other risk pools. The commission suggested that disability and survivor's benefits would have to be reduced if the privatization plan proceeds.

This vision is of a retirement program designed for the benefit of the worker who retires—only. A program with that focus would work against, not for, African Americans because of the higher morbidity rates in middle age and the smaller share of African Americans who live to retirement.

MYTH #2

African Americans have less education, and so are in the work force longer, than whites, and yet Social Security only credits 35 years of work experience in figuring benefits. Tanner says, "benefits are calculated on the basis of the highest 35 years of earnings over a worker's lifetime. Workers must still pay Social Security taxes during years outside those 35, but those taxes do not count toward or earn additional benefits. Generally, those low-earnings years occur early in an individual's life. That is particularly important to African Americans because they are likely to enter the workforce at an earlier age than whites...."

This claim misinterprets the benefit formula for Social Security. Yes, African Americans on average are slightly less educated than whites. The gap is mostly because of a higher college completion rate for white men compared to African-American men. But the education argument fails to acknowledge that white teenagers have a significantly higher labor force participation rate (at 46%) than do African-American teens (29%). The higher labor force participation of white teenagers helps to explain why young white adults do better in the labor market than young African-American adults. (The racial gaps in unemployment are considerably greater for teenagers and young adults than for those over 25.)

These differences in early labor market experiences mean that African-American men have more years of zero earnings than do whites. So while the statement about education is true, the inference from education differences to work histories is false. By taking only 35 years of work history into account in the benefit formula, the Social Security formula is progressive. It in effect ignores years of zero or very low earnings. This levels the playing field among long-time workers, putting African Americans with more years of zero earnings

on par with whites. By contrast, a private system based on total years of earnings would exacerbate racial labor market disparities.

MYTH #3

A third claim put forward by critics of Social Security is that African-American retirees are more dependent on Social Security than whites. Tanner writes: "Elderly African Americans are much more likely than their white counterparts to be dependent on Social Security benefits for most or all of their retirement income." Therefore, he concludes, "African Americans would be among those with the most to gain from the privatization of Social Security—transforming the program into a system of individually owned, privately invested accounts." Law professor and senior policy advisor to Americans for Tax Reform Peter Ferrara adds, "the personal accounts would produce far higher returns and benefits for lower-income workers, African Americans, Hispanics, women and other minorities."

It's true that African-American retirees are more likely than whites to rely on Social Security as their only income in old age. It's the sole source of retirement income for 40% of elderly African Americans. This is a result of discrimination in the labor market that limits the share of African Americans with jobs that offer pension benefits. Privatizing Social Security would not change labor market discrimination or its effects.

Privatizing Social Security would, however, exacerbate the earnings differences between African Americans and whites, since benefits would be based solely on individual savings. What would help African-American retirees is not privatization, but rather changing the redistributive aspects of Social Security to make it even more progressive.

The current formula for Social Security benefits is progressive in two ways: low earners get a higher share of their earnings than do higher wage earners and the lowest years of earning are ignored. Changes in the formula to raise the benefits floor enough to lift all retired Social Security recipients out of poverty would make it still more progressive. Increasing and updating the Supplemental Security Income payment, which helps low earners, could accomplish the same goal for SSI recipients. (SSI is a program administered by Social Security for very low earners and the poor who are disabled, blind, or at least 65 years old.)

The proponents of privatization argue that the heavy reliance of African-American seniors on Social Security requires higher rates of return—returns that are only possible by putting money into the stock market. Yet given the lack of access to private pensions for African-American seniors and their low savings from lifetimes of low earnings, such a notion is perverse. It would have African Americans gamble with their only leg of retirement's supposed three-legged stool—pension, savings, and Social Security. And, given the much higher risk that African Americans face of both death before retirement and of disability, it would be a risky gamble indeed to lower those benefits while jeopardizing their only retirement leg.

Privatizing the retirement program, and separating the integrated elements of Social Security, would split America. The divisions would be many: between those more likely to be disabled and those who are not; between those more likely to die before retirement and those more likely to retire; between children who get survivors' benefits and the elderly who get retirement benefits; between those who retire with high-yield investments and those who fare poorly in retirement. The "horizontal equity" of the program (treating simi-

lar people in a similar way) would be lost, as volatile stock fluctuations and the timing of retirement could greatly affect individuals' rates of return. The "vertical equity" of the program (its progressive nature, insuring a floor for benefits) would be placed in greater jeopardy with the shift from social to private benefits.

Social Security works because it is "social." It is America's only universal federal program. The proposed changes would place Social Security in the same political space as the rest of America's federal programs—and African Americans have seen time and again how those politics work.

ARTICLE 4.9   *May/June 2004*

BUSH STRIKES OUT ON HEALTH CARE

BY ELISE GOULD

In his State of the Union address in January, President Bush claimed to be addressing the twin crises of rising health care costs and declining access. He touted the Medicare bill Congress passed late last year for adding a prescription drug benefit for seniors, creating tax-free health savings accounts, and generally "strengthening Medicare." He then made some new proposals, including a tax credit to help uninsured people buy health insurance and a tax deduction to encourage people to buy catastrophic (or high-deductible) health insurance policies.

Dollars & Sense asked Economic Policy Institute economist Elise Gould to explain what these programs are—or are not—likely to accomplish.

PRIVATE INSURERS AND PRESCRIPTION DRUGS: STRIKE ONE

The 2003 Medicare Modernization Act is an inadequate, poorly-devised excuse for Medicare expansion. Its key provisions include new money for private insurers involved with Medicare, a prescription drug benefit, and tax-advantaged Health Savings Accounts. Originally scored at $395 billion, now estimated to cost $534 billion, the bill makes big payments to private insurance and pharmaceutical companies, but provides little bang for the buck for Medicare beneficiaries.

One aspect of the new law has received almost no attention: it raises payments to private insurers to entice them into the business of providing insurance for the Medicare population. Actually, Medicare is already partially privatized. For a number of years, the government has contracted with private insurance companies to offer their own Medicare plans to seniors. As it turned out, many of these companies, unable

to turn a profit, ended up dropping their Medicare plans. (Meantime, traditional Medicare has rolled right along, with an excellent track record of beneficiary satisfaction and a super-low overhead cost under 4%.) The new, higher payments included in the 2003 law are designed to attract private companies back into the Medicare business. Proponents argue that private industry is more efficient than government and that privatization will lower Medicare's costs. But if private insurance companies are so efficient, why do they need higher reimbursement rates?

In one respect, private insurers may prove to be cheaper—but not because they're more efficient. Private insurers can tailor their plans—what's covered, what's not, whether patients have a choice of specialists, and so forth—to attract the healthiest of the Medicare population and discourage sicker elders from signing on. Of course, the healthiest are also the least expensive to insure. Splitting the Medicare pool in this way decreases the viability of the system in the long run.

What about the prescription drug benefit? It's full of holes—literally. There's the so-called donut hole in the coverage: for seniors who spend between $2,250 and $5,100 annually on prescription drugs, the amount they spend above $2,250 is entirely out-of-pocket.

Then there are the rate increases. The premiums and deductibles for the new drug coverage are expected to rise at average annual rates of 7.5% and 8.6%, respectively, from 2006 to 2013. This far exceeds the annual cost-of-living adjustments Social Security recipients get, which have averaged just 2.4% over the past 10 years. Medicare Part B (the section that provides coverage for doctor visits) has built-in protections that keep out-of-pocket expenses from rising faster than seniors' Social Security checks; the prescription drug benefit, however, includes no such protection. Even with the new benefit, then, drug costs will eat up a growing share of Medicare beneficiaries' incomes over time.

The new law also fails to treat "dual eligibles"—that is, low-income seniors eligible for both Medicare and Medicaid—fairly. The law prohibits the use of federal Medicaid dollars to pay for prescription drugs not covered by the new Medicare drug plan. This means that individuals currently on Medicaid can actually lose some of their existing coverage.

If the prescription drug benefit is offering less-than-meets-the-eye to seniors, then who does benefit from the massive new expenditure? Primarily, the pharmaceutical companies. The new law specifically prohibits the government from negotiating lower prices with drug companies. The Medicare population accounts for about half the prescription drug market. If the government were allowed to negotiate over prices—the same type of negotiation that goes on between private insurers and providers already—costs of the program would go down substantially.

Private insurers also stand to gain. The new prescription drug benefit will not be administered as part of traditional Medicare. Instead, seniors who want the benefit will have to choose a private drug plan; the plans will in turn be paid by Medicare. It's no surprise that the drug benefit is structured so as to accelerate the privatization of Medicare.

Instead of an inadequate program that wastes billions of dollars subsidizing private insurers and pharmaceutical companies, the government should offer a drug benefit that helps people who most need the care and cannot afford it.

HEALTH SAVINGS ACCOUNTS: STRIKE TWO

The new law also provides for health savings accounts (HSAs). HSAs provide tax benefits for individuals and families who buy eligible high-deductible health insurance plans—those with an annual deductible of at least $1,000 (for individuals, or $2,000 for a family). If you purchase such a plan, which typically has relatively low premiums, you can contribute to an HSA up to a set maximum. HSA contributions are fully tax deductible. Nor do you pay any tax—even on accrued interest—when you withdraw funds from the account to pay medical expenses.

HSAs were billed as a health cost-containment vehicle and a savings mechanism designed to help people prepare for future medical expenses. Their most likely primary use, however, will be as a generous tax shelter for the upper-income set. Consider two people with HSAs, a higher-income person in the 35% tax bracket and a lower-income person in the 10% bracket. The lower-income person pays 90 cents for every dollar she puts in her HSA then withdraws for medical bills, while the higher-income person pays only 65 cents. (Assuming that the lower-income person has any extra money to contribute to the HSA in the first place!) Clearly, higher-income families have much more to gain from these accounts than middle- or low-income families. And unlike many tax deductions, there is no phase-out range or maximum income

limit. Further, wealthy people who have exhausted their other tax-advantaged savings vehicles or who have income too high to qualify for traditional IRAs will be most likely to participate. Since people over 65 can withdraw money from their accounts tax-free for any reason—not only for medical expenses—with no penalty, HSAs subsidize the retirement savings of wealthy people at the expense of lost tax revenue.

Because the benefits of an HSA come through a tax deduction, they are of no use to the many Americans who do not file taxes or who have little tax liability. A married couple with two children would receive no tax benefit whatsoever from contributing to an HSA unless their income was at least $40,200—more than twice the poverty level.

HSAs are not an effective means of cost containment as they create conflicting incentives. It's true that moving people to high-deductible plans ought to induce lower spending on health care. But by giving people a tax break when they spend money on health care, this plan reduces the cost-containment advantage of high-deductible insurance.

Nor is encouraging people to move to high-deductible plans good for the health insurance system as a whole. High-deductible plans have lower premiums and are a good deal for healthy people who don't need much care. When the healthy are siphoned off into these plans, risk pools become unbalanced and costs rise for everyone else. The result: it gets harder and harder for the less healthy to afford adequate coverage.

TAX PROPOSALS: STRIKE THREE

New Bush administration proposals for improving health care access suffer from the same problems. The president proposes an income tax deduction for high-deductible health insurance premiums. Only families with income tax liability gain from the proposal; it will do little to reduce the number of uninsured, about half of whom are from households with income too low to benefit from the deduction at all.

The Health Insurance Tax Credit (HITC), another administration proposal introduced in the Senate this March, is intended to help the uninsured obtain coverage. The HITC would provide low-income Americans with a tax credit of up to $1,000 for individuals and $500 per child to assist them in buying private health insurance. Individuals with incomes up to $30,000 and families with incomes up to $60,000 who have no job-based or government health insurance are eligible for the credit, which is refundable—in other words, those with little or no income tax liability will receive the amount of the credit as a direct payment from the government.

The HITC has three major problems as a vehicle for widening health insurance access: it doesn't help the sick, it isn't age adjusted, and it simply isn't generous enough. The HITC applies only to the purchase of individual or non-group health coverage. People who are already sick have an extremely difficult time getting insurance in the individual market. When they are not turned down outright, the premiums are prohibitively high, and insurers often add riders that disallow coverage on pre-existing conditions and reserve the right not to renew. The benefit isn't age adjusted, but premiums are. So the HITC disproportionately benefits younger people, the least in need of health insurance.

Non-group insurance is expensive: premiums and deductibles are higher and overall plan benefits are less generous than for group plans. In one market, premiums for non-group family plans average $13,214 a year. Even with the maximum $3,000 per family credit, eligible families would still have to pay over $10,000 a year for coverage—far beyond the means of most low- and moderate-income families. And while non-group health plans are a poor substitute for employer-provided health insurance, tax preferences for these plans may give companies an excuse to stop offering insurance to their employees.

A WHOLE NEW BALLGAME

If the administration really wants to lower the number of uninsured, there are better ways than through the tax system.

For the estimated cost of $95 billion in the first five years, researchers estimate the HITC and the new tax deduction for high-deductible plan premiums combined will insure an additional 1.3 million people—barely a dent in the estimated 43 million uninsured Americans. Why not expand Medicaid to cover more people, encourage the creation of risk pools to cover the sick, provide an affordable safety net for the unemployed—or dare to think about a single-payer system?

Sources: U.S. Congressional Budget Office, "Estimating the Cost of the Medicare Modernization Act," testimony before the House Ways and Means Committee, 3/24/04; U.S. Treasury Dept., "General Explanations of the Administration's Fiscal Year 2005 Revenue Proposals," February 2004; Kaiser Family Foundation, Employer Health Benefits 2003 Annual Survey; Kaiser Family Foundation, "Coverage and Cost Impacts of the President's Health Insurance Tax Credit and Tax Deduction Proposals," March 2004; Massachusetts Blue Cross and Blue Shield; U.S. Census Bureau, "Health Insurance Coverage in the United States: 2002," September 2003.

ARTICLE 4.10   *May/June 2004*

THE CASE AGAINST PRIVATIZING NATIONAL SECURITY

BY ANN MARKUSEN

In the past 20 years, this country has undergone a transformation in the way it prepares for, conducts, and mops up after war. The Pentagon has overseen a large-scale effort to outsource all aspects of its operations to private corporations. But despite the claims of privatization proponents, there's scant evidence that private firms perform better or at lower cost than public-sector agencies. More troubling, as corporations cash in on lucrative contracts, they encroach on the political process, driving up military spending and influencing military and foreign policy.

THE GROWING "SHADOW PENTAGON"

National defense is one of the most heavily outsourced activities in the U.S. federal government. From 1972 to 2000, private contractors' share of all defense-related jobs climbed from 36% to 50%. While the country's public-sector defense workforce remains large—about 2.2 million in 2000—its "shadow workforce," the true number of people supported by federal government spending and mandates, is far larger. (See Table 1.)

Of the dozens of major military contract firms in the United States today, Lockheed Martin, Boeing, and Northrop Grumman are the largest three—they divvied up $50 billion of the $209 billion the Pentagon awarded in prime contracts in 2003, according to defense analyst William Hartung—but lesser-known info-tech and engineering companies like Computer Sciences Corporation, BDM International, and Science Applications International Corporation are emerging as major Department of Defense (DOD) suppliers, each with billions of dollars in defense business annually.

Despite the popular image of a defense contract as a contract for building large weapons systems like aircraft, missiles, or tanks, contracts for services are actually more typical. Service workers—not production workers—accounted for nearly three out of four contract-created jobs in 1996, up more than 50% since 1984. A growing legion of contracted employees install, maintain, trouble-shoot, operate, and integrate military hardware. Similarly, research and development work is increasingly farmed out. (Navy technical centers outsourced 50% of research, development, test, and evaluation work by 1996, up from 30% in 1970.) And other, lower-skill, service contract firms perform a panoply of other functions, from base maintenance and catering and support, to security detail and military training.

TABLE 1
ESTIMATED FULL-TIME EQUIVALENT FEDERAL CIVIL SERVICE,
CONTRACT, AND GRANT JOBS BY CATEGORY, 1996

Federal Agency	Civil Service Jobs	Contract Jobs	Grant Jobs*	Ratio of Civil Service to Contract + Grant Jobs
Defense	778,900	3,634,000	53,000	1:4.7
Energy	19,100	633,000	40,200	1:37
NASA	20,100	350,600	26,900	1:19
Total Defense-Related	818,100	4,617,600	120,100	1:5.8
All Other Federal	1,073,900	1,017,400	2,292,900	1:3.1

*Jobs created by money given as a grant rather than a contract for performance of services. The grant category includes research grants to universities.

Source: Paul Light, The True Size of Government, Washington, DC: Brookings Institution Press, 1999.

ECONOMIC EXPECTATIONS

According to economic theory, it's competition, not privatization per se, that is expected to produce cost savings and performance improvements. Competition is key because private contractors are profit-seeking firms whose first loyalties are to their shareholders. Without competition, and in the absence of close monitoring, the corporations have every incentive to raise prices and hide information about their products and services. Defense economists suggest competition should generate efficiencies, but only under certain conditions: four or more firms competing for a given job, ongoing competition over time, clarity by the government buyer about task and performance requirements, and active, sustained government monitoring.

That's the theory. In the real world of military contracting, these conditions are rarely met. Most contracts that are opened to competing bids have fewer than three bidders. Once signed, contracts last for long periods, insulating firms from ongoing competitive pressures. The bidding process itself may be distorted in that firms "low-ball" bids, knowing they can negotiate add-ons later. And with the dramatic consolidation of the industry in the mid-1990s, and the shrinking number of large prime contractors, collusion among firms is a recurrent problem.

Several Pentagon contracts are "cost-plus," meaning the companies recoup their costs, including a portion of overhead, and are guaranteed a percentage of the costs as profit—a recipe for cost inflation. For example, Halliburton subsidiary Kellogg Brown & Root was given a 10-year multibillion dollar contract to provide logistical support services to U.S. troops overseas. The contract guarantees the firm will receive 1% of total costs as profit. In addition, KBR is eligible for a bonus payment of up to 2%. The firm has a long record of cost overruns in Kosovo, and its performance to date in Iraq has been weak. KBR admitted to overcharging the government by $61 million for gasoline, and its own internal audit of its Iraq operations reveals serious problems including a failure to control subcontractor costs and widespread loss of supplies and equipment, according to the *Wall Street Journal*.

THE EVIDENCE ON EXPECTED GAINS FROM PRIVATIZATION

Given the colossal sum of government dollars doled out in defense contracts, you'd think Congress and the Pentagon would carefully track cost and performance outcomes. But Pentagon records are sketchy and largely hidden from public view. Even the U.S. General Accounting Office (GAO), the investigative arm of Congress, has had difficulty prying data from the Pentagon. What's more, the few assessments that do exist focus on competitions between public and private bidders (where a government agency bids for work in competition with a private entity), and not private-private competitions, or the 50% of DOD purchases that are sole-sourced, simply given to a contractor with no competitive bidding process at all.

Some have estimated that the DOD saves 20% to 30% from public-private competitions, but those approximations are based on savings estimates at the initial bidding stage. In other words, they look at the promise of savings, not actual savings over time—a poor measure, since cost overruns are common and contracts are often renegotiated or otherwise changed after they're awarded.

The few existing studies of longer-term outcomes—conducted mainly by the Center for Naval Analysis (CNA), a federally funded research and development center, and the GAO—offer mixed results.

A CNA study of surface ships found that readiness was about the same whether the work was done in a public Navy yard or a private yard; a study of Navy maintenance work over time found that for a period of around two years, the contractors' performance was worse than that of the Navy in-house team, but that overall, the contractors performed better than the Navy team.

CNA insists that public-private competitions do generate bids and plans which would, if implemented, save the Pentagon money. But CNA analyses are emphatic that "competition produces the savings and not outsourcing per se." Its simulations suggest that 65% of total savings should in theory be achieved simply by the exercise of competing, even if no private firm receives a contract.

GAO is less sanguine about the potential for cost savings. The agency investigated some of the Pentagon's savings estimates and concluded that they were overstated because "DOD has not fully calculated either the investment costs associated with undertaking these competitions or the personnel separation costs likely to be associated with implementing them." DOD had assumed it would cost just $2,000 per position to conduct a competition, but in actuality the costs run from $7,000 to $9,000. In a later review of the Pentagon's claim that it had saved $290 million through public-private competition in 1999, the GAO concluded that it was difficult to determine how much had actually been saved. A large part of the problem, again, is that the DOD does not systematically track or update its savings estimates once contracts are underway.

GAO also cautions that savings from outsourcing come chiefly from cuts in personnel costs. We cannot know whether these cuts normally take the form of wage and benefit reductions, the use of temporary workers, cuts to the full-time workforce, or some combination, because private-sector firms refuse to share personnel information, calling it proprietary.

The large role of labor-cost savings in Pentagon outsourcing should give policymakers pause. It's troubling that the Pentagon does not monitor the pay and working conditions of its "shadow employees." If private prison administrators are required to share employment data with evaluators, why shouldn't Pentagon contractors face the same requirement?

In sum, the jury's still out on whether outsourcing military work produces efficiencies, and little is known about how savings that are achieved may result from cutting wages. Furthermore, no study has included the cost of competent oversight in the outsourcing calculus, or looked systematically at performance outcomes.

CORRUPTION AND POLICY INFLUENCE

Beyond efficiency and performance concerns, the increasing reliance on for-profit firms for national defense creates deeper political and institutional problems—namely, the capture of public decision-making by private military interests.

Through lobbying, advertising, and heavy campaign contributions, the private defense sector calls for weapons systems and defense initiatives that generate lucrative contracts. Since the end of the Cold War, private military contractors have formed a powerful lobby to protect obsolete Cold War weapons systems. For example, during the Reagan years, strenuous lobbying overcame even the highly mobilized and scientifically well-informed opposition to the B-1 bomber and the Star Wars program, two of the most costly weapons programs in the postwar period. In the 1990s, lobbyists undermined important initiatives to control the export of conventional arms, and recently the aerospace industry—led by Lockheed Martin—pushed hard to bring Poland, Hungary, and the Czech Republic into NATO in the expectation that these countries would then upgrade their militaries with costly new hardware. In general, the defense industry's leverage in Congress makes it difficult for the nation to shift resources toward peacekeeping missions, negotiated settlements, and the use of economic development in place of regional warfare.

As John Donahue summarizes in *The Privatization Decision*:

In any contractual relationship between government and

private business, a key question becomes who is representing the broader public interests. Unless there are sturdy provisions to prevent it—and even if all parties are immune to corruption—the natural outcome is an alliance between private-sector suppliers and government officials at the taxpayers' expense.

Less visible than the congressional lobbyists and trade groups, but just as significant, contractors employ their superior technical expertise to sell Pentagon procurement managers and top military leaders on pricey and risky new projects. Sitting on Pentagon advisory committees helps, as does the firms' insulation from public scrutiny. The quickening pace of privatization in research and development has left the government without the expertise to assess and monitor contractors' proposals.

WHAT'S DRIVING DEFENSE PRIVATIZATION?

The political, intellectual, and financial impetus for government privatization began in the 1970s and received its major political boost from the Reagan administration, which shrank government even as it increased defense expenditures by 50% in real terms. The Clinton administration's reversal of the Carter-Reagan military buildup had the unintended consequence of unleashing a hungry pro-privatization lobby onto the political scene—the mid-1990s reduction of the defense budget sent private contractors scrambling for new markets. At the same time, a raft of mergers consolidated the industry into a powerful handful of giant firms, all focused on developing new streams of government revenue. Their efforts on Capitol Hill dovetailed with and drew life from the 20-year ideological assault on public-sector provision of goods and services. During the Clinton years, insiders also adopted and capitalized on the "reinventing government" agenda spearheaded by Vice President Al Gore at the federal level.

Since the 1990s, private business groups, DOD advisory boards and key managers, and both the Clinton and Bush administrations have heightened calls to privatize national-security activity. For Pentagon managers, privatization offers a means of coping with a "go it alone" defense doctrine that deploys U.S. armed forces around the world with little international support.

Advocacy groups heavily populated by large defense contractors issue a stream of pronouncements and publications urging privatization. They recommend outsourcing functions outright rather than relying on public-private competitions (which give public agencies a chance to bid for projects), and back the wholesale privatization of complex business areas that currently involve large numbers of government employees.

One such task force, the Defense Science Board Task Force on Outsourcing and Privatization, issued studies in 1996 claiming that $10 billion to $30 billion could be saved through privatizing DOD's support and maintenance services.

Needless to say, they offered inadequate evidence to support these multibillion-dollar savings estimates. The panel that released the first study was headed by the CEO of military contractor BDM International.

At about the same time, Business Executives for National Security (BENS), a group founded in 1982 as a watchdog organization to monitor the Pentagon on weapons costs and nuclear, chemical, and biological warfare, transformed itself into an outspoken advocate of outsourcing. In 1996, BENS launched a high-profile commission to "promote outsourcing and privatization, closing unneeded military bases and implementing acquisition reform" with a self-described membership of "business leaders, former government officials and retired military officers." The commission published op-eds and position papers claiming the Pentagon civilian workforce is bloated. It decried what it misleadingly described as the bleeding away of private-sector defense jobs. (BENS used 1988 as its baseline; the year was an anomaly that included a spike in Reagan-era defense contracts.) It also claimed the Pentagon lags behind private corporations in outsourcing, and that the United States lags behind Europeans in privatization. Neither assertion is borne out by the evidence.

Under Clinton, Secretary of Defense William Cohen and other top DOD officials echoed BENS' calls for a "Revolution in Military Business Affairs." Dr. Jacques Gansler, President Clinton's undersecretary of defense for acquisition and technology, frequently spoke out in favor of outsourcing and a business approach:

> To meet the challenge of modernization, the Department of Defense ... must do business more like private business.... My top priority, as Under Secretary of Defense, is to make the Pentagon look much more like a dynamic, restructured, reengineered, world-class commercial sector business.

In February 2001, just after George W. Bush took office, a defense reform conference organized by the Aerospace Industries Association of America and Boeing, Lockheed Martin, Northrop Grumman, Raytheon, TRW, Inc., and BAE Systems met to set the agenda for the new administration. It attracted 500 participants and drew up a "Blueprint for Action" to slash bureaucracies, reduce "cycle times" and restore operational and financial strength to the defense industrial base. Also in February 2001, a BENS initiative,

"Improving the Business End of the Military," identified activities the DOD can discontinue and "replace with world class business models," turning entire functions (housing, communications, power utilities, logistics systems) over to the private sector.

Since George W. Bush took office, the military budget has grown from $300 billion to $400 billion, not counting the $200 billion in supplemental expenditures for Iraq and Afghanistan. The spending hike has set off a feeding frenzy among contractors, some of which have seen double-digit growth in profits.

The Bush administration is intensifying efforts to transfer work from inside the Pentagon to private contractors. The DOD is expected to put 225,000 jobs up for competition between public employee groups and private companies by the end of Bush's first term. Many more jobs have been displaced through direct outsourcing. The Bush push appears to be driven by a combination of ideology and political calculation, reinforced by defense-sector campaign contributions and the accelerating revolving door between the Pentagon and private contractors.

But this strategy poses serious risks and may threaten the possibility of society exercising democratic control over the evolution and use of military force. George Washington University political scientist Deborah Avant stresses that privatizing security "almost inevitably redistributes power over the control of violence both within governments and between states and non-state actors." In the United States, the private delivery of services has strengthened the executive branch, diminished the control of Congress, and reduced transparency. And, she warns, the process is cumulative—as private security companies are integrated into military efforts, the companies gain greater influence over foreign and military policy-making.

This article was adapted from a longer article published in the journal *Governance*, Vol. 16, No. 4 (October, 2003).

Sources: Deborah Avant, The Market for Force: Private Security and Political Change, manuscript under review, 2004; "The Revolution in Business Affairs: Realizing the Potential," Conference Summary, CNA Corporation, Alexandra, VA: 1998; John Donahue, *The Privatization Decision: Public Ends, Private Means,* New York: Basic Books, 1989; William D. Hartung, "Making Money on Terrorism," *The Nation*, February 5, 2004; Paul Light, The True Size of Government, Washington, DC: Brookings Institution Press, 1999.

CHAPTER 5

MONETARY POLICY AND FINANCIAL MARKETS

INTRODUCTION

Ben Bernanke has replaced Alan Greenspan as the man behind the curtain of the Federal Reserve Board. But unless he actually possesses the wizard-like powers the business press sometimes attributed to Greenspan, it is doubtful that working people will fare any better. In his final year, Greenspan himself worried that under his tenure inequality had worsened to levels that threaten our democratic institutions, and that the unprecedented level of U.S. reliance on foreign borrowing has become unsustainable.

But why should it matter who chairs the Federal Reserve Board? The Fed is charged with using monetary policy to keep inflation in check and provide liquidity to keep the economy going, or bolster a flagging economy. The Fed is supposed to use its three tools—the reserve requirement, the discount and federal funds rates, and open market operations—to manipulate banking activity, control the money supply, and direct the economy to everyone's benefit.

It all sounds value-free. But what the Fed really does is serve those who hold financial assets. And that is just what's wrong with Fed monetary policy. When it comes to making monetary policy, the Fed puts the interests of bondholders first, well before those of job seekers and workers. Investors look to the Fed to protect the value of their stocks and bonds by keeping inflation low—and if that means keeping a cap on employment growth, so be it.

That is why monetary policy is not just a matter for financial market junkies, but for anyone concerned with the social policies it holds hostage. As Doug Orr and Ellen Frank argue in this chapter, "Whenever any policy is proposed, be it in health care, housing or transportation, the first question politicians ask is, 'What will the bond market think about it?'" The authors go on to show just how monetary policy under Greenspan has worked against most of us and even helped push the economy into a slowdown in 2000 (Article 5.3).

Other articles in this chapter look closely at diverse aspects of Fed policy-making. Doug Orr explains in everyday language what money is and how the Fed attempts to control the money supply (Article 5.1). Arthur MacEwan compares monetary and fiscal policy, highlighting the greater powers of fiscal policy to counteract recessions (Article 5.4). Ellen Frank describes how changes in the interest rate the Fed charges on loans to commercial banks affect those banks' financial positions, as well as market-wide interest rates (Article 5.5).

Several articles address the context in which the Fed operates. In Article 5.2, James K. Galbraith explains how the value of the dollar, the world's reserve currency, depends on the willingness of foreign central banks and international investors to hold U.S. assets, and how that willingness is being eroded by the deteriorating U.S. trade position. Economic journalist William Greider worries that Bernanke will jack up short-term interest rates in the name of fighting inflation in order to control the housing bubble (just as Greenspan had to control the stock bubble) and risk throwing the economy into a recession that would cripple those worst off in our economy. But Greider says that there are far better ways for the Fed to defuse the housing bubble. (Article 5.6) Bob Pollin closes the chapter with his proposal for transforming the Fed into a democratically controlled investment bank that serves the interests of all of us (Article 5.7).

DISCUSSION QUESTIONS

1) (Article 5.1) What are the mechanisms the Fed uses to "control" the creation of money by the banking system. Why, according to Orr, is the Fed's control over the creation of money "limited"?

2) (Article 5.2) According to Galbraith, how has the United States becoming a debtor nation threatened the status of the dollar as the world's reserve currency? How serious a threat is this for the U.S. economy?

3) (Article 5.3) According to Orr and Frank, monetary policy serves the interests of bondholders at the expense of people seeking work and of everyone who benefits from social spending. What evidence do they provide to show that Fed policy has this class character? Do you find it convincing?

4) (Article 5.4) What advantage is there in using monetary policy to slow down the economy? Why might fiscal policy be a more effective tool for lifting the economy out of a recession?

KEY TO COLANDER

E = *Economics*   M = *Macroeconomics*

These readings complement E27, E28, and E34, or M11, M12, and M19.

Articles 5.1, 5.3, 5.4, 5.5, and 5.6 look at the working of monetary policy, who it serves, and the differences between monetary and fiscal policy. They fit with chapter E27 and E28 or M11 and M12. Article 5.2 takes up a complication of conducting monetary policy in an international economy, and fits with chapter E34 or M19. Pollin's discussion of transforming the Fed in Article 5.7 would work with any of these chapters.

5) (Article 5.5) How does the discount rate affect the financial position of commercial banks and market interest rates?

6) (Article 5.6) Why is Greider convinced that lowering interest rates would be a more effective way to defuse the housing bubble than raising short-term interest rates?

7) (Article 5.7) What are the chief elements of Pollin's proposal to transform the Fed and how would it affect the focus of the Fed and its decision-making? Do you think his proposals would be effective?

ARTICLE 5.1

November/December 1993

WHAT IS MONEY?

BY DOUG ORR

We all use money every day. Yet many people do not know what money actually is. There are many myths about money, including the idea that the government "prints" all of it and that it has some intrinsic value. But actually, money is less a matter of value, and more a matter of faith.

Money is sometimes called the universal commodity, because it can be traded for all other commodities. But for this to happen, everyone in society must believe that money will be accepted. If people stop believing that it will be accepted, the existing money ceases to be money. Recently in Poland, people stopped accepting the zloty, and used vodka as money instead.

In addition to facilitating exchanges, money allows us to "store" value from one point in time to another. If you sell your car today for $4,000, you probably won't buy that amount of other products today. Rather, you store the value as money, probably in a bank, until you want to use it.

The "things" that get used as money have changed over time, and "modern" people often chuckle when they hear about some of them. The Romans used salt (from which we get the word "salary"), South Sea Islanders used shark's teeth, and several societies actually used cows. The "Three Wise Men" brought gold, frankincense and myrrh, each of which was money in different regions at the time.

If money does not exist, or is in short supply, it will be created. In POW camps, where guards specifically outlaw its existence, prisoners use cigarettes instead. In the American colonies, the British attempted to limit the supply of British pounds, because they knew that by limiting the supply of money, they could hamper the development of independent markets in the colonies. Today, the United States uses a similar policy, through the International Monetary Fund, in dealing with Latin America.

To overcome this problem, the colonists began to use tobacco leaves as money. This helped the colonies to develop, but it also allowed the holders of large plots of land to grow their own money! When the colonies gained independence, the new government decreed gold to be money, rather than tobacco, much to the dismay of Southern plantation owners. Now, rather than growing money, farmers had to find or buy it.

To aid the use of gold as money, banks would test its purity, put it in storage, and give the depositor paper certificates of ownership. These certificates, "paper money," could then be used in place of the gold itself. Since any bank could store gold and issue certificates, by the beginning of the Civil War, over 7,000 different types of "paper money" were in circulation in the United States, none of it printed by the government.

While paper money is easier to use than gold, it is still risky to carry around large amounts of cash. It is safer to store the paper in a bank and simply sign over its ownership to make a purchase. We sign over the ownership of our money by writing a check. Checking account money became popular when the government outlawed the printing of paper money by private banks in 1864.

HOW BANKS CREATE MONEY

Banks are central to understanding money, because in addition to storing it, they help to create it. Bankers realize that not everyone will withdraw their money at the same time, so they loan out much of the money that has been deposited. It is from the interest on these loans that banks get their profits, and through these loans the banking system creates new money.

If you deposit $100 cash in your checking account at Chase Manhattan Bank, you still have $100 in money to use, because checks are also accepted as money. Chase must set aside some of this cash as "reserves," in case you or other depositors decide to withdraw money as cash. Current regulations issued by the Federal Reserve Bank (the Fed) require banks to set aside three cents out of each dollar. So Chase can make a loan of $97, based on your deposit. Chase does not make loans by handing out cash but instead by putting $97 in the checking account of the person, say Emily, taking out the loan. So from your initial deposit of $100 in cash, the economy now has $197 in checking account money.

The borrower, Emily, pays $97 for some product or service by check, and the seller, say Ace Computers, deposits the money in its checking account. The total amount of checking account money is still $197, but its location and ownership have changed. If Ace Computer's account is at Citibank, $97 in cash is transferred from Chase to Citibank. This leaves just $3 in cash reserves at Chase to cover your original deposit. However, Citibank now has $97 in "new" cash on hand, so it sets aside three cents on the dollar ($2.91) and loans out the rest, $94.09, as new checking account money. Through this process, every dollar of "reserves" yields many dollars in total money.

If you think this is just a shell game and there is only $100 in "real" money, you still don't understand money. Anything that is accepted as payment for a transaction is "real" money. Cash is no more real than checking account money. In fact, most car rental companies will not accept cash as payment for a car, so for them, cash is not money!

Today, there is $292 billion of U.S. currency, i.e. "paper money," in existence. However, somewhere between 50% to 70% of it is held outside the United States by foreign banks and individuals. The vast majority of all money actually in use in the United States is not cash, but rather checking account money. This type of money, $726 billion, was created by private banks, and was not "printed" by anyone. In fact, this money exists only as electronic "bits" in banks' computers. (The less "modern" South Sea Islanders could have quite a chuckle about that!)

The amount of money that banks can create is limited by the total amount of reserves, and by the fraction of each deposit that must be held as reserves. Prior to 1914, bankers themselves decided what fraction of deposits to hold as reserves. Since then, this fraction has been set by the main banking regulator, the Fed.

Until 1934, gold was held as reserves, but the supply of gold was unstable, growing rapidly during the California and Alaska "gold rushes," and very slowly at other times. As a result, at times more money was created than the economy needed, and at other times not enough money could be created. Starting in 1934, the U.S. government decided that gold would no longer be used as reserves. Cash, now printed by the Fed, could no longer be redeemed for gold, and cash itself became the reserve asset.

Banks, fearing robberies, do not hold all of their cash reserves in their own vaults. Rather, they store it in an account at a regional Fed bank. These accounts count as reserves. What banks do hold in their vaults is their other assets, such as Treasury bonds and corporate bonds.

THE FED AND BANK RESERVES

The only role of the government in creating money is through the Fed. If the Fed wants to expand the money supply, it must increase bank reserves. To do this, the Fed buys Treasury bonds from a bank, and pays with a check drawn on the Fed itself. By depositing the check in its reserve account at the Fed, the bank now has more reserves, so the bank can now make more loans and create new checking account money.

By controlling the amount of reserves, the Fed attempts to control the size of the money supply. But as recent history has shown, this control is limited. During the recent recession, the Fed created reserves, but many banks were afraid to make loans, so little new money was created. During the late 1970s, the Fed tried to limit the amount of money banks could create by reducing reserves, but banks simply created new forms of money, just like the POW camp prisoners. In 1979, there was only one form of checking account money. Today, there are many, with odd names such as NOWs, ATSs, repos, and money market deposit accounts.

These amorphous forms of money function only because we believe they will function, which is why the continued stability of the banking system is so critical. Banks do not have cash reserves to cover all checking account money. If, through a replay of the savings & loan debacle, we lose faith in the commercial banking system and all try to take out our "money" as cash, the banks will become insolvent (fail), and the money they have created will simply disappear. This would create a real crisis, since no market economy can function without its money.

THE DECLINE OF THE DOLLAR SYSTEM

BY JAMES K. GALBRAITH

Today, the U.S. dollar is the world's reserve currency. Nations around the world invest most of their foreign exchange reserves in dollar assets. The international economic position of the United States depends on this.

So long as foreign central banks and international investors are willing to take and hold U.S. assets (including stocks, bonds, and cash) this system works—and shamefully to the interest of Americans. Their demand keeps the value of the dollar high. This means that we have been able to consume comfortably, and in exchange for very little effort, the products of hard labor by poor people. (As the supplier of liquidity to the world system, our situation is akin to that of, say, Australia in the late 19th century when gold fields were discovered, except that, in our case, no actual effort is required to extract the gold.) And meanwhile (thanks to ample cheap imports), we are not obliged to invest unduly in maintaining our own industrial base, which has substantially eroded since the 1970s. We could afford to splurge on new technologies and telecommunications systems whose benefits were, to a very great extent, figments of the imagination. And even when the bubble burst in those sectors, life went on, for most Americans, substantially undisturbed—at least for now.

But for how long can this system endure? There can be no definitive answer; the few economists who have worried about this issue are far from being in agreement. On one side, it is argued that the dominant currency holds a "lock-in advantage"; that is, there are economies (reduced transaction costs and reduced risk) associated with keeping all reserves in one basket. The United States in particular is in a strong position to pressure foreign central banks—notably Japan's—to absorb the dollars that private parties may not wish to hold, at least within limits.

Furthermore, oil is bought and sold in dollars. As a result, oil importers must buy dollars in order to buy oil, and oil exporters accumulate dollars as they sell oil. To some extent this arrangement further strengthens the dollar—though it is not obvious why it requires anyone to hold dollars for very long, once they start falling in value.

Against this, the question remains: As the U.S. trade position continues to erode, will foreigners be willing to add to their holdings of dollar assets by enough to allow the United States to return to full employment? The amount to be absorbed at present—the trade deficit at full employment—is in the range of half a trillion dollars per year. This was easily handled when dollar asset prices were rising. But now that these prices are falling, they are not as attractive as

they once were. If foreigners are not willing to absorb all the dollars we need to place, and if asset prices do not quickly fall to the point where U.S. stocks appear cheap to investors, dollar dumping is, sooner or later, inevitable.

To keep the dollar's fall from getting out of hand, the United States will be strongly tempted to slow the rate at which new U.S. assets reach the world system, by restricting its imports. Having renounced the traditional tools of trade protectionism, it can only do this by raising interest rates, holding down economic growth, and keeping incomes, and therefore imports, well below the full-employment level. In that situation—which may actually already have arrived—the United States joins Brazil and other developing nations as a country effectively constrained by its debts. Indeed, the world prognosis from that point forward becomes grim, since high levels of American demand have been just about the only motor of growth and development (outside, perhaps, of China and India) in recent years.

THE UNITED STATES AS A DEBTOR NATION

There are economists who advocate dollar devaluation, believing that the richer countries of the world would quickly rally to purchase increasing quantities of made-in-America exports, thus reversing the manufacturing decline of the past 20 years. But this is very unlikely. Exports to the rich regions may not be very price-sensitive.

And exports to the developing regions are very sensitive to income and credit conditions, which would get worse. At least in the short and medium term, there is no foolproof adjustment process to be had by these means. Where a high dollar provides U.S. consumers with cheap imports and capital inflows to finance domestic activity, a falling dollar would have opposite effects. A falling dollar would raise the price of imports into the United States, especially from the richer countries. Meanwhile, a declining dollar would hit at the value of developing countries' reserves and their access to credit, and so it would diminish their demand for our exports. (It would help, in some cases, on their debts.) The most likely outcome from dollar devaluation is a general deepening of the world slump, combined with pressure on American banks and markets as global investors seek safer havens in Europe.

This specter of financial vulnerability means that for the United States, the combination of falling internal demand, falling asset prices, and a falling dollar represents a threat that can best be described as millennial. (My colleague Randall Wray has called it the "perfect fiscal storm.") The consequences at home would include deepening unemployment. There would be little recovery of privately financed investment, amid a continued unraveling of plans—both corporate and personal—that had been based on the delirious stock market valuations of the late 1990s. The center of the world banking industry would move, presumably to continental Europe. Over time, the United States could lose both its position as the principal beneficiary of the world financial order and its margin of maneuver on the domestic scene. This would be not unlike what happened to the United Kingdom from 1914 to 1950.

It is not obvious that senior financial policymakers in the United States have yet grasped this threat, or that there is any serious planning under way to cope with it—apart from a simpleminded view among certain strategic thinkers about the financial advantages of the control of oil. Instead it appears that the responsible officials are confining themselves to a very narrow range of Third-World debt management proposals, whose premises minimize the gravity of the issue and whose purpose is to keep the existing bonds of debt peonage in place as long as possible.

The alternative? It would involve rebuilding a multilateral monetary system, demolished for the benefit of the private commercial banks in 1973. The way forward would probably entail new regional systems of financial stabilization and capital control, such as the Asian Monetary Fund proposed by Japan in 1997. Such a course would be unpalatable to current American leadership. But we may find, down the road, that for the sake of our own prosperity, let alone that of the rest of the world, there is no other way.

Adapted from "The Brazilian Swindle and The Larger International Monetary Problem," published by the Levy Economics Institute in 2002. The full article is available at <www.levy.org>.

FOCUS ON THE FED
THE BOND MARKET VERSUS THE REST OF US

BY DOUG ORR AND ELLEN FRANK

Why should anyone involved in environmental issues, or education reform efforts, or efforts to house the homeless, or anyone else, care about monetary policy? After all, it only affects the financial markets, right? *Wrong*. Monetary policy is holding all other social policy hostage, and is part of the cause of the rapid increase in income inequality in the United States. Whenever any policy change is proposed, be it in health care, housing or transportation, the first question politicians ask is, "What will the bond market think about this?"

"The bond market" is a euphemism for the financial sector of the U.S. economy and the Federal Reserve Bank (the Fed), which regulates that sector. The Fed is the central bank of the U.S. government. It controls monetary policy, and has been using its power to help the banking industry and the holders of financial assets, while thwarting government attempts to deal with pressing social problems.

Since 1979, the Fed has had an unprecedented degree of independence from government control. This independence had put it in a position to veto any progressive fiscal policy that the Congress might propose. To understand how this situation developed, we must understand the function of banks, the structure of the Fed, and the role of monetary policy.

BANKS AND INSTABILITY

Government regulates the banking industry because private sector, profit-driven banking is inherently unstable. Banks do more than just store money—they help create it. If you deposit a dollar in the bank, you still have that dollar. Commercial banks will set aside three cents as "reserves" to "cover" your deposit, and the remaining 97 cents is loaned out to someone else who now has "new money." By making loans, banks create new money and generate profit. The drive to maximize profits often leads banks to become overextended: making too many loans and holding too few reserves. This drive for profits can undermine a bank's stability.

If depositors think the bank is holding too few reserves, or is making overly speculative loans, they might try to withdraw their money as cash. Large numbers of depositors withdrawing cash from a bank at the same time is called a "run on the bank." Since banks only hold 3% of their deposit liabilities as cash, even a moderate-sized "run" would be enough to drain the bank of its cash reserves. If a bank has no reserves, it is insolvent and is forced to close. At that point, all remaining deposits in the bank cease to exist, and depositors lose their money.

The failure of a bank affects more than just that bank's depositors. One bank's excesses tend to shake people's faith in other banks. If the run spreads, "bank panics" can occur. During the 1800s, such panics erupted every 10 to 15 years, bankrupting between 10% and 25% of the banks in the United States and creating a recession each time.

THE CREATION OF THE FED
The panic of 1907 bankrupted some of the largest banks and led to demands for bank reforms that would stabilize the system. Reform proposals ranged from doing almost nothing to nationalizing the entire banking industry. As a compromise, the Federal Reserve was created in 1913. The U.S. government saw the Fed as a way for bankers to regulate themselves, and structured the Federal Reserve System so that it could be responsive to its main constituents: banks and other financial-sector businesses that are now called, euphemistically, "the bond market." While ideally it should serve the interests of the general public when it conducts monetary policy, in reality the Fed balances two, occasionally conflicting goals: maintaining the stability of "the bond market" and maximizing financial-sector profits. Over time, Congress and the President have varied the degree of independence that they have given to the Fed to choose between these goals.

Initially, the Fed enjoyed a high degree of independence. Unfortunately, it was more successful in aiding bank profits than in stabilizing the system. During the 1920s, the Fed allowed member banks to engage in highly speculative activities, including using depositor's money to play the stock market. While many banks were very profitable, speculative excesses caused almost 20% of the banks in existence in 1920 to fail during the following decade. With the onset of the Great Depression, between 1929 and 1933, more than 9,000 banks, 38% of the total, failed. Since the Fed had not achieved its first goal, in 1935 Congress responded with laws that put many new regulations on banks, and reduced the Fed's independence.

FED INDEPENDENCE LOST
Under the new regulations, commercial banks were restricted to taking deposits and making commercial loans. Thus, the only opportunity for making a profit was to maintain a "spread" between the interest rate paid on deposits and that charged on loans. Loans are made for relatively long terms, and deposits are not. If the short-term interest rate on deposits varies widely, the spread will grow and shrink, which makes bank profits unstable. In order to stabilize bank profits, during the 30 years after 1935, the Treasury mandated that the Fed keep this rate approximately constant.

Under this arrangement, Congress indirectly controlled monetary policy. If Congress wanted to stimulate the economy it could increase government spending or cut taxes. Both led to an increase in spending and an increase in the demand for money. To keep interest rates, which are the price of money, from rising, the Fed must increase the supply of money. Thus, the Fed "accommodated" fiscal policy decisions made by Congress and the President.

During most of this period, growth was moderate and prices were stable. The Fed went along because this arrangement did not threaten bank profits. Starting in the mid-1960s, however, stimulative fiscal policy started to push up the inflation rate, which did threaten bank profits. A confrontation over Fed independence ensued and grew in intensity throughout the 1970s.

INFLATION'S IMPACT
Contrary to the view commonly propagated by the media, inflation does not affect everyone equally. In fact, there are very clear winners and losers. Inflation is an increase in the average level of prices, but some prices rise faster than average and some rise slower. If the price of something you are selling is rising faster than average, you win. Otherwise, you lose. Inflation redistributes income, but in an arbitrary manner. This uncertainty makes inflation unpopular, even to the winners. However, one industry always loses from unexpected inflation, and that industry is finance.

Banks make loans today that will be repaid, with interest, in the future. If inflation reduces the value of those future payments, the banks' profits will be reduced. So bankers are interested in the "real interest rate," that is, the actual (nominal) interest rate on the loan minus the rate of inflation. If the interest rate on commercial bank loans is 7% and the rate of inflation is 3%, the real rate of interest is 4%. In the early postwar period, real interest rates were relatively stable at about 2%.

From 1965 on, unexpected increases in inflation reduced the real interest rate. This cheap credit was a boon to home buyers, farmers, and manufacturers, but it greatly reduced bank profits. Banks wanted inflation cut. The Keynesian view of monetary policy offered a simple but unpopular solution: raise interest rates enough to cause a recession. High unemployment and falling incomes would take the steam out of inflation.

Putting people out of work to help bankers would be a hard sell. The Fed needed a different story to justify shifting its policy from stabilizing interest rates to fighting inflation. That story was monetarism, a theory that claims that changes in the money supply affect prices, but nothing else in the economy.

THE MONETARIST EXPERIMENT
On October 6, 1979, Fed Chair Paul Volcker, using monetarist theory as a justification, announced that the Fed would no longer try to keep interest rates at targeted levels. He argued that Fed policy should concentrate on controlling inflation, and to do so he would now focus on limiting the money supply growth rate. Since neither Congress nor the President attempted to overrule Volcker, this change ushered in an era of unprecedented independence for Fed monetary policy.

During the next three years, the Fed reduced the rate of growth in the money supply, but this experiment did not yield the results predicted by the monetarists. Instead of a swift reduction in the rate of inflation, the most immediate outcome was a rapid rise in the real interest rate and the start of the worst recession since the Great Depression.

As the Keynesian view predicted, the recession occurred because high interest rates slowed economic growth and increased unemployment. In 1979, the unemployment rate was 5.8%. By 1982 it had reached 10.7%, the first double-digit rate since the Depression. With fewer people working and buying products, the inflation rate, which had been 8.7% in 1979, finally started to slow in 1981 and was approaching 4% by the end of 1982. Tight money policies by the Fed kept nominal interest rates from falling as fast as inflation. This raised real interest rates (nominal rates minus inflation) on commercial loans from 0.5% in 1979 to 10% in 1982.

The Fed's fight against inflation had a severe impact on the entire economy. All businesses, especially farming and manufacturing, run on credit. The rise in interest rates, combined with lower prices, squeezed the profits of farmers and manufacturers.

Both of these industries rely heavily on exports, and so were also hurt by the negative effect of high interest rates on the competitiveness of U.S. exports. Real interest rates in the United States were the highest in the world, thereby attracting financial investment from abroad. In order for foreigners to buy financial assets in the United States, they first had to buy dollars. This demand for dollars drove up their value in international markets. While a "strong" dollar means imports are relatively cheap, it also means that U.S. exports are expensive. Foreign countries could not afford to buy our "costly" agricultural and manufactured exports. As a result, during this period, bankruptcy rates in these two industries were massive, higher than during the 1930s.

Despite its high cost to the rest of the economy, the monetarist experiment did not benefit many banks. Initially, the high real interest rates appeared to help bank profits. Regulations capped the interest rates banks could pay on deposits, but rates charged on loans were not regulated. This increased the profit on loans. Many investors, however, started moving their deposits to less regulated financial intermediaries, such as mutual funds, that could pay higher rates on deposits. In addition, the recession forced many borrowers to declare bankruptcy and default on their loans. Both of these factors pushed banks toward insolvency.

REVERSING COURSE

It was bank losses, rather than the pain in the rest of the economy, that led Volcker to announce in September 1982 that he was abandoning monetarism. His new policy aimed to provide enough reserves to keep most banks solvent and to allow a *slow* recovery from the recession. Unemployment remained high for the next five years, so inflation continued to slow. Real interest rates stayed near 8% through 1986, so interest-sensitive industries, such as farming and manufacturing, did not take part in the recovery.

Volcker made his allegiance to the banking industry very clear during a meeting, in February 1985, with a delegation of state legislators, laborers, and farmers who were demanding easier money and lower interest rates. He told them, "Look, your constituents are unhappy, mine aren't."

Yet by 1985, the crisis in the savings and loan industry was spreading into commercial banking. To provide cash ("liquidity") to the banks, Volcker allowed the money supply to grow by 12% during 1985 and by 17% in 1986. Monetarists raised the specter of a return to double-digit inflation. Instead, the rate of inflation continued to slow, demonstrating that a simple link between the money supply and inflation does not exist.

THE VETO

Despite the failure and subsequent abandonment of monetarist policies, the Fed still uses monetarist *theory* to justify its continued focus on "fighting inflation." The myth that monetary policy only affects inflation provides a convenient "cover" that allows the Fed to serve its narrow constituency: "the bond market." During 1998, nominal interest rates appeared low, but because inflation is so low, real interest rates on commercial loans were 6.8%—3.2 times the post-World War II average. Real interest rates remain high because "the bond market" worries about any possible increase in future inflation.

IN 1995 THE WEALTHIEST 10% OF HOUSEHOLDS OWNED 89.8% OF ALL BONDS, 88.4% OF ALL STOCKS, 88.5% OF FINANCIAL TRUSTS, AND 91% OF OTHER BUSINESS EQUITY.

Fighting inflation benefits the bond market. However, despite the near-depression that monetarism caused in the 1980s and the extremely slow rate of economic growth that has occurred in the 1990s, the Fed continues to claim that fighting inflation serves the interests of the entire country. The public's widespread belief in this myth denies progressives in Congress the support they need to force the Fed back into accommodating fiscal policy. It also provides support for those in Congress that want to block any expansion of social programs.

If Congress decides to spend more for environmental clean-up, housing the homeless, or education, "the bond market" will raise the specter of renewed inflation. The Fed will then raise interest rates, as it did in June 1999, as a "preemptive strike" to prevent inflation. The increase in interest rates, if large enough, will slow the economy, increase unemployment, reduce government revenues, and return the federal budget to a deficit. Since Congress is aware of this probable outcome, and knows it will be incorrectly blamed for it, Congress won't pass any legislation "the bond market" doesn't like. This is how the bond market holds Congress hostage. As long as Congress and the President allow the Fed to follow an inflation-fighting policy, the Fed can maintain a veto threat over the elected government.

The Fed has also played a large role in the rapid increase in income and wealth inequality that started in the 1980s and has accelerated in the 1990s. The two decades following World War II are often called the "golden age" of the U.S. economy. On average, Gross Domestic Product (GDP) grew 4.2% each year, unemployment averaged 4.6%, and real commercial interest rates averaged 2.1%. Average real wages, that is, wages adjusted for inflation, grew at an annual rate of 2.1%, rising from $8.34 an hour in 1950 to $12.75 in 1970 (both measured in 1998 dollars). This period saw the creation of a true middle class in the United States.

In the two decades since 1980, GDP growth has averaged 2.6% each year, unemployment has averaged 6.6%, and real interest rates have averaged 5.9%. Average real wages *declined* every year from 1980 to 1996. In fact, the real wage in 1996 was exactly the same as in 1968. If wages had continued to grow at 2.1%, the average wage today would be almost twice what it is. Without the slow growth policies of the Fed and the anti-labor policies started under Reagan, the average income of the majority of the people in the United States would be twice as large. Instead, we've seen a hollowing out of the middle class, and a rapid transfer of wealth and income to those already wealthy.

By focusing on inflation rather than interest rates, the media deflect attention from a critical social issue—how high interest rates transfer income from the indebted middle class to the very rich. The social consequences of high interest rates can be gauged by looking at the share of interest income in total U.S. personal income. Between 1980 and 1989, real interest rates rose from 1.8% to 6.1%. The share of income received as interest rose from 11% to 15.2%. As rates came back down slightly in the mid-1990s, so did the share of income going to interest.

WHERE DO INTEREST PAYMENTS GO?

If ownership of financial assets was evenly distributed among households, the growth in interest income would not be of much importance. When increases in interest rates outstripped wage and salary gains, the typical household would simply gain on the asset side what they were losing on the liability side. An increase in the size of their mortgage payment would be matched by an increase in their interest income.

But ownership of financial assets is heavily concentrated. A mere 7% of families with incomes of $100,000 or more con-

trol nearly half of total household net worth. Yet this number understates the concentration of financial wealth. Almost 80% of families in the United States have almost no assets, outside the equity in their homes and vehicles. As a result, despite the massive increase in financial asset values during the 1990s, median net worth was no higher in 1995 than it was in 1989. Almost all of the growth in net worth accrued to the few owners of financial assets.

Detailed studies of wealth data collected by the Fed report that in 1995 the wealthiest 10% of households owned 89.8% of all bonds, 88.4% of all stocks, 88.5% of financial trusts, and 91% of other business equity. Despite the media hype about the "democratization" of the stock market, between 1989 and 1995 the concentration of stock ownership increased. In 1995 only 15.3% of households held stocks directly and only 12% owned shares in mutual funds outside of their retirement accounts.

The "poorest" nine-tenths of the U.S. population—that is, most of us—have virtually no financial assets. Such families gain little from rising interest rates. But the higher mortgage, credit card, and auto payments that result take a real toll on living standards. Each uptick in the real interest rate entails a transfer of income from the lowest 90% of the population to the highest 10%. And most of that income goes to the very, very wealthy who are yet another part of "the bond market" served by the Fed.

Economist James Galbraith has called today's high interest rates a form of taxation without representation. The term is apt. Tax increases are passed by Congress, which has at least some public oversight. Interest rate hikes are decided by the Fed, an institution over which the President, Congress and the public have virtually no control.

Like taxes, rising interest rates are a drain on the resources and income of the vast majority of U.S. households. But unlike tax revenues that can be used to provide education, environmental clean-up, homeless shelters, roads, airports, and other infrastructure, interest payments flow into the pockets of the very rich, who become ever so much richer.

Resources: Arthur B. Kennickell, Martha Starr-McCluer, and Annika E. Sunden, "Family Finances in the U.S.: Recent Evidence from the Survey of Consumer Finances," *Federal Reserve Bulletin* (Jan. 1997); Lawrence Mishel, Jared Bernstein, and John Schmitt, *The State of Working America 1998-99*, 1999.

HOW DO FISCAL AND MONETARY POLICY COMPARE?

BY ARTHUR MacEWAN

The Federal Reserve influences the economy through monetary policy—the actions the Fed takes to affect the cost and availability of credit. For example, in March of this year, the Fed, led by its chairman Alan Greenspan, decided that it was time to slow economic growth. So it induced banks and other lenders to raise their interest rates. Higher interest rates mean fewer businesses and individuals will take out loans and spend the borrowed money. Lower spending means slower economic growth.

The federal government can also influence economic growth and the demand for goods and services through fiscal policy—the way it taxes and spends. If the government wants to slow down the economy, for example, it can raise taxes and reduce its own spending. Less money ends up in people's hands if the government hires fewer construction workers to build roads, or if it cuts back on education programs.

One problem with fiscal policy is that changing the budget takes time—except for programs whose spending levels change automatically when the economy does, like unemployment compensation. To slow down the economy, Congress has to pass new laws raising taxes—certainly a "no no" these days—or cutting spending. Then the President has to accept Congress's new law, which might require negotiations, or more legislative action. All this is to say that the political process involves considerable delays and might result in no action at all.

Monetary policy is different because the Fed does not have to bother with this messy political process that we call democracy. It is "independent" since its members, appointed by the President, serve long terms. They decide whether to ease or tighten the availability of credit, without any role for Congress or the President. To be sure, the "independence" of the Fed is not enshrined in the Constitution. Yet for Con-

> THE FED DOES NOT HAVE TO BOTHER WITH THIS MESSY POLITICAL PROCESS THAT WE CALL DEMOCRACY.

gress and the President to pass new laws which directed or restricted the Fed's action would be a serious disruption of well-established policy.

The law governing the Fed says that it should pursue both stable prices (low inflation) and full employment. In fact, the Fed focuses almost exclusively on the goal of stable prices. If unemployment has to rise to meet this goal, well, too bad. It is easy to see why the Fed does its work best when it doesn't have to worry about getting democratic approval.

Fiscal policy is somewhat more constrained by democratic processes than is monetary policy. For example, conservative attacks on Medicare and Social Security have not gotten very far because these programs are very popular.

But the recent mania to balance the budget makes it difficult to use fiscal policy to stimulate economic expansion by increasing spending. This may present some serious problems during economic downturns. The monetary policy of the Fed, it turns out, is not nearly so effective in stimulating economic expansion during a recession as it is in slowing growth during relatively good times. In a recession, the Fed can induce commercial banks to lower their interest rates. But if the recession leads investors to worry that demand for products and services will fall, the lower interest rates might not reignite economic growth. What's the point, for example, in building a new office building when it doesn't look like it will be possible to rent out the space in existing buildings for quite a while?

In a recession, then, trying to use monetary policy to get the economy going can be like pushing on a string. It simply won't do any good. Fiscal policy, however, might directly create demand, present businesses with the reality of a new expansion, and generate a new period of investment and growth.

THE DISCOUNT RATE

BY ELLEN FRANK

Dear Dr. Dollar:

The Federal Reserve keeps fussing with the "discount rate" and everybody thinks it's important. This is, if I understand it right, the rate banks charge each other for overnight loans. Now presumably someone makes money on the interest that's charged and someone loses money (or makes less) when the rate is lowered. But no one screams. Why not? If it's because the charges among banks just cancel one another out, then why does the rate even matter? Or is it that the Federal Reserve itself charges this interest, in which case the taxpayers lose when the rate it lowered?
—*Peter Marcuse, New York*

To answer your question, it helps to understand how the U.S. Federal Reserve system works. The quasi-public Federal Reserve has two parts, neither of which is actually part of the federal government. First, there are the district banks—12 Federal Reserve Banks scattered across the country, charged with regulating and overseeing the commercial banks in their region and each wholly owned by those banks. Then there is the Board of Governors, a seven-member board with a vast research staff, based in Washington, D.C., and chaired by Alan Greenspan.

Every six weeks, the board and the presidents of the regional banks meet together as the so-called *Federal Open Market Committee* (FOMC), where they set targets for the *fed funds rate*—a rate that commercial banks charge one another for overnight loans. After the fed funds target is announced, the district banks will generally raise or lower the *discount rate*—the rate that commercial banks pay when they borrow from their local Fed—so that the two rates stay roughly equal.

In order to reduce the fed funds rate, the FOMC directs traders at the New York Federal Reserve Bank to buy U.S. Treasury bills on the financial markets.

The Fed creates new money—quite literally, since paper printed by the Fed *is* money—to pay for these bills. When this new money enters the economy, it tends to be deposited in banks that, suddenly awash in cash, must find borrowers for it if they are to earn a profit. (To raise interest rates the FOMC does the opposite, selling U.S. Treasury bills and taking cash out of circulation.)

Since the district banks are owned not by the federal government but by the commercial banks, reductions in the discount rate do not affect the public treasury. And since commercial banks are both borrowers and the lenders in the fed funds market, gains and losses for the banks do tend, as you suspect, to cancel out. The point of reducing the fed funds rate, though, is to drive down other interest rates. If the financial markets are swimming in cheap cash, then competition for borrowers ought to push down rates on auto loans, business loans, mortgages, rates on bonds, and so forth.

Financial firms earn money by charging interest. In general, they prefer high interest rates to low. But they prefer low interest rates to watching their business dry up and their clients default on loans. Banks recognize that in a recession, lower interest rates may be necessary to spur growth and prevent bankruptcies. They accept the Fed's authority to reduce rates and print new money when circumstances warrant it. And they also know that the Fed, traditionally, has been their advocate—if not their mouthpiece—in Washington.

The district banks are owned outright by the finance industry and appointees to the Board of Governors nearly always have close industry ties. Greenspan himself has a well-established record as an "inflation hawk" who tends to err on the side of high interest rates. Moreover, in his nearly 12 years as Fed chair, Greenspan has presided

over the slow erosion of the Fed's policy authority, so that a lower fed funds rate often does not translate into lower interest rates for businesses and consumers. Over the past year, for example, the FOMC cut its target fed funds rate from 6.0% to 1.75%, yet rates on home mortgages have fallen by only one percentage point. If the Fed really wanted to bring down long-term interest rates (like mortgage rates), it could sell not only short-term Treasury bills but also long-term bonds. The Fed could use a variety of other means to lower interest rates set in other markets (like the bond market), but such policies could eat into the finance industry's earnings. Instead, the Fed's recent interest rate reductions have meant that banks pay lower rates on deposits, while earning fairly high rates on loans to consumers and businesses.

If the recession persists and competition for credit-worthy customers intensifies, however, lending rates will fall and banks will feel the pinch of the Fed's cheap credit policy. But don't expect to see Citigroup lambasting the Fed on the *New York Times* editorial page or lobbying Congress to oust Greenspan. The banks have a more direct avenue for airing their complaints. Every six weeks, on the day before the FOMC meets to set interest rate policy, the Board meets with the Federal Advisory Council—a group of private bankers from each of the 12 Fed districts—to hear their advice on how high interest rates should be.

Economist Edwin Dickens from Drew University, who has done extensive archival research on the Fed, notes that banks often "are adamant that they can't take the hit in income" if the Fed cuts rates. Records show that they have often thwarted rate cuts, even in recessions. So if lowered rates begin to squeeze financial earnings, the finance industry won't scream. Who needs to scream when you can whisper?

BERNANKE'S DILEMMA

BY WILLIAM GREIDER

If Ben Bernanke is unlucky, he may inherit the whirlwind when he succeeds Alan Greenspan as Federal Reserve chairman early next year. The Greenspan Fed is once again pursuing a high-risk strategy while concealing its real intentions from the public: raising short-term interest rates in the name of fighting inflation, but actually aiming to defuse the price bubble in housing. The last time the Fed tried this maneuver, it was hoping to subdue the stock market bubble. That gambit ended badly: shareholders lost $6 trillion, and instead of subsiding gently, the bubble collapsed and the economy went into recession.

This time, as sophisticated financial-market analysts understand, the Fed's true objective is asset deflation—though neither Greenspan nor Bernanke will acknowledge even that a housing bubble exists. Raising short-term rates, the Fed assumes, will induce financial markets to raise rates on long-term loans like mortgages, and higher interest on mortgages would definitely dampen housing prices.

Trouble is, the Fed strategy has so far failed utterly. Long-term rates are not rising. If Bernanke persists with Greenspan's strategy, short-term rates may rise higher than long-term rates. That unnatural condition means the imminent threat of recession, which is what has occurred repeatedly when the Fed has induced this state of inverted short-term and long-term rates.

A recession, as always, imposes the worst pain and loss on the weakest parties—the newly unemployed, families already struggling with debt, and small businesses already squeezed by energy costs and other negatives. Thorstein Veblen called it "the slaughter of the innocents." It's simply wrong for the Fed to put the real, Main Street economy at

risk in order to solve a financial problem, the housing bubble, that Greenspan, Bernanke and their colleagues at the Fed won't even acknowledge exists, let alone admit their culpability in creating.

If Bernanke, like Greenspan, is convinced that long-term rates need to rise, there's a better way to do it—an ingenious strategy proposed by Paul McCulley, Fed watcher at PIMCO, the giant bond investment house. Contrary to conventional thinking, McCulley suggests the Fed can effectively force long-term rates to rise if it now starts to *reduce* short-term rates. Inflation vigilantes in the bond market would be alarmed, McCulley explains, believing that the central bank has given in to the return of price inflation that depresses the value of long-term financial assets. In that event, bond-market players would bid up bond rates to protect themselves. Pushing long-term rates up would address the housing bubble; doing so without raising short-term rates would be easier on the Main Street economy.

The logic is persuasive, but don't count on Bernanke to grasp it. Like Greenspan, he belongs to the orthodox school: Markets are logical and efficient, so there should be no need for central bankers to game or surprise market players to induce them to react one way or another. Holding firm to their economic principles—in this case, protecting the interests of the wealth holders and financial markets—is often more important to central bankers than protecting the economic well-being of the overall society.

But perhaps Bernanke will turn out to be a more supple thinker than the excessively admired Greenspan. We will soon find out.

TRANSFORMING THE FED

BY ROBERT POLLIN

The U.S. financial system faces deep structural problems. Households, businesses, and the federal government are burdened by excessive debts. The economy favors short-term speculation over long-term investment. An unrepresentative and unresponsive elite has extensive control over the financial system. Moreover, the federal government is incapable of reversing these patterns through its existing tools, including fiscal, monetary, and financial regulatory policies.

I propose a dramatically different approach: transforming the Federal Reserve System (the "Fed") into a public investment bank. Such a bank would have substantial power to channel credit in ways that counter financial instability and support productive investment by private businesses. The Fed would use its powers to influence how and for what purposes banks, insurance companies, brokers, and other lenders loan money.

The U.S. government has used credit allocation policies, such as low-cost loans, loan guarantees, and home mortgage interest deductions, extensively and with success. Its primary accomplishment has been to create a home mortgage market that, for much of the period since World War II, provided non-wealthy households with unprecedented access to home ownership.

I propose increasing democratic control over the Federal Reserve's activities by decentralizing power to the 12 district Fed banks and instituting popular election of their boards of directors. This would create a mechanism for extending democracy throughout the financial system.

My proposal also offers a vehicle for progressives to address two separate but equally serious questions facing the U.S. economy:

- how to convert our industrial base out of military production and toward the development and adoption of environmentally benign production techniques; and
- how to increase opportunities for high wage, high productivity jobs in the United States. The U.S. needs such jobs to counteract the squeeze on wages from increasingly globalized labor and financial markets.

Transforming the Federal Reserve system into a public investment bank will help define an economic path toward democratic socialism in the United States.

My proposal has several strengths as a transitional program. It offers a mechanism for establishing democratic control over finance and investment—the area where capital's near-dictatorial power is most decisive. The program will also work within the United States' existing legal and institutional framework. We could implement parts of it immediately using existing federal agencies and with minimal demands on the federal budget.

At the same time, if an ascendant progressive movement put most of the program in place, this would represent a dramatic step toward creating a new economic system. Such a system would still give space to market interactions and the pursuit of greed, but would nevertheless strongly promote general well-being over business profits.

HOW THE FED FAILS

At present the Federal Reserve focuses its efforts on managing short-term fluctuations of the economy, primarily by influencing interest rates. When it reduces rates, it seeks to increase borrowing and spending, and thereby stimulate economic growth and job opportunities. When the Fed perceives that wages and prices are rising too fast (a view not necessarily shared by working people), it tries to slow down borrowing and spending by raising interest rates.

This approach has clearly failed to address the structural problems plaguing the financial system. The Fed did nothing, for example, to prevent the collapse of the savings and loan industry. It stood by while highly speculative mergers, buyouts, and takeovers overwhelmed financial markets in the 1980s. It has failed to address the unprecedented levels of indebtedness and credit defaults of private corporations and households.

NEW ROLES FOR THE FED

Under my proposal, the Federal Reserve would shift its focus from the short to the long term. It would provide more and cheaper credit to banks and other financiers who loan money to create productive assets and infrastructure—which promote high wage, high productivity jobs. The Fed would make credit more expensive for lenders that finance speculative activities such as the mergers, buyouts, and takeovers that dominated the 1980s.

The Fed would also give favorable credit terms to banks that finance decent affordable housing rather than luxury housing and speculative office buildings. It would make low-cost credit available for environmental research and development so the economy can begin the overdue transition to environmentally benign production. Cuts in military spending have idled many workers and productive resources, both of which could be put to work in such transformed industries.

Finally, the Fed would give preferential treatment to loans that finance investment in the United States rather than in foreign countries. This would help counter the trend of U.S. corporations to abandon the domestic economy in search of lower wages and taxes.

The first step in developing the Fed's new role would be for the public to determine which sectors of the economy should get preferential access to credit. One example, suggested above, is industrial conversion from military production to investment in renewable energy and conservation.

Once the public establishes its investment goals, the Fed will have to develop new policy tools and use its existing tools in new ways to accomplish them. I propose that a transformed Federal Reserve use two major methods:

- set variable cash ("asset reserve") requirements for all lenders, based on the social value of the activities the lenders are financing; and
- increase discretionary lending activity by the 12 district Federal Reserve banks.

VARYING BANKS' CASH REQUIREMENTS

The Fed currently requires that banks and other financial institutions keep a certain amount of their assets available in cash reserves. Banks, for example, must carry three cents in cash for every dollar they hold in checking accounts. A bank cannot make interest-bearing loans on such "reserves." I propose that the Fed make this percent significantly lower for loans that finance preferred activities than for less desirable investment areas. Let's say the public decides that banks should allocate 10% of all credit to research and development of new environmental technologies, such as non-polluting autos and organic farming. Then financial institutions that have made 10% of their loans in environmental technologies would not have to hold any cash reserves against these loans. But if a bank made no loans in the environmental area, then it would have to hold 10% of its total assets in reserve. The profit motive would force banks to support environmental technologies without any direct expenditure from the federal budget.

All profit-driven firms will naturally want to avoid this reserve requirement. The Fed must therefore apply it uniformly to all businesses that profit through accepting deposits and making loans. These include banks, savings and loans, insurance companies, and investment brokerage houses. If the rules applied only to banks, for example, then banks could circumvent the rules by redefining themselves as another type of lending institution.

LOANS TO BANKS THAT DO THE RIGHT THING

The Federal Reserve has the authority now to favor some banks over others by making loans to them when they are short on cash. For the most part, however, the Fed has cho-

sen not to exercise such discretionary power. Instead it aids all banks equally, through a complex mechanism known as open market operations, which increases total cash reserves in the banking system. The Fed could increase its discretionary lending to favored banks by changing its operating procedures without the federal government creating any new laws or institutions. Such discretionary lending would have several benefits.

First, to a much greater extent than at present, financial institutions would obtain reserves when they are lending for specific purposes. If a bank's priorities should move away from the established social priorities, the Fed could then either refuse to make more cash available to it, or charge a penalty interest rate, thereby discouraging the bank from making additional loans. The Fed, for example, could impose such obstacles on lenders that are financing mergers, takeovers, and buyouts.

In addition, the Fed could use this procedure to more effectively monitor and regulate financial institutions. Banks, in applying for loans, would have to submit to the Fed's scrutiny on a regular basis. The Fed could more closely link its regulation to banks' choices of which investments to finance.

Implementing this procedure will also increase the authority of the 12 district banks within the Federal Reserve system, since these banks approve the Fed's loans. Each district bank will have more authority to set lending rates and monitor bank compliance with regulations.

The district banks could then more effectively enforce measures such as the Community Reinvestment Act, which currently mandates that banks lend in their home communities. Banks that are committed to their communities and regions, such as the South Shore Bank in Chicago, could gain substantial support under this proposed procedure.

OTHER CREDIT ALLOCATION TOOLS

The Fed can use other tools to shift credit to preferred industries, such as loan guarantees, interest rate subsidies, and government loans. In the past the U.S. government has used these techniques with substantial success. They now primarily support credit for housing, agriculture, and education. Indeed, as of 1991, these programs subsidized roughly one-third of all loans in the United States.

Jesse Jackson's 1988 Presidential platform suggested an innovative way of extending such policies. He proposed that public pension funds channel a portion of their money into a loan guarantee program, with the funds used to finance investments in low cost housing, education, and infrastructure.

There are disadvantages, however, to the government using loan guarantee programs and similar approaches rather than the Fed's employing asset reserve requirements and discretionary lending. Most important is that the former are more expensive and more difficult to administer. Both loan guarantees and direct government loans require the government to pay off the loans when borrowers default. Direct loans also mean substantial administrative costs. Interest subsidies on loans are direct costs to government even when the loans are paid back.

In contrast, with variable asset reserve requirements and discretionary lending policies, the Fed lowers the cost of favored activities, and raises the cost of unfavored ones, without imposing any burden on the government's budget.

INCREASING PUBLIC CONTROL

The Federal Reserve acts in relative isolation from the political process at present. The U.S. president appoints seven members of the Fed's Board of Governors for 14 year terms, and they are almost always closely tied to banking and big business. The boards of directors of the 12 district banks appoint their presidents, and these boards are also composed of influential bankers and business people within each of the districts.

The changes I propose will mean a major increase in the central bank's role as an economic planning agency for the nation. Unless we dramatically improve democratic control by the public over the Fed, voters will correctly interpret such efforts as an illegitimate grasp for more power by business interests.

Democratization should proceed through redistributing power downward to the 12 district banks. When the Federal Reserve System was formed in 1913, the principle behind creating district banks along with the headquarters in Washington was to disperse the central bank's authority. This remains a valuable idea, but the U.S. government has never seriously attempted it. Right now the district banks are highly undemocratic and have virtually no power.

One way to increase the district banks' power is to create additional seats for them on the Open Market Committee, which influences short-term interest rates by expanding or contracting the money supply.

A second method is to shift authority from the Washington headquarters to the districts. The Board of Governors would then be responsible for setting general guidelines, while the district banks would implement discretionary lending and enforcement of laws such as the Community Reinvestment Act.

The most direct way of democratizing the district banks would be to choose their boards in regular elections along with other local, regional, and state-wide officials. The boards would then choose the top levels of the banks' professional staffs and oversee the banks' activities.

HISTORICAL PRECEDENTS

Since World War II other capitalist countries have extensively employed the types of credit allocation policies proposed here. Japan, France, and South Korea are the outstanding success stories, though since the early 1980s globalization and deregulation of financial markets have weakened each of their credit policies. When operating at full strength, the Japanese and South Korean programs primarily supported large-scale export industries, such as steel, automobiles, and consumer electronics. France targeted its policies more broadly to coordinate Marshall Plan aid for the development of modern industrial corporations.

We can learn useful lessons from these experiences, not least that credit allocation policies do work when they are implemented well. But substantial differences exist between experiences elsewhere and the need for a public investment bank in the United States.

In these countries a range of other institutions besides the central bank were involved in credit allocation policies. These included their treasury departments and explicit planning agencies, such as the powerful Ministry of International Trade and Industry (MITI) in Japan. In contrast, I propose to centralize the planning effort at the Federal Reserve.

We could create a new planning institution to complement the work of the central bank. But transforming the existing central banking system rather than creating a new institution minimizes both start-up problems and the growth of bureaucracies.

A second and more fundamental difference between my proposal and the experiences in Japan, France, and South Korea is that their public investment institutions were accountable only to a business-oriented elite. This essentially dictatorial approach is antithetical to the goal of increasing democratic control of the financial system.

The challenge, then, is for the United States to implement effective credit allocation policies while broadening, not narrowing, democracy. Our success ultimately will depend on a vigorous political movement that can fuse two equally urgent, but potentially conflicting goals: economic democracy, and equitable and sustainable growth. If we can meet this challenge, it will represent a historic victory toward the construction of a democratic socialist future.

Resources: Robert Pollin, "Transforming the Federal Reserve into a Public Investment Bank: Why it is Necessary; How it Should Be Done," in G. Epstein, G. Dymski and R. Pollin, eds., *Transforming the U.S. Financial System,* M.E. Sharpe, 1993.

CHAPTER 6

UNEMPLOYMENT AND INFLATION

INTRODUCTION

On the day the Bureau of Labor Statistics announced that the April 2003 unemployment rate had jumped to 6%—after the economy had lost a half million jobs over the previous three months—the stock market rallied. The stock market's reaction confused David Johnson, a Dallas stockbroker, business analyst, and commentator on the public radio program "Marketplace."

"A lot of times you look at the market reactions," Johnson confessed to his radio listeners, "and it looks like the market always tries to do whatever it can to confound the greatest number of people."

But it's really no surprise that stock prices should go up as the number of jobs shrinks and unemployment rates rise. The explanation comes down to the trade-off between inflation and unemployment. Standard macroeconomic textbooks depict that tradeoff as a "Phillips curve" in which rising employment (or falling unemployment rates) pushes up prices.

Why does this textbook trade-off affect the stock market? The answer, as Economist Robert Pollin points out, is that it is "all about class conflict." Wall Street investors, out to protect the value of their assets and their investment profits, are hyper-concerned with price stability, and this pits them against workers on Main Street, who care about employment and wage growth. Higher unemployment rates and fewer jobs eat away at the bargaining power of workers, keeping wage growth and inflation in check, and corporate profit margins wide.

Pollin captures that dynamic in "The 'Natural Rate' of Unemployment." As he sees it, the unemployment rate consistent with price stability, the so-called "natural rate," declined dramatically in the 1990s because workers' economic power eroded during the decade (Article 6.1).

Chris Tilly attributes the long-term decline in pay, benefits, and working conditions for U.S. workers to slower economic growth, the business offensive against workers' protections, such as unions and the minimum wage, and businesses pushing more risks onto workers in the form of temporary work, mass layoffs, and reduced benefits (Article 6.2).

The current economic recovery took nearly four years to replace the jobs lost in the preceding recession, something every other U.S. economic recovery accomplished within two and a half years from the onset of the recession. Of course, that is counting jobs by the payroll survey favored by most economists. The Bush administration and the editors of the *Wall Street Journal* favor using the household survey, which shows the recovery creating more new jobs. But, as John Miller points out, when used appropriately, both surveys tell the same sad story of a recovery that has performed poorly by historical standards (Article 6.3). "Offshoring by the Numbers" reports on how much of that dismal job growth is due to the shipping abroad of manufacturing jobs as well as back office and other white collar jobs (Article 6.4). William Rodgers looks closely at the gains African Americans made during the 1990s boom that partially narrowed the racial gap in employment and earnings. Unfortunately, most of those gains have been washed away in this decade's economic slowdown (Article 6.5). Attenio Davis laments that young African Americans are leaving the deindustrialized North in search of low-paying service jobs in the South—the mirror image of the choices that her mother's generation made (Article 6.6).

Finally, Bryan Snyder takes a careful look at the real costs of inflation. He argues that while higher inflation erodes the value the of financial assets held by Wall Street investors, there is little evidence that inflation actually slows the investment and economic growth that make life on Main Street better (Article 6.7).

DISCUSSION QUESTIONS

1) (Article 6.1) What is the concept of the NAIRU, or natural rate of unemployment? Is there a natural rate? What is it?
2) (Article 6.1) Given the class conflict inherent in the trade-off between inflation and unemployment, what policies might lead to an improved standard of living in today's economy?
3) (Article 6.2) What forces have led to a raw deal for workers over the long run?
4) (Article 6.3) How have the "paradox of corporate thrift," the "neoliberal paradox," and the "Arkansas paradox" complicated the task of winning a fair deal for workers?
5) (Article 6.3) What are the chief differences in the Payroll

---

KEY TO COLANDER
E = *Economics*   M = *Macroeconomics*

This entire chapter is keyed to chapter E29 or M13. Articles 6.1, 6.2, and 6.7 expose the class conflict that underlies the tradeoff between inflation and unemployment, the topic of chapter E29 or M13. Articles 6.3, 6.4, 6.5, and 6.7 fit squarely with the discussion of inflation and unemployment in chapter E29 or M13 and can also be used with chapter E22 or M6. Article 6.4 also goes with the discussion of outsourcing in E2, E21, or M2.

and Household surveys of employment. How different is the picture of the current recovery painted by each survey. Which survey do you regard as more accurate and why?

6) (Article 6.4) "Offshoring" was one of the hot button words of last year's presidential campaign. How much of the failure of the current recovery to create jobs (at the usual pace) is due to outsourcing overseas? And what, if

anything, should be done about it?

7) (Article 6.7) In what ways has the jobless recovery hit African Americans especially hard? What needs to be done to address the lingering racial disparities in the labor market?

8) (Article 6.6) What are the costs of higher inflation? And according to Snyder's evidence, what is the relationship between inflation and growth?

ARTICLE 6.1   *September/October 1998*

THE "NATURAL RATE" OF UNEMPLOYMENT
IT'S ALL ABOUT CLASS CONFLICT

BY ROBERT POLLIN

In 1997, the official U.S. unemployment rate fell to a 27-year low of 4.9%. Most orthodox economists had long predicted that a rate this low would lead to uncontrollable inflation. So they argued that maintaining a higher unemployment rate—perhaps as high as 6%—was crucial for keeping the economy stable. But there is a hitch: last year the inflation rate was 2.3%, the lowest figure in a decade and the second lowest in 32 years. What then are we to make of these economists' theories, much less their policy proposals?

Nobel prize-winning economist Milton Friedman gets credit for originating the argument that low rates of unemployment would lead to accelerating inflation. His 1968 theory of the so-called "natural rate of unemployment" was subsequently developed by many mainstream economists under the term "Non-Accelerating Inflation Rate of Unemployment," or NAIRU, a remarkably clumsy term for expressing the simple concept of a threshold unemployment rate below which inflation begins to rise.

According to both Friedman and expositors of NAIRU, inflation should accelerate at low rates of unemployment because low unemployment gives workers excessive bargaining power. This allows the workers to demand higher wages. Capitalists then try to pass along these increased wage costs by raising prices on the products they sell. An inflationary spiral thus ensues as long as unemployment remains below its "natural rate."

Based on this theory, Friedman and others have long argued that governments should never actively intervene in the economy to promote full employment or better jobs for workers, since it will be a futile exercise, whose end result will only be higher inflation and no improvement in job opportunities. Over the past generation, this conclusion has had far-reaching influence throughout the world. In the United

States and Western Europe, it has provided a stamp of scientific respectability to a whole range of policies through which governments abandoned even modest commitments to full employment and workers' rights.

This emerged most sharply through the Reaganite and Thatcherite programs in the United States and United Kingdom in the 1980s. But even into the 1990s, as the Democrats took power in the United States, the Labour Party won office in Britain, and Social Democrats won elections throughout Europe, governments remained committed to stringent fiscal and monetary policies, whose primary goal is to prevent inflation. In Western Europe this produced an average unemployment rate of over 10% from 1990-97. In the United States, unemployment rates have fallen sharply in the 1990s, but as an alternative symptom of stringent fiscal and monetary policies, real wages for U.S. workers also declined dramatically over the past generation. As of 1997, the average real wage for nonsupervisory workers in the United States was 14% below its peak in 1973, even though average worker productivity rose between 1973 and 1997 by 34%.

Why have governments in the United States and Europe remained committed to the idea of fiscal and monetary stringency, if the natural rate theory on which such policies are based is so obviously flawed? The explanation is that the natural rate theory is really not just about predicting a precise unemployment rate figure below which inflation must inexorably accelerate, even though many mainstream economists have presented the natural rate theory in this way. At a deeper level, the natural rate theory is bound up with the inherent conflicts between workers and capitalists over jobs, wages, and working conditions. As such, the natural rate theory actually contains a legitimate foundation in truth amid a welter of sloppy and even silly predictions.

THE "NATURAL RATE" THEORY IS ABOUT CLASS CONFLICT

In his 1967 American Economic Association presidential address in which he introduced the natural rate theory, Milton Friedman made clear that there was really nothing "natural" about the theory. Friedman rather emphasized that: "by using the term 'natural' rate of unemployment, I do not mean to suggest that it is immutable and unchangeable. On the contrary, many of the market characteristics that determine its level are man-made and policy-made. In the United States, for example, legal minimum wage rates ... and the strength of labor unions all make the natural rate of unemployment higher than it would otherwise be."

In other words, according to Friedman, what he terms the "natural rate" is really a social phenomenon measuring the class strength of working people, as indicated by their ability to organize effective unions and establish a livable minimum wage.

Friedman's perspective is supported in a widely-read 1997 paper by Robert Gordon of Northwestern University on what he terms the "time-varying NAIRU." What makes the NAIRU vary over time? Gordon explains that, since the early 1960s, "The two especially large changes in the NAIRU... are the increase between the early and late 1960s and the decrease in the 1990s. The late 1960s were a time of labor militancy, relatively strong unions, a relatively high minimum wage and a marked increase in labor's share in national income. The 1990s have been a time of labor peace, relatively weak unions, a relatively low minimum wage and a slight decline in labor's income share."

In short, class conflict is the spectre haunting the analysis of the natural rate and NAIRU: this is the consistent message stretching from Milton Friedman in the 1960s to Robert Gordon in the 1990s.

Stated in this way, the "Natural Rate" idea does, ironically, bear a close family resemblance to the ideas of two of the greatest economic thinkers of the left, Karl Marx and Michal Kalecki, on a parallel concept—the so-called "Reserve Army of Unemployed." In his justly famous Chapter 25 of Volume I of *Capital*, "The General Law of Capitalist Accumulation," Marx argued forcefully that unemployment serves an important function in capitalist economies. That is, when a capitalist economy is growing rapidly enough so that the reserve army of unemployed is depleted, workers will then utilize their increased bargaining power to raise wages. Profits are correspondingly squeezed as workers get a larger share of the country's total income. As a result, capitalists anticipate further declines in profitability and they therefore reduce their investment spending. This then leads to a fall in job creation, higher unemployment, and a replenishment of the reserve army. In other words, the reserve army of the unemployed is the instrument capitalists use to prevent significant wage increases and thereby maintain profitability.

Kalecki, a Polish economist of the Great Depression era, makes parallel though distinct arguments in his also justly

famous essay, "The Political Aspects of Full Employment." Kalecki wrote in 1943, shortly after the 1930s Depression had ended and governments had begun planning a postwar world in which they would deploy aggressive policies to avoid another calamity of mass unemployment. Kalecki held, contrary to Marx, that full employment can be beneficial to the profitability of businesses. True, capitalists may get a smaller share of the total economic pie as workers gain bargaining power to win higher wages. But capitalists can still benefit because the size of the pie is growing far more rapidly, since more goods and services can be produced when everyone is working, as opposed to some significant share of workers being left idle.

But capitalists still won't support full employment, in Kalecki's view, because it will threaten their control over the workplace, the pace and direction of economic activity, and even political institutions. Kalecki thus concluded that full employment could be sustainable under capitalism, but only if these challenges to capitalists' social and political power could be contained. This is why he held that fascist social and political institutions, such as those that existed in Nazi Germany when he was writing, could well provide one "solution" to capitalism's unemployment problem, precisely because they were so brutal. Workers would have jobs, but they would never be permitted to exercise the political and economic power that would otherwise accrue to them in a full-employment economy.

Broadly speaking, Marx and Kalecki do then share a common conclusion with natural rate proponents, in that they would all agree that positive unemployment rates are the outgrowth of class conflict over the distribution of income and political power. Of course, Friedman and other mainstream economists reach this conclusion via analytic and political perspectives that are diametrically opposite to those of Marx and Kalecki. To put it in a nutshell, in the Friedmanite view mass unemployment results when workers demand more than they deserve, while for Marx and Kalecki, capitalists use the weapon of unemployment to prevent workers from getting their just due.

FROM NATURAL RATE TO EGALITARIAN POLICY

Once the analysis of unemployment in capitalist economies is properly understood within the framework of class conflict, several important issues in our contemporary economic situation become much more clear. Let me raise just a few:

1 Mainstream economists have long studied how workers' wage demands cause inflation as unemployment falls. However, such wage demands never directly cause inflation, since inflation refers to a general rise in prices of goods and services sold in the market, not a rise in wages. Workers, by definition, do not have the power to raise prices. Capitalists raise prices on the products they sell. At low unemployment, inflation occurs when capitalists respond to workers' increasingly successful wage demands by raising prices so that they

can maintain profitability. If workers were simply to receive a higher share of national income, then lower unemployment and higher wages need not cause inflation at all.

2 There is little mystery as to why, at present, the so-called "time-varying" NAIRU has diminished to a near vanishing point, with unemployment at a 25-year low while inflation remains dormant. The main explanation is the one stated by Robert Gordon—that workers' economic power has been eroding dramatically through the 1990s. Workers have been almost completely unable to win wage increases over the course of the economic expansion that by now is seven years old.

3 This experience over the past seven years, with unemployment falling but workers showing almost no income gains, demonstrates dramatically the crucial point that full employment can never stand alone as an adequate measure of workers' well-being. This was conveyed vividly to me when I was working in Bolivia in 1990 as part of an economic advising team led by Keith Griffin of the University of California-Riverside. Professor Griffin asked me to examine employment policies.

I began by paying a visit to the economists at the Ministry of Planning. When I requested that we discuss the country's employment problems, they explained, to my surprise, that the country *had no employment problems*. When I suggested we consider the situation of the people begging, shining shoes, or hawking batteries and Chiclets in the street just below the window where we stood, their response was that these people *were* employed. And of course they were, in that they were actively trying to scratch out a living. It was clear that I had to specify the problem at hand far more precisely. Similarly, in the United States today, we have to be much more specific as to what workers should be getting in a fair economy: jobs, of course, but also living wages, benefits, reasonable job security, and a healthy work environment.

4 In our current low-unemployment economy, should workers, at long last, succeed in winning higher wages and better benefits, some inflationary pressures are likely to emerge. But if inflation does not accelerate after wage increases are won, this would mean that businesses are not able to pass along their higher wage costs to their customers. Profits would therefore be squeezed. In any case, in response to *either* inflationary pressures or a squeeze in profitability, we should expect that many, if not most, segments of the business community will welcome a Federal Reserve policy that would slow the economy and raise the unemployment rate.

Does this mean that, as long as we live in a capitalist society, the control by capitalists over the reserve army of labor must remain the dominant force establishing the limits of workers' strivings for jobs, security, and living wages? The challenge

for the progressive movement in the United States today is to think through a set of policy ideas through which full employment at living wages can be achieved and sustained.

Especially given the dismal trajectory of real wage decline over the past generation, workers should of course continue to push for wage increases. But it will also be crucial to advance these demands within a broader framework of proposals. One important component of a broader package would be policies through which labor and capital bargain openly over growth of wages and profits after full employment is achieved. Without such an open bargaining environment, workers, with reason, will push for higher wages once full employment is achieved, but capitalists will then respond by either raising prices or favoring high unemployment. Such open bargaining policies were conducted with considerable success in Sweden and other Nordic countries from the 1950s to the 1980s, and as a result, wages there continued to rise at full employment, while both accelerating inflation and a return to high unemployment were prevented.

Such policies obviously represent a form of class compromise. This is intrinsically neither good nor bad. The question is the terms under which the compromise is achieved. Wages have fallen dramatically over the past generation, so workers deserve substantial raises as a matter of simple fairness. But workers should also be willing to link their wage increases to improvements in productivity growth, i.e., the rate at which workers produce new goods and services. After all, if the average wage had just risen at exactly the rate of productivity growth since 1973 and not a penny more, the average hourly wage today for nonsupervisory workers would be $19.07 rather than $12.24.

But linking wages to improvements in productivity then also raises the question of who controls the decisions that determine the rate of productivity growth. In fact, substantial productivity gains are attainable through operating a less hierarchical workplace and building strong democratic unions through which workers can defend their rights on the job. Less hierarchy and increased workplace democracy creates higher morale on the job, which in turn increases workers' effort and opportunities to be inventive, while decreasing turnover and absenteeism. The late David Gordon of the New School for Social Research was among the leading analysts demonstrating how economies could operate more productively through greater workplace democracy.

But improvements in productivity also result from both the public and private sector investing in new and better machines that workers put to use every day, with the additional benefit that it means more jobs for people who produce those machines. A pro-worker economic policy will therefore also have to be concerned with increasing investments to improve the stock of machines that workers have at their disposal on the job.

In proposing such a policy approach, have I forgotten the lesson that Marx and Kalecki taught us, that unemployment serves a purpose in capitalism? Given that this lesson has become part of the standard mode of thinking among mainstream economists ranging from Milton Friedman to Robert Gordon, I would hope that I haven't let it slip from view. My point nevertheless is that through changing power relationships at the workplace and the decision-making process through which investment decisions get made, labor and the left can then also achieve a more egalitarian economy, one in which capitalists' power to brandish the weapon of unemployment is greatly circumscribed. If the labor movement and the left neglect issues of control over investment and the workplace, we will continue to live amid a Bolivian solution to the unemployment problem, where full employment is the by-product of workers' vulnerability, not their strength.

Resources: A longer version of this article appears as "The 'Reserve Army of Labor' and the 'Natural Rate of Unemployment': Can Marx, Kalecki, Friedman, and Wall Street All Be Wrong?," *Review of Radical Political Economics*, Fall 1998. Both articles derive from a paper originally presented as the David Gordon Memorial Lecture at the 1997 Summer Conference of the Union for Radical Political Economics. See also Robert Pollin and Stephanie Luce, *The Living Wage: Building A Fair Economy*, 1998; David Gordon, *Fat and Mean*, 1997; David Gordon, "Generating Affluence: Productivity Gains Require Worker Support," *Real World Macro*, 15th ed., 1998.

ARTICLE 6.2

July/August 2003

RAW DEAL FOR WORKERS

BY CHRIS TILLY

Few people have seen the inside of a "secondary meat processor"—a factory where large cuts of beef are turned into hamburger patties, roast beef, and other beef products. The workers who process beef do not have it easy. Many stand for long hours on wet floors. They are in constant contact with raw meat. In a typical plant the temperature ranges from 50° down to 3°F. Some workers rake 30-pound beef slabs from a huge bin onto a scale. Others heave giant roasts from one transmission belt to another. The work is repetitive and boring, but at the same time requires extreme attention to detail because of the potential for injury as well as food safety regulations. At one typical plant, entry-level pay is $7.75 an hour, or $16,000 a year—a poverty-level wage. There is no question that meat processors are getting a raw deal.

But the raw deal for workers is not limited to those workers who deal with raw meat. Pay, opportunities, and job quality have gotten worse for most workers in the United States over the past 30 years, across most sectors of the economy.

Obviously, the 2001 recession and the current jobless recovery have meant two-plus years of severe job shortages. But the deterioration of U.S. labor market conditions is a longer-term phenomenon. The spread of second-class jobs in the past three decades relates to fundamental changes in the economy and society, including sluggish productivity growth and employer assaults on workers' rights and protections.

The strongest evidence for the raw deal comes from looking at how workers were doing at the peak of the 1990s boom, three years ago. It was the longest boom in recorded U.S. history (lasting from March 1991 to March 2001). The expansion drove unemployment down to its lowest level in 30 years and spurred talk about a "new economy" that would turn productivity growth into endless prosperity. It should have been the best of times. But as a glance at the numbers reveals, it was not the best of times for working people.

WHY THE RAW DEAL?

Why are workers getting such a raw deal? First, the economic pie is growing more slowly. Productivity growth during the "new economy" 1990s was only two-thirds as fast as in the "old economy" 1960s. That reflects the fact that companies have not invested as much in upgrading their equipment and training their workers as they once did—although the numbers are up compared to the 1980s, when productivity growth was even slower.

Why are these investments down? Businesses make an investment when they expect a payoff. But total global demand for goods and services grew only about half as fast in the 1980s and 1990s as it did in the 1960s and 1970s, and the increasing globalization of trade and investment meant that businesses were much more likely to face new competitors.

Second, over the last 20 years, businesses have aggressively attacked the protections that workers had built up for themselves. They have busted and blocked unions, shredded the unspoken agreements that governed many non-union workplaces, and lobbied to weaken pro-worker legislation. One consequence of these efforts: private sector workers are now less than one-third as likely to belong to a union now as they were in the mid-1950s. The minimum wage is only worth about two-thirds as much as it was at its high point in the late 1960s (after taking inflation into account). Because the low-wage workforce includes disproportionate numbers of women and people of color, the minimum wage and unions particularly benefit these groups.

Republican presidents have joined in the attacks on these protections. Every Republican administration since Ronald Reagan has doggedly opposed minimum wage increases. When Reagan fired striking air traffic controllers in 1981, he set a precedent for the permanent replacement of strikers. George W. Bush out-did Reagan in 2002 when he demanded that the Department of Homeland Security not have civil service protections and announced plans to privatize half of the federal workforce. Republicans in the White House have also stacked the National Labor Relations Board (NLRB), other federal agencies, and the courts with anti-labor appointees. As a result, these agencies offer at best weak enforcement of labor protections. To provide two recent examples: the NLRB recently ruled that unions have no right to hand out leaflets in company parking lots, and the Supreme Court ruled in 2002 that if a company terminates an undocumented worker, it need not pay the worker his or her back pay. Further, under-funding of the Occupational Safety and Health Administration (OSHA) has reduced inspections in hazardous workplaces—like meat processors. Self-styled New Democrats have backed many of these changes in the name of aiding business.

> WHY ARE BUSINESSES ATTACKING WORKER PROTECTIONS AND DEMANDING THAT WORKERS BEAR MORE RISK? BECAUSE THEY *CAN*.

Of course, at the same time as corporations have attacked rank-and-file workers' protections, they have increased the rewards to top executives and stockholders. CEO pay kept growing through 2001, even while profits and stock values declined.

The third reason for the raw deal is that businesses have pushed more and more risk onto workers. The most extreme example of this is the growth of temporary work, which has expanded more than twenty-fold since the late 1960s. (Temporary work has been shrinking for the last two years—which of course is exactly the point: you hire temporary workers so you can dump them when the economy goes south.) But beyond the temps themselves, the frequency of mass layoffs highlights the fact that really, almost all jobs are temporary today.

Benefits are another area where workers bear more and more risk. Twenty-five years ago, most workers with pensions had "defined benefit" plans which specified the amount they would be paid upon retirement. Today, fewer than half of all workers are covered by any retirement plan, and fewer than one in five has a defined-benefit pension plan. Businesses prefer to offer defined-contribution plans like 401(k)s which require employee contributions and tie retirement income to market returns. In the last two years, we saw the

results for those who had invested their 401(k) savings in Wall Street. Similarly, employers who offer health insurance have made workers take on more and more of the cost of health benefits—with the result that a growing number of workers decide they can't afford their health plan and go without coverage.

BECAUSE THEY CAN

Why are businesses attacking worker protections and demanding that workers bear more risk? The first answer that many people give is "globalization"—and the increased competition that comes with it. Globalization has certainly had an important impact, but it does not offer an adequate explanation for business's newly combative stance. After all, it is the National Restaurant Association—representing an industry that experiences absolutely no global competition—that has fought hardest to keep the minimum wage low. To a large extent, businesses have gone on the offensive not because they *must*, but because they *can*.

Of course, businesses have always had the ability to lobby against the minimum wage, to cut health benefits, and to run anti-union campaigns. What has changed is the social acceptability of such actions. Princeton economist Paul Krugman recently argued that this is what accounts for the stratospheric rise of CEO pay: businesses have torn up the old social contract that placed important restraints on corporate self-seeking. Once a few large companies did this, the pressure mounted for other companies to go along or else face a competitive disadvantage, both in the stock market and in the market for goods and services. And as the social contract got rewritten, the government stopped enforcing the old rules. Cases in point are recent changes by the Supreme Court, the NLRB, and OSHA, mentioned earlier.

What can be done about this raw deal? It's tempting to think about the Arnold Schwarzenegger solution. In the 1986 movie *Raw Deal* ("They gave him a raw deal. *Nobody* gives him a raw deal."), Schwarzenegger used fists, guns, and explosives to wipe out the Chicago mob. But leveling the playing field for workers is no Hollywood action film. Complicating the task of winning a fairer share are three paradoxes.

THREE PARADOXES

The first is the *paradox of corporate thrift*. Again, businesses are spending less on investments in equipment and training, and are also doing their best to keep wages and benefits low, all because the demand for the goods and services they sell is not growing very fast. For any business individually, this kind of thrift makes sense. But the paradox is that for businesses taken as a whole, it's counterproductive. Because if businesses are keeping down their own spending, and giving workers as little as possible, the overall result is to keep down the demand for goods and services. It's a vicious circle.

Handing another million dollars to a CEO is not a good way to stimulate the economy. True, some CEOs, like

Tyco's Dennis Kozlowski, found creative ways to spend the money—on art, furniture, boats, and travel. But in general, rich people save most of their income. If you took a million dollars of executive pay and divided it among 1,000 poor families, you would get a lot more economic impact.

The second paradox is what University of Massachusetts economist James Crotty calls the *neoliberal paradox*. With slow global growth and increased global competition, it's become harder for most businesses to keep profits up. But at the same time, changes in the stock market mean that investors now demand consistently high profits. The growth of large institutional investors and the invention of the hostile takeover have made it possible for investors to threaten companies with takeover or destruction unless they generate high returns. Crotty points out that profit for nonfinancial corporations actually peaked in 1997. But corporations knew what would happen if they told their shareholders this bad news. In this context, the pressures for accounting games and even fraud became irresistible.

These first two paradoxes point out that the economy is far too important to let businesses run it. But when we think about how to take more control away from businesses, we run into the third paradox, the *Arkansas Traveler paradox*, named for an old song in which a traveler comes upon a man whose roof is leaking in a rainstorm. When the traveler asks him why he doesn't fix the roof, he says, "I can't fix it when it's raining." Asked why he doesn't then repair the roof when it's sunny, he replies, "When it's sunny, there's no need to fix it."

Similarly, when the economy is booming, workers have more economic leverage. Businesses run up against labor shortages, so they're more willing to make concessions to in order to ensure they can get the workers they need. It's a good time to organize a union, push for a higher minimum wage, or demand that employers provide a training program. Governments have the money to enforce regulations or to help pay for training.

But when the economy is booming, many workers don't see as much need to band together to defend their interests. Why form a union or lobby for a higher minimum wage when you can hop to a better paying job? Why push for a training program when even unskilled workers are getting jobs? The 1990s may not have amounted to a workers' paradise, but employment rates and wages were relatively edenic compared to the two decades that came before.

On the other hand, when the economy crashes, all of a sudden even the corporate media and mainstream politicians begin to focus on all the ways that business falls short. But when businesses are struggling for survival, they will fight desperately against any attempt to give workers a bigger share. The large numbers of unemployed job seekers put a damper on any attempts to organize unions or boost minimum wages. Governments face budget shortfalls, so they are not inclined to take on new activities.

The only way out of this box is not economic, but political. We have to build a movement that sees beyond the current situation in any given year. In the boom years, we have to remember all the problems of a business-dominated economy and use our economic leverage to strengthen institutions and business practices that help workers. In the bust years, like now, we have to keep in mind that economic resources will soon enough be growing again, and put in place rules that will more equitably distribute and effectively use them. We know what rules make a difference: the most important are strong wage floors and collective bargaining protections. By making businesses work under a better set of rules, we can actually help grow those resources by steering the economy out of the paradox of thrift and the neoliberal paradox.

If the problem is a raw deal, the solution is a new New Deal. The New Deal of the 1930s and 1940s saved U.S. capitalism from itself. It looks like we're going to have to do it again.

MISSING JOBS STILL LOST

BY JOHN MILLER

"MISSING JOBS FOUND"

... It turns out that this economic expansion is different from those in the past, but not in the way that many thought. New jobs are being created as usual, but they are different kinds of jobs. The U.S. economy is undergoing a structural change as more people become self-employed or form partnerships, rather than working for large corporations.

This transformation confounds the government's employment surveyors because they rely on the payroll data of about 400,000 existing companies ...

These [new] jobs show up in the "household survey." The government collects this data from workers rather than companies, and while it is more volatile month-to-month due to the smaller sample size (60,000 households), over the past three years it consistently told us that something unusual is happening. If you believe the payroll figures, the U.S. still has to create 700,000 more new jobs before it will return to the peak pre-recession level of 2001. But according to what individual Americans are saying, we've already surpassed that level by two million jobs.

In short, these are good times for most American workers ...

—The Wall Street Journal, *October 11, 2004*

The Bush administration may have struck out trying to find weapons of mass destruction in Iraq, but the *Wall Street Journal* editors say they have found the jobs that have gone missing during this jobless economic recovery.

Using the household survey of employment as their Geiger counter, the Journal's editors claim to have unearthed hundreds of thousands of new jobs overlooked by the traditional payroll survey of employment favored by the Bureau of Labor Statistics, the Congressional Budget Office, and most economists. With those extra jobs, the household survey has the Bush administration adding jobs to the economy, not losing them, and the recovery, as of September, creating 1,628,000 jobs on top of replacing the jobs lost since the last recession began, in March 2001. That picture is far more to the liking of the Journal's editors than the one painted by the payroll survey, which depicts the Bush administration as losing jobs and the recovery still down 940,000 jobs since the onset of the recession some three and a half years ago. Replacing the jobs lost to the recession is something the average postwar recovery managed to accomplish within two years.

But the truth is that, when used appropriately, the payroll and household employment surveys tell "the same (sad) story," in the words of Cleveland Federal Reserve Bank economists Mark Schweitzer and Guhan Venkatu. "Both surveys," they note, "show that employment has performed poorly in this recovery relative to the usual post-World War II experience." By historical standards, over four million jobs remain missing in today's economy.

WHY THE PAYROLL SURVEY IS MORE ACCURATE THAN THE HOUSEHOLD SURVEY

Federal Reserve Board Chair Alan Greenspan feels the Journal editors' pain. Still, he can't bring himself to endorse using the household survey to measure monthly employment growth. Earlier this year, Greenspan told Congress, "Having looked at both sets of data ... it's our judgment that as much as we would like the household data to be the more accurate, regrettably that turns out not to be the case."

Why do Alan Greenspan, the Bureau of Labor Statistics (BLS) that conducts both surveys, and the nonpartisan Congressional Budget Office regard the payroll survey to be "the more accurate," to provide "more reliable information," and to "better reflect the state of the labor market" than the household survey?

The first reason is statistical reliability. The payroll or establishment survey, which the BLS calls the Employment Statistics Survey, asks employers at about 400,000 worksites how many people they employ. The payroll sample includes every firm with 1,000 employees or more and covers about one-third of the total number of workers. The household survey—its formal name is the Current Population Survey—asks people in 60,000 households about their employment status. That is a small fraction of the total number of workers; the sample size of the payroll survey is 600 times larger. As a result, the household survey is subject to a large sampling error, about three times that of the payroll survey on a monthly basis.

Second, the payroll survey is better anchored in a comprehensive count of employment than the household survey. The household survey checks its result against a direct count of employment only once a decade when the decennial census is completed. On the other hand, every year the BLS adjusts the payroll survey's estimate of employment to correspond to the unemployment insurance tax records that nearly all employers are required to file. The preliminary revision based on the March 2004 benchmark added 236,000 workers, or a two-tenths of one percent increase in employment. The *Journal* suggests the revision shows the payroll numbers to be faulty; on the contrary, it should be taken as sign of their reliability, especially since the household survey is "benchmarked" but once a decade.

Beyond statistical reliability, the two surveys differ conceptually as well. Some of those differences narrow the gap between the job count of the two surveys, while others widen that gap. For instance, the two surveys treat multiple jobholders differently. The payroll survey counts each job reported by employers, even if the same worker holds two jobs. The household survey, on the other hand, counts multiple jobholders as employed only once. Also, while the household survey sample is quite limited, it does equally well counting jobs at new firms and long-established firms. The more thorough payroll survey only slowly integrates new firms into its sample, which can present problems in periods of rapid job growth. Finally, the household survey counts the self-employed, while the payroll survey of business establishments does not.

It is this third point that the Journal editors have seized on to explain why the payroll survey has undercounted the growth of jobs in the current recovery. They put it this way: "[W]hen a higher ratio of people make their livelihood as independent consultants to their old company, or as power sellers on eBay, they don't show up in the establishment survey."

Perhaps—if it were true that a higher ratio of people are self-employed. But even Harvard economist Robert Barro, a senior fellow at the conservative Hoover Institute, isn't buying it. In his March *Wall Street Journal* op-ed piece, Barro called "the large expansion of self-employment" explanation "a non-starter." Self-employment in the household survey just hasn't risen that much. As a ratio of household employment, self-employment rose somewhat after 2002, but even now that ratio is barely above its level at the onset of the recession in 2001, and it remains well below its level throughout most of the 1990s. What's more, an increase in self-employment is common in a weak labor market and typically disappears as labor market conditions improve and many of the self-employed find wage and salary employment. Finally, Barro estimates that "self-employment and other measurable differences between the two surveys explain only 200,000 to 400,000 of the extra three million jobs in the household survey."

THE SAME SAD STORY

Even the household survey indicates this recovery has done far less to create jobs than other postwar recoveries. According to the household survey, the current recovery had added just 1.5% to total employment by January 2004, some 26 months after the recession officially ended in November 2001. Other postwar recoveries added an average of 5.5% to the number of jobs over the same period. The payroll survey paints an even more dismal picture: it shows the U.S. economy losing 0.5% off its job base during 26 months of

recovery, while prior recoveries since 1949 added an average of 6.9% to employment in that amount of time.

Economists Schweitzer and Venkatu agree that it is more sensible to compare each employment survey to its own results during other postwar business cycles rather than to the other survey. They compare the ratio of employment (measured by the household survey) to total population in this recovery with the average pattern over postwar business cycles. In a recession, the employment-population ratio typically declines for about a year and a half and then returns to its previous level within about three years. But in this recovery, the employment-population ratio has declined nearly continuously. As a result, after three years of economic recovery, that ratio now stands at 62.3% (in September 2004), a full two percentage points below its 2001 pre-recession level of 64.3%.

By that standard, the U.S. economy is still missing 4,252,000 jobs—the number required to simply return to the employment-population ratio in 2001, and to equal the performance of the average postwar recovery. Schweitzer and Venkatu conclude that "both measures [the payroll survey and the household survey] show a surprisingly similar picture of the weak labor market performance that has prevailed during this recovery relative to previous business cycle periods."

The continuous decline in the ratio of employment to population makes clear why the unemployment rate is not higher, given the weak labor market. It is not because new jobs have gone uncounted; after all, unemployment rates are derived from the household survey. Rather, it is because many people have stopped looking for jobs and thus have dropped out of the unemployment statistics. The labor force participation rate—the fraction of the population either working or looking for work—has fallen sharply since George Bush took office; if it had stayed at its January 2001 level, the official unemployment rate would be 7.4%.

STILL MISSING

By any measure—the payroll survey, the household survey, or even the unemployment rate—the *Wall Street Journal* has not managed to locate the missing jobs in the U.S. economy. An honest inspection of the data reveals what most working people already know: when it comes to creating jobs, this recovery is the weakest since the Great Depression. That truth will continue to go missing on the editorial pages of the *Wall Street Journal*.

Sources: "Missing Jobs Found," *Wall Street Journal* 10/11/04; Mark Schweitzer and Guhan Venkatu, "Employment Surveys Are Telling the Same (Sad) Story," Economic Commentary (Federal Reserve Bank of Cleveland, 5/15/04); Robert Barro, "Go Figure," *Wall Street Journal*, 3/9/04; Bureau of Labor Statistics, "Employment from the BLS household and payroll surveys: summary of recent trends," 10/8/04; Elise Gould, "Measuring Employment Since the Recovery: A comparison of the household and payroll surveys," (Economic Policy Institute, December 2003); Steven Hipple, "Self-employment in the United States: an update," *Monthly Labor Review*, July 2004.

OFFSHORING BY THE NUMBERS

BY ANGEL CHEN AND ADRIA SCHARF

Offshoring has attracted a lot of attention lately from the presidential candidates, the media, economists, and workers. From all the talk, you'd think that offshoring represents the single largest threat to U.S. jobs. But according to new Bureau of Labor Statistics (BLS) data, a small fraction—just 2.5%—of jobs lost to mass layoffs in a recent period involved the relocation of work overseas.

The Department of Labor's BLS only began tracking overseas relocation of work in January and included the statistics for the first time in a quarterly report on layoffs released in June. Of the 182,456 private-sector nonfarm workers who lost their jobs in mass layoffs between January and March of 2004, 4,633 of these job separations (or 2.54% of the total) involved the movement of work from within the United States to locations outside of the country. (These figures exclude layoffs caused by vacation and seasonal factors. See Table 1.) Of the 34 reported cases of mass layoffs in which work was relocated overseas, 62% involved juggling work within companies, while 38% involved shifting work to a different company.

The BLS estimates are minuscule in comparison to other widely cited figures on international outsourcing. For example, Goldman Sachs estimates that about 300,000 to 500,000 jobs were offshored in the last three years, and Cambridge, Mass.-based Forrester Research projects 3.3 million jobs will move abroad by 2015.

Why the disparity? Without question, the BLS figures understate the magnitude of the trend. Because the bureau only tracks layoffs in large companies in which 50 or more people are laid off for more than 30 days, its data do not reflect job losses in small establishments, smaller-scale layoffs, or layoffs in the public sector or agriculture. (According to one study, mass layoffs account for only about one in five layoffs.) Moreover, neither the BLS nor anyone else tracks a major dimension of offshoring: the creation of new jobs abroad that do not directly result in layoffs at home (e.g., when a growing company decides to open its new call center in Mumbai rather than in Cleveland).

In sum, the BLS data capture only part of the offshoring phenomenon. So it would be a mistake to take these figures as an assurance that offshoring fears are overblown. We would do better to join Brian Deese and John Lyman of the Center for American Progress in calling for "much better data" on the subject.

Still, the low percentage of work lost to overseas relocations as a portion of all mass layoffs suggests that other factors are playing far more significant a hand in the job loss picture (See Table 2). As a proportion of total job separations, "company reorganization" and "labor disputes" are the two

TABLE 1: EXTENDED MASS LAYOFFS AND SEPARATIONS, FIRST QUARTER 2004

	Number of Mass Layoff "Events"		Job Separations from Mass Layoffs	
Total in private nonfarm sector, excluding seasonal and vacation events	869		182,456	
Overseas relocations	34	3.9%	4,633	2.5%
Within company	21	2.4%	2,976	1.6%
Different company	13	1.5%	1,657	0.9%

Note: Questions on movement of work were not asked of employers when the reason was either seasonal work or vacation period.

Source: Bureau of Labor Statistics (June 10, 2004).

TABLE 2: REASON FOR LAYOFF

	Number of Mass Layoff "Events"	Job Separations from Mass Layoffs
Total, private nonfarm	1,204	239,361
Bankruptcy	28	8,422
Business ownership change	31	4.217
Contract cancellation	29	4,238
Contract completed	170	51,795
Environment-related	0	0
Financial difficulty	84	15,755
Import competition	14	1,182
Labor dispute	4	21,293
Natural disaster	0	0
Product line discontinued	8	1,675
Reorganization in company	162	26,982
Seasonal work	332	56,478
Slack work	146	16,999
Vacation period	3	427
Weather-related	15	1,382
Other	56	11,004
Not reported	115	15,656

Note: Data on automation, material shortage, model changeover, and plant or machine repair are omitted because they do not meet BLS or state agency disclosure standards. All data in this table are preliminary.

Source: Bureau of Labor Statistics (June 10, 2004).

most significant reasons that employers cite for issuing mass layoffs, other than seasonal cycles and contract completion—a reminder that ordinary downsizing and the ongoing war on workers merit at least as much attention and concern as the offshoring phenomenon.

Sources: Brian Deese and John Lyman. "The Offshoring Numbers Game," Center for American Progress, June 28, 2004; "Extended Mass Layoffs Associated With Domestic And Overseas Relocations, First Quarter 2004," Bureau of Labor Statistics, June 10, 2004; "Putting Layoffs in Context," Employment Policy Foundation, April 9, 2001.

ARTICLE 6.5

BLACK WORKERS NEED MORE THAN AN ECONOMIC BOOM

BY WILLIAM M. RODGERS III

At the end of the 1990s economic boom, Hugh Price, the former president of the Urban League, reflected, "The truth is that for black Americans the 'glass'–their overall situation–is both half-empty and half-full." That glass is even less full today, as many of the gains African Americans made during the boom decade have melted away.

During the 1990s economic expansion, the longest on record, the U.S. unemployment rate fell from 6.8% in March 1991 to 4.3% in March 2001. Over those 10 years, the economy created almost 24 million jobs, an average of 200,000 jobs a month. That was enough to more than comfortably absorb the 150,000 new entrants into the labor force each month, pushing the jobless rate to 4.5% or below for 34 months.

Many hoped that the sustained economic boom would make a significant dent in the nation's persistent racial inequality. From the end of World War II to the 1990s, the unemployment rate for blacks had typically been twice that of whites, and black earnings had been 25% less than white earnings. The 1990s boom did substantially improve the absolute and relative economic positions of African Americans, although not as much as some had hoped. By the end of the boom, the ratio of black to white unemployment rates had fallen below the two-to-one ratio, and the black unemployment rate fell below 10% for a sustained period. The earnings of African Americans, particularly of young African Americans, increased. But during the short economic recession that began in March 2001, and the jobless recovery that has followed, much of the hard-fought progress made by blacks has eroded.

Below, we look at why the absolute and relative gains that African Americans made were less than hoped for during the 1990s boom and especially fragile in the period of economic decline that followed. Given that the economic boom of the 1990s by itself was not sufficient to put African Americans on an equal footing with white workers over the long term, we also look at the public policies that would be necessary to sustain the gains that blacks are likely to make during the next economic expansion.

A BOOM FOR SOME

African Americans, particularly those who are young and low skilled, typically make the greatest advances during boom years, when labor markets tighten. However, a closer look at the numbers calls into question whether the boom years were as good for African Americans as they should have been. In 2000, 63.6% of the 16-and-over African-American male civilian population were employed, up slightly from 63.4% in 1979. For young African Americans, the data provide an even bleaker picture. In 2000, only 52% of young African-American men with no more than a high school education were employed, compared to 62% in 1979. Studies have shown that the decline in the level of employment for inner-city black youth could not be explained by demographic shifts (like the growth of the suburbs) and labor market trends (such as the decline in manufacturing jobs) alone. A study by the Urban Institute suggests that the growing incarceration rate of young black men is undermining their labor market position. Young black men with histories of incarceration are more likely targets of workplace discrimination. Furthermore, more stringent enforcement of child support orders may have created the unintended side effect of reducing incentives for young African-American men to enter the formal economy.

A lesson of the boom is that sustained economic growth is one condition for lessening racial inequality, but is not by itself sufficient to erase it. Economic growth must be supplemented with public policies that attack the discrimination and structural impediments that make minorities second-class labor.

THEN COMES THE BUST

Many economists predicted that the boom would break down discrimination and other structural barriers to success. They hoped that young workers would gain enough experience to reduce the adverse effects of a future recession on their earnings and employment rates. The hope was that instead of taking two steps back during a recession, young African-American workers might only take one step back.

The first few months of the 2001 recession seemed to fulfill this hope. As the economic slowdown took hold, the employment-population ratio for whites fell by 0.7%, while the African-American ratio declined by only 0.3%. (The employment-population ratio measures the share of the civilian population that is employed. It has an advantage over the unemployment rate because it captures people who have given up their search for employment.) But the greater hit that white workers took was likely due to their overrepresentation in the manufacturing and information technology (IT) sectors where in the latter, jobs melted away with the dot-com bust. But as the downturn worsened, the African-American employment ratio began to fall faster. By the recession's end in November 2001, their employment-population ratio had fallen by almost 2%, compared to a 1.2% decline in the white ratio. This return to the "typical" pattern of recessions, where the least skilled are the first fired, continued during the jobless recovery. Today, the African-American unemployment rate has been above 10% for 23 of the past 24 months. The jobless rate of African-American teenagers, which reached a still-too-high historical low of 20% in April 2000 and averaged 29% during the recession, is 30.8% today, almost twice the white teenage unemployment rate.

SUSTAINED ECONOMIC GROWTH IS ONE CONDITION FOR LESSENING RACIAL INEQUALITY, BUT IS NOT BY ITSELF SUFFICIENT TO ERASE IT.

Most discouragingly, education no longer provides African Americans a strong protection during periods of economic downturn and stagnation. In December 2000 the unemployment rates of white and African-American college graduates were virtually indistinguishable, both below 2.0%. A year later, when the recession officially ended, jobless rates for both groups had risen to 2.7%. By 2004, however, the white college-graduate unemployment rate had fallen to 2.0%, while the African-American rate jumped to 5.0%.

Why do minorities have such fragile and persistently low employment rates? Although racial differences in educational attainment have narrowed over the past few decades, the remaining differences in the years and quality of education remain major contributors to racial differences in labor market outcomes. In its 1999 report "Futurework: Trends and Challenges for the 21st Century," the U.S. Department of Labor identified several additional factors. Employer perceptions, racial discrimination, limited early work experience, spatial mismatch between where jobs are and where minority workers live, and involvement with crime all contribute to racial inequality in the labor market, according to the report. These are all factors that even the best economy in decades cannot undo.

LOOKING TO THE FUTURE

If even the best economy in 30 years did little to correct persistent racial unemployment and earnings gaps, and what gains did come were fragile, will strong economic growth in the future do any better? If we can't rely on future growth alone, how can we make any positive changes that do stick? Economists are deeply split on this issue. Some argue that improving the education system is key. Others would strengthen the government's ability to protect workers from discrimination, bad working conditions, and inappropriate workplace policies. Still others continue to believe that economic growth alone is the key to eliminating racial differences in the labor market. This debate should not be cast as a zero-sum game. None of these policies alone are likely to be effective.

A number of economists have analyzed data from the National Longitudinal Survey of Youth, which has been following a cohort of young men and women since 1979, and concluded that the wage gap between African Americans and whites is fully explained by racial differences in test scores. Wage differences are due solely to pre-market factors such as racial differences in school quality, and parent's education and occupation, these economists contend—not to discrimination and other problems in labor markets.

Continued discrimination in the labor market, however, is well documented, for example, by Phillip Moss and Chris Tilly's research on employer preferences. Research on housing and credit markets also finds evidence of discrimination—and if there is wide consensus on the presence of racial discrimination in these other markets, it is hard to believe that the labor market is immune.

SUMMING UP

To generate a boom that lessens racial inequality, government must adopt a range of policies that have disproportionately positive impacts on African Americans even if they are race-neutral. This includes not only improving education and training opportunities, but also implementing the appropriate monetary and fiscal policies. For example, the dollar value of the 2001 and 2003 tax cuts should have been tilted more toward lower and middle-income households. These are the families that ultimately bore the brunt of the recession and the weak recovery as well as of rising energy and health care costs. They are more likely to spend a tax cut than to save it, which would have provided the economy with more stimulus.

But even during a vigorous 1990s-style boom, there remains ample room for race-specific approaches to addressing inequality. Even in a robust economy, vigorous enforcement of affirmative action, anti-discrimination laws, and support of minority and women-owned business creation are necessary.

"We know," Hugh Price has noted, "that there are many ways government at the national, state, and local levels can assist individuals and the private sector in reducing the 'empty' portion of the 'glass' black America holds, and making it more and more full. That is the task ahead."

Resources: Harry J. Holzer and Paul Offner, *Left Behind in the Labor Market: Recent Employment Trends Among Young Black Men*, 2002; Phillip Moss and Chris Tilly, *Stories Employers Tell: Race, Skill, and Hiring in America*, 2000; William M. Rodgers III, "Male Sub-Metropolitan Black-White Wage Gaps: New Evidence for the 1980s," *Urban* Studies, 34, (8): 1201-1213, 1997; U.S. Department of Labor, "Futurework: Trends and Challenges for the 21st Century," 1999.

Article 6.6

May/June 2004

WHERE IS THE NORTH OF TODAY?

BY ATTIENO DAVIS

Ellen Williams was 16 years old when she left Butler County, Georgia, one of the innumerable backwoods Georgia counties with Jim Crow and "Negroes Need Not Apply," no indoor plumbing and one-room schoolhouses. When she arrived in Boston in 1946, she thought she'd died and gone to heaven. Though she'd left her family behind, her dream of accessing just a bit of the pie seemed realizable at last.

Momma never quite achieved her dream, but she did have a job for 41 years, a job that helped stabilize our lives. When she retired in the early 1990s, that job provided her a pension she lives on today, back in her beloved Georgia. My mother worked for Raytheon and was a member of the International Brotherhood of Electrical Workers. She never had a car until the early '70s, but she said she never thought of herself as poor because she had a good job, which gave her a sense of hope.

I understood as a girl that the job was the key to my family's security. Momma could pay our rent, buy groceries, pay the insurance man, and take my sister and me to the doctor. Raytheon was a cornerstone in my family's life.

Momma made sure that her family members in the South did okay, regularly sending money home to help out. Our three-bedroom apartment was a temporary home to at least three other extended family members who fled the economically depressed South in the 1960s. Two of them also managed to get jobs at Raytheon.

It was a struggle for women working in the plants. Promotions weren't as forthcoming, especially if you were Black. Momma said the combined issue of race and gender was a problem even in the union. But she was a card-carrying member of IBEW, and she supported the union for the job security it gave her. She said, "The union was my key. We had health care, vacation, pension, and the union protected my rights." With the union's support, she took community college courses and broke ground to become one of Raytheon's first women inspectors.

None of my daughters or nieces have worked in manufacturing jobs, and none of them have been union members. They've worked at hotels and in stores. One niece went to community college in a certified nursing assistant program, and got a job at a unionized hospital—but it was a temporary contract job for six months, not a permanent union job. Now she works in a nursing home.

Many younger members of my family have moved south again because that's where the jobs are. But companies have a "let me hold my nose, I think I smell a union" attitude. Some of these young people have gone to college and found better-paying jobs—but not everyone can go to college, and the jobs for those without college now have no benefits and no union. Unlike their parents, they can't have a car or purchase a home. No matter what they do, a stable life seems to always be just beyond.

Today as I watch young people of color enter the workforce, it's almost as if we've come full circle, back to that same place my mother started out. She left a state with no opportunity for her and moved to a state with abundant good jobs. The young Black adults coming up today all live in states with a shrinking base of options for those without college educations—but there is now nowhere to move to find abundant good jobs. Where's their boost up the ladder?

July/August 1994, revised and excerpted February 1999

WHAT ARE THE REAL COSTS OF INFLATION —AND TO WHOM?

BY BRYAN SNYDER

As the American economy rolls along in a continuing boom, almost weekly the media speculate on when Federal Reserve Bank Chairman Alan Greenspan will decide to cool things down in order to stave off even a hint of rising inflation. Although workers are benefiting from low unemployment and the first real wage increases in two and a half decades, the Federal Reserve views these gains as a danger sign.

A powerful array of moneyed interests lurks behind Greenspan's attitudes. Financiers with large investments see the specter of inflation as a threat to their interests and to the economy as a whole. Because inflation erodes the value of financial assets, they argue that it discourages the investment that is needed for stable long-term economic growth. They prefer a modest growth rate of 3% or less maintained over time, which would achieve a "safe" level of wage gains and unemployment.

But is controlling inflation worth the high costs to workers of suffering from lower wages and more job insecurity? The evidence shows that price increases are not the enemy of long-term growth that financiers would have us believe. What's more, according to research by Thomas Michl of Colgate University, the other costs of moderate inflation are either avoidable or bearable. For most people, the treatment prescribed by the Fed for inflation is much more painful than the malady itself.

COUNTING THE COSTS OF INFLATION

Michl analyzed the costs of inflation by first determining which costs are avoidable and which are not. Falling real incomes are a cost of inflation that the right policies can rectify. If an economy has a moderate rate of inflation, such as 7% to 10% annually, someone living on fixed Social Security benefits would watch the actual buying power of his or her fixed income erode in direct proportion to that rate of inflation. To compensate for this, the government has built a COLA (Cost of Living Adjustment) into the Social Security benefit structure to keep real incomes constant or close to it. Likewise, employers can often anticipate moderate levels of inflation and float their pay scales accordingly.

In the area of taxation, rising wages could potentially push individuals into higher income tax brackets. This "bracket creep" could reduce workers' after-tax real wages (wages adjusted for inflation). Indexing the tax structure to the rate of inflation can take care of this problem. The 1986 Tax Reform Act does this for personal exemptions.

There is also concern that inflation depresses the housing market. Historically, banks were reluctant to give mortgage loans when the interest on their loans might be wiped out by inflation. But banks have learned to compensate for the possibility of future inflation by using variable-rate mortgages. Banks could also avoid this impact of inflation by having mortgage payments that rise gradually over time, along with expected inflation. In addition, elements of the tax code, such as deductions for mortgage interest payments, facilitate first-time mortgages.

According to Michl, some costs are less easy to offset, but that doesn't necessarily mean they're significant. A particularly good example of this is inflation's "shoe leather" costs.

Shoe leather costs result from the fact that high levels of inflation make it expensive for capitalists to keep a lot of cash on hand to cover transactions. Rather than let their cash grow less valuable, when there's high inflation they will keep their money in bank accounts that offer interest rates at least equal to the inflation rate. This keeps the value of their money constant.

The story goes that this "parking" of working funds in bank accounts leads to increased expenses (transaction costs), due to the extra time spent running to and from the bank making withdrawals and deposits, which wears down "shoe leather." This is an unavoidable cost of inflation, but it's relatively small. Michl reports that, when annual inflation is 10%, shoe leather costs would amount to $7.28 billion or 0.13% of a $5.5 trillion Gross National Product. Innovation and technological change within the banking system, including electronic fund transfers, have made these costs all but evaporate in recent years, as banks now offer firms instantly accessible interest-bearing accounts and decentralized service.

THE GROWTH QUESTION

A larger concern is whether or not inflation retards economic growth. Does inflation create uncertainty about future inflation, making capitalists reduce their level of investment and slowing economic growth in the long run? The conventional wisdom of mainstream economics answers a nervous *yes*.

Yet as Michl argues, the evidence shows that inflation and growth tend to go together in industrial societies. Between 1955 and 1973, countries such as Japan, Korea, Israel, Brazil, and Turkey had rapid rates of growth as well as relatively high inflation.

Economist Ross Levine tried to determine whether there is a correlation between rates of inflation and rates of investment and growth. Using data from 119 countries from 1969 through 1989, Levine and his colleagues found that "... inflation is not significantly negatively correlated with long-run growth.... Given the uncharacteristically unified view among economists and policy analysts that countries with high inflation rates should adopt policies to lower inflation in order to promote prosperity, the inability to find simple cross-country regressions supporting this contention is both surprising and troubling."

Wall Street's argument that inflation will hurt long-term investment runs like this: Inflation reduces the incentive to save money, because if you're locked into a bank account or fixed-rate investment that yields interest at a lower rate than inflation, the value of your money will deteriorate. It also reduces the incentive to lend money, as the debt will be repaid in the future when money is less valuable. To compensate for these disincentives, financial institutions raise interest rates to the level of inflation or above. Because this rise in interest rates raises the cost of borrowing money, some argue that it hurts long-term investment.

That would be true if interest rates largely determined investment. But other factors, such as sales growth and how much cash a firm has on hand, are more powerful determinants of investment than interest rates. For example, while the East Asian economies grew rapidly during the 1980s and early 1990s, their interest rates remained high, but still were below profit rates, and did not significantly stunt economic growth.

In the case of the bond market, in which bond buyers lend the government money, fears of inflation can cause a drop in bond prices and a rise in interest rates. Inflation erodes the value of bonds, as it allows the government to pay off its debt in cheaper dollars in the future. Falling bond prices in turn have prompted a hike in interest rates to appease skittish buyers. It's not surprising, then, that the bond market has put so much political pressure on the federal government to ward off inflation.

SOCIAL WELFARE, WEALTH, AND INFLATION

If they see it coming, policymakers can compensate for inflation in order to maintain real incomes. But when inflation is not anticipated and mechanisms are not in place to keep the value of assets and liabilities constant, then inflation will alter the distribution of income within society.

Specifically, inflation can shift real incomes from creditors (lenders) to debtors (borrowers). Unanticipated inflation allows debtors (such as the U.S. government, in the case of bonds) to pay off debts in less valuable currency, while eroding the rate of return lenders can realize from loans. For instance, if a bank Certificate of Deposit (CD) offers a fixed annual interest rate of 7%, and suddenly the rate of inflation rises to 7% that year, the investor would make no money since the CD's value eroded at the same rate that the interest accumulated. This cost of inflation falls on the wealthiest households, who derive the bulk of their incomes from returns on investments rather than from their labor.

A 1979 study by Joseph Minarik analyzed the effects of inflation on the distribution of incomes in the 1970s. Households with the lowest incomes actually gained slightly due to windfalls on fixed home mortgages. However, the richest 20% of households suffered a substantial loss. In fact, the study found that for those making between $200,000 and $500,000 a year, a modest 2% increase in inflation caused a 17% reduction in real income.

Because of this disproportionate impact of inflation on the wealthiest members of society, there is a consensus among the country's elite that the government should declare it to be Public Enemy Number One. Tom Michl puts it this way: "To the extent that the wealthiest citizens, who depend on interest and capital income substantially more than the average citizen, are also disproportionately represented in the political process (and who would seriously dispute that), this creates a very strong bias toward disinflationary economic policies."

> INFLATION CAN SHIFT REAL INCOMES FROM CREDITORS TO DEBTORS, BY ALLOWING DEBTORS TO PAY OFF DEBTS IN LESS VALUABLE CURRENCY, ERODING THE RATE OF RETURN FROM LOANS.

The vast majority of Americans can live with moderate levels of inflation, when properly COLA-ed or indexed, and would prosper with high rates of economic growth. For them, the therapy for inflation—a sustained regimen of tight money, slow economic growth, and wages which fall or grow only slightly even during boom times—is the real burden.

Resources: Thomas Michl, "Assessing the Costs of inflation and Unemployment," discussion paper, 1994; Ross Levine and David Renelt, "A Sensitivity Analysis of Cross Country Growth Regressions," *American Economic Review* 82 (4 September 1992); Ross Levin and Sara Zervos, "What Have We Learned about Policy and Growth from Cross Country Regressions?" *American Economic Review* 83 (2 May 1993).

CHAPTER 7

PERSPECTIVES ON MACROECONOMIC POLICY

INTRODUCTION

A few years back, political economist Bob Sutcliffe developed a sure-fire economic indicator that he called the Marx/Keynes ratio—the ratio of references to Karl Marx to references to John Maynard Keynes in Paul Samuelson's *Economics*, the best-selling introductory economics textbook during the decades following World War II. In a recession or a period of sluggish economic growth, the Marx/Keynes ratio would climb, as social commentators and even economists fretted over the future of capitalism. In economic booms, however, Marx's predictions of the collapse of capitalism disappeared from the pages of Samuelson's textbook, while the paeans to Keynesian demand-management policies multiplied.

Today Sutcliffe's ratio wouldn't work very well. Marx has been pushed off the pages of most introductory macroeconomics textbooks altogether, and even Keynes has been given only a minor role. Mainstream textbooks now favor the "New Classical" economics, which depicts the private economy as inherently stable and self-regulating, and dismiss Keynesian demand-management policies as ineffectual or counterproductive. Our authors disagree. In this chapter, they reintroduce schools of thought that have been removed from economics textbooks in recent decades and critically assess New Classical economics.

John Miller and Gina Neff start with a down-to-earth account of New Classical "rational expectations" models, in which markets clear instantaneously and bungling government bureaucrats always make a mess of things. Drawing on the writings of Keynesian and New Keynesian economists, Miller and Neff argue that rational expectations models are contradicted by the historical record, which shows that bigger government has brought milder, not more severe, business cycle fluctuations (Article 7.1).

Robert Pollin (Article 7.2) attacks the underpinnings of the neoliberal policy prescription for the global economy. As he sees it, the unfettered globalization of free markets will be unable to resolve three basic problems: an ever-larger reserve army of the unemployed that reduces the bargaining power of workers in all countries (the Marx problem); the inherent instability and volatility of investment and financial markets (the Keynes problem); and the erosion of the protections of the welfare state (the Polanyi problem).

Ellen Frank explains the development of Keynesian economic institutions in the United States and their subsequent dismantling under the Clinton administration. She also introduces the radical insight of Keynes—"that real wealth lies in the people, resources, and productive apparatus of a society and that citizens can, through the collective power of government, harness those resources for internal development." (Article 7.3)

Alejandro Reuss provides a primer on Marxist economics. Marx rejected the idea of a self-equilibrating economy, and argued that capitalism was inherently dynamic and unstable. Reuss describes some of Marx's key ideas, including the nature of capitalist exploitation, and what Marx saw as two ingredients of an eventual crisis of capitalism: overproduction and the falling rate of profit (Article 7.4). Rick Wolff explains why Marxian class analysis remains relevant today (Article 7.6).

Randy Albelda offers a feminist analysis of poverty and gender. Feminist economists have illuminated the ways in which having and caring for children alters the economic status of women—including those who are not mothers but are still relegated to poorly-paid care-giving jobs. Feminist economists, argues Albelda, provide the best understanding of the obstacles low-income families face and the options that might improve their position in today's economy (Article 7.5).

KEY TO COLANDER

E = *Economics*   M = *Macroeconomics*

These articles fit with chapters E25-E26 and E22, or M9-M10 and M6.

Article 7.1 complements chapter E25 or M9, especially its presentation of the classical range of the aggregate supply/aggregate demand model.

Article 7.2 works well with any of these chapters.

Article 7.3 works with chapters E25-E26 or M9-M10, or the discussion of debt and deficits in E31 or M15.

Articles 7.4, 7.5, and 7.6 can be introduced with the Appendix to chapter E22 or M6, "Nonmainstream Approaches of Macroeconomics." They can also go with any discussion of the instabilities and inequalities of the modern macroeconomy.

Article 7.6 fits well with any discussion of the philosophical foundations of capitalism in the early chapters, as well as with the Appendix to chapter E22 or M6.

DISCUSSION QUESTIONS

1) (Article 7.1) How do classical economists argue that macroeconomies are inherently stable, and that government intervention is ineffective or counterproductive? Are their arguments convincing?

2) (Article 7.1) Why are Keynesians convinced that markets don't clear instantaneously, and that government intervention can and must stabilize market economies? Evaluate the evidence for their position.

3) (Article 7.2) Summarize the Marx, Keynes, and Polanyi problems. Why does Pollin think that neoliberal globalization policies will be unable to resolve them?

4) (Article 7.3) What do the terms "fiscal policy," "automatic stabilizer," "cyclical deficit," and "federal deficit" mean? How do they relate to Keynesian policy-making?

5) (Article 7.3) How did the Democrats bring down Keynes?

6) (Article 7.3) What would a macroeconomic policy that captured Keynes's radical insights look like?

7) (Article 7.4) In Marxist theory, how is a dynamic capitalist economy felled by instability? What roles do a "falling rate of profit," a "reserve army of the unemployed," and "overproduction" play in Marx's theory of how capitalism will fall into a crisis? Do you think today's macroeconomy displays any of those tendencies?

8) (Article 7.5) How does feminist economics' focus on gender challenge other theories of poverty? How are feminist theories of poverty different from Keynesian, Marxist, Institutionalist, and neoclassical analyses?

9) (Article 7.6) How does Wolff's class analysis of today's economy differ from the one presented in your textbook?

ARTICLE 7.1

May/June 1996, revised April 2002

THE REVENGE OF THE CLASSICS

BY JOHN MILLER AND GINA NEFF

Nineteen ninety-five was not a good year for the welfare state. A Gingrich-led Congress attempted to pull the plug on universal entitlements for the poor, from welfare to Medicaid. And the Royal Swedish Academy of Science awarded the Nobel Prize in economics to Robert Lucas, a 58-year-old University of Chicago economist, for his "insights into the difficulties of using economic policy to control the economy."

Using sophisticated mathematics and economic models, Lucas has persuaded much of the economics profession that the economic policies John Maynard Keynes developed to combat the Great Depression—the economic underpinnings of the welfare state and the mixed economy—are ineffective.

What would Lucas do instead? Forsake those policies, dismantle the welfare state, and embrace the market. That was a job that, back in the mid-1990s, Gingrich and his crowd seemed only too happy to take up. They were glad to join forces with a Federal Reserve Board (the "Fed") already under the influence of the conservative counterrevolution in macroeconomics, led initially by Milton Friedman, another University of Chicago monetary theorist, and then by Lucas.

The Fed has accepted the futility of using monetary policy to promote long-run employment, leaving inflation alone as the ultimate target of its policies. In addition, the Fed's practice of making early announcements of changes in monetary policy, which is probably a good thing, can be directly attributed to Lucas. He has argued that unannounced changes provoke instability in the private sector instead of muting it.

Lucas and his school of followers call themselves New Classical economists. Like the classical economists who predated Keynes, these modern conservatives believe the economy possesses powerful self-correcting forces that guarantee full employment. Their vision of a stable market economy rests on three building blocks: rational expectations, market clearing, and imperfect information.

Let's look first at rational expectations, a notion which does seem rational enough. After all, every one of our economic actions is directed toward the future. Using whatever economic information we can get our hands on about prices, growth, and other economic activity, we predict our economic future. And usually we are good at it. When fellow workers are getting laid off at the company we are employed in, for instance, chances are that buying an expensive house is not at the top of our to-do list.

When we do get things wrong, we reevaluate our predictions. And, says Lucas, we keep up this process of prediction and evaluation until there is no way to improve those predictions, ensuring that we won't consistently make the same forecasting mistakes. In that way we form what Lucas calls "rational expectations." As he sees it, people act much like experienced bettors at the track. They get good at picking horses, but are never able to pick the winning horse every time.

Lucas has made a career out of expressing these ideas in mathematical terms. He argues that predictions about the rates of interest, unemployment, and inflation shape how consumers, workers, and business people decide their economic future. From consumers buying a new home to workers looking for a new job to bosses hiring or laying off employees, rational expectations theory seeks to describe what motivates economic actors.

ADAM SMITH RETURNS

But Lucas does not stop there—with merely a theory of how people make economic decisions. New Classical economic theory also assumes that markets "clear" instantaneously. In the bat of an eye, prices adjust so that how much sellers bring to market just matches whatever buyers take away. For instance, in a labor market, wages (the price of labor) fall quickly enough to guarantee that every worker willing to work (or sell their labor) at the going wage finds a job with an employer (or buyer of labor). For New Classical economists that constitutes full employment. Only workers unwilling to work at the market clearing wage are out of a job. Those workers are voluntarily unemployed—they chose not to work and brought unemployment upon themselves.

The point here is simple: Market capitalism is stable. "Price flexibility" and "market clearing" guarantee a booming full-employment economy—one that does not need economic policymaking to stabilize it. In fact, in Lucas's framework, government attempts to fine tune the economy actually backfire.

> WHILE KEYNESIANS MAY ACCEPT THE IDEA OF RATIONALLY FORMED EXPECTATIONS, THEY FIND THE IDEAS OF FLEXIBLE PRICES AND CLEARING MARKETS PREPOSTEROUS.

Here's why. If people expect the government to change economic policy, they too change their economic actions. That is rational expectations at work. And when prices and wages adjust instantaneously as people scramble to match their economic actions to their new expectations, those adjustments nullify the government's actions.

For instance, suppose the Fed tries to reduce unemployment by increasing the money supply, in the hope of raising spending and putting people to work. Lucas's rational workers anticipate that more spending and hiring will bring not only higher wages but also instantaneously higher prices, leaving their purchasing power unchanged. In this world people are not forced to work to avoid starving, but rather choose to offer their services only when their inflation-adjusted wages are sufficiently high. So no rational worker is lured into the market. The Fed's actions fail to lower unemployment, and succeed only in driving up prices.

As far-fetched as this theory might seem, the stagflation (simultaneous stagnation and inflation) of the 1970s lent these ideas plausibility. New Classical economics gathered adherents as Keynesian policies seemed increasingly ineffectual.

In New Classical economics, meddlesome government is not only ineffective, it is the enemy. Why does Lucas's inherently stable capitalism suffer through the ups and downs of the business cycle? His answer: Washington types trying to fine tune the economy. This is where imperfect information, the third building block of Lucas' theory, enters the model. Even Lucas's rational actors in this market-clearing world possess only limited information and can be fooled by bungling bureaucrats and re-election minded politicians who launch surprise (unannounced) changes in government policy.

People know the economy around them—their own wages or profits, the prices of the products they sell and those that they buy—better than what is going on across the economy. So if the Federal Reserve, without announcing it, increases the money supply in order to beef up spending and lower unemployment, even people with rational expectations can be confounded. They see their prices or wages go up, but don't anticipate prices going up elsewhere in the economy.

And that causes a problem. Corporate managers, for instance, hike up production, thinking that a higher price must signal a soaring demand for their products. Output rises across the economy. But soon inventories pile up, because the price increases were due to general inflation rather than greater demand. Corporate managers realize that the higher production levels were unwarranted, and they order a cutback—below even the initial output. The economy contracts, causing a recession.

What can return stability to the economy? Forsaking government intervention into the economy. In Lucas's world, unannounced changes in government policy cause the ups and downs of the business cycle. And announced changes in government policies are fully anticipated and therefore ineffective. For Lucas, the only rational course of action is to turn our backs on active government attempts to soften the blows of the market economy.

KEYNESIAN CRITICS

Not all economists are convinced by Lucas's arguments or support the draconian policy implications of New Classical economics. The proponents of Keynesian economic policy have been among the most vocal critics. While Keynesians may accept the idea of rationally formed expectations, they find the ideas of flexible prices and clearing markets preposterous. One Nobel laureate, James Tobin, called these ideas a "great myth"—powerful in its effect on how we see the economy, but nonetheless a myth.

Another Keynesian Nobel winner, Franco Modigliani, railed that it is as if "what happened in the United States in the 1930s was a severe attack of contagious laziness." For these dyed-in-the-wool Keynesians, the private economy will not necessarily be driven toward full employment even in the long run and Keynes's fundamental message still holds: "a modern monetized economy needs to be stabilized, can be stabilized, and should be stabilized" by government intervention.

More recently, "New Keynesian" economists have fashioned a different critique of New Classical economics. These modern Keynesians accept not only the idea that people form rational expectations about what will happen in the economy, but also the idea that in the long run the private economy tends toward full employment. Still, they argue that for good economic reasons, wages and prices are "sticky" and much slower to adjust than Lucas suggests. For instance, given the high cost of negotiating a wage settlement, most labor contracts are long term. In the United States, nearly 80% of union contracts are for three years and only about two-fifths of them contain cost-of-living adjustments. Corporations also often rely on long-term pricing agreements to afford them the price stability necessary to bid on contracts.

Thus, while the economy might eventually reach the full employment outcome Lucas's model predicts, the wait is likely to be intolerably long. What's needed is active government intervention designed for the workable policy time frame of three to five years, for as Keynes once wrote, "in the long run we are all dead."

More fundamentally, Lucas's way of thinking exaggerates the amount of power people really have over their economic lives. Economist E. Ray Canterbery writes mockingly that in the New Classical school, "The marginal blue collar worker on his way to the factory anticipates an increase in the money supply then fully anticipates the inflation within his monetarist model ... and a fall in the real interest rates and a fall in real wages. The worker does a U-turn, drives home, and voluntarily disemploys himself." In New Classical economics bosses raise their workers' wages when the economy is doing well rather than pocketing the extra profits. And workers have the power to choose whether or not to work, to ask for higher wages when they expect inflation to go up, or to move into a different industry when they fear the worst for their own job. This is indeed a great myth.

Perhaps the most mythical aspect of New Classical economics is its claim that capitalism is stable—that if only policy makers would cease their interventions, economic stability would be assured and full employment guaranteed. But the instability of capitalism has been with us since long before Keynesian economic policy, which after all was a response to the Great Depression of the 1930s.

And that instability will worsen if New Classical economics is able to undo what Keynesian policy makers have done to mitigate the instability of capitalism since World War II. Current economic anxiety will heighten as workers struggle with real-life adjustments like stagnant wages and rising layoffs. At the same time, Lucas and his New Classical followers will continue to construct mathematical paeans to the rationality of these adjustments and the inherent stability of capitalism, even if that stability is evident only in their seminar rooms and the the Royal Swedish Academy of Science.

Resources: Robert J. Gordon, *Macroeconomics*, 6th ed., 1994; Robert Lucas, *Studies in Business Cycle Theory*, 1989; N. Gregory Mankiw, "A Quick Refresher Course in Macroeconomics," *Journal of Economic Literature*, December 1990; James Tobin, *Asset Accumulation and Economic Activity*, 1980; *The End of Economic Man*, reviewed by E. Ray Canterbery in *Challenge*, Nov./Dec. 1995.

WHAT'S WRONG WITH NEOLIBERALISM?

THE MARX, KEYNES, AND POLANYI PROBLEMS

BY ROBERT POLLIN

During the years of the Clinton administration, the term "Washington Consensus" began circulating to designate the common policy positions of the U.S. administration along with the International Monetary Fund (IMF) and World Bank. These positions, implemented in the United States and abroad, included free trade, a smaller government share of the economy, and the deregulation of financial markets. This policy approach has also become widely known as *neoliberalism*, a term which draws upon the classical meaning of the word *liberalism*.

Classical liberalism is the political philosophy that embraces the virtues of free-market capitalism and the corresponding minimal role for government interventions, especially as regards measures to promote economic equality within capitalist societies. Thus, a classical liberal would favor minimal levels of government spending and taxation, and minimal levels of government regulation over the economy, including financial and labor markets. According to the classical liberal view, businesses should be free to operate as they wish, and to succeed or fail as such in a competitive marketplace. Meanwhile, consumers rather than government should be responsible for deciding which businesses produce goods and services that are of sufficient quality as well as reasonably priced. Businesses that provide overexpensive or low-quality products will then be out-competed in the marketplace regardless of the regulatory standards established by governments. Similarly, if businesses offer workers a wage below what the worker is worth, then a competitor firm will offer this worker a higher wage. The firm unwilling to offer fair wages would not survive over time in the competitive marketplace.

This same reasoning also carries over to the international level. Classical liberals favor free trade between countries rather than countries operating with tariffs or other barriers to the free flow of goods and services between countries. They argue that restrictions on the free movement of products and money between countries only protects uncompetitive firms from market competition, and thus holds back the economic development of countries that choose to erect such barriers.

Neoliberalism and the Washington Consensus are contemporary variants of this longstanding political and economic philosophy. The major difference between classical liberalism as a philosophy and contemporary neoliberalism

as a set of policy measures is with implementation. Washington Consensus policy makers are committed to free-market policies when they support the interests of big business, as, for example, with lowering regulations at the workplace. But these same policy makers become far less insistent on free-market principles when invoking such principles might damage big business interests. Federal Reserve and IMF interventions to bail out wealthy asset holders during the frequent global financial crises in the 1990s are obvious violations of free-market precepts.

Broadly speaking, the effects of neoliberalism in the less developed countries over the 1990s reflected the experience of the Clinton years in the United States. A high proportion of less developed countries were successful, just in the manner of the United States under Clinton, in reducing inflation and government budget deficits, and creating a more welcoming climate for foreign trade, multinational corporations, and financial market investors. At the same time, most of Latin America, Africa, and Asia—with China being the one major exception—experienced deepening problems of poverty and inequality in the 1990s, along with slower growth and frequent financial market crises, which in turn produced still more poverty and inequality.

If free-market capitalism is a powerful mechanism for creating wealth, why does a neoliberal policy approach, whether pursued by Clinton, Bush, or the IMF, produce severe difficulties in terms of inequality and financial instability, which in turn diminish the market mechanism's ability to even promote economic growth? It will be helpful to consider this in terms of three fundamental problems that result from a free-market system, which I term "the Marx Problem," "the Keynes problem," and "the Polanyi problem." Let us take these up in turn.

THE MARX PROBLEM

Does someone in your family have a job and, if so, how much does it pay? For the majority of the world's population, how one answers these two questions determines, more than anything else, what one's standard of living will be. But how is it decided whether a person has a job and what their pay will be? Getting down to the most immediate level of decision-making, this occurs through various types of bargaining in labor markets between workers and employers. Karl Marx argued that, in a free-market economy generally, workers have less power than employers in this bargaining process because workers cannot fall back on other means of staying alive if they fail to get hired into a job. Capitalists gain higher profits through having this relatively stronger bargaining position. But Marx also stressed that workers' bargaining power diminishes further when unemployment and underemployment are high, since that means that employed workers can be more readily replaced by what Marx called "the reserve army" of the unemployed outside the office, mine, or factory gates.

Neoliberalism has brought increasing integration of the world's labor markets through reducing barriers to international trade and investment by multinationals. For workers in high-wage countries such as the United States, this effectively means that the reserve army of workers willing to accept jobs at lower pay than U.S. workers expands to include workers in less developed countries. It isn't the case that businesses will always move to less developed countries or that domestically produced goods will necessarily be supplanted by imports from low-wage countries. The point is that U.S. workers face an increased *credible* threat that they can be supplanted. If everything else were to remain the same in the U.S. labor market, this would then mean that global integration would erode the bargaining power of U.S. workers and thus tend to bring lower wages.

But even if this is true for workers in the United States and other rich countries, shouldn't it also mean that workers in poor countries have greater job opportunities and better bargaining positions? In fact, there are areas where workers in poor countries are gaining enhanced job opportunities through international trade and multinational investments. But these gains are generally quite limited. This is because a long-term transition out of agriculture in poor countries continues to expand the reserve army of unemployed and underemployed workers in these countries as well. Moreover, when neoliberal governments in poor countries reduce their support for agriculture—through cuts in both tariffs on imported food products and subsidies for domestic farmers—this makes it more difficult for poor farmers to compete with multinational agribusiness firms. This is especially so when the rich countries maintain or increase their own agricultural supports, as has been done in the United States under Bush. In addition, much of the growth in the recently developed export-oriented manufacturing sectors of poor countries has failed to significantly increase jobs even in this sector. This is because the new export-oriented production sites frequently do not represent net additions to the country's total supply of manufacturing firms. They rather replace older firms that were focused on supplying goods to domestic markets. The net result is that the number of people looking for jobs in the developing countries grows faster than the employers seeking new workers. Here again, workers' bargaining power diminishes.

This does not mean that global integration of labor markets must necessarily bring weakened bargaining power

and lower wages for workers. But it does mean that unless some non-market forces in the economy, such as government regulations or effective labor unions, are able to counteract these market processes, workers will indeed continue to experience weakened bargaining strength and eroding living standards.

THE KEYNES PROBLEM

In a free-market economy, investment spending by businesses is the main driving force that produces economic growth, innovation, and jobs. But as John Maynard Keynes stressed, private investment decisions are also unavoidably risky ventures. Businesses have to put up money without knowing whether they will produce any profits in the future. As such, investment spending by business is likely to fluctuate far more than, say, decisions by households as to how much they will spend per week on groceries.

But investment fluctuations will also affect overall spending in the economy, including that of households. When investment spending declines, this means that businesses will hire fewer workers. Unemployment rises as a result, and this in turn will lead to cuts in household spending. Declines in business investment spending can therefore set off a vicious cycle: the investment decline leads to employment declines, then to cuts in household spending and corresponding increases in household financial problems, which then brings still more cuts in business investment and financial difficulties for the business sector. This is how capitalist economies produce mass unemployment, financial crises, and recessions.

Keynes also described a second major source of instability associated with private investment activity. Precisely because private investments are highly risky propositions, financial markets have evolved to make this risk more manageable for any given investor. Through financial markets, investors can sell off their investments if they need or want to, converting their office buildings, factories, and stock of machinery into cash much more readily than they could if they always had to find buyers on their own. But Keynes warned that when financial markets convert long-term assets into short-term commitments for investors, this also fosters a speculative mentality in the markets. What becomes central for investors is not whether a company's products will produce profits over a long term, but rather whether the short-term financial market investors *think* a company's fortunes will be strong enough in the present and immediate future to drive the stock price up. Or, to be more precise, what really matters for a speculative investor is not what they think about a given company's prospects per se, but rather what they think *other investors are thinking*, since that will be what determines where the stock price goes in the short term.

Because of this, the financial markets are highly susceptible to rumors, fads, and all sorts of deceptive accounting practices, since all of these can help drive the stock price up in the present, regardless of what they accomplish in the longer term. Thus, if U.S. stock traders are convinced that Alan Greenspan is a *maestro*, and if there is news that he is about to intervene with some kind of policy shift, then the rumor of Greenspan's policy shift can itself drive prices up, as the more nimble speculators try to keep one step ahead of the herd of Greenspan-philes.

Still, as with the Marx problem, it does not follow that the inherent instability of private investment and speculation in financial markets are uncontrollable, leading inevitably to persistent problems of mass unemployment and recession. But these social pathologies will become increasingly common through a neoliberal policy approach committed to minimizing government interventions to stabilize investment.

THE POLANYI PROBLEM

Karl Polanyi wrote his classic book *The Great Transformation* in the context of the 1930s depression, World War II, and the developing worldwide competition with Communist governments. He was also reflecting on the 1920s, dominated, as with our current epoch, by a free-market ethos. Polanyi wrote of the 1920s that "economic liberalism made a supreme bid to restore the self-regulation of the system by eliminating all interventionist policies which interfered with the freedom of markets."

Considering all of these experiences, Polanyi argued that for market economies to function with some modicum of fairness, they must be embedded in social norms and institutions that effectively promote broadly accepted notions of the common good. Otherwise, acquisitiveness and competition—the two driving forces of market economies—achieve overwhelming dominance as cultural forces, rendering life under capitalism a Hobbesian "war of all against all." This same idea is also central for Adam Smith. Smith showed how the invisible hand of self-interest and competition will yield higher levels of individual effort that increases the wealth of nations, but that it will also produce the corruption of our moral sentiments unless the market is itself governed at a fundamental level by norms of solidarity.

In the post-World War II period, various social democratic movements within the advanced capitalist economies adapted the Polanyi perspective. They argued in favor of government interventions to achieve three basic ends: stabilizing overall demand in the economy at a level that will provide for full employment; creating a financial market environment that is stable and conducive to the effective allocation of investment funds; and distributing equitably the rewards from high employment and a stable investment process. There were two basic means of achieving equitable distribution: relatively rapid wage growth, promoted by labor laws that were supportive of unions, minimum wage standards, and similar interventions in labor markets; and welfare state policies, including progressive taxation and redistributive programs such as Social Security. The political ascendancy of these ideas was the basis for a dramatic increase in the role of government in the post-World War II capitalist economies.

As one indicator of this, total government expenditures in the United States rose from 8% of GDP in 1913, to 21% in 1950, then to 38% by 1992. The International Monetary Fund and World Bank were also formed in the mid-1940s to advance such policy ideas throughout the world—that is, to implement policies virtually the opposite of those they presently favor. John Maynard Keynes himself was a leading intellectual force contributing to the initial design of the International Monetary Fund and World Bank.

FROM SOCIAL DEMOCRACY TO NEOLIBERALISM

But the implementation of a social democratic capitalism, guided by a commitment to full employment and the welfare state, did also face serious and persistent difficulties, and we need to recognize them as part of a consideration of the Marx, Keynes, and Polanyi problems. In particular, many sectors of business opposed efforts to sustain full employment because, following the logic of the Marx problem, full employment provides greater bargaining power for workers in labor markets, even if it also increases the economy's total production of goods and services. Greater worker bargaining power can also create inflationary pressures because businesses will try to absorb their higher wage costs by raising prices. In addition, market-inhibiting financial regulations limit the capacity of financial market players to diversify their risk and speculate.

Corporations in the United States and Western Europe were experiencing some combination of these problems associated with social democratic capitalism. In particular, they were faced with rising labor costs associated with low unemployment rates, which then led to either inflation, when corporations had the ability to pass on their higher labor costs to consumers, or to a squeeze on profits, when competitive pressures prevented corporations from raising their prices in response to the rising labor costs. These pressures were compounded by the two oil price "shocks" initiated by the Oil Producing Exporting Countries (OPEC)—an initial four-fold increase in the world price of oil in 1973, then a second four-fold price spike in 1979.

These were the conditions that by the end of the 1970s led to the decline of social democratic approaches to policy-making and the ascendancy of neoliberalism. The two leading signposts of this historic transition were the election in 1979 of Margaret Thatcher as Prime Minister of the United Kingdom and in 1980 of Ronald Reagan as the President of the United States. Indeed, it was at this point that Mrs. Thatcher made her famous pronouncement that "there is no alternative" to neoliberalism.

This brings us to the contemporary era of smaller government, fiscal stringency and deregulation, i.e., to neoliberalism under Clinton, Bush, and throughout the less-developed world. The issue is not a simple juxtaposition between either regulating or deregulating markets. Rather it is that markets have become deregulated to support the interests of business and financial markets, even as these same groups still benefit greatly from many forms of government support, including investment subsidies, tax concessions, and rescue operations when financial crises get out of hand. At the same time, the deregulation of markets that favors business and finance is correspondingly the most powerful regulatory mechanism limiting the demands of workers, in that deregulation has been congruent with the worldwide expansion of the reserve army of labor and the declining capacity of national governments to implement full-employment and macroeconomic policies. In other words, deregulation has exacerbated both the Marx and Keynes problems.

Given the ways in which neoliberalism worsens the Marx,

Keynes, and Polanyi problems, we should not be surprised by the wreckage that it has wrought since the late 1970s, when it became the ascendant policy model. Over the past generation, with neoliberals in the saddle almost everywhere in the world, the results have been straightforward: worsening inequality and poverty, along with slower economic growth and far more unstable financial markets. While Margaret Thatcher famously declared that "there is no alternative" to neoliberalism, there are in fact alternatives. The experience over the past generation demonstrates how important it is to develop them in the most workable and coherent ways possible.

ARTICLE 7.3   *February 2000, revised May 2001*

LIFE AFTER KEYNES

BY ELLEN FRANK

Current conventional wisdom has it that business cycles are obsolete; promarket policies have swept recessions into history's proverbial dustbin. The generation of policymakers nurtured on notions of government economic management after World War II is retiring or dying off, replaced by "new economy" enthusiasts like Bill Clinton, who famously declared in 1996 that "the age of big government is over."

But what happens if the economy slips?

The old-fashioned big-government programs that pulled the United States through many an economic downturn have, in the last decade, been mostly dismantled. Many presume that the government will pick its recession-fighting tactics up again, should the economy falter—priming the economic pump by cutting taxes and raising spending, as Reagan did in the 1980s and Bush in the 1991 recession. Indeed, Treasury Secretary Larry Summers defended the Clinton administration's plan to pay off the federal debt by contending that Clinton was merely "reloading the fiscal cannon": saving against the bad times when heavy federal spending and borrowing might really be needed.

But the tools of macroeconomic management are not so easily discarded and taken up again; not, at least, in the U.S. political environment. From the 1930s, efforts to push through programs to ameliorate recessions and relieve unemployment in this country have been fraught with controversy and fiercely contested.

During the 1930s President Franklin Roosevelt's "New Deal" attempted to implement the "Keynesian Revolution"—the programs proposed by British economist John Maynard Keynes to end depressions, such as public works programs financed through deficit spending. Roosevelt, to

be sure, pressed throughout the 1930s to expand federal jobs programs, but did not actually succeed until the Second World War. After the war, it took years of careful and deliberate effort to craft the political and intellectual infrastructure for continued Keynesian policy in the United States. That infrastructure is now largely gone. Putting it back together again will not be easy.

THE KEYNESIAN CONSENSUS

When Richard Nixon declared in 1972 that "we are all Keynesians now," it seemed that the consensus for active, government management of the economy in the manner of Keynes was unshakable. Just a few years after Nixon's speech, Congress passed the Humphrey-Hawkins Act which committed the federal government to use its virtually unlimited taxing and spending powers to avert economic downturns and promote full employment.

In fact, though, the Keynesian consensus was already shattering. In 1967, the influential American Economic Association elected arch-conservative and Keynesian nemesis Milton Friedman as its president. In 1969, the prestigious *American Economic Review* published a paper by Robert Lucas outlining the new theory of rational expectations which purported to "prove" that government macroeconomic policy was useless.

Keynes had taught that the cycle of economic boom and bust could be eliminated with judicious government spending to create demand for goods and workers. By running deficits, governments could fuel economic growth, borrowing idle funds (or printing new money) to pay the employees that private businesses put to work. Known as fiscal stabilization policy or expansionary macroeconomic policy, these tools proved highly effective in combating business cycles. Even those initially hostile to Keynesian ideas in the 1930s could not deny the evidence of World War II when, thanks to massive government spending, the U.S. economy went from deep depression to rapid boom virtually overnight.

But support forged during the war for federal involvement in taming the business cycle and creating full employment proved hard to sustain once the war ended. The American version of Keynesianism, though tepid and watered-down compared to European programs or to Keynes' own proposals, was sufficiently left-wing to galvanize unending hostility in the deeply conservative pro-business arena of U.S. politics. Continued government spending after the war faced determined opposition from businesses who decried swollen government budgets as "creeping socialism" and complained that government programs amounted to "unfair competition" with the private sector. In 1954, one radical economist pronounced Keynesianism in the United States "deader than the dodo."

THE CENTRAL INSIGHT OF KEYNESIAN THOUGHT WAS THAT REAL WEALTH LIES IN THE PEOPLE, RESOURCES, AND PRODUCTIVE APPARATUS OF A SOCIETY.

To be sure, business leaders supported the federal highway program, cold war military build-up of weapons, and the Korean and Vietnam wars. But they did not support the deficit financing of these ventures, nor did they back using federal programs as tools of macroeconomic management. By the early 1960s, even moderate gestures toward fiscal stabilization had become a hard sell in Congress. Keynesian economists worried openly about "implementation lags"—the yawning gap between the onset of a recession and the time it might take Congress to do something.

FULL-EMPLOYMENT BUDGETING

Throughout the 1960s and 1970s, coalitions of liberals and moderates tried to stem the backlash, quietly constructing a macroeconomic policy infrastructure that would weave some basic fiscal stabilization into the fabric of federal law. Under the Johnson and Nixon administrations, federal entitlement programs—Social Security, Medicaid, Medicare, Food Stamps, and the plethora of welfare programs—were enacted or vastly expanded. Economists called these automatic stabilizers, because, as enacted, eligible applicants could not be denied benefits for lack of funding. Thus government's mandated spending levels would rise and fall predictably with the unemployment rate. Entitlements legally committed the government to increase spending during economic downturns, regardless of, or despite, sentiment in Congress for Keynesian fiscal policies. Thus the government would automatically send money into the economy via these social programs during downturns.

These programs were neither massive nor generous—especially compared with their European counterparts—but taken together they provided a bedrock level of federal spending in lean years as well as a minimal guaranteed income to prevent wages from plummeting in a recession.

With the sole exception of Reagan's tax cut and military build-up in the early 1980s, automatic increases in entitlement spending have been the only significant source of fiscal stimulus in the United States since 1973. During the recession of 1991, for example, virtually all of the $47 billion increase in the federal deficit came about because of increased welfare and Social Security spending.

Furthermore, Keynesian-trained economists insisted that the budget deficits that resulted when recessions suddenly swelled welfare and Social Security rolls should not really count as deficits at all. In annual economic reports, the president's economic advisors carefully distinguished between a structural deficit—in which the government's budget was out of balance even with a booming economy—and a cyclical deficit—where the deficit soared unavoidably due to rising entitlements and falling tax collections. Full-employment budgeting—the position that balancing the federal budget should take a back seat to expanded financing of entitlements during a recession—sustained Keynesian fiscal policy even during the Reagan-Bush years.

THE END OF MACROECONOMIC POLICY

Though Reagan is credited with killing Keynesian economics, neither the Bush nor Reagan administrations were able to dismantle the policy apparatus inherited from the 1970s. Despite substantial cuts in the average benefit for many welfare programs, for example, total spending on entitlement programs rose throughout the 1980s, contributing (along with tax cuts and a military build-up) to the largest peacetime deficits ever run by the U.S. government. AFDC, Food Stamps, WIC and other programs, though perhaps stingier than before, enlarged their spending with each downward shift in the economy during the 1980s. Deficits ballooned and a Democratic House resisted major changes in entitlements.

Reagan's budget director, David Stockman, contended in 1984 that Reagan's huge deficits were a deliberate strategy to discredit Keynesian policy and part of a larger plan to undermine Congressional support for further expansions of federal spending. While this may well have been Reagan's intention, Keynesian economics was not finished, politically, until Bill Clinton's watch.

Upon attaining a legislative majority in 1994, conservatives in Congress singlemindedly set about dismantling the key legislative vestiges of Keynesian economic policy in the United States. Welfare reform, their most important victory, is instructive. When the Personal Responsibility Act passed in 1996, much was made of the five-year lifetime limit on welfare benefits, the work requirements, and so forth. Rarely noted was the fact that the legislation transformed the fiscal nature of most federal welfare programs. Welfare benefits are no longer an entitlement. Annual spending levels are now capped and will not rise with the unemployment rate unless Congress specifically allocates new funds. It was this provision of the legislation that led official Peter Edelman to resign from the Department of Health and Human Services in protest when Clinton signed the legislation.

The Food Stamp and Medicaid programs remain entitlements in theory, still available to all comers. But in enacting the 1996 reforms, Congress turned responsibility for managing these programs over to local officials who have been known to turn away applicants not already receiving welfare. Meanwhile, conservatives lobby intensely to privatize and effectively dismantle Social Security—the largest of all federal entitlement programs—though so far without success.

Republican leadership had hoped to bury Keynesian stabilization policy altogether by passing a constitutional amendment requiring an annually balanced federal budget, which would put an end once and for all to full-employment budgeting. The amendment failed by one vote to pass the Senate, but conservatives scored a partial victory with the Balanced Budget Agreement of 1997, committing Congress and the administration to balance the budget each year for the next decade, regardless of the state of the economy. Whether the agreement survives an economic downturn remains to be seen, but the strident antideficit rhetoric of the last decade will certainly make stabilization policies a tough, if not an impossible, sell.

Under Clinton, the outlook for macroeconomic policy grew bleak indeed. Clinton attributed the economic boom to tough spending caps and fiscal restraint and made a fetish of further fiscal austerity. White House press releases conceived the future exclusively in terms, not simply of budgetary balance, but of burgeoning surpluses and massive debt repayment. Rather than fight recessions or expand jobs programs, $3.5 trillion of tax revenue would buy back federal bonds from financial institutions. Clinton's millennial State of the Union address laid out the goal of Clintonomics: "Make America debt-free for the first time since 1835." Candidate Al Gore assured voters that he planned to reduce the debt "even if the economy slows." Sounding uncannily like the ghost of Herbert Hoover or Calvin Coolidge, Gore maintained that a recession would provide "an opportunity" to cut government spending "just like a corporation has to cut expenses if revenues fall." When Bill Bradley floated a modest proposal to use surplus funds for health care, Gore attacked the idea as "fiscally irresponsible," and warned it might plunge the U.S. economy in recession. Hillary Clinton, running for the Senate from New York, declared that most problems facing the country "cannot be solved by government" and staunchly supported running budget surpluses to pay off the national debt. When Democrats are hawking debt reduction and warning that deficits cause recessions, Keynesian policy has truly drawn its last gasp.

It is no good thinking these statements can be unsaid, conveniently forgotten when the next recession revives talk of an active, proemployment government. The political programs that buttressed American Keynesianism are gone. The intellectual backing and public rhetoric that sustained Keynesian ideas no longer exist or are dwarfed by the editorial pages of the *Wall Street Journal*. College economics textbooks, through which hundreds of thousands of voters and policymakers learn the rudiments of macroeconomics, barely bother with Keynes these days—or with recessions for that matter. The hottest new text by Gregory Mankiw (for which Prentice-Hall paid an unprecedented $1.4 million advance) does not even mention economic downturns until a few pages at the very end.

LIFE AFTER KEYNES

So what if the "new economy" turns out to be the same old economy? The last U.S. recession officially ended in 1991. In the eight years since, GDP has grown steadily and unemployment rates have fallen. If this is just the start of an endless millennial boom, there is no reason to worry. But what if the United States is on the brink of a Y2K recession? This is not the first time in history that Americans have lived through a prolonged boom—the economy grew for eight years straight in the 1960s—but it is the first time since the Depression that politicians and policymakers have rested their hopes so utterly on the boom's continuing.

Many on the left, of course, do not mourn Keynes' passing. Keynes, after all, despised the British Labor party and proudly proclaimed his allegiance to "the educated bourgeoisie." Socialists have long argued that Keynesian programs were meant not to help workers or humanize the economy, but to placate and defuse a potentially powerful workers' movements awakened by the Depression. Environmentalists too criticize Keynesian thinking for its mindless worship of economic growth, its predilection to solve all economic problems with more production, more work, more growth, more stuff.

But Keynes' understanding of capitalist economies was, nevertheless, profoundly radical. Any effort to construct a new kind of economic policy in the future will need to build on and attend to his fundamental insights. Keynes understood that the matters of debt and budget deficits, of interest payments and paper wealth that so obsess private business people and financial interests are, ultimately, irrelevant to all but the wealthy elite. The central insight of Keynesian thought was that real wealth lies in the people, resources, and productive apparatus of a society and that citizens can, through the collective power of government, harness those resources for internal development.

In the early years of the New Deal, government jobs programs funded public art works, community theaters, oral history projects, and the creation of hiking trails in national forests—programs that would warm the hearts of environmentalists and radicals alike. The government disbanded the efforts in the face of business opposition. In the end, Americans got a timid version of Keynesianism, complete with probusiness tilt and antigovernment bias, that flexed the collective muscle of government weakly indeed and only at the federal level. The most U.S. Keynesians managed to accomplish was to secure a minimal living standard for the very poor and very old, and to provide a fair number of makeshift defense jobs for the otherwise unemployed.

Should the boom prove not to be eternal, it is inevitable that many voices will call to reestablish the dismantled and discredited programs of postwar American Keynesianism. It will be wasted breath. The real challenge for the new millennium will be to forge a post-Keynesian economic policy. This will entail thinking about how citizens can harness their collective power to produce more leisure rather than more jobs, more equity rather than more income, more conservation rather than more production, more satisfaction rather than more consumption, more quality rather than more quantity.

OPENING PANDORA'S BOX
THE BASICS OF MARXIST ECONOMICS

BY ALEJANDRO REUSS

In most universities, what is taught as "economics" is a particular brand of orthodox economic theory. The hallmark of this school is a belief in the optimal efficiency (and, it goes without saying, the equity) of "free markets."

The orthodox macroeconomists—who had denied the possibility of general economic slumps—were thrown for a loop by the Great Depression of the 1930s, and by the challenge to their system of thought by John Maynard Keynes and others. Even so, the orthodox system retains at its heart a view of capitalist society in which individuals, each equal to all others, undertake mutually beneficial transactions tending to a socially optimal equilibrium. There is no power and no conflict. The model is a perfectly bloodless abstraction, without all the clash and clamor of real life.

KARL MARX AND THE CRITIQUE OF CAPITALIST SOCIETY

One way to pry open and criticize the orthodox model of economics is by returning to the idiosyncrasies of the real world. That's the approach of most of the articles in this book, which describe real-world phenomena that the orthodox model ignores or excludes. These efforts may explain particular facts better than the orthodoxy, while not necessarily offering an alternative general system of analysis. They punch holes in the orthodox lines but, ultimately, leave the orthodox model in possession of the field.

This suggests the need for a different conceptual system that can supplant orthodox economics as a whole. Starting in the 1850s and continuing until his death in 1883, the German philosopher and revolutionary Karl Marx dedicated himself to developing a conceptual system for explaining the workings of capitalism. The system which Marx developed

and which bears his name emerged from his criticism of the classical political economy developed by Adam Smith and David Ricardo. While Marx admired Smith and Ricardo, and borrowed many of their concepts, he approached economics (or "political economy") from a very different standpoint. He had developed a powerful criticism of capitalist society before undertaking his study of the economy. This criticism was inspired by French socialist ideas and focused on the oppression of the working class. Marx argued that wage workers—those working for a paycheck—were "free" only in the sense that they were not beholden to a single lord or master, as serfs had been under feudalism. But they did not own property, nor were they craftspeople working for themselves, so they were compelled to sell themselves for a wage to one capitalist or another. Having surrendered their freedom to the employer's authority, they were forced to work in the way the employer told them while the latter pocketed the profit produced by their labor.

Marx believed, however, that by creating this oppressed and exploited class of workers, capitalism was creating the seeds of its own destruction. Conflict between the workers and the owners was an essential part of capitalism. But in Marx's view of history, the workers could eventually overthrow the capitalist class, just as the capitalist class, or "bourgeoisie," had grown strong under feudalism, only to supplant the feudal aristocracy. The workers, however, would not simply substitute a new form of private property and class exploitation, as the bourgeoisie had done. Rather, they would bring about the organization of production on a cooperative basis, and an end to the domination of one class over another.

This line of thinking was strongly influenced by the ideas of the day in German philosophy, which held that any new order grows in the womb of the old, and eventually bursts forth to replace it. Marx believed that the creation of the working class, or proletariat, in the heart of capitalism was one of the system's main contradictions. Marx studied capitalist economics in order to explain the conditions under which it would be possible for the proletariat to overthrow capitalism and create a classless society. The orthodox view depicts capitalism as tending towards equilibrium (without dynamism or crises), serving everyone's best interests, and lasting forever. Marx saw capitalism as crisis-ridden, full of conflict, operating to the advantage of some but not others, and far from eternal.

CLASS AND EXPLOITATION

Marx studied history closely. Looked at historically, he saw capitalism as only the latest in a succession of societies based on exploitation. When people are only able to produce the bare minimum needed to live, he wrote, there is no room for a class of people to take a portion of society's production without contributing to it. But as soon as productivity exceeds this subsistence level, it becomes possible for a class of people who do not contribute to production to live by appropriating the surplus for themselves. These are the masters in slave societies, the lords in feudal societies, and the property owners in capitalist society.

Marx believed that the owners of businesses and property—the capitalists—take part of the wealth produced by the workers, but that this appropriation is hidden by the appearance of an equal exchange, or "a fair day's work for a fair day's pay."

Those who live from the ownership of property—businesses, stocks, land, etc—were then a small minority and now are less than 5% of the population in countries like the United States (Marx wrote before the rise of massive corporations and bureaucracies, and did not classify managers and administrators who don't own their own businesses as part of the bourgeoisie.) The exploited class, meanwhile, is the vast majority who lived by earning a wage or salary—not just the "blue collar" or industrial workers but other workers as well.

Marx's view of how exploitation happened in capitalist society depended on an idea, which he borrowed from Smith and Ricardo, called the Labor Theory of Value. The premise of this theory, which is neither easily proved nor easily rejected, is that labor alone creates the value which is embodied in commodities and which creates profit for owners who sell the goods. The workers do not receive the full value created by their labor and so they are exploited.

Students are likely to hear in economics classes that profits are a reward for the "abstinence" or "risk" of a businessperson—implying that profits are their just desserts. Marx would argue that profits are a reward obtained through the exercise of power—the power owners have over those who own little but their ability to work and so must sell this ability for a wage. That power, and the tribute it allows owners of capital to extract from workers, is no more legitimate in Marx's analysis than the power of a slaveowner over a slave.

A slaveowner may exhibit thrift and take risks, after all, but is the wealth of the slaveowner the just reward for these virtues, or a pure and simple theft from the slave?

As Joan Robinson, an important 20th-century critic and admirer of Marx, argues, "What is important is that owning capital is not a productive activity. The academic economists, by treating capital as productive, used to insinuate the suggestion that capitalists deserve well by society and are fully justified in drawing income from their property."

THE FALLING RATE OF PROFIT

Marx believed that his theory had major implications for the crises that engulf capitalist economies. In Marx's system, the value of the raw materials and machinery used in the manufacture of a product does not create the extra value that allows the businessman to profit from its production. That additional value is created by labor alone.

Marx recognized that owners could directly extract more value out of workers in three ways: cutting their wages, lengthening their working day, or increasing the intensity of their labor. This need not be done by a direct assault on the workers. Capitalists can achieve the same goal by employing more easily exploited groups or by moving their operations where labor is not as powerful. Both of these trends can be seen in capitalism today, and can be understood as part of capital's intrinsic thirst for more value and increased exploitation.

With the mechanization of large-scale production under capitalism, machines and other inanimate elements of production form a larger and larger share of the inputs to production. Marx believed this would result in a long-term trend of the rate of profit to fall as less of production depended on the enriching contribution of human labor. This, he believed, would make capitalism increasingly vulnerable to economic crises.

MARX'S DISCUSSIONS OF CAPITALISM'S IRRESISTIBLE EXPANSIVE IMPULSE SEEM AS APT TODAY AS THEY DID 150 YEARS AGO.

This chain of reasoning, of course, depends on the Labor Theory of Value (seeing workers as the source of the surplus value created in the production process) and can be avoided by rejecting this theory outright. Orthodox economics has not only rejected the Labor Theory of Value, but abandoned the issue of "value" altogether. After lying fallow for many years, value analysis was revived during the 1960s by a number of unorthodox economists including the Italian economist Piero Sraffa. Marx was not the last word on the subject.

UNEMPLOYMENT, PART I:
THE "RESERVE ARMY OF THE UNEMPLOYED"

Marx is often raked over the coals for arguing that workers, under capitalism, were destined to be ground into ever more desperate poverty. That living standards improved in rich capitalist countries is offered as proof that his system is fatally flawed. While Marx was not optimistic about the prospect of workers raising their standard of living very far under capitalism, he was critical of proponents of the "iron law of wages," such as Malthus, who held that any increase in wages above the minimum necessary for survival would simply provoke population growth and a decline in wages back to subsistence level.

> AS AESTHETICALLY APPEALING AS THE CLOCKWORK HARMONY OF THE ORTHODOX MODEL MAY BE, THIS IS PRECISELY ITS FAILING.

Marx emphasized that political and historical factors influencing the relative power of the major social classes, rather than simple demographics, determined the distribution of income.

One economic factor to which Marx attributed great importance in the class struggle was the size of the "reserve army of the unemployed." Marx identified unemployment as the major factor pushing wages down—the larger the "reserve" of unemployed workers clamoring for jobs, the greater the downward pressure on wages. This was an influence, Marx believed, that the workers would never be able to fully escape under capitalism. If the workers' bargaining power rose enough to raise wages and eat into profits, he argued, capitalists would merely substitute labor-saving technology for living labor, recreating the "reserve army" and reasserting the downward pressure on wages.

Though this has not, perhaps, retarded long-term wage growth to the degree that Marx expected, his basic analysis was visionary at a time when the Malthusian (population) theory of wages was the prevailing view. Anyone reading the business press these days—which is constantly worrying that workers might gain some bargaining power in a "tight" (low unemployment) labor market, and that their wage demands will provoke inflation—will recognize its basic insight.

UNEMPLOYMENT, PART II: THE CRISIS OF OVERPRODUCTION

Marx never developed one definitive version of his theory of economic crises (recessions) under capitalism. Nonetheless, his thinking on this issue is some of his most visionary. Marx was the first major economic thinker to break with the orthodoxy of "Say's Law." Named after the French philosopher Jean-Baptiste Say, this theory held that each industry generated income equal to the output it created. In other words, "supply creates its own demand." Say's conclusion, in which he was followed by Smith, Ricardo, and orthodox economists up through the Great Depression, was that while a particular industry such as the car industry could overproduce, no generalized overproduction was possible. In this respect, orthodox economics flew in the face of all the evidence. In his analysis of overproduction, Marx focused on what he considered the basic contradiction of capitalism—and, in microcosm, of the commodity itself—the contradiction between "use value" and "exchange value." The idea is that a commodity both satisfies a specific need (it has "use value") and can be exchanged for other articles (it has "exchange value"). This distinction was not invented by Marx; it can be found in the work of Smith. Unlike Smith, however, Marx emphasized the way exchange value—what something is worth in the market—overwhelms the use value of a commodity. Unless a commodity can be sold, the portion of society's useful labor embodied in it is wasted (and the product is useless to those in need). Vast real needs remain unsatisfied for the majority of people, doubly so when—during crises of overproduction—vast quantities of goods remain unsold because there is not enough "effective demand."

It is during these crises that capitalism's unlimited drive to develop society's productive capacity clashes most sharply with the constraints it places on the real incomes of the majority to buy the goods they need. Marx developed this notion of a demand crisis over 75 years before the so-called "Keynesian revolution" in economic thought (whose key insights were actually developed before Keynes by the Polish economist Michal Kalecki on the foundations of Marx's analysis).

Marx expected that these crises of overproduction and demand would worsen as capitalism developed, and that the crises would slow down more and more the development of society's productive capacities (what Marx called the "forces of production"). Ultimately, he believed, these crises would be capitalism's undoing. He also pointed to them as evidence of the basic depravity of capitalism. "In these crises," Marx writes in the *Communist Manifesto*,

> there breaks out an epidemic that, in all earlier epochs would have seemed an absurdity, the epidemic of overproduction. Society suddenly finds itself put back into a state of momentary barbarism; it appears as if a famine, a universal war of devastation had cut off the supply of every means of subsistence; industry and commerce seem to be destroyed; and why? Because there is too much civilization, too much means of subsistence, too much industry, too much commerce ...
>
> And how does the bourgeoisie get over these crises? On the one hand by enforced destruction of productive force; on the other hand, by the conquest of new markets, and by the more thorough exploitation of old ones.

This kind of crisis came so close to bringing down capitalism during the Great Depression that preventing them became a central aim of government policy. While government intervention has managed to smooth out the business cycle, especially in the wealthiest countries, capitalism has hardly become crisis-free.

While the reigning complacency about a new, crisis-free capitalism is much easier to sustain here than in, say, East

Asia, capitalism clearly has not yet run up against any absolute barrier to its development. In fact, Marx's discussions (in the *Communist Manifesto* and elsewhere) of capitalism's irresistible expansive impulse—capital breaking down all barriers, expanding into every crevice, always "thirsting for surplus value" and new fields of exploitation—seem as apt today as they did 150 years ago.

MARX AS PROPHET

Marx got a great deal about capitalism just right—its incessant, shark-like forward movement; its internal chaos, bursting forth periodically in crisis; its concentration of economic power in ever fewer hands. Judged on these core insights, the Marxist system can easily stand toe-to-toe with the orthodox model. Which comes closer to reality? The capitalism that incessantly bursts forth over new horizons, or the one that constantly gravitates towards comfortable equilibrium? The one where crisis is impossible, or the one that lurches from boom to bust to boom again? The one where perfect competition reigns, or the one where a handful of giants towers over every industry?

In all these respects, Marx's system captures the thundering dynamics of capitalism much better than the orthodox system does. As aesthetically appealing as the clockwork harmony of the orthodox model may be, this is precisely its

failing. Capitalism is anything but harmonious.

There was also a lot that Marx, like any other complex thinker, predicted incorrectly, or did not foresee. In this respect, he was not a prophet. His work should be read critically, and not, as it has been by some, as divine revelation. Marx, rather, was the prophet of a radical approach to reality. In an age when the "free market" rides high, and its apologists claim smugly that "there is no alternative," Joan Robinson's praise of Marx is apt: "[T]he nightmare quality of Marx's thought gives it … an air of greater reality than the gentle complacency of the orthodox academics. Yet he, at the same time, is more encouraging than they, for he releases hope as well as terror from Pandora's box, while they preach only the gloomy doctrine that all is for the best in the best of all *possible* worlds."

Resources: Joan Robinson, *An Essay on Marxian Economics* (Macmillan, 1952); "Manifesto of the Community Party," and "Crisis Theory (from Theories of Surplus Value)," in Robert C. Tucker, ed., *The Marx-Engels Reader* (W.W. Norton, 1978); Roman Rosdolsky, *The Making of Marx's 'Capital'* (Pluto Press, 1989); Ernest Mandel, "Karl Heinrich Marx"; Luigi L. Pasinetti, "Joan Violet Robinson"; and John Eatwell and Carlo Panico, "Piero Sraffa"; in John Eatwell, Murray Milgate, and Peter Newman, eds., *The New Palgrave: A Dictionary of Economics* (Macmillan, 1987).

ARTICLE 7.5

September/October 2002

UNDER THE MARGINS
FEMINIST ECONOMISTS LOOK AT GENDER AND POVERTY

BY RANDY ALBELDA

For all the hype about welfare-to-work, most former welfare recipients are still living in poverty. It is true that, since the advent of 1990s-style "welfare reform," families no longer on welfare are earning more, on average, than those still on welfare. But more often than not, the jobs that former welfare mothers find don't provide employer-sponsored health insurance, vacation time, sick leave, or wages sufficient to support their families. In fact, the percentage of families who are "desperately" poor (with incomes at or below 50% of the official poverty line) has gone up since the mid-1990s, and so has the percentage of former welfare recipients who report hardships such as difficulty feeding their families or paying bills. And remember: All of this occurred during a so-called economic boom.

So why does the emphasis on work (and now marriage) continue to dominate the welfare debate? In large part, this

is because the poverty "story" of the last 20 years—created and perpetuated by conservative ideologues and politicians—blames poor people for their own poverty. Women supposedly have too many children without husbands, poor black urban dwellers exhibit pathological behaviors, and liberal welfare policies—by expanding government spending and providing an attractive alternative to jobs and marriage—have made matters worse.

At least one group of theorists—feminist economists—says it isn't so. It is women's particular economic role in capitalism—as caregiver—that shapes their relationship to the labor market, men, and the state. Feminist economists have shown how having and caring for children affects the economic status of women—including women who are not mothers but are still relegated to poorly paid care-giving jobs. While their voices are largely ignored in research and policy circles, feminist economists' analyses provide the best understanding of the obstacles low-income families face and the range of policy options that might work.

WOMEN AND POVERTY

Almost everywhere, women are the majority of poor adults. Recently, a group of sociologists from several U.S. universities looked at poverty in eight industrialized nations. Using a relative poverty measure (half of median family income), they found that, in the 1990s, women's poverty rates exceeded men's in all countries but Sweden. Further, they found that single-mother poverty rates—even in countries with deep social welfare systems—are exceptionally high. (See Figure 1.)

In the United States in 2000, women comprised just over half of the adult population but constituted 61% of all poor adults. (The U.S. poverty income threshold is based on an absolute dollar figure determined in the 1960s and since indexed for inflation.) Toss in children, and the data are even grimmer; 16.2% of all children were poor, while over one-third of all single-mother families were poor. Together, women and children comprised 76% of the poor in the United States, far surpassing their 62% representation in the population as a whole.

Since the late 1950s (when the data were first collected), single-mother families in the United States have never constituted more than 13% of all families; however, they form just under half of all poor families. Figure 2 depicts the proportion of all families—and all poor families—that are single-mother families. The steepest increase occurred in the late 1960s on the heels of the War on Poverty, as poverty rates for everyone were falling.

ECONOMIC THEORY AND POVERTY

From Adam Smith onward, most economists have understood poverty by looking at labor markets, labor-market inequality, and economic growth. According to this approach, it is underemployment or the lack of employment—and the resulting lack of income—that causes poverty. A brief summary of the dominant economic theories in the last half of the 20th century illustrates the point.

Keynesian economic theory argues that the lack of demand in the economy as a whole leads to unemployment. When investors and consumers can't jumpstart the economy, we need fiscal or monetary economic stimuli to induce demand. It was this wisdom that has guided economists to promote economic growth as a way to reduce poverty, arguing that "a rising tide lifts all boats"—as, for example, during the Kennedy and Johnson administrations.

Marxian theorists say that, under capitalism, unemployment cannot be totally eliminated because it is a necessary component of capitalist production that serves to "discipline" workers. Unless we make radical changes to the economic system, there will always be families that are without employment and therefore poor.

Like Marxian economists, *institutional* economists also believe that economic outcomes aren't simply the result of pure market forces; cultural, social, and political forces also come into play. In the 1970s, economists Peter Doeringer and Michael Piore identified distinct labor-market segments. Younger workers, workers of color, and women tend to end up in what they call the "secondary labor market"—characterized by low wages, few promotional opportunities, and easy-to-acquire skills—more than other workers. These workers are particularly vulnerable to unemployment and hence more likely to be poor. The way to relieve poverty is to help these workers move into better jobs, or to create policies that make their jobs better.

These understandings of poverty offer little or no gender analysis—presumably what ails men is equally applicable to women. Analyses of insufficient (aggregate) demand, unemployment, and labor-market inequality rarely mention women or discuss how and why gender matters—unless feminist scholars provide them.

Neoclassical (mainstream) economists also argue that poverty is caused by lack of employment and low wages—but they consider workers responsible for their own wage levels. Workers who choose not to pursue edu-

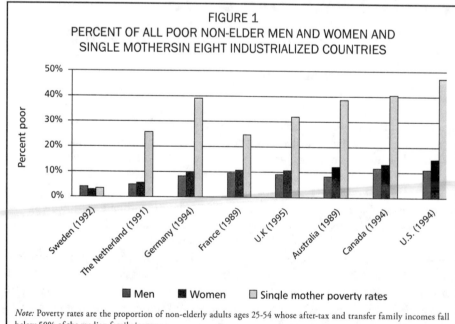

FIGURE 1
PERCENT OF ALL POOR NON-ELDER MEN AND WOMEN AND SINGLE MOTHERSIN EIGHT INDUSTRIALIZED COUNTRIES

■ Men ■ Women ☐ Single mother poverty rates

Note: Poverty rates are the proportion of non-elderly adults ages 25-54 whose after-tax and transfer family incomes fall below 50% of the median family income.

Source: Table 1, in Karen Christopher et al., "Gender Inequality in Poverty in Affluent Nations: The Role of Single Motherhood and the State," in Karen Vleminckx and Timothy Smeeding, eds., *Child Well-Being, Child Poverty and Child Policy in Modern Nations* (London: Policy Press, 2001).

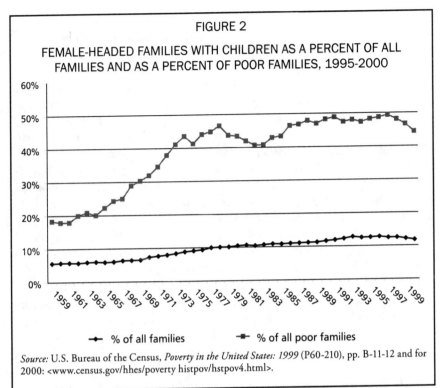

FIGURE 2

FEMALE-HEADED FAMILIES WITH CHILDREN AS A PERCENT OF ALL FAMILIES AND AS A PERCENT OF POOR FAMILIES, 1995-2000

→ % of all families   ■ % of all poor families

Source: U.S. Bureau of the Census, *Poverty in the United States: 1999* (P60-210), pp. B-11-12 and for 2000: <www.census.gov/hhes/poverty histpov/hstpov4.html>.

cation, training, or on-the-job experience will participate in the labor force less often than more highly trained and skilled workers, be less productive, and receive lower wages. Unlike the political economy theorists just discussed, many non-feminist economists—the most well known being Nobel Prize winner Gary Becker—have tackled the topic of women's lower wages. But they consistently conclude that women's lack of employment, or employment at low wages, results from rational individual choice. Only policies that boost incentives for individuals to invest in themselves (like tax credits for education) will alleviate poverty.

GENDER MATTERS

It is true that one reason women are poor is that they are not in the labor force or are underemployed. But while employment is an important underpinning to understanding poverty, it is not the same for women as for men.

Most economists who study labor markets assume that workers in capitalist economies are "unencumbered"—that they don't have significant constraints on their time outside of paid work. Encumbered workers are treated as a "special case"—worthy of examination, but understood and analyzed as an exception rather than the rule.

Since the beginnings of capitalism, however, female workers have almost always been "encumbered." And women's role as caregivers—their main encumbrance—has shaped their participation in the economy, as feminist historians and economic historians have shown. Historically, women's economic opportunities have been severely constricted, with race, age, and marital status sending important market "signals" about where women could or should be employed. For

example, until the 1960s, many professional and some clerical jobs had "marriage bars," i.e., employers refused to hire married women on the assumption that they did not need the salaries these jobs paid, and would not stick around once they had children. Similarly, before anti-discrimination laws were enacted, many workers of color could not get jobs as managers in many professions, or even as sales clerks if the business catered to a white clientele.

For more than a century, this labor market "ordering" has given rise to employment, income, and wage policies that reinforce and reproduce women's political and economic dependence on men (and non-whites' inferior status in relation to whites). These policies assume that the standard family is a heterosexual married couple with a lone male breadwinner employed in industrial production. For example, in order to collect unemployment insurance benefits, workers must work a minimum number of hours and receive a minimum amount of earnings. Because many women work part-time and earn low wages, they are much less likely to qualify for benefits than men. Similarly, Social Security benefits are based on previous earnings over a sustained period of employment. Women who have spent most of their adult lives as caregivers are thus ineligible for benefits on their own, and must rely on their husbands' contributions instead.

Men's and women's employment patterns are very different. Women's labor force participation rates are lower than men's, and women's employment experiences in economic downturns often differ from men's. Women's job options and choices are also highly influenced by care-giving responsibilities; mothers are more likely than fathers to trade higher-paying jobs for jobs that are closer to childcare, have more flexible schedules, or require fewer hours.

In addition to shaping women's paid labor-market activities, care work has been economically, socially, and politically undervalued, as feminist economists point out. This is true both when that work is done in the home for free and when others do it for low pay. Among the few jobs immigrant women and women of color can almost always find are low-paying care-work jobs, and they are disproportionately represented in those jobs. For example, in 2001, women were 47% of all workers but 97% of child care workers, 93% of registered nurses, 90% of health aides, and 72% of social workers. Black workers comprised 11% of the workforce but were 33% of health aides, 23% of licensed practical nurses, and 20% of cleaning service workers. This type of occupational "stereotyping" reinforces the care-giving roles that women and people of color fill, and the low pay (relative to jobs with similar skill requirements) reinforces women's dependence on men and racial inequality. Economist Nancy Folbre, in her 2001 book *The Invisible Heart: Economics and Family Values*, calls this the "care penalty."

It is because of their low-paid and unpaid care work, then, that women are particularly economically vulnerable and much more likely to be poor than are men. The role of care giving—as distinct from other factors like employment, economic growth, and labor-market inequality—helps to explain not only women's employment patterns but also women's poverty. So theories of poverty that rely on analyses of employment that assume all people are men—or that women are a special case of men—are not only incomplete, they are wrong.

FEMINIST ANALYSES OF POVERTY

It is no coincidence that, when there has been a viable women's movement—in the early part of the 20th century and in the late 1960s—feminists and women researchers have paid particular attention to poor women.

Documenting poor families: early efforts

In the early 20th century, there was a good deal of concern about how women fit into the capitalist economy. Social scientists living in or near poor communities—often in settlement houses established by women reformers—conducted surveys of women workers, mostly through government-sponsored research. Many of the surveys found that the biggest problems faced by two-parent families were a lack of employment and insufficient wages. Researchers readily recognized that families headed by women were constrained by women's role as caregiver and women's low wages. Instead of advocating more employment for women, they promoted relatively meager levels of public assistance.

In the 1910s and 1920s, women reformers were key players not only in doing research but also in creating policies directed toward poor women and children. These women imposed white middle-class values about child-rearing, hygiene, and education; their construction of "deservingness" replicated and reinforced the ways in which women and men, immigrants and non-immigrants, were supposed to act. At the same time, they successfully implemented income supplement programs for single-mother families at the state level, and they were instrumental in incorporating AFDC (Aid to Families with Dependent Children) into the Social Security Act of 1935. Feminist poverty researchers and reformers did not emerge again until the late 1960s.

Sisterhood may be powerful, but motherhood is not: recent efforts

The women's movement of the late 1960s and 1970s laid some important foundations for understanding women's poverty, even though its main economic strategies were aimed at improving the wages of women who were employed. Feminists fought for affirmative action, which was most successful in creating opportunities for college-educated women. Today, women hold 46% of executive and professional jobs—exactly their representation in all jobs—and comprise just under 30% of all doctors and lawyers. Feminists also organized for comparable worth, which was intended to lift wages for low-income women by recognizing and rewarding the skill level and effort needed to perform low-paying women's jobs (including care-giving ones).

At the same time, feminist scholars called attention to women's "double day" (now called "work/family conflict") and theorized about the role of care work and reproduction in capitalist economies. From the outset, feminist analysts understood that "housework" was work and a vital component of capitalist production. This intellectual work paralleled "wages for housework" campaigns that were launched in Italy, Canada, Great Britain, and the United States.

Using these tools to reinterpret poverty was not hard. Among the first to apply a feminist analysis to women's poverty was sociologist Diana Pearce, in an 1978 article entitled "The Feminization of Poverty: Women, Work, and Welfare." Pearce called attention to the fact that women were disproportionately represented among the poor. Her phrase—"the feminization of poverty"—became very popular in feminist circles as well as in the mainstream press.

Economist Nancy Folbre followed up with a theoretical framework directly linking women's care work as mothers to their poverty. In her 1985 article, "The Pauperization of Motherhood: Patriarchy and Social Policy in the U.S.," she argued that, when the costs of raising children are shifted onto women, women (and children) become dependent on men. Then, when fathers abandon their families, women and children are consigned to poverty. Folbre also argues that public policies around divorce, child support, unemployment insurance, and welfare reinforce this relationship. For example, welfare policies—even before the 1990s reforms—never provided enough income for women to support their families without working "under the table" or getting unreported income, paying a big price for not being married.

Single mothers especially bear the burden of these policies in the form of incredibly high poverty rates. But, Folbre points out, the benefits of care labor—healthy, productive children who become tax-paying adults—are enjoyed by all of society, not merely the mothers who provided the care. If society recognized the value of women's care work and compensated them for it, then fewer women would be poor.

Current trends

Currently, some feminist scholars are addressing the ways that gender influences government allocation of income supports (like pensions, unemployment insurance, and welfare) and non-cash assistance (e.g., education and child care). Sociologist Ann Orloff and political scientists Diane Sainsbury and Jane Lewis argue that state welfare policies (construed broadly) embody deeply gendered notions of citizenship and need. Much of this work is theoretical and does not explicitly address poverty. However, it helps to explain the lack of policies that would correct women's poverty.

Other researchers are focusing on how people's capacity—access to health and education, living conditions, how they are treated in a society—affects their potential to generate income and causes poverty. Building on the work of economist Amartya Sen, feminist economists in the United States have shown that it is unreasonable and unlikely to expect single mothers to "work" their way out of poverty—because women earn lower wages than men, because they have care-giving responsibilities, and because the additional costs associated with caring for children restrict their capacity to be employed even while family needs remain high. For example, Barbara Bergmann and Trudi Renwick developed budgets for low-income families in the 1990s. Chris Tilly and I have demonstrated that the income needs of single-mother families far exceed their earnings possibilities—even with full-time employment. This work refutes the claims of liberals who supported welfare reform in the naïve belief that welfare recipients could easily substitute earnings for public assistance.

Finally, feminist economists are documenting how low-income women—especially single-mother families in which the same adult is both caregiver and breadwinner—relate to the labor market, fathers, and the state. Using longitudinal data, feminist social scientists Roberta Spalter-Roth and Heidi Hartmann found that many poor single-mother families either combine government assistance with wages (under or above the table) or cycle between the two. This research is confirmed and extended by feminist sociologists like Kathryn Edin and Laura Lein, who, through extensive interviews with poor single mothers, documented the particular ways and times that poorly paying jobs as well as men and their incomes drift in and out of women's lives. These studies make it clear that women's employment is not family-sustaining, and that, to survive, single-mother families need a sane combination of earnings, child support, *and* government assistance. In contrast to the narrowly focused, incentive-based literature that characterizes poor women's behavior as pathological, these approaches demonstrate that poor women's lives are dynamic yet fragile, and that the decisions they make are creative, adaptive, and almost always child-centered.

WHO CARES?

Despite their efforts, feminist scholars have not had much impact on the poverty literature—at least not in economics—nor have they influenced policies intended to alleviate poverty. Much (though not all) poverty research is grant-funded, and it tends to focus narrowly on evaluating the individual impact of welfare reform, mostly by looking at welfare "leavers." These factors discourage the use of feminist analysis, since most funding goes either to conservative think tanks with a specific ideological aversion to feminism

or to "liberal" think tanks that have made their fortunes in mainstream analysis fitted to their main consumer—the federal government.

Further, these conventional studies often preclude the larger political economy approach taken by feminists. Welfare reform is a mechanism of social control over poor single women—especially women of color—that is part of a larger conservative agenda to justify if not exacerbate economic inequality, assure a large pool of low-wage labor, and silence important political movements. Feminist analysis suggests the need for policies that would not only reduce poverty but also change women's (and people of color's) relationship to the labor market, (white) men, and the state, thus loosening the grip of economic dependence. This isn't in line with the right-wing agenda at all.

However, feminist economic analysis has been very useful to activists who are trying to help poor women. For example, in the mid-1990s, Wider Opportunity for Women (WOW), a feminist group based in Washington, D.C., started conducting family economic self-sufficiency standard projects. Currently, WOW operates projects in 40 states and D.C. The studies demonstrate how much income a single-mother family needs to survive, and are being used as organizing tools in the states.

During the mid-1990s welfare reform debates and now in discussions about reauthorization of Temporary Assistance for Needy Families (TANF), feminist scholars—connected informally through the "Women's Committee of 100"—have argued that raising children is work and that responsible legislation should recognize unpaid work as work. The Committee has called for a caregiver's allowances (see "Wages for Housework," article 1.5, and <www. welfare2002.org>). And while Congress has not embraced these ideas, a TANF reauthorization bill sponsored by Representative Patsy Mink (D-Hawaii) in the spring of 2002 garnered support from close to 90 members of the House.

Feminist economists argue that the role of economists is to understand how societies do or do not provide for people's needs. Through their research and skills, they provide the tools for activists to argue that women's employment status and care-giving responsibilities place many at the bottom of the economic pecking order. At the same time, feminist economists are connecting their work directly to social movements, lending their expertise—and their own voices—to living wage campaigns, efforts to improve compensation for child care workers and home health aides, and efforts to eliminate poverty, not welfare.

Resources: Kathryn Edin and Laura Lein, *Making Ends Meet: How Single Mothers Survive Welfare and Low Wage Work* (Russell Sage Foundation, 1997); Nancy Folbre, "The Pauperization of Motherhood: Patriarchy and Social Policy in the U.S.," *Review of Radical Political Economics*, vol. 16, no. 4 (1984): 72-88; Nancy Folbre, *The Invisible Heart: Economics and Family Values* (New York: The New Press, 2001); Jane Lewis, "Gender and the Development of Welfare Regimes," *Journal of European Social Policy* 3 (1992): 159-73; Alice

O'Connor, *Poverty Knowledge: Social Science, Social Policy, and the Poor in Twentieth Century U.S. History* (Princeton, N.J.: Princeton University Press, 2001); Ann Orloff, "Gender and the Social Rights of Citizenship: The Comparative Analysis of Gender Relations and Welfare States," *American Sociological Review* 58 (1993): 303-28; Diana Pearce, "The Feminization of Poverty: Women, Work, and Welfare," *Urban and Social Change Review* (February 1978); Trudi Renwick and Barbara Bergmann, "A Budget-based Definition of Poverty with an Application to Single-parent Families," *Journal of Human Resources* 28, no. 1 (1993): 1-24; Diane Sainsbury, *Gender, Equality, and Welfare States* (Cambridge: Cambridge University Press, 1996); Amartya K. Sen, *Development as Freedom* (New York: Alfred A. Knopf, 1999); Roberta SpalterRoth et al., *Welfare That Works: The Working Lives of AFDC Recipients* (Washington, D.C.: Institute for Women's Policy Research, 1995); Chris Tilly and Randy Albelda, "Family Structure and Family Earnings: The Determinants of Earnings Differences among Family Types," *Industrial Relations* 33, no. 2 (1994): 151-167; U.S. Census, *Current Population Surveys* <www.census. gov/hhes/income/histinc/histpovtb.html>; Bureau of Labor Statistics, *Employment and Earnings*, Table 11 <*www.bls.gov/ cps/home.htm#charemp.§§*>

March/April 2005

MARXIAN CLASS ANALYSIS AND ECONOMICS

BY RICHARD WOLFF

Class analysis predates economics. Long before modern economics emerged, ancient Greek thinkers, for example, analyzed their society by *classifying* people into groups by wealth. They viewed understanding the relationships between classes as crucial to improving their society and debated whether wealth should be distributed equally. While class analysis has a long history, no single definition of class has prevailed. Alongside *property* definitions (rich and poor), social theorists have used definitions based on the *power* that various groups wielded and have debated whether power is or should be distributed unequally (to elites, to kings, and so on) or equally (in various versions of democracy).

For Adam Smith and David Ricardo, originators of modern economics, class analysis was central. Here is how Ricardo opened his *Principles of Political Economy and Taxation* (1817): "The produce of the earth ... is divided among three classes of the community ...". He defined these classes as owners of the land, owners of capital (machines, tools, etc.), and owners of labor power who do the work. He continued, "To determine the laws which regulate this distribution is the principal problem in Political Economy." Like many thinkers before and since, Ricardo believed that understanding a society required identifying its main classes and recognizing the nature of their interdependence and conflicts. Class and class differences were the core concerns of economics at the discipline's founding.

Why then do today's dominant economic theories—the neoclassical and Keynesian economics traditions—ignore class analysis? They do that in reaction to what Marx did with class analysis after Ricardo. Building on but also differing from Smith and Ricardo, Marx took class analysis in new directions. He also linked his new class analysis to a fundamental critique of capitalism; Smith and Ricardo had used their class analyses to celebrate capitalism.

Marx was a radical who criticized his society's unequal distributions of property and power. Like other social critics, he favored collective ownership of property, egalitarian income distribution, and democracy as basic component of social justice. Marx inherited the ancient concept of classes based on property. He made use of Smith's and Ricardo's economics because he valued their class analyses. He also appreciated the power definition of class. But Marx believed that the received definitions of class were inadequate. He developed a new class analysis to equip mass movements for social justice with new insights and strategies for constructing just, egalitarian and democratic societies.

In his new class analysis, Marx defined class not in terms of wealth, income, or power, but rather in terms of the *surplus*. He argued that in all societies, a portion of the people applied brain and muscle to produce a quantity of goods that *exceeded* what they themselves consumed plus what went to replenish the raw materials and equipment used up in the production process. That excess he called a surplus. Societies differed in how they organized this surplus: who produced it, who got it, and what they did with it.

By focusing on the surplus, Marx had changed the very meaning of class. In his work, it referred less and less to groups of *people* (the rich, the poor, labor, management, the rulers, the powerless, and so on). Instead, it increasingly referred to the economic *processes* of producing, appropriating, and distributing the surplus that occur in every society. A "class structure" came to mean a particular set of these processes. Because the dominant class structure in Marx's time was capitalist, it was the particular capitalist processes of surplus production, appropriation, and distribution that he analyzed.

Capitalism is still dominant, and Marx's analysis still applies. Here is a capsule summary. Capitalists promise workers wages in return for producing an output which the capitalists own, immediately and entirely. The capitalists sell the output in markets and pocket the revenues. One portion of capitalists' revenues provides workers their promised wages, which workers then use to buy back *from* the capitalists a portion of what they had produced *for* the capitalists. After paying wages and replenishing materials used up in production, the remaining revenues comprise the capitalists' surplus. The workers produce the surplus; the capitalists appropriate it.

As Marx stressed, capitalism resembles feudalism and slavery in this organization of the surplus. Slaves produced more than they got back from their slave masters; feudal serfs kept part of their product for themselves and delivered the rest—the surplus—as rents to feudal lords. Whenever workers produce a surplus *that other people get,* Marx labeled that "exploitation." Thus, in his scheme, the transitions from slavery and feudalism that established capitalism had not freed workers from exploitation.

Marx's surplus-based concept of class turned out to be a powerful analytical tool that those in the Marxist tradition have used to make sense of a wide range of political and economic questions. One fruitful area of research has focused on how changes in economic, political, and cultural conditions affect the size of the surplus pumped out of the workers, how workers and capitalists struggle over that size, and how the supplies, demands, and prices of goods and services in the market reflect and affect those class struggles. For example, falling food and clothing prices make it easier for capitalists to lower the money wages they pay and thereby extract more surplus from workers. To take another example, if political and cultural developments encourage workers' class consciousness to grow—if they come to understand surplus and exploitation—they may reduce the surplus they deliver to capitalists or even demand the right to appropriate the surplus themselves.

Marxian analysis also follows the surplus after the capitalists appropriate it. Competition among capitalists and their struggles with workers impose demands on the surplus. Thus, for example, capitalists distribute some of the surplus to pay supervisors to squeeze more surplus from workers. Capitalists distribute another portion of the surplus to attorneys to fend off lawsuits, another portion to pay managers who buy new machines to overcome competitors, and so on.

Class-analytical economics distinguishes workers who *produce* the surplus ("productive workers") from those who *provide the conditions* that capitalists need to keep appropriating it ("unproductive workers" such as supervisors, lawyers, and managers). Since productive workers create the surplus that capitalists then distribute to unproductive workers, these two groups relate differently to class processes even though members of both are wage-earners. Thus, Marxian economists can ask and answer questions about class differences among different groups of workers that other economists, lacking an analysis of class in surplus terms, cannot ask let alone answer.

Marxian economics also explores interactions among class processes. How surpluses get produced and appropriated shapes how those surpluses are then distributed and vice versa. For example, intensified exploitation (e.g., speed-ups, closer supervision, or cuts in paid time off) produces stress that often requires capitalists to devote more of the surplus for programs like counseling that help workers cope with alcoholism, absenteeism, and so on. Similarly, when capitalists distribute more of the surplus to buy new machines, that usually changes the number of workers hired, the intensity of their labor, and the resulting rate of their exploitation. Class analysis further shows how commodity prices, enterprise profits, and individual incomes depend on and influence class processes. For example, when workers succeed in raising their wages at the expense of capitalists' surpluses, capitalists often respond by automation, outsourcing to cheaper workers abroad, layoffs, or still other strategies that change individual incomes, corporate profits, prices, and government tax revenues both at home and abroad.

Those in the Marxist tradition also study the interactions among politics, culture, and capitalist class processes. For example, capitalists spend part of their surpluses on campaign contributions and lobbyists to shape government policies in the interests of exploiting more surplus from their workers, of beating out their capitalist competitors, and so on. Needless to say, such distributions out of the surplus have a heavy impact on politics in capitalist societies. Another example: When Wal-Mart recently found its surpluses hurt by employees' class action suits over discrimination and unfair labor practices, it decided to distribute more of its huge surpluses to "media expenditures." In plain English, this money aims to influence what TV programs we see, how newspapers shape stories, what messages films emphasize, and so forth. Beyond Wal-Mart's image, these distributions of the surplus help to shape the larger culture and thereby the development of the societies whose media Wal-Mart intends to "engage."

Marxian economists recognize that capitalism often yields rising output and consumption levels. But their analyses typically underscore the contradictions and injustices of capitalism's uneven distributions of its costs and benefits and demonstrate how the economic problems of capitalism, including unemployment, waste of natural and human resources, and cyclical instability, emerge in part from the system's particular class structure.

An analysis of class in terms of surplus has also allowed thinkers in the Marxian tradition to develop an economics of post-capitalism. A post-capitalist economy begins when revolutionary economic change brings about an end to exploitation, not merely changes in its form. Then, the workers who produce the surplus will also be the people who appropriate and distribute that surplus. In a sense, productive workers become their own board of directors; they collectively appropriate their own surpluses within enterprises. Imagine that Monday through Thursday, the workers produce output. Fridays they perform three very different activities collectively: return a portion of their output to themselves as individual wages, replenish the used-up means of production, and devote what remains—the surplus—to maintain this new class structure. Such a nonexploitative class structure is what Marxian class analysis means by *communism*. Of course, a nonexploitative class structure is no automatic utopia; it will have its distinctive economic, political, and cultural problems, but they will differ from those of capitalism.

Marxian economists argue about how class processes interact with other economic, political, and cultural processes to shape the evolution of capitalist societies. They differ as well in their analyses of nonexploitative class structures—past, present, and future. Generations of these debates have yielded a complex, sophisticated, and diverse Marxian class analytical economics that offers distinctive understandings of capitalism and the communist alternative.

Yet Marxian class analysis is now largely excluded from books, newspapers, classrooms, and most people's consciousness by the neoclassical and Keynesian economics orthodoxies. Instead of welcoming debate among alternative kinds of economics, most orthodox economists endorse the silencing of alternatives generally and Marxian class analysis in particular. Neither neoclassical nor Keynesian economics argues about the production, appropriation, and distribution of surpluses. They simply deny that surpluses or class processes exist. Students mostly study neoclassical or Keynesian models of how economies work. Practical economists apply the models to statistics and statistics to the models. The public hears their conclusions not as results of one kind of (class-blind) economics but rather as *the* truth of economic science, applicable always and everywhere.

Nonetheless, Marxian class analyses thrive despite their exclusion from the mainstream. Capitalism's problems plus the struggles and oppositions they provoke continue to generate critics. Many find capitalism's inequalities of wealth, income, and power unacceptable. Some find their way to Marxian class analyses focused on the social organization of the surplus as a key to the insights and strategies needed to take societies beyond capitalism.

CHAPTER 8
INTERNATIONAL TRADE AND FINANCE

INTRODUCTION

When it comes to the global economy, most textbooks line up behind the "Washington Consensus"—a package of free trade and financial liberalization policies that the U.S. Treasury Department, the International Monetary Fund (IMF), and the World Bank have spun into the prevailing prescriptions for the world's developing economies. Mainstream textbook discussions of exchange rates, international trade, and economic development policies almost always promote a market-dictated integration into the world economy. Outside the classroom, however, popular discontent with the Washington Consensus has spawned a worldwide movement calling into question the myth of self-regulating markets on which these policies rest.

While the doctrines of free trade and financial liberalization are seldom questioned in mainstream economics textbooks, both are scrutinized here. Arthur MacEwan gives an overview of the process of globalization today, what is new and what continues long-established patterns, and the difficulties opposition groups face coming to grips with the power and the complexity of these forces (Article 8.1). MacEwan's second article shows how industrialized economies developed by protecting their own manufacturing sectors—never preaching the "gospel of free trade" until they were highly developed. Today, he argues, these countries prescribe free trade not because it's the best way for others to develop, but because it gives U.S. corporations free access to the world's markets and resources, which in turn strengthens the power of business against workers (Article 8.2). Keith Yearman and Amy Gluckman explore the perils of trade liberalization by looking closely at the effects of the expiration of the 30-year-old Multifiber Agreement which will likely cost the jobs of millions of garment workers across the global economy (Article 8.3). In another article, MacEwan explains the ins and outs of the trade deficit and the threat it poses for the U.S. economy (Article 8.4). Economist Thomas Palley argues that even China, with the fastest growing economy in the world and one of the chief beneficiaries of the expiration of the Multifiber Agreement, will eventually have to turn away from a policy of export-led growth to one led by meeting domestic demand (Article 8.8).

John Miller debunks the Economic Freedom Index that the Heritage Foundation and other backers of neoliberal globalization use to argue that economic freedom and prosperity go hand-in-hand. Miller argues that the Index measures neither freedom nor prosperity, but rather corporate and entrepreneurial freedom from accountability (Article 8.5). Miller then follows up with an analysis of the imperial financial policies that lie behind the unprecedented current

account deficit and the decline of the dollar, and examines the worries that both pose for the U.S. and global economies (Article 8.6).

Other articles look at the institutions of the global economy. Deborah James explains why the December 2006 meeting of the World Trade Organization (WTO) in Hong Kong had little chance of overcoming the obstacles that had stalled earlier meetings: First World leaders demanding that developing countries lower tariffs and other barriers to trade and open up their economies to multinational corporations, while at the same time refusing to give up their agricultural subsidies. As James documents, these obstacles have led the United States and the European Union to direct an increasing number of the WTO's major decision-making to its General Council Meetings in Geneva, where the big powers have more sway (Article 8.7). Aldo Caliari argues that the Central American Free Trade Agreement (CAFTA), modeled after NAFTA and another step toward a Free Trade Area of the Americas, will hobble the ability of national governments to confront economic crises, build political coalitions, and properly compensate their public employees (Article 8.8).

We close the chapter with a debate about fair trade and farm subsidies (Article 8.12). Gawain Kripke, a senior policy analyst at Oxfam America, argues that fairer trade rules would provide enormous benefits to the world's poorest people. Dean Baker and Mark Weisbrot, co-directors of the Center for Economic and Policy Research, maintain that while ending agricultural subsidies for wealthy nations

---

KEY TO COLANDER
E = Economics   M = Macroeconomics

The articles in this chapter are linked to chapters E32-33 and E21, or M16-M18, which take up macroeconomic policies in developing countries and international policy issues.

Articles 8.7-8.12 fit with chapters E32-33 and E21, or M16-M18. They take a critical look at the most powerful institutions of the global economy, such as the World Trade Organization, the World Bank, and the IMF, the devastating impact their policies have had on the developing world, and what would constitute genuine reform of the global economy.

Articles 8.1-8.4 take on the advocacy of trade liberalization found in most economics textbooks, and should be read with E21 and E33, or M17-M18.

Articles 8.5 and 8.6 delve into the U.S. trade deficit and its impact on the global economy They go with E33 and E34 or M17 and M18.

would make them less hypocritical, it wouldn't do much to help the developing world.

DISCUSSION QUESTIONS

1) (Article 8.1) According to MacEwan, what aspects of today's globalization are new and what continues earlier trends? How might opposition forces best push for a more democratic and equitable globalization process?

2) (Article 8.2) MacEwan claims that the "infant industry" argument for trade protection is much more widely applicable than standard theory suggests. To what countries and industries might it apply in today's world economy? Explain your answer.

3) (Article 8.2) Free trade, MacEwan argues, gives business greater power relative to labor. Why is this so? Is it a good reason to oppose free trade?

4) (Article 8.3) What are the likely effects of the expiration of the Multifiber Agreement on garment workers in the developing world? How will expiration of the Agreement affect First World workers and investors?

5) (Article 8.4) What is a current account deficit and what causes it? When does a current account deficit become a problem?

6) (Article 8.5) According to Miller, how does the Economic Freedom Index misrepresent the relationship between economic freedom, on the one hand, and prosperity and economic growth, on the other hand? What do you think is the actual relationship between these factors?

7) (Article 8.6) What economic and political forces enable the United States to run an unprecedented current account deficit that is now the equivalent of 1% of the world's GDP? Which of the three prospects for the U.S. economy that Miller outlines at the close of his article—a dollar crisis, a long slow decline in the value of the dollar, or a dollar propped up through repeated interest rate hikes—do you think is most likely (or do you a different scenario is more likely)?

8) (Article 8.7) According to James, what are the chief conflicts between developing countries and developed countries that were brought up at the Hong Kong meeting of the WTO?

9) (Article 8.8) Why does Caliari think that CAFTA is a bad deal for Central America?

10) (Article 8.9) Why does Palley think that China, which has been an export-led growth success story, will have to shift to a domestic-led growth strategy?

11) (Article 8.10) The anti-sweatshop movement demands that certain companies (such as colleges selling insignia clothing) see that the goods they sell are manufactured subject to certain labor standards. Explain what this movement is trying to do in terms of consumer sovereignty and solving information problems. When some economists say that the movement is about back-door trade protectionism, what do they mean? Do you agree with them?

12) (Article 8.12) Who do you find more convincing in the debate about fair trade, Kripke or Baker and Weisbrot? Do you think fairer trade rules pay off for poor countries? If not, what policies would do a better job of improving the lot of poor people in the developing world?

WHAT IS GLOBALIZATION?

BY ARTHUR MacEWAN

Ever since Adam and Eve left the garden, people have been expanding the geographic realm of their economic, political, social and cultural contacts. In this sense of extending connections to other peoples around the world, globalization is nothing new. Also, as a process of change that can embody both great opportunities for wealth and progress and great trauma and suffering, globalization at the beginning of the 21st century is following a well established historical path. Yet the current period of change in the international system does have its own distinctive features, not the least important of which is the particular sort of political conflict it is generating.[1]

"GREATEST EVENTS" AND "DREADFUL MISFORTUNES"

We are fond of viewing our own period as one in which great transformations are taking place, and it is easy to recite a list of technological and social changes that have dramatically altered the way we live and the way we connect to peoples elsewhere in the world. Yet, other surges of globalization in the modern era have been similarly disruptive to established practices. The first surge by which we might mark the beginning of modern globalization came with the invasion of the Western Hemisphere by European powers and with their extension of ocean trade around Africa to Asia. Adam Smith, writing *The Wealth of Nations* in 1776, did not miss the significance of these developments:

The discovery of America, and that of a passage to the East Indies by the Cape of Good Hope, are the two greatest and most important events recorded in the history of mankind... By uniting, in some measure, the most distant parts of the world, by enabling them to relieve one another's wants, to increase one another's enjoyments, and to encourage one another's industry, their general tendency would seem to be beneficial.

Alongside of what Adam Smith saw as the great gains of globalization (not his term!), were the slaughter, by battle and disease, of millions of Native Americans, the enslave- ment and associated deaths of millions of Africans, and the subjugation of peoples in Asia. Smith did recognize the "dreadful misfortunes" that fell upon the peoples of the East and West Indies as a result of these "greatest events" (though he does not mention Africans in this expression of concern). He saw these misfortunes, however, as arising "rather from accident than from any thing in the nature of the events themselves."

The first stage of modern globalization illustrates not only the combined great gains and "dreadful misfortunes" that have characterized globalization but also the vast scope of the process. The political and economic changes that fol- lowed from the European conquest of the Americas and for- ays into Asia are relatively well known. Equally momentous were the huge cultural transformations that were tied to the great expansion of economic contacts among the continents. Peoples moved, or they were moved by force. As they came to new locations and in contact with other peoples, almost every aspect of their lives was altered—from what people eat ("Ital- ian" spaghetti with tomato sauce comes from Asia, the spa- ghetti, and America, the tomatoes) to their music (jazz is now the best known example, blending the backgrounds of dif- ferent continents to emerge in America) to religion (the cross accompanied the sword in the era of colonial conquest).

The second great surge of modern globalization came in the 19th century, both as product and cause of the Industrial Revolution. On the one hand, the expansion of industry gen- erated large reductions in transport costs that brought huge increases in international commerce. On the other hand, for the emerging commercial centers of Europe and North America, the opening of foreign markets and access to for- eign sources of raw materials fueled (sometimes literally) the expansion of industry. Great Britain, as the "workshop of the world," was at the center of these changes and over the course of the century saw its foreign trade increase three times as rapidly as national income.

Britain during the 19th century provided a foreshadow- ing of current-day globalization as it officially touted "free

---

[1] We usually measure "the extent of economic connections" by levels of imports and exports relative to total production or by the level of international invest- ment relative to total production. For example, in 1913, US exports were 6% as large as Gross Domestic Product (GDP); the figure had fallen to 4.6% in 1950, but was up to 7.1% in 1973 and 10.6% in 1999. For Europe, the figures are: 22% in 1913, 16.7% in 1950, 21.8% in 1973, and 32.1% in 1999. Interestingly, Japan, for which exports were 20% of GDP in 1913, saw this figure remain relatively stable at around 10% of GDP in the latter half of the 20th century. Fig- ures on foreign investment are harder to come by for the early part of the 20th century, but they seem to show a similar pattern. In recent years, the foreign investment figures show strong increases of economic connections. In the 1985-90 period, for the world as a whole, foreign direct investment (i.e., not including financial investments) were 5.4% of the level of GDP in the countries making the investments and 6.0% of GDP in the countries receiving the investments; in the 1996-98 period, the figures had risen to 8.2% and 8.4%, respectively.

trade" as the proper mode of organization for commerce—not just for itself, but for the entire world. The gospel of "free trade" was then carried around the globe by the British navy, and heroic ideological gymnastics allowed a growing colonial empire to be included under this same rubric. As the British historian E. J. Hobsbawm has commented, "British industry could grow up, by and large, in a protected home market until strong enough to demand free entry into other people's markets, that is 'Free Trade'." In today's globalization it is the United States, a country that also attained its economic power on the foundation of protectionism, that preaches the gospel of "free trade" to the rest of the world.

Current day globalization is, by and large, a continuation of the process that began in the 19th century (which in turn had its roots in the great transformation that began along with the 16th century). Two world wars and the Great Depression disrupted the progress of globalization for some sixty years and shifted its center from Britain to the United States, but it is now back on track. By the 1980s, the extent of economic connections that had been established among the world's national economies by 1913 had been reattained, and in subsequent years international trade and investment have continued to expand their roles in the economies of most nations.

HOMOGENIZATION AND COMPETITION

Change in the world economy today, however, is not simply an extension of what went on in earlier periods, not simply a quantitative extension of well established trends. What distinguishes the current era from earlier phases of globalization is that now capitalism is ubiquitous. Virtually everywhere, production takes place for profit and is based on wage labor. In the 19th century, capitalism may have provided the leading dynamic of the international economy, but in many parts of the world—most everywhere outside of Europe and North America—a great deal of economic activity was organized through families (peasant farms or shops), under semi-feudal conditions, or through slavery. These activities were all connected to markets and to a world capitalist system, but they were not capitalist in themselves. Certainly there are important aspects of life and work today which take place outside of markets and are not directly capitalist—for example, work in the home, interactions within governments, volunteer activity, and some other forms of production. Yet capitalism holds sway, dominating and defining economic relationships in almost all parts of the world.

The ubiquity of capitalism gives a new character to the economic connections among peoples in distant parts of the world. There has, in particular, been a grand homogenization, both of consumer markets and of production activity. Wal-Mart and McDonald's establish themselves in Mexico to sell the same sorts of products in the same way as in the United States. At the same time, Mexican workers at the Ford plant in Hermosillo produce the same cars that are produced in US factories and they do so with equipment and procedures that are among the most "modern" in the world. Also on the production side, plants in Mexico and the United States are sometimes integrated with one another in a "global assembly line," with Mexican workers engaged in the labor intensive aspects of the operation and US workers engaged in the more highly skilled activities; for example, in clothing production, design and cutting is done in the United States while the pieces are stitched together on the Mexican side of the border.

Mexico, because of its proximity to the United States and the reduction of trade restrictions between the two countries, presents an extreme example of the cross-border integration of production. Yet in broad terms, we are presented today with a new international organization of production, as people on different corners of the globe produce the same sorts of products with the same technologies and often for the same employers—though the ultimate employers often operate through local subcontractors.

The homogenization of the world economy creates a new set of relationships, a direct competition, among workers in different parts of the world. Although such competition always existed, it is much more extensive and intense than in the past and, most important, it takes place between workers whose wages are dramatically different from each other. It is one thing when US and Canadian workers, who have very similar wages and standards of living, are in competition with each other. It is quite another thing when the US and Canadian workers are in competition with Mexican workers.

This new relationship among workers in different countries presents obvious problems for the workers in the rich countries: they simply cannot compete with workers who, using the same equipment and methods of production (i.e., the same technology), are paid far, far lower wages. Yet similar, though perhaps less obvious, problems exist for the low-wage workers as well. With wage labor markets existing throughout most of the world, virtually all workers are placed in competition with one another. While workers in Bangladesh may be willing to accept very low wages to assemble clothing for the European market, they are always faced with the prospect that Vietnamese workers may accept even lower wages. Or Indonesian workers, who assemble sports shoes for the US market, may face the prospect of production innovations that will substitute machinery and skilled workers for unskilled workers on an assembly line, making it profitable for the firms to move their production back to the United States.

In a capitalist world, where many different sites around the world provide firms with the labor markets they need, those firms can have a great advantage over workers. That advantage, however, depends upon "free trade," the elimination of government barriers to the movement of goods and funds across national boundaries. Free trade has given firms the option of either moving themselves or moving their sources of supply in response to cost differences (wage differences, but also other cost differences). Free trade, however, does not include the reduction—let alone the elimination—of barriers to the movement of workers. So labor does not enjoy the same freedom in the globalized economy as does capital. Since "freedom" means having alternatives, and having alternatives means having power, a system that enhances the freedom of firms relative to the freedom of labor means giving businesses more power relative to labor. (Even were barriers to migration to be reduced, there are still substantial costs to labor movement compared to capital movement; and capital's advantage, while reduced, would not be eliminated.)

The drive for free trade existed, as pointed out above, in the British-led globalization of the 19th century, but the United States has been able to push the concept to a whole new level. In part, free trade is important for the power it confers on business, but it is also important as ideology. The ideology of free trade has provided the defining rationale for the North American Free Trade Agreement (NAFTA), the Free Trade Agreement of the Americas (FTAA), the World Trade Organization (WTO), and the programs pushed on low income countries by the International Monetary Fund (IMF) and the World Bank. The opening of markets, the opening of sources of supply, the spread of private economic activity—all of this is supposed to provide a new era of rapid economic growth for the world and serve the needs of the poor as well as the rich.

NOT SO FAST

The concept of free trade has a certain intuitive appeal. After all, if the firms and people of a nation are free to buy their supplies from the lowest-cost source of supply, then they will be able to buy more and satisfy their needs more thoroughly than if their government limits the sources from which they can buy those supplies (bans imports) or imposes extra costs (tariffs) on supplies from abroad. For low income countries, desperate for economic growth, it would seem absurd for their governments to place restrictions on imports, forcing firms and people to waste resources on expensive domestic goods. Moreover, it only takes a moment's reflection to note the huge gains we attain from international commerce: not only the banana I eat for breakfast and a good portion of the oil that fuels my car and heats my home, but also the ideas and culture from elsewhere in the world—to say nothing of the competitive pressures from abroad that help drive economic advances in my own country. For a small country, the gains from foreign commerce are a virtual necessity.

Another moment's reflection, however, reveals that things are not so simple. Free trade is not the only way to engage extensively in international commerce. In fact, none of the countries we now denote as "developed" attained their development through free trade, though all engaged extensively in international commerce. There are, it seems, some substantial advantages to having the production of certain kinds of goods take place within a country, as compared to obtaining those same goods from abroad. The US textile industry in the 19th century, the US auto industry through most of the 20th

century, the Japanese computer industry in the mid-20th century, the South Korean steel and ship building industries later in the 20th century—all generated broad economic gains in terms of the transformation of technology and the formation of a skilled work force that far surpassed the costs that arose from the government protection they received in their early stages of expansion. None of this provides a justification for protectionism in general; continuing protection of sugar and steel production in the United States imposes costs with no off-setting benefits (except to those directly engaged in the industries). Yet the experience of two centuries of capitalist development does demonstrate the fallacy of the free trade argument. Efforts by the US government to push free trade on low income countries today may make sense from the perspective of the interests of US firms, but it is hardly a prescription for economic advancement in low income countries.

But there is more. Globalization as it is being organized under the banner of free trade is doing nothing to reduce the "development gap," the huge difference in material well-being between the peoples of the rich nations and the peoples of most of the rest of the world. In fact, there is some evidence that under the regime of increasingly open world markets, the "development gap" is increasing. Worse yet: there is a good deal of evidence that free trade globalization is contributing to increasing inequality within nations, not only within the low income countries of the "South" but also within the United States and the other high income countries of the "North."

As the international economy is increasingly organized in a way that enhances the power of firms and tends to undermine the power of labor, it is certainly likely that greater inequality would be the outcome. Unfortunately, available data do not allow us to draw strong conclusions about what has been happening to world income inequality in recent decades. What we do know is that income distribution in today's world is already grossly unequal, with hundreds of millions of people living at the edge of subsistence, while the elites in all countries live in obscene luxury. We also know that, although some low income countries have made substantial gains (South Korea and some other countries of East Asia), the current surge of globalization has provided no general relief for the world's poor. Furthermore, we know that globalization—new patterns of international trade and investment—has disrupted people's lives, pushed people out of their traditional lines of work, shifted the location of economic activity, and forced people to adopt new patterns of consumption. All of this makes many people's lives very unpleasant, regardless of what can be uncovered with the aggregate statistics regarding income distribution and economic growth.

WHAT ELSE IS NEW?

One might well absorb this summary of change in the world economy and respond with the comment: So, what else is new? It does seem that periods of great change in the world economy, whatever immediate benefits they may generate for the elite and whatever their long run benefits for society in general, are accompanied by severe disruptions, hardships and inequalities. Current day experience seems to fit well with the pattern established in the 16th and 19th centuries, to say nothing of earlier eras of imperial expansion. (Many commentators quite reasonably reject the term "globalization" in favor of "imperialism" precisely because the latter term underscores the great inequalities of power and income that are always so important in international affairs.)

Yet perhaps there is something new in the current era in the particular type of political response to globalization that has been generated in recent years. The "dreadful misfortunes" of earlier eras have also generated political responses—sometimes in the form of spontaneous rebellion, sometimes as more organized resistance and revolution, and sometimes as waves of new oppositional organizations and alliances. The political response to globalization at the beginning of the 21st century, however, has some distinguishing characteristics that are worth emphasizing.

Most important, parts of the response to globalization are themselves global. The coming out "party" for the anti-globalization movement in Seattle in the fall of 1999 involved people and organizations from all over the world. As a coordinated effort by groups from many rich countries and many poor countries, the action in Seattle—and the ones that have followed in Washington, Quebec, Prague, Puerto Allegre, and elsewhere—suggest something is different about the nature of political action. Many times, opposition movements based on national identities have, at least implicitly, been in conflict with one another; at other times, organizations in rich countries have opted to "support" groups in poor countries, but not as a joint and coordinated effort. While progressive movements have always talked about their internationalism, this time around the talk may translate more effectively into practice.

Also, the globalization of political opposition to globalization has included steps by labor unions, which have long adhered to highly nationalist positions. So far, more of the new internationalism of the US labor movement has been in the realm of rhetoric rather than practice, but US unions have made some important efforts at cross border organizing—in the form, for example, of supporting efforts of Mexican workers to organize firms in their country that supply the US market. (NAFTA, while allowing corporations, the organizations of capital, to operate in both the United States and Mexico, as well as Canada, makes no parallel provision for unions, the organizations of labor.) The rhetoric of internationalism, too, is important, especially because it marks such a departure from the past practices of the US labor movement. Some critics complain that the new-found interest of the US labor movement in conditions abroad arises from its own immediate concerns, the competition from low-cost imports, instead from a concern for workers elsewhere in the world. But that is just the point. If global-

ization forces US unions to secure the interests of their own members by pursuing a new internationalism, then that is certainly a change of significance.

The organized opposition to globalization goes far beyond the labor movement, however, involving a wide spectrum of social movements. Environmental and women's organizations, peasant groupings, student-based action committees, and others have all been a part of the actions. In addition, well established non-governmental organizations such as Oxfam, while not engaged in the protest actions in Seattle and elsewhere, have been a part of the general opposition to globalization. Not only is this opposition based on a wide range of social movements, but these different movements have at least begun to work in alliance with one another. Some aspects of this alliance, particularly that between environmental groups and labor unions, suggest a major shift from past conflicts.

Opposition actions have taken place in a wide spectrum of countries. On the one hand, there have been the much publicized actions led by young, often middle-class activists in the United States, focused on meetings of the principal international economic agencies such as the IMF, World Bank, and WTO. On the other hand, there have been actions in India, where peasant organizations have demonstrated against the international pharmaceutical and seed companies that are trying to use the internationalization of patent regulations to secure their control of world markets. While these geographically disparate actions are not coordinated through any cohesive international organization, they are part of an interconnected movement.

The opposition that has developed to globalization is not a cohesive movement, and it is not so well developed that we can have confidence in its lasting impact. Furthermore, it has many problems. Opposition to globalization sometimes is expressed as an opposition to connections with other peoples rather than as an opposition to the way those connections are exacerbating inequalities of power and income. Thus xenophobic protectionism is sometimes just below the surface of protest actions. By and large, however, the opposition to globalization appears to be based on an internationalism that may provide a basis for a progressive, and perhaps lasting, movement.

The more serious problems of this opposition arise from the difficulties in coming to grips with the power and complexity of the globalization process itself. A small example is provided by efforts in the rich countries to respond to the proliferation of imports of goods produced in "sweat shop" conditions in low income countries. Protests against the companies that utilize these shops—firms such as Nike and Gap—are met with the response that workers in these "sweat shops" are eager to obtain their jobs because these jobs are significantly better in terms of pay and working conditions than other available jobs. What's more, the response is often true. A sophisticated movement can come to terms with this reality by emphasizing the need to alter the context that impoverishes workers in low income countries and by stressing that such a context is most effectively transformed through political struggle. Also, by focusing on workers' right to political freedom—in particular, the right to organize unions—rather than on particular aspects of workers' conditions, anti-sweat shop activists can have a positive impact.

The "sweat shop" example helps clarify that globalization is not simply a collection of practices, not simply a peculiar set of connections among peoples around the globe. It is part of the long historical development and spread of capitalism. Within the framework of capitalism, it is difficult to solve problems that are based on the inequality of income and power, because those problems are generated by the system itself. Nonetheless, capitalism is not an immutable system, and it is probably not a permanent system. The oppositional struggles are not only responses to globalization, but they are part of the process of globalization itself. They will play a role in shaping events and in shaping the entire nature of the process. And they will contribute to answering the question: What is globalization?

Reprinted with permission from *Radical Teacher*, Issue 61, 2001.

ARTICLE 8.2

November/December 1991, updated July/August 2002

THE GOSPEL OF FREE TRADE
THE NEW EVANGELISTS

BY ARTHUR MacEWAN

In the early 1990s, the passage of the North American Free Trade Agreement marked a new epoch of U.S. economic expansion into the Americas. Today, the chimes of "free trade" are ringing out even more loudly in corporate America, as neoliberal economic policies—such as the Free Trade Area of the Americas—continue to make their way around the world.

With his article, "The Gospel of Free Trade," published in November 1991, Arthur MacEwan helped Dollars & Sense *readers to demystify the role of trade in the development of domestic economies. Drawing on the lessons of economic history, MacEwan shows that "free trade" is not the best route to economic prosperity for nations.*

Just as British corporations cheered in favor of free trade in the 19th century, the largest U.S. corporations today are pushing to reduce restraints on trade and investment. The result: downward pressure on wages and social welfare programs in both rich and poor countries, and a reduced capacity of citizens across the globe to control their own economic conditions. —Darius Mehri

Free trade! It's the cure-all for the 1990s. With all the zeal of Christian missionaries, the U.S. government has been preaching, advocating, pushing, and coercing around the globe for "free trade."

While a Mexico-U.S.-Canada free trade pact is the immediate aim of U.S. policy, George Bush has heralded a future free trade zone from the northern coast of Canada to the southern tip of Chile. For Eastern Europe, U.S. advisers prescribe unfettered capitalism and ridicule as unworkable any move toward a "third way." Wherever any modicum of economic success appears in the Third World, free traders extol it as one more example of their program's wonders.

Free traders also praise their gospel as the proper policy at home. The path to true salvation—or economic expansion, which, in this day and age, seems to be the same thing—lies in opening our markets to foreign goods. Get rid of trade barriers, allow business to go where it wants and do what it wants. We will all get rich.

Yet the history of the United States and other advanced capitalist countries teaches us that virtually all advanced capitalist countries found economic success in protectionism, not in free trade. Likewise, heavy government intervention has characterized those cases of rapid and sustained economic growth in the Third World.

Free trade, does, however, have its uses. Highly developed nations can use free trade to extend their power and their control of the world's wealth, and business can use it as a weapon against labor. Most important, free trade can limit efforts to redistribute income more equally, undermine progressive social programs, and keep people from democratically controlling their economic lives.

A DAY IN THE PARK

At the beginning of the 19th century, Lowell, Massachusetts, became the premier site of the country's textile industry. Today, thanks to the Lowell National Historical Park, you can tour the huge mills, ride through thee canals that redirected the Merrimack River's power to the mills, and learn the story of the textile workers, from the Yankee "mill girls" of the 1820s through the various waves of immigrant laborers who poured into the city over the next century.

During a day in the park, visitors get a graphic picture of the importance of 19th-century industry to the economic growth and prosperity of the United States. Lowell and the other mill towns of the era were centers of growth. They not only created a demand for Southern cotton, they also created a demand for new machinery, maintenance of old machinery, parts, dyes, skills, construction materials, construction machinery, more skills, equipment to move the raw materials and products, parts maintenance for that equipment, and still more skills. The mill towns also created markets—concentrated groups of wage earners who needed to buy products to sustain themselves. As centers of economic activity, Lowell and similar mill towns contributed to U.S. economic growth far beyond the value of the textiles they produced.

The U.S. textile industry emerged decades after the industrial revolution had spawned Britain's powerful textile industry. Nonetheless, it survived and prospered. British linens inundated markets throughout the world in the early 19th century, as the British navy nurtured free trade and kept ports open for commerce. In the United States, however, hostilities leading up to the War of 1812 and then a substantial tariff made British textiles relatively expensive. These limitations on trade allowed the Lowell mills to prosper, acting as a catalyst for other industries and helping to create the skilled work force at the center of U.S. economic expansion.

FREE TRADE FORCES DOWN THE GENERAL LEVEL OF WAGES ACROSS THE BOARD, EVEN OF THOSE WORKERS NOT DIRECTLY AFFECTED BY IMPORTS.

Beyond textiles, however, tariffs did not play a great role in the United States during the early 19th century. Southern planters had considerable power, and while they were willing to make some compromises, they opposed protecting manufacturing in general because that protection forced up the price of the goods they purchased with their cotton revenues. The Civil War wiped out Southern opposition to protectionism, and from the 1860s through World War I, U.S. industry prospered behind considerable tariff barriers.

DIFFERENT COUNTRIES, SIMILAR STORIES

The story of the importance of protectionism in bringing economic growth has been repeated, with local variations, in almost all other advanced capitalist countries. During the late 19th century, Germany entered the major league of international economic powers with substantial protection and government support for its industries. Likewise, in 19th-century France and Italy, national consolidation behind protectionist barriers was a key to economic development.

Only Britain—which entered the industrial era first—might be touted as an example of successful development without tariff protection. Yet, in addition to starting first, Britain built its industry through the expansion of its empire and the British navy, hardly prime ingredients in any recipe for free trade.

Japan provides a particularly important case of successful government protection and support for industrial development. In the post-World War II era, when the Japanese established the foundations for the modern "miracle," the government rejected free trade and extensive foreign investment and instead promoted its national firms.

In the 1950s, for example, the government protected the country's fledgling auto firms from foreign competition. At first, quotas limited imports to $500,000 (in current dollars) each year; in the 1960s, prohibitively high tariffs replaced the quotas. Furthermore, the Japanese allowed foreign investment only insofar as it contributed to developing domestic industry. The government encouraged Japanese companies to import foreign technology, but required them to produce 90% of parts domestically within five years.

The Japanese also protected their computer industry. In the early 1970s, as the industry was developing, companies and individuals could only purchase a foreign machine if a suitable Japanese model was not available. IBM was allowed to produce within the country, but only when it licensed basic patents to Japanese firms. And IBM computers produced in Japan were treated as foreign-made machines.

Today, while Japan towers as the world's most dynamic industrial and financial power, one looks in vain for the role free trade played in its success. The Japanese government provided an effective framework, support, and protection for the country's capitalist development.

Likewise, in the Third World, capitalism has generated high rates of economic growth where government involvement, and not free trade, played the central role. South Korea is the most striking case. "Korea is an example of a country that grew very fast and yet violated the canons of conventional economic wisdom," writes Alice Amsden in *Asia's Next Giant: South Korea and Late Industrialization*, widely acclaimed as the most important recent book on the Korean economy. "In Korea, instead of the market mechanism allocating resources and guiding private entrepreneurship, the government made most of the pivotal investment decisions. Instead of firms operating in a competitive market structure, they each operated with an extraordinary degree of market control, protected from foreign competition."

With Mexico, three recent years of relatively moderate growth, about 3-4% per year, have led the purveyors of free trade to claim it as one of their success stories. Yet Mexico has been opening its economy increasingly since the early 1980s, and most of the decade was an utter disaster. Even if the 1980s are written off as the cost of transition, the recent success does not compare well with what Mexico achieved in the era when its government intervened heavily in the economy and protected national industry. From 1940 to 1980, with policies of state-led economic development and extensive limits on imports, Mexican national output grew at the high rate of about 6% per year.

The recent Mexican experience does put to rest any ideas that free market policies will improve the living conditions for the masses of the people in the Third World. The Mexican government has paved the road for free trade policies by reducing or eliminating social welfare programs. In addition, between 1976 and 1990, the real minimum wage declined by 60%. Mexico's increasing orientation toward foreign trade has also destroyed the country's self-sufficiency in food, and the influx of foreign food grains has forced small farmers off the land and into the ranks of the urban unemployed.

THE USES OF FREE TRADE

While free trade is not the best economic growth or development policy, the largest and most powerful firms in many countries find it highly profitable. As Britain led the cheers for free trade in the early 19th century, when its own industry was already firmly established, so the United States—or at least many firms based in the United States—finds it a profitable policy in the late 20th century.

For U.S. firms, access to foreign markets is a high priority. Mexico may be relatively poor, but with a population of 85 million it provides a substantial market. Furthermore, Mexican labor is cheap; using modern production techniques, Mexican workers can be as productive as workers in the United States. For U.S. firms to obtain full access to the Mexican market, the United States must open its borders to Mexican goods. Also, if U.S. firms are to take full advantage of cheap foreign labor and sell the goods produced abroad to U.S. consumers, the United States must be open to imports.

On the other side of the border, wealthy Mexicans face a choice between advancing their interests through national development or advancing their interests through ties to U.S. firms and access to U.S. markets. For many years, they chose the former route. This led to some development of the Mexican economy but also—due to corruption and the massive power of the ruling party—created huge concentrations of wealth in the hands of a few small groups of firms and individuals. Eventually, these groups came into conflict with their own government over regulation and taxation. Having benefited from government largesse, they now see their fortunes in greater freedom from government control and, particularly, in greater access to foreign markets and partnerships with large foreign companies. National development is a secondary concern when more involvement with international commerce will produce greater riches quicker.

In addition, the old program of state-led development in Mexico ran into severe problems. These problems came to the surface in the 1980s with the international debt crisis. Owing huge amounts of money to foreign banks, the Mexican government was forced to respond to pressure from the International Monetary Fund, the U.S. government, and large international banks. That pressure meshed with the pressure coming from Mexico's own richest elites, and the result has been the move toward free trade and a greater opening of the Mexican economy to foreign investment.

Of course, in the United States, Mexico, and elsewhere, advocates of free trade claim that their policies are in everyone's interest. Free trade, they point out, will mean cheaper products for all. Consumers in the United States, who are mostly workers, will be richer because their wages will buy more. In both Mexico and the United States, they argue, rising trade will create more jobs. If some workers lose their jobs because cheaper imported goods are available, export industries will produce new ones.

Such arguments obscure many of the most important issues in the free trade debate. Stated, as they usually are, as universal truths, these arguments are plain silly. No one, for example, touring the Lowell National Historical Park could seriously argue that people in the United States would have been better off had there been no tariff on textiles. Yes, in 1820, they could have purchased textile goods more cheaply, but the cost would have been an industrially backward, impoverished nation. One could make the same point with the Japanese auto and computer industries, or indeed with numerous other examples from the last two centuries of capitalist development.

In the modern era, even though the United States already has a relatively developed economy with highly skilled workers, a freely open international economy does not serve the interests of U.S. workers, though it will benefit large firms. U.S. workers today are in competition with workers around the globe. Many different workers in many different places can produce the same goods and services. Thus, an international economy governed by the free trade agenda will bring down wages for U.S. workers.

The problem is not simply that of workers in a few industries—such as auto and steel—where import competition is the most obvious and immediate problem. A country's openness to the international economy affects the entire structure of earnings in that country. Free trade forces down the general level of wages across the board, even of those workers not directly affected by imports. The simple fact is that when companies can produce the same products in several different places, it is owners who gain because they can move their factories and funds around much more easily than workers can move themselves around. Capital is mobile, labor is much less mobile. Businesses, not workers, gain from having a larger territory in which to roam.

CONTROL OVER OUR ECONOMIC LIVES

But the difficulties with free trade do not end with wages. Free trade is a weapon in the hands of business when it opposes any progressive social programs. Efforts to place environmental restrictions on firms are met with the threat of moving production abroad. Higher taxes to improve the schools? Business threatens to go elsewhere. Better health and safety regulations? The same response.

Some might argue that the losses from free trade for people in the United States will be balanced by gains for most people in poor countries—lower wages in the United States, but higher wages in Mexico. Free trade, then, would bring about international equality. Not likely. In fact, as pointed out above, free trade reforms in Mexico have helped force down wages and reduce social welfare programs, processes rationalized by efforts to make Mexican goods competitive on international markets.

Gains for Mexican workers, like those for U.S. workers, depend on their power in relation to business. Free trade and the imperative of international "competitiveness" are just as much weapons in the hands of firms operating in Mexico as they are for firms operating in the United States. The great mobility of capital is business' best trump card in dealing with labor and popular demands for social change—in the United States, Mexico, and elsewhere.

None of this means that people should demand that their economies operate as fortresses, protected from all foreign economic incursions. There are great gains that can be obtained from international economic relations—when a nation manages those relations in the interests of the great majority of the people. Protectionism often simply supports narrow vested interests, corrupt officials, and wealthy industrialists. In rejecting free trade, we should move beyond traditional protectionism.

Yet, at this time, rejecting free trade is an essential first step. Free trade places all the cards in the hands of business. More than ever, free trade would subject us to the "bottom line," or at least the bottom line as calculated by those who own and run large companies.

For any economy to operate in the interest of the great majority, people's conscious choices—about the environment, income distribution, safety, and health—must command the economy. The politics of democratic decision-making must control business. In today's world, politics operates primarily on a national level. To give up control over our national economy—as does any people that accepts free trade—is to give up control over our economic lives.

Resources: The New Gospel: North American Free Trade," *NACLA's Report on the Americas* 24(6), May 1991; Robert Pollin and Alexander Cockburn, "Capitalism and its Specters: The World, the Free Market and the Left," *The Nation*, 25 February 1991; P. Armstrong, A. Glyn, and J. Harrison, *Capitalism Since World War II*, 1984.

September/October 2005

FALLING OFF A CLIFF

BY KEITH YEARMAN AND AMY GLUCKMAN

January 1, 2005, was just another New Years' Day for most Americans, but for millions of garment workers in developing countries around the globe, from Lesotho to Bangladesh to Jamaica, the date symbolizes cataclysm. On that day, a 30-year-old international trade arrangement known as the Multifiber Agreement (MFA) was officially ended. Under the MFA's quotas, which guaranteed them a share of the world clothing market, and with the encouragement of international financial institutions, dozens of poor countries had developed apparel industries. Now, stores in Europe and the United States are likely to be deluged with clothing made in China and India, and millions of garment workers elsewhere are likely to be unceremoniously dumped into the ranks of the unemployed. The sweatshop jobs may have paid little, and the apparel industries may have contributed little to nations' genuine economic development. Nonetheless, you can hardly blame Bangladeshi or Salvadoran workers for feeling jerked around by shifts in global trade policy over which they have virtually no say.

OKAY, WE'LL EXPORT GARMENTS

Though most people have probably never heard of the MFA, to see its impact one only has to open the bedroom closet. The MFA imposed a global quota system for textile and apparel production, limiting the output of manufacturing giants such as China while allowing substantial clothing industries to develop in small countries which would not have been able to compete otherwise.

Nearly 50 nations were given market access to the United States and Europe under the MFA. For example, "Cambodia ... this year can export to the U.S. 1,721,232 cotton pillowcases, 72 silk dresses, and 37,896 playsuits—in all, $1.4 billion worth of clothing and textiles," *BusinessWeek* reported in 2003. The agreement was not originally aimed at boosting Third World economies. In the 1960s, the Kennedy administration implemented a quota system to protect domestic cotton producers. This was expanded in the 1974 MFA to include textiles and clothing of all materials (hence a "multifiber" agreement). "The original idea of the quotas was to afford some protection to the declining textile industries of the developed countries. The reality was different. With quotas effectively guaranteeing market access, manufacturing sprang up in such unlikely places as Jamaica and Sri Lanka, which before the quotas had no significant textile industry," notes *BusinessWeek*.

The MFA guaranteed market access for these nations, and the neoliberal policies imposed on them by international institutions such as the IMF helped too. For example, the elimination of agricultural price-stabilization programs and the removal of tariffs and quotas on food imports in many countries over the past 20 years has forced countless farmers off their lands and into the urban economy, where a formal garment factory job, however low-paid and tedious, can look a lot better than eking out a living in the informal sector. Under the structural adjustment programs many nations adopted as a condition of refinancing their foreign loans, governments privatized public-sector enterprises, often resulting in mass layoffs and further softening labor markets.

Large supplies of desperate workers, cheap financing for factory construction (for example, from the U.S. Agency for International Development), and guaranteed market access led many nations to become dependent on their textile exports for jobs and revenues. In 2001 clothing and textiles accounted for nearly 80% of Bangladesh's total exports, up from 39% in 1990. Other countries that have become deeply dependent on clothing exports include Cambodia (72.5%), El Salvador (60.2%), Mauritius (56.6%), the Dominican Republic (50.9%), Sri Lanka (49.8%), and Honduras (41.3%).

THEN THE RULES CHANGE

Now that they've followed the neoliberal prescription to switch from an economic development model that emphasizes production for domestic markets ("import substitution") to one that focuses on building up export industries like apparel, these countries are about to have the ground ripped out from under them. In the United States, textile and garment manufacturing has continued its long-term decline even under the MFA; it's now small enough to provide little incentive for continued quotas. So the United States has gone along with a decade-long phase-out of the MFA, which had been attacked all along by the business press, by many economists, and by clothing retailers as "nonsense" and a barrier to free trade.

Ironically, in the 1990s smaller nations *sought* removal of the quota system. After all, the MFA's original purpose had been to protect textile manufacturing in the rich countries from growing Third World exports, and many of these countries believed they would gain even more market share once the quotas were dropped. At the time the phase-out plan was signed in 1994, China was not a member of the World Trade Organization or its predecessor, the GATT, and was thus not allotted a quota. But once China joined the WTO in 2001, it stood to dominate the world textile trade. So instead of

shifting opportunity in the textile industry from rich nations to poor ones as advertised, the elimination of quotas is likely only to shift production out of lots of developing countries and into just a few: India and particularly China.

It seems implausible that smaller nations would not have realized the threat China posed. Plans for bringing China into the world trading system had been afoot for years. As early as July 1994, for example, German Chancellor Helmut Kohl announced he would give China "full support" in its attempt to join the new WTO. China had already come to dominate production of many manufactured goods. And the country spent the years leading up to the MFA's expiration building textile factories. "Hundreds of new textile mills are now sprouting up in Changzhou and Guangdong provinces, alongside megafactories that will dwarf anything found in Latin America," the *Wall Street Journal* reported in 2004. China also has a massive base of cheap labor to staff these megafactories. China's textile wages are not the lowest in the world, but its relatively low wages, in combination with factors such as a strong infrastructure and the domestic technical expertise the country has built up under its proactive industrial policy, give it an insuperable edge over most other developing countries.

FORECAST: DISASTER

Quota removal, which smaller nations once welcomed, now poses a grave danger. The predictions for the post-quota world are quite literally of disaster: projections suggest as many as 30 million jobs will be lost worldwide.

The most dire forecasts are for Bangladesh. "At stake are 1.8 [million] jobs in the factories and as many as 15 [million] more in related industries, from button-making to insurance underwriting," notes the *Financial Times*. Projections are that the country will lose 40% of its total exports and face social upheaval, with a massive number of newly unemployed workers who have no social security, welfare, or unemployment benefits.

The forecast for Mongolia is dim: tens of thousands of jobs are likely to be lost there as a result of the quota expiration. Likewise a number of African and Caribbean countries: "Among the people who will be destroyed by this are the African and Caribbean people who have been building investments based on the special quotas," former U.S. trade negotiator Seth Bodnar told the *Miami Herald*. Latin America is projected to lose at least half of its 500,000 garment jobs by 2010. And the U.S. colony Saipan, long a major center for textile production, has already seen four plants close in 2005, with nearly 1,600 jobs lost. Saipan's garment sales are projected to drop by 50% in 2005.

There's a technical term for what these nations are facing: falling off a cliff.

Actually, the destruction began even before last January 1, as companies readied for the MFA's termination by shedding hundreds of thousands of jobs around the world. In the months and years prior to the expiration of the quota system, for example, 6,000 Salvadorans and 235,000 Brazilians lost their textile jobs. Sara Lee closed factories in the mainland United States, Puerto Rico, Honduras, and Mexico, and laid off more than 4,000 employees, in what was described in the business press as a quota move.

Chinese-made garments are now flooding markets. To point this out has been derided in the *Wall Street Journal* as "hysteria," but the facts speak for themselves:

- After quotas on baby clothes ended, China's exports to the United States rose 826%. Soft luggage exports rose fivefold. Production of these items in Mexico, Thailand and Indonesia has dropped by half.
- During the first three months of 2005, exports of Chinese-made cotton knit shirts and blouses to the U.S. rose 1,250%. In January 2004 (under quotas), China shipped 941,000 knit shirts to the United States. In January 2005, it shipped 18.2 million.
- During the first three months of 2005, exports of Chinese-made trousers to the United States increased by 1,500% and exports of underwear by 300%.
- From 2001 to 2003, during the partial phaseout of quotas, China's share of the United States sock market jumped from 2% to 40%.

The World Bank estimates that China's share of the global trade in textiles will grow from 17% to around 45% in just a few years. Over the same period, U.S. clothing importers expect they will go from buying goods in about 50 countries down to less than 10.

A SMALL BACKLASH

In the United States, 12,000 textile jobs were lost in January 2005 alone, and projections suggest more than 500,000 jobs will disappear over the next few years. A strong backlash from unions, the textile industry, and Congress has forced the Bush administration to take advantage of a clause in the MFA phase-out agreement that allows countries to reimpose some quotas. The curbs are temporary though, lasting for just a few years, and granting China a yearly quota increase of 7.5%. China may challenge the new quotas, but even if they remain, this essentially amounts to a brief stay of execution. Economist Dean Baker of the Center for Economic and Policy Research believes that there is no chance of reviving an MFA-type quota agreement in the long run. Given that, he says, "the best thing that could be argued is that the proponents of getting rid of the MFA should feel an obligation to provide special assistance to the victims of their policy. This could take the form of debt forgiveness, for example, or relaxing the new WTO rules governing intellectual property."

For investors in clothing retailers and manufacturers, the expiration of the MFA means good times ahead. Thirty million textile workers, on the other hand, have just been shoved off the cliff. The institutions that regulate global trade, the powerful nations that dominate them, and the corporations whose interests they promote are committed to reshaping global trade rules along neoliberal lines, even if the changes cause upheaval for tens of millions of workers worldwide. There's nothing inherently wrong with clothes being manufactured in China or India rather than in Mauritius or Bangladesh. But there is something wrong with a global trade regime that pushes millions of poor workers into one sector then, with little ado, kicks them out of it.

Sources: Magnusson, P. et al., "Where Free Trade Hurts," *Business-Week* 12/15/03; "A New Silk Road" (editorial), *Wall Street Journal,* 12/29/04; Buerk, R., "Social Upheaval Feared When End of Import Quotas Hits Bangladesh," *Financial Times,* 7/24-25/04; Fritsch, Peter, "Looming Trouble," *WSJ,* 11/20/03; Brooke, James, "Down and Almost Out in Mongolia," *New York Times,* 12/29/04; Barboza, D. and Becker, E. "Free of Quota, China Textiles Flood the US," *NYT,* 3/10/05; Brooke, James, "Trade Quotas? Ah, the Good Old Days," *NYT,* 4/9/05; Bussey, Jane, "Asian Countries Gain Larger Share of Global Clothing Business," *Miami Herald,* 4/28/03; King Jr., Neil, "Stitch in Time," *WSJ,* 6/16/04; McGregor, R. and Harney, A., "China Gets Set to Clothe America When Quotas End," *FT,* 7/20/04; Thompson, Ginger, "Fraying of a Latin Textile Industry," *NYT,* 3/25/05; Lapper, R., "Garment Companies Fight Back for Share of Market," *FT,* 7/27/04; Beales, R. and Grant J., "Sara Lee Will Cut 4,000 Jobs in Quota Move," *FT,* 6/12-13/04; Adamy, Janet, "Sara Lee to Close 5 Clothing Plants and Cut 4,175 Jobs," *WSJ,* 6/11/04; King Jr., Neil, "U.S. Sock Makers Ask White House to Rein in China," *WSJ,* 6/29/04; Harney, A., "US Set for Further Curbs on Chinese Imports," *FT,* 11/15/04; "Protectionist Piffle" (editorial), *FT,* 4/27/05.

UNDERSTANDING THE TRADE DEFICIT

BY ARTHUR MacEWAN

Dear Dr. Dollar

Can you explain what trade deficits are? Who owes what to whom or is it just an accounting device?

—*Jack Miller, Indianapolis, Ind.*

I see that the United States has had a negative international trade balance for years. What happens to those dollars we've sent overseas?

—*Bill Clark, Chillicothe, Ohio*

Americans collectively import more goods and services from foreigners than we export, we are said to have a *trade deficit*. Paying for the things we import accounts for most of the flow of dollars out of the United States. However, money flows out of the country for other reasons as well. The U.S. government provides foreign aid and supports overseas military bases; immigrants to the United States send dollars back to their families; foreigners who own U.S. businesses or financial assets take income out of the country.

When these factors are added to the trade deficit, the net outflow of dollars is called the *current account deficit*. In 2002, the U.S. trade deficit amounted to $418 billion, and the current account deficit totaled $480 billion. Data for 2003 is not yet available, but preliminary reports indicate the current account deficit will be at least $550 billion.

Once the dollars leave the country, three things can happen.

First, foreigners can use dollars to purchase U.S. assets: stocks, bonds, bank deposits, government debt, real estate, businesses. When Toyota buys land and equipment for a factory in the United States, when a British investment fund buys stock in a U.S. corporation, when a German bank purchases U.S. Treasury bonds, then the United States is said to be

"financing" its current account deficit by selling assets. In 2002, foreigners acquired $612 billion in U.S. assets.

The United States has run persistent and increasing current account deficits since the 1980s, and foreigners have used the dollars to stake significant claims on U.S. assets. At the end of 2002, the value of U.S. assets owned by foreigners exceeded the value of foreign assets owned by U.S. residents by $2.4 trillion. This is the reason the United States is often said to be a debtor nation, with a net debt to the rest of the world of $2.4 trillion. But this "debt" is denominated in our own currency. For that reason, it does not pose the same risks for the United States as developing countries with large debts—which

OVER THE PAST FEW YEARS, THE DOLLAR LOST ABOUT ONE-THIRD OF ITS VALUE RELATIVE TO THE EURO.

must be repaid in dollars or euro—face.

Foreign central banks provide a second outlet for dollars that leave the United States. The dollar is the most widely used international currency, and many less-developed countries have sizable dollar-denominated debts. Governments sometimes hang on to whatever dollars fall into their hands, parking them in liquid assets like U.S. bank accounts or U.S. government bonds to earn interest. In 2002, foreign governments held almost $95 billion in dollar reserves, which they will use to cover future deficits, repay debts, intervene in financial markets, or simply to exert influence in negotiations with the United States.

If you've followed the arithmetic so far,

you will have figured out that in 2002, on balance, more dollars flowed back into the United States to purchase assets then flowed out. This allowed U.S. companies to buy assets overseas, almost $200 billion worth.

As long as the country's large current account deficit is financed by these capital inflows, it is not necessarily a problem. But a third possible consequence of the massive U.S. current account deficit is that foreigners will lose confidence in the U.S. economy and stop purchasing U.S. assets. If this happens, the supply of dollars in the global banking system will exceed demand and the exchange value of the dollar will fall.

Some people believe this is already happening. Over the past few years, the dollar lost about one-third of its value relative to the euro. This could signify that foreigners are shifting from U.S. to euro-based assets. If the era of dollar supremacy is indeed coming to a close, the value of the dollar will continue to fall. What this would mean for the U.S. and world economies is difficult to predict. A sustained loss of confidence in the dollar could have many potentially serious ramifications.

Imports would grow more expensive, infuriating our trading partners, who depend on the U.S. market for their goods. With less foreign demand for U.S. assets, stock prices might tumble and interest rates rise. United States-based banks and corporations would find it harder to buy foreign assets and expand overseas. The dollar has been in trouble before and, in the past, the U.S. government pressured other countries to buy or hold dollars and prop up its value. Whether other countries agree to this will depend, ultimately, on whether the United States and other major economic powers are still talking to one another.

FREE, FREE AT LAST

BY JOHN MILLER

HAIL ESTONIA!

For the first time in the 11 years that the Heritage Foundation and *The Wall Street Journal* have been publishing the Index of Economic Freedom, the U.S. has dropped out of the top 10 freest economies in the world. ...

The 2005 Index, released today, ranks Hong Kong once again as the world's freest economy, followed by Singapore and Luxembourg. But it is Estonia at No. 4 that makes the point. This former Soviet satellite is a model reformer, setting the standard for how fast countries can move ahead in the realm of economic liberalization. ...

The U.S. ... scores well. But worrying developments like Sarbanes-Oxley in the category of regulation and aggressive use of antidumping law in trade policy have kept it from keeping pace with the best performers in economic freedom. Most alarming is the U.S.'s fiscal burden, which imposes high marginal tax rates for individuals and very high marginal corporate tax rates. ...

Policy makers who pay lip service to fighting poverty would do well to grasp the link between economic freedom and prosperity. This year the Index finds that the freest economies have a per-capita income of $29,219, more than twice that of the "mostly free" at $12,839, and more than four times that of the "mostly unfree." Put simply, misery has a cure and its name is economic freedom.

—Wall Street Journal *op-ed by Mary Anastasia O'Grady, January 4, 2005*

I must be confused. I somehow thought that an Economic Freedom Index would showcase countries that are reducing the democratic deficits of the global economy by giving people more control over their economic lives and the institutions that govern them. In the hands of the *Wall Street Journal* and the Heritage Foundation, Washington's foremost right-wing think tank, however, an economic freedom index merely measures corporate and entrepreneurial freedom from accountability. Upon examination, the index turns out to be a poor barometer of either freedom more broadly construed or of prosperity.

The index does not even pretend that its definition of economic freedom has anything to do with political freedom. Take the two city-states, Hong Kong and Singapore, which top the index's list of free countries. Both are only "partially free" according to *Freedom in the World*, an annual country-by-country assessment published by the nonpartisan think tank Freedom House, which the *Journal*'s editors themselves

have called "the Michelin Guide to democracy's development." Hong Kong is still without direct elections for its legislature or its chief executive, and a proposed internal security law threatens press and academic freedom as well as political dissent. In Singapore, freedom of the press and the right to demonstrate are limited; films, TV, and other media are censored; preventive detention is legal; and you can do jail time for littering.

Moving further down the list of "free" countries, the rankings are no better correlated with any ordinary definition of "freedom," as economic journalist Robert Kuttner pointed out when the index was first published in 1997. For instance, Bahrain (#20), where the king holds an effective veto over parliament and freedom of expression is limited, ranks higher than Norway (#29), whose comprehensive social insurance and strong environmental regulation drag down its score. Likewise, Kuwait, an emirship no one would term free or democratic, is tied (at #54) with Costa Rica, long the most vigorous democracy in Latin America.

These results are not surprising, however, given the index's premise: the less a government intervenes in the economy, the higher its freedom ranking. Specifically, the index breaks "economic freedom" down into 10 components: trade policy; fiscal burden of government; level of government intervention; monetary policy; financial liberalization; banking and finance policies; labor market policies; enforcement of property rights; business, labor, and environmental regulations; and size of the black market. In other words, minimum-wage laws, environmental regulations, or requirements for transparency in corporate accounting make a country less free, whereas low business taxes, harsh debtor laws, and little or no regulation of occupational health and safety make a country more free.

Consider that the index docks the United States' ranking for passing Sarbanes-Oxley, a law that seeks to improve corporate accounting practices and to make CEOs responsible for their corporations' profit reports. The segment of the U.S. population whose economic freedom this law erodes is tiny, but it's obviously that segment—not workers and not even shareholders—whose freedom counts for the folks at the *Journal* and at Heritage.

The rather objective-looking list that results from assessing the 10 components ranks 155 countries from freest (Hong Kong and Singapore) to most repressive (Burma and North Korea). The index then becomes a tool its authors can use to hammer home their message: economic freedom (as they define it) brings prosperity. As they point out, "the freest economies have a per-capita income more than twice that of the 'mostly free' and more than four times that of the 'mostly unfree.'"

Not so fast. For one thing, the index's creators used some oddball methods that compromise its linkage of prosperity to economic freedom.

For instance, according to the index, the fiscal burden of the Swedish and Danish welfare states is smaller than that of the United States, even though U.S. government spending is more than 20 percentage points lower relative to Gross Domestic Product (GDP, or the size of the economy). This bizarre result comes about because the index uses the change in government spending, not its actual level, to calculate fiscal burden.

To measure the tax side of a country's fiscal burden, the index uses the top rate of the personal and corporate income taxes—and that's equally misleading. Besides ignoring the burden of other taxes, these two figures don't get at *effective* tax rates, which also depend on what share of corporate profits and personal income is actually taxed. On paper, U.S. corporate tax rates are higher than those in Europe, as the *Journal* is quick to point out. But nearly half of U.S. corporate profits go untaxed. The average rate of taxation on U.S. corporate profits currently stands at 15%, far below the top corporate tax rate of 35%. And relative to GDP, U.S. corporate income taxes are no more than half those of other OECD countries.

The index's treatment of government intervention is flawed as well, for it fails to count industrial policy as a form of intervention. This is a serious mistake: it means that the index overestimates the degree to which some of the fastest growing economies of the last few decades, such as in Taiwan and South Korea, relied on the market and underestimates the positive role that government played in directing economic development in those countries by guiding investment and protecting infant industries.

The treatment of informal markets is downright strange. The index considers a large informal sector to indicate less economic freedom because government restrictions must have driven that economic activity underground. (Of course, you could take the opposite view: since the informal sector is for the most part unregulated, countries with larger informal sectors are, by the index's definition, more free!) But this way of looking at it biases the index. Developing countries tend to have large informal sectors while developed economies usually have small informal sectors. That means the index systematically lowers the economic freedom index of developing countries while boosting the scores of developed countries, thus artificially correlating income levels with economic freedom. Even right-wing economist Stefan Karlsson of the libertarian Ludwig Von Mises Institute has criticized the index on this point. Thanks in part to this bias, Estonia, Chile, and Bahrain are the only middle-income countries to make it into the top 20.

Whatever the biases in the index do to cement a tight relationship between economic freedom and income, they can't produce a tight correlation between economic freedom and *growth*. The fastest-growing countries are mostly unfree. Take China, India, and Vietnam, three of the fastest-growing countries in the world. They are way down in the rankings, at #112, #118, and #137 respectively. While all three countries have adopted market reforms in recent years that have improved their standing in the index, their trade policies and regulations remain "repressive." And there are plenty of relatively slow growers among the countries high up in the index, including Estonia (#4), the *Journal's* poster child for economic freedom. How free or unfree a country is according to the index seems to have little to do with how quickly it grows.

An "Economic Freedom Index" that tells us little about economic growth or political freedom is a slipshod measure that would seem to have no other purpose other than to sell the neoliberal policies that stand in the way of most people gaining control over their economic lives and obtaining genuine economic freedom in today's global economy.

Resources: Mary Anastasia O'Grady, "Hail Estonia!" *Wall Street Journal*, 1/4/05; *The 2005 Index of Economic Freedom* (Heritage Foundation, 2005); Johan Fernandez, "Malaysia climbs up economic freedom index," *The Star Online*, 1/25/05; "Freedom & Growth: No Siamese twins," *The Economic Times*, 5/27/02; Robert Kuttner, "A Weird Set of Values," *The American Prospect*, 12/7/97; Stefan M. I. Karlsson, "The Failings of the Economic Freedom Index," (Ludwig Von Mises Institute, 1/21/05); "Freedom in the World 2005: Civic Power and Electoral Politics," (Freedom House, 2005) <www.freedomhouse.org/research/survey2005.htm>.

DOLLAR ANXIETY

REAL REASONS TO WORRY

BY JOHN MILLER

The value of the dollar is falling. Does that mean that our economic sky is falling as well? Not to sound like Chicken Little, but the answer may well be yes. If an economic collapse is not in our future, then at least economic storm clouds are gathering on the horizon.

It's what lies behind the slide of the dollar that has even many mainstream economists spooked: an unprecedented current account deficit—the difference between the country's income and its consumption and investment spending. The current account deficit, which primarily reflects the huge gap between the amount the United States imports and the amount it exports, is the best indicator of where the country stands in its financial relationship with the rest of the world.

At an estimated $670 billion, or 5.7% of gross domestic product (GDP), the 2004 current account deficit is the largest ever. An already huge trade deficit (the amount exports fall short of imports) made worse by high oil prices, along with rock bottom private savings and a gaping federal budget deficit, have helped push the U.S. current account deficit into uncharted territory. The last time it was above 4% of GDP was in 1816, and no other country has ever run a current account deficit that equals nearly 1% of the world's GDP. If current trends continue, the gap could reach 7.8% of U.S. GDP by 2008, according to Nouriel Roubini of New York University and Brad Setser of University College, Oxford, two well-known finance economists.

Most of the current account deficit stems from the U.S. trade deficit (about $610 billion). The rest reflects the remittances immigrants send home to their families plus U.S. foreign aid (together another $80 billion) less net investment income (a positive $20 billion because the United States still earns more from investments abroad than it pays out in interest on its borrowing from abroad).

The current account deficit represents the amount of money the United States must attract from abroad each year. Money comes from overseas in two ways: foreign investors can buy stock in U.S. corporations, or they can lend money to corporations or to the government by buying bonds. Currently, almost all of the money must come from loans because European and Japanese investors are no longer buying U.S. stocks. U.S. equity returns have been trivial since 2000 in dollar terms and actually negative in euro terms since the dollar has lost ground against the euro.

In essence, the U.S. economy racks up record current account deficits by spending more than its national income to feed its appetite for imports that are now half again exports. That increases the supply of dollars in foreign hands.

At the same time, the demand for dollars has diminished. Foreign investors are less interested in purchasing dollar-dominated assets as they hold more of them (and as the self-fulfilling expectation that the value of the dollar is likely to fall sets in). In October 2004 (the most recent data available), net foreign purchases of U.S. securities—stocks and bonds—dipped to their lowest level in a year and below what was necessary to offset the current account deficit. In addition, global investors' stock and bond portfolios are now overloaded with dollar-denominated assets, up to 50% from 30% in the early '90s.

Under the weight of the massive current account deficit, the dollar has already begun to give way. Since January 2002, the value of the dollar has fallen more than 20%, with much of that dropoff happening since August 2004. The greenback now stands at multiyear lows against the euro, the yen, and an index of major currencies.

Should foreign investors stop buying U.S. securities, then the dollar will crash, stock values plummet, and an economic downturn surely follow. But even if foreigners continue to purchase U.S. bonds—and they already hold 47% of U.S Treasury bonds—a current account deficit of this magnitude will be a costly drag on the economy. The Fed will have to boost interest rates, which determine the rate of return on U.S. bonds, to compensate for their lost value as the dollar slips in value and to keep foreigners coming back for more. In addition, a falling dollar makes imports cost more, pushing up U.S inflation rates. The Fed will either tolerate the uptick in inflation or attempt to counteract it by raising interest rates yet higher. Even in this more orderly scenario of decline, the current expansion will slow or perhaps come to a halt.

IMPERIAL FINANCE

You can still find those who claim none of this is a problem. Recently, for example, the editors of the *Wall Street Journal* offered worried readers the following relaxation technique—a version of what former Treasury Secretary Larry Summers says is the sharpest argument you typically hear from a finance minister whose country is saddled with a large current account deficit.

First, recall that a large trade deficit requires a large surplus of capital flowing into your country to cover it. Then ask yourself, would you rather live in a country that continues to attract investment, or one that capital is trying to get out of? Finally, remind yourself that the monetary authorities control the value of currencies and are fully capable of halting the decline.

Feel better? You shouldn't. Arguments like these are unconvincing, a bravado borne not of postmodern cool so much as the old-fashioned, unilateral financial imperialism that underlies the muscular U.S. foreign policy we see today.

True, so far foreigners have been happy to purchase the gobs of debt issued by the U.S. Treasury and corporate America to cover the current account deficit. And that has kept U.S. interest rates low. If not for the flood of foreign money, Morgan Stanley economist Stephen Roach figures, U.S. long-term interest rates would be between one and 1.5 percentage points higher today.

The ability to borrow without pushing up interest rates has paid off handsomely for the Bush administration. Now when the government spends more than it takes in to prosecute the war in Iraq and bestow tax cuts on the rich, savers from foreign shores finance those deficits at reduced rates. And cash-strapped U.S. consumers are more ready to swallow an upside-down economic recovery that has pushed up profit but neither created jobs nor lifted wages when they can borrow at low interest rates.

How can the United States get away with running up debt at low rates? Are other countries' central banks and private savers really the co-dependent "global enablers" Roach and others call them, who happily hold loads of low-yielding U.S. assets? The truth is, the United States has taken advantage of the status of the dollar as the currency of the global economy to make others adjust to its spending patterns. Foreign central banks hold their reserves in dollars, and countries are billed in dollars for their oil imports, which requires them to buy dollars. That sustains the demand for the dollar and protects its value even as the current account imbalance widens.

The U.S. strong dollar policy in the face of its yawning current account deficit imposes a "shadow tax" on the rest of the world, at least in part to pay for its cost of empire. "But payment," as Robert Skidelsky, the British biographer of Keynes, reminds us, "is voluntary and depends at minimum on acquiescence in U.S. foreign policy." The geopolitical reason for the rest of the capitalist world to accept the "seignorage of the dollar"—in other words, the advantage the United States enjoys by virtue of minting the reserve currency of the international economy—became less compelling when the United States substituted a "puny war on terrorism" for the Cold War, Skidelsky adds.

The tax does not fall only on other industrialized countries. The U.S. economy has not just become a giant vacuum cleaner that sucks up "all the world's spare investible cash," in the words of University of California, Berkeley economist Brad DeLong, but about one-third of that money comes from the developing world. To put this contribution in perspective: DeLong calculates that $90 billion a year, or one-third of the average U.S. current account deficit over the

IF THE UNITED STATES WAS AN EMERGING MARKET

If the United States was a small or less-developed country, financial alarm bells would already be ringing. The U.S. current account deficit is well above the 5%-of-GDP standard the IMF and others use to pronounce economies in the developing world vulnerable to financial crisis.

Just how crisis-prone depends on how the current account deficit affects the economy's spending. If the foreign funds flowing into the country are being invested in export-producing sectors of the economy, or the tradable goods sectors, such as manufacturing and some services, they are likely over time to generate revenues necessary to pay back the rest of the world. In that case, the shortfall is less of a problem. If those monies go to consumption or speculative investment in non-tradable (i.e., non-export producing) sectors such as a real estate, then they surely will be a problem.

By that standard, the U.S. current account deficit is highly problematic. Economists assess the impact of a current account deficit by comparing it to the difference between net national investment and net national savings. (Net here means less the money set aside to cover depreciation.) In the U.S. case, that difference has widened because saving has plummeted, not because investment has picked up. Last year, the United States registered its lowest net national savings rate ever, 1.5%, due to the return of large federal budget deficits and anemic personal savings. In addition, U.S. investment has shifted substantially away from tradable goods as manufacturing has come under heavy foreign competition toward the non-traded goods sector, such as residential real estate whose prices have soared in and around most major American cities.

Capital inflows that cover a decline in savings instead of a surge in investment are not a sign of economic health nor cause to stop worrying about the current account deficit.

last two decades, is equal to the income of the poorest 500 million people in India.

The rest of the world ought not to complain about these global imbalances, insist the strong dollar types. That the United States racks up debt while other countries rack up savings is not profligacy but a virtue. The United States, they argue, is the global economy's "consumer of last resort." Others, especially in Europe, according to U.S. policymakers, are guilty of "insufficient consumption": they hold back their economies and dampen the demand for U.S. exports, exacerbating the U.S. current account deficit. Last year U.S. consumers increased their spending three times as quickly as European consumers (excluding Britain), and the U.S. economy grew about two and half times as quickly.

GLOBAL UPRISING

Not surprisingly, old Europe and newly industrializing Asia don't see it that way. They have grown weary from all their heavy lifting of U.S. securities. And while they have yet to throw them overboard, a revolt is brewing.

Those cranky French are especially indignant about the unfairness of it all. The editors of Le Monde, the French daily, complain that "The United States considers itself innocent: it refuses to admit that it lives beyond its means through weak savings and excessive consumption." On top of that, the drop of the dollar has led to a brutal rise in the value of the euro that is wiping out the demand for euro-zone exports and slowing their already sluggish economic recoveries.

Even in Blair's Britain the Economist, the newsweekly, ran an unusually tough-minded editorial warning: "The dollar's role as the leading international currency can no longer be taken for granted. ... Imagine if you could write checks that were accepted as payment but never cashed. That is what [the privileged position of the dollar] amounts to. If you had been granted that ability, you might take care to hang to it. America is taking no such care. And may come to regret it."

But the real threat comes from Asia, especially Japan and China, the two largest holders of U.S. Treasury bonds. Asian central banks already hold most of their reserves in dollar-denominated assets, an enormous financial risk given that the value of the dollar will likely continue to fall at current low interest rates.

In late November, just the rumor that China's Central Bank threatened to reduce its purchases of U.S. Treasury bonds was enough to send the dollar tumbling.

No less than Alan Greenspan, chair of the Fed, seems to have come down with a case of dollar anxiety. In his November remarks to the European Banking Community, Greenspan warned of a "diminished appetite for adding to dollar balances" even if the current account deficit stops increasing. Greenspan believes that foreign investors are likely to realize they have put too many of their eggs in the dollar basket and will either unload their dollar-denominated investments or demand higher interest rates. After Greenspan spoke, the dollar fell to its lowest level against the Japanese yen in more than four years.

A ROUGH RIDE FROM HERE

The question that divides economists at this point is not whether the dollar will decline more, but whether the descent will be slow and orderly or quick and panicky. Either way, there is real reason to believe it will be a rough ride.

First, a controlled devaluation of the dollar won't be easy to accomplish. Several major Asian currencies are formally or informally pegged to the dollar, including the Chinese yuan. The United States faces a $160 billion trade deficit with China alone. U.S. financial authorities have exerted tremendous pressure on the Chinese to raise the value of their currency, in the hope of slowing the tide of Chinese imports into the United States and making U.S. exports more competitive. But the Chinese have yet to budge.

Beyond that, a fall in the dollar sufficient to close the current account deficit will slaughter large amounts of capital. The Economist warns that "[i]f the dollar falls by another 30%, as some predict, it would amount to the biggest default

in history: not a conventional default on debt service, but default by stealth, wiping trillions off the value of foreigners' dollar assets."

Even a gradual decline in the value of dollar will bring tough economic consequences. Inflation will pick up, as imports cost more in this bid to make U.S. exports cheaper. The Fed will surely raise interest rates to counteract that inflationary pressure, slowing consumer borrowing and investment. Also, closing the current account deficit would require smaller government deficits. (Although not politically likely, repealing Bush's pro-rich tax cuts would help.)

What will happen is anyone's guess given the unprecedented size of the U.S. current account deficit. But there is a real possibility that the dollar's slide will be anything but slow or orderly. Should Asian central banks stop intervening on the scale needed to finance the U.S. deficit, then a crisis surely would follow. The dollar would drop through the floor; U.S. interest rates would skyrocket (on everything from Treasury bonds to mortgages to credit cards); the stock market and home values would collapse; consumer and investment spending would plunge; and a sharp recession would take hold here and abroad.

The Bush administration seems determined to make things worse. Should the Bush crew push through their plan to privatize Social Security and pay the trillion-dollar transition cost with massive borrowing, the consequences could be disastrous. The example of Argentina is instructive. Privatizing the country's retirement program, as economist Paul Krugman has pointed out, was a major source of the debt that brought on Argentina's crisis in 2001. Dismantling the U.S. welfare state's most successful program just might push the dollar-based financial system over the edge.

The U.S. economy is in a precarious situation held together so far by imperial privilege. Its prospects appear to fall into one of three categories: a dollar crisis; a long, slow, excruciating decline in value of the dollar; or a dollar propped up through repeated interest rates hikes. That's real reason to worry.

Sources: "Dollar Anxiety," editorial, Wall Street Journal, 11/11/04; D. Wessel, "Behind Big Drop in Currency: U.S. Soaks Up Asia's Output," WSJ, 12/2/04; J. B. DeLong, "Should We Still Support Untrammeled International Capital Mobility? Or are Capital Controls Less Evil than We Once Believed," Economists' Voice, 2004; R. Skidelsky, "U.S. Current Account Deficit and Future of the World Monetary System" and N. Roubini and B. Setser "The U.S. as A Net Debtor: The Sustainability of the U.S. External Imbalances," 11/04, Nouriel Roubini's Global Macroeconomic and Financial Policy site <www.stern.nyu.edu/globalmacro>; Rich Miller, "Why the Dollar is Giving Way," Business Week, 12/6/04; Robert Barro, "Mysteries of the Gaping Current-Account Gap," Business Week, 12/13/04; D. Streitford and J. Fleishman, "Greenspan Issues Warning on Dollar," L.A. Times, 11/20/04; S. Roach, "Global: What Happens If the Dollar Does Not Fall?" Global Economic Forum, Morgan Stanley, 11/22/04; L. Summers, "The U.S. Current Account Deficit and the Global Economy," The 2004 Per Jacobsson Lecture, 10/3/04; "The Dollar," editorial, The Economist, 12/3/04; "Mr. Gaymard and the Dollar," editorial, Le Monde, 11/30/04.

WILL THE WTO STRIKE OUT IN HONG KONG?

BY DEBORAH JAMES

This December, delegates from 148 countries will meet to shape the future of the world's nearly 6 billion people. From December 13 to 18, the World Trade Organization will hold its sixth major meeting, known as a ministerial, in Hong Kong, China, to negotiate on such crucial matters as the fate of public services, the global food supply, and jobs and development.

The WTO is the global promoter and enforcer of the ideology that "free trade" is the best way to foster economic growth and, hence, development. The theory might sound great if you don't look at the record. For example, in the 25 years Latin American governments have submitted to the prescription to open their economies up to free flows of goods and capital, economic growth has ground to a near halt, marking only about a half a percent per capita income growth per year. That's left 222 million people—an outrageous 43% of the region's population—impoverished. In fact, the fastest growing economies in Latin America are those that are rejecting orthodox "free trade" doctrine, primarily Venezuela and Argentina. And in China, growing rural poverty is linked to the country's 2001 accession to the WTO, according to a study the World Bank released last February.

Moreover, the fine print of WTO agreements often turns out to have more to do with protecting the interests of multinational corporations and specific sectors in the economies of the rich countries than with actual adherence to the doctrine of free trade. Ten years into the WTO process, for example, the United States and the European Union are still refusing to give up their agricultural subsidies, which have swamped poor countries with artificially cheap food imports and forced countless farmers off the land across the global South.

Six years ago, the world watched as activists from across the United States shut down the third WTO ministerial meeting in Seattle. Yet while the WTO remains a grave threat to communities, the environment, democracy, and global development, only a handful of organizations are gearing up for the Hong Kong ministerial.

STRIKE ONE, STRIKE TWO

By 1999, developing country governments had begun to recognize that the WTO, though masquerading as a neutral arbiter of trade rules, was actually facilitating a giant corporate power grab, threatening democracy, natural resources, and labor rights across the globe. Over 50,000 people came to Seattle to say no to the WTO's corporate agenda, successfully shutting down the meetings on the first day, November 30, 1999. Activists wanted to build a world where life values—like the right to good jobs, clean water, health care, education, democracy and sovereignty—trumped the money values of the WTO. Emboldened by massive civil society resistance, the African, Caribbean, and other least-developed country representatives literally walked out of the meetings, causing the negotiations to collapse. *Strike one.*

The fourth ministerial took place in 2001 in Qatar, a country where free-speech rights are effectively nonexistent. The rich countries promised that this round of negotiations would focus on development and the needs of the poorest countries—an implicit acknowledgment of the unfairness of the existing system. But behind closed doors and out of the civil-society and media spotlight, hard pressure could be applied. Few countries actually participated in the negotiations, but the United States and the EU bullied and arm-twisted all member countries into signing onto a largely corporate trade agenda—and thus succeeded in launching the so-called Doha Development Round, a misnomer of epic proportions.

In 2003 the process moved to Cancún, Mexico, where the rich countries sought to expand the scope of the WTO, pressing for agreements in new areas such as investment at the fifth ministerial. But they didn't count on the rise of a remarkable new alliance: Brazil, India, South Africa, China, Indonesia, Venezuela, and 14 other countries created a negotiating block representing over half of the world's population. This "Group of 20" argued that the unfair global agricultural system had to be cleaned up first, before new issues could come onto the table. The tragic suicide of Korean farmer Lee Kyung Hae brought the collective rage of the outside civil-society mobilization inside the closed gates of the negotiating halls. Most important, the least developed countries stood their ground against the intransigence of the rich countries and refused to accept an expansion in the scope of WTO agreements without a genuine development agenda. *Strike two.*

Then, in the summer of 2004, a funny thing happened. Major WTO decisions are supposed to be made at the biannual ministerial meetings, but those gatherings kept striking out. So the United States and the EU turned a General Council meeting in Geneva into a decision-making forum where, out of sight of teeming protests and behind closed doors in invitation-only "green rooms," the WTO was saved from a third strike. The United States and the EU pulled India and Brazil (along with Australia) into a meeting of the so-called Five Interested Parties (FIPs). With false assurances that agriculture would be fairly reformed, they cobbled together a minimal consensus to get the negotiations back on track. After subduing Brazil and India, they pressured the rest of the members of the WTO into going along with the new patched-up framework agreement—sight unseen. Thus the WTO was given a walk, and is up at bat at the next ministerial this December.

The WTO convened another General Council meeting in Geneva this July that was supposed to be a major step forward. Fortunately, there was anything but consensus. When WTO spinmeisters start to downplay expectations for upcoming meetings, that usually means the "free trade" juggernaut is stalled. That's good news: global justice activists have reached a broad consensus that blocking any new agreements within the existing WTO framework is critical. But as with the passage of CAFTA in the U.S. Congress this summer, you never know what kinds of buy-offs, procedural tricks, or pork barrel the Bush administration is willing to parlay to get a deal.

Here is a preview of what is at stake in the negotiations this December in three key areas: public services, agriculture, and jobs.

TAKING THE PUBLIC OUT OF PUBLIC SERVICES

Traditionally, international trade agreements were focused primarily on trade in goods. But in recent years, corporations and their government allies have fought to expand the scope of these agreements to include services as well. The U.S. government's agenda is to gain access to the world's financial and energy services markets for U.S. corporations. This would give the green light for U.S. banks like Citigroup and JP Morgan Chase to control the world's capital and banking industries. And it would allow U.S. corporations like Halliburton and Bechtel to control the world's energy services—everything that has to do with getting oil out of the earth and into the market. Also on the chopping block are education, water, and health care—in other words, the services that citizens of rich and poor countries alike expect their governments to provide to all, not merely to those who can afford to purchase them in the marketplace.

Evidently, developing countries aren't lining up fast enough to privatize their public services. (Sometimes privatizations have been halted by public pressure; for example, in Cochabamba, Bolivia, massive protest forced the government to reverse the handover of the city's water system to a private corporation in 2000.) In response, the United States and the EU are pushing for an inflexible new bargaining framework, known as benchmarking, that would set a high bar for the level of privatization countries must allow. Developing-country negotiators have vehemently rejected the benchmarking proposal at WTO meetings this summer and fall. But they face great pressure to open up their public

services to privatization and liberalization, especially since the 2004 framework agreement linked negotiations over services to the rest of the WTO agenda, essentially telling poor countries that they will not get any of the changes they seek in areas like agricultural subsidies unless they concede on services.

Even more controversial are the negotiations around what the WTO calls Mode 4, or the "natural movement of persons." Developing countries generally want more access for their citizens to migrate freely and to work in the United States and the EU. India, for example, has made the permanent codification of the current standard of 65,000 H1B visas for highly-educated workers to enter the United States a principal demand (admittedly a move some consider strange as a key development strategy for a country of more than a billion people). But easing immigration is not exactly popular in the United States or Europe. Some labor rights groups are concerned that H1B visas amount to an "internal outsourcing" where U.S. jobs physically stay in the country but are filled by foreigners. And immigrants' rights activists are sounding the alarm bells about the lack of labor rights for immigrants allowed in on H1B visas. In any case, U.S. and EU negotiators have made only vague and minimal commitments to the developing countries on this issue.

FOOD: TO EAT OR TO EXPORT?

Since the U.S. government abolished its supply management program in 1996, agricultural oversupply has led to a price collapse. To bail out the system, the government instituted subsidies to farmers, which disproportionately benefit large-scale agribusiness over family farmers. This crazy regime allows giant corporations like Monsanto and ConAgra to dump artificially cheap food in developing countries, undercutting local markets and pushing farmers off the land.

Export subsidies are supposed to be phased out under the WTO and other free-trade regimes. But the rich countries, with stunning hypocrisy, have largely won exemptions for the types of subsidies they use, while pushing to prohibit the subsidies and regulations used by poor countries to protect their domestic agriculture sectors. For example, about 70% of U.S. agricultural subsidies fall into a loophole category called the Green Box. Another loophole, the Blue Box, originally covered only those farm subsidies that were linked to limits on crop production, to address the vicious circle of oversupply, price drop, subsidy, oversupply, and so on. Far from being phased out, though, the Blue Box was actually expanded in the July 2004 framework agreement to cover subsidies without production limits—in order to accommodate some of the subsidies in the 2002 U.S. farm bill, according to the advocacy group Focus on the Global South.

Developing countries have been demanding that the EU and the United States cut back their agricultural subsidy programs and provide market access for products like Central American sugar and Brazilian orange juice. But with agribusiness in control of several key red states and the farm bill coming up for reauthorization in Congress, it's unlikely the Bush administration will negotiate seriously on these issues in the near future.

KICKING AWAY THE LADDER OF DEVELOPMENT

In another key area of negotiation, the WTO is pressuring governments to lower tariffs on industrial products and natural resources (Non-Agricultural Market Access, or NAMA, in WTO-speak). Using tariffs to protect new and developing industries against competition from foreign products is a cornerstone of industrial policy, one that every developed country has used. But now rich countries want to prohibit the use of this tool, effectively kicking away the ladder of development they themselves ascended. According to the Third World Network, this would de-industrialize many middle-income countries and prevent the industrialization of most of Africa.

Not only would massive tariff reductions allow floods of cheap imported products into poor countries, putting their own industries out of business, it would also starve many small nations of the revenues they need to finance health care and education. Tariffs are nothing but taxes on corporations for the privilege of selling a product in a foreign country. NAMA, then, can be understood as a massive corporate tax abolition scheme.

NAMA negotiators also want to eliminate so-called "non-tariff barriers" such as bans on importing bacteria-contaminated food or mandates that government agencies use energy from renewable sources, purchase Fair Trade Certified coffee, or buy from companies that use sweatshop-free labor. The NAMA framework deems these and other food-safety, health, environmental, and labor regulations to be unfair trade barriers—unfair, in other words, to products that damage the environment, human health, or labor rights. U.S. negotiators are also pushing within NAMA to eliminate tariffs completely on forest, fishery, and mining products. Both tariffs and regulations are tools governments can use to conserve resources and promote environmentally sustainable development; the prospect of eliminating them has environmentalists spinning.

LAST CHANCE AT BAT?

The Doha round negotiations have missed just about every major deadline thus far: talks were supposed to have been wrapped up by January 2005, yet are still stalled over disagreements on the basic framework. The new deadline of December 2006 is not far off, considering that most of the heavy lifting is still to be completed.

A meeting of the WTO General Council this October was suspended to allow for the big powers plus India and Brazil—the FIPs—to hammer out the elusive agricultural compromise. A new draft framework is expected by December 15; early "pre-drafts" demonstrate an alarming trend in favor of rich country corporate interests. If developing country governments, supported by global civil society, can stand up to the arm-twisting and the outrageous demands coming from the United States and the EU, the Hong Kong ministerial could fall apart—a tremendous blow to the WTO's credibility. Then, perhaps, citizens and activists around the globe could declare, "Three strikes and you're out!"

ARTICLE 8.8

July/August 2005

CAFTA'S DEBT TRAP

BY ALDO CALIARI

The proposed Central American Free Trade Agreement (CAFTA) would create a trade and investment block that includes the United States, Costa Rica, El Salvador, Guatemala, Honduras, Nicaragua, and the Dominican Republic. Modeled on the failed 11-year-old North American Free Trade Agreement (NAFTA), the deal aims to liberalize trade among the signatory countries by removing barriers to the flow of goods, services, and capital. CAFTA is widely viewed as a stepping stone to the creation of a larger Free Trade Area of the Americas. The Senate voted to pass CAFTA in June, and the House is expected to follow suit.—Eds.

Critics of the Central American Free Trade Agreement have focused on concerns that the treaty will devastate Central American farmers by forcing them to compete with heavily subsidized U.S. agribusiness. Others point out that the deal will perpetuate low-road development based on poverty wages and lax environmental enforcement, while undermining governments' authority to ensure basic services. These are all valid concerns, but CAFTA poses yet another danger that deserves equal attention.

Rules buried in the technical language of the investment chapter of the agreement would make it more difficult for the six Central American nations to escape their heavy debt burdens or recover from debt crises should they, for example, find themselves unable to meet their obligations to holders

of government bonds and other creditors. The investment provisions of CAFTA—like the 1994 North American Free Trade Agreement between the United States, Canada, and Mexico—are based on the argument that strong investment protections encourage foreign private investment. CAFTA subscribes to this same precept, and, like NAFTA, it would require governments to comply with a long list of investor protections and even grant foreign private investors the right to sue governments for damages if those obligations are violated.

Both treaties require governments to treat foreign investors at least as favorably as domestic investors, a principle known as "national treatment." Governments must also ensure "most favored nation" treatment for other treaty members, meaning they cannot give special preferences to, or discriminate against, the investors of any one country that is a party to the agreement. As a result, member governments can no longer favor domestic interests or investors even to support social goals or other national interests.

But whereas NAFTA's investor protections explicitly exclude "sovereign debt" (the bonds, loans, and other securities issued from or guaranteed by national governments) from investor protection rules, CAFTA specifically includes these forms of public liabilities.

As the U.S. House deliberates on CAFTA, it's important for the public to recognize that in subjecting government bonds and other forms of sovereign debt to stringent investment protections, the deal would place huge constraints on indebted countries' ability to prevent or survive debt crises —and to protect the basic needs of their citizens.

NATIONAL TREATMENT AND MOST FAVORED NATION STATUS

The "national treatment" and "most favored nation" principles were originally born in agreements dealing with trade in goods, only later extending to investment. Their application to sovereign debt introduces a number of serious problems.

1. CAFTA dismantles essential tools governments need to recover from crisis.

Requiring that foreign creditors be offered favorable treatment equal to domestic creditors is dangerous for the developing-country members of CAFTA, since they all, with the exception of Honduras, owe a significant share of public debt to domestic creditors. In some countries, including Costa Rica, domestic debt is actually higher than external debt.

When undergoing a debt restructuring, a government makes an "offer" to all creditors, typically reducing the value of outstanding bonds and loans substantially. Once the offer is agreed to, the country can regain its footing and restart the flow of investment.

There are a variety of reasons why a country might want to offer domestic creditors preferential conditions in restructuring its sovereign debt. In a financial crisis, domestic creditors often take a double hit. They're forced to accept a reduction

in the value of their loans, and they face high interest rates and other costs. Yet domestic capital markets are critical in a recovery. By addressing the needs of domestic investors first, a country will be better able to return to domestic capital markets quickly during what is likely to be a sustained interruption in access to foreign capital. This can feed a resumption of growth, which, in turn, can facilitate repayment of other obligations and reverse the precipitous fall in a country's standard of living that typically accompanies a debt crisis. Even the International Monetary Fund (IMF), a staunch defender of the rights of foreign private investors, acknowledges that "the restructuring of certain types of domestic debt may have major implications for economic performance, as a result of its impact on the financial system and the operation of domestic capital markets."

Prioritizing domestic debt may also be necessary to protect a country's banking system. Argentinean economist José Luis Machinea has pointed out that sovereign debt restructuring has a double impact on domestic holders of debt: On the one hand, the value of their bonds is reduced. On the other, they suffer the general impact of the crisis on the real economy and on their access to finance. The IMF has stated that in crises, affording special treatment to domestic debt might help protect "a core of the banking system by ensuring the availability of assets required for banks to manage capital, liquidity, and exposure to market risks."

More generally, countries may need to provide special treatment to domestic debtors as part of their national development strategy—that is, for the same legitimate reasons that can lead them to accord special treatment to domestic industries.

2. CAFTA prevents states from paying salaries and pensions.

Under CAFTA, member governments would no longer be able to prioritize domestic debts consisting of, among other things, wages, salaries, and pensions. This could have dire ramifications for state workers. According to the national treatment principle, governments are bound to treat these obligations the same way they treat foreign debts held by transnational banks and foreign investors. If the state has only enough resources to cover a portion of its debts, it will be prohibited from choosing to direct those funds first to wages and salaries. In this way, too, CAFTA would deal a setback to national governments' ability to prioritize their obligations to the basic human rights of their citizens and put their own economic development above the claims of foreign creditors.

Unlike a private corporation in bankruptcy, an indebted nation has human rights obligations and social responsibilities toward its people. That's why civil society groups have called for developing new debt-crisis protocols that take into account the broader mission of the state and its role in society. Models already exist—for example, Chapter 9 of the U.S. bankruptcy code which applies to municipalities.

Even the IMF's proposed rules for restructuring sovereign debt excluded "wages, salaries and pensions" from their application.

3. *It reduces the leverage of domestic debtors.*

A government's debt restructuring offer can take on added clout if it has first cut a deal with supportive domestic creditors. Giving these domestic creditors preferential terms is a way for the state to win back their support. If the principles of national treatment are applied to sovereign debt, however, any incentive offered to domestic creditors would have to be offered to the foreign creditors as well, effectively foreclosing this avenue of recovery.

Argentina's offer of preferential conditions to domestic creditors was a crucial element in enhancing the government's leverage in negotiating with its foreign private creditors after it suffered the largest sovereign default in history in December 2001. In September 2003, the government released its initial proposed debt restructuring conditions, which included a 75% cut in the value of its bonds. Some groups of bondholders quickly rejected this offer, claiming that it was woefully insufficient and, in light of the country's latest growth figures, below what the country could repay. The creditors also strongly lobbied the G7 group of industrialized countries, which, both directly and through the IMF, put more pressure on Argentina to sweeten its offer. With pressure mounting from the G7 and the IMF, Argentina turned to its domestic pension funds. By granting domestic pension funds preferential conditions, Argentina was able to reach an agreement with them. The funds held more than 17% of the country's total debt and their coming on board was a critical first step in Argentina's eventually garnering the support of a full 76% of its creditors.

The government's ability to treat domestic bondholders differently from foreign ones was crucial to reaching an agreement with the majority of creditors. This option would have been out of the question if the government had been bound by CAFTA's national treatment principle.

INVESTOR-STATE LAWSUITS

Under CAFTA, governments that violate these investor protections can face expensive lawsuits. As under NAFTA and numerous bilateral investment treaties, CAFTA grants private foreign investors the right to bypass domestic courts and sue governments in international tribunals.

Such "investor-state lawsuits" are highly controversial for a number of reasons. First, many arbitration tribunals operate with an absolute lack of transparency, having no obligation to disclose relevant documents or allow any form of public participation. The system for choosing arbitrators has also drawn criticism, as the arbitrators can be chosen from the ranks of practicing investment lawyers, with no obligation to appoint people who will be independent, that is, who have no stake in the treaty interpretation. These unelected tribunals may well rule on difficult questions with far-reaching social and economic implications that rightfully belong under the domestic jurisdiction of states.

* * * * *

CAFTA's application of investor protections to sovereign debt would suppress the few options available to countries trying to prevent or exit from debt crises. History shows that the inability to exit a crisis situation causes economic losses far outweighing any commercial gains achieved through a free trade agreement.

Central American activists are already calling on their governments to reject CAFTA. In the United States, activists must also urge Congress to reject CAFTA because in addition to all the concerns that have been voiced already, it will tightly tie the hands of member countries in dealing with their large stocks of external debt.

An earlier version of this article appeared in *Foreign Policy In Focus* <www.fpif.org>, June 2005.

CHINA AND THE GLOBAL ECONOMY

BY THOMAS I. PALLEY

Over the last twenty years China has undergone a massive economic transformation. A generation ago, China's economy was largely agricultural; today, the country is an industrial powerhouse experiencing rapid economic growth. Now, however, many economists question the sustainability of China's development model. Ironically, this debate has been triggered by recent acceleration in China's growth, which exceeded 9% in both 2003 and 2004. Some analysts claim this acceleration is being driven by a private investment bubble and by misdirected state investment, posing the risks of inflation and a hard landing when the bubble pops.

China's development model is indeed unsustainable—but not for the reasons most economists suggest. It is not overinvestment or excessive growth that is the problem. Instead, it is China's impact on the global economy. China's export-led development model threatens to trigger a global recession that will rebound and hit China itself. In short, in the same kind of scenario that Keynes addressed in the 1930s, China has failed to develop the demand side of its economy, and so its massive production growth threatens to swamp a weakening demand picture worldwide, with potentially severe consequences for both China and its customers.

A BRIEF REVIEW OF CHINA'S DEVELOPMENT MODEL

Broadly speaking, China's development model aims to reduce the size of the centrally planned economy and increase the size of market-based private sector activity. The first step in this transition was taken with the historic 1979 reforms of the agricultural sector, which allowed small farmers to produce for the market. Since then, the government has allowed private sector activity to spread more widely by removing controls on economic activity; at the same time, it is privatizing state owned enterprises (SOEs) on a limited basis.

This spread of market-centered activity has been accompanied by both external and internal capital accumulation strategies. The external strategy rests on foreign direct investment (FDI) and export-led growth. The internal strategy uses credit creation by state-controlled banks to fund SOEs and infrastructure investment.

Though FDI is small relative to total Chinese fixed asset accumulation, it serves a number of important functions. Construction and operation of foreign-owned plants has created employment. FDI has also brought capital goods and high technology into the country, and the inflow has been financed by foreign multinational companies (MNCs).

Industrialization inevitably requires importing capital goods from developed economies. Most poor countries have borrowed to pay for these capital goods, which has constrained their growth and made them vulnerable to ever-fluctuating global currency markets. In China, FDI has been a form of self-financing development that short-circuits these foreign financing problems.

Significantly, FDI has provided a key source of export earnings, since a significant portion of MNC output in China is exported. In 2004, MNCs provided 57% of total exports. These exports earnings have bolstered China's balance of payments and ensured external investor confidence.

Low-wage labor plus the advanced technology and capital that FDI has brought into the country have made China the world's low-cost manufacturing leader. With exports booming, foreign MNCs have been willing to continue building new plants in China. This has given rise to an anomalous situation in which low-income China has been a lender (in the form of its trade surplus) to the high-income United States. Normally, it is expected that high-income households save and lend to low-income households. However, there is a logic to this situation. Exports and a trade surplus (i.e., Chinese savings) are the price that China pays for getting foreign MNCs to invest there. For the Chinese government this is a deal worth striking, since China gains productive capacity, high technology, and jobs. It also gains foreign exchange from the trade surplus, which provides protection against the vagaries of the international economy.

This external capital accumulation strategy has been complemented by an internal strategy predicated on state-directed bank credit expansion. The state-owned banking system has been used to fund large industrial and infrastructure investment projects, as well as to maintain employment in unprofitable SOEs. This has helped support aggregate demand and avoid a precipitous collapse of employment in the SOE sector. With no alternative places to invest their money, Chinese savers have effectively been forced to finance these state investments; the government keeps interest rates low by fiat and thus controls the interest cost of these public investments.

EXTERNAL CONTRADICTIONS: LIMITS TO EXPORT-LED GROWTH

Though highly successful to date, China's development strategy is ultimately fundamentally flawed. China has become such a global manufacturing powerhouse that it is now driving the massive U.S. trade deficit and undermining the

U.S. manufacturing sector. This threatens the economic health of its major customer. China is putting pressure on the European Union's manufacturing sector, slowing economic growth there as well. The contradiction in China's model, then, is that China's success threatens to undermine the U.S. economy, which has provided the demand that has fueled that success.

China's trade surpluses with the United States have been growing rapidly for several years. In 2004, the United States' bilateral trade deficit with China was $162.0 billion, representing 38.8% of the U.S. trade deficit with all non-OPEC countries. The bilateral China deficit is growing fastest, too: by 30.5% from 2003 to 2004, compared to 16.8% growth in the non-China, non-OPEC trade deficit.

The U.S. trade deficit threatens to become a source of financial instability. More important, the deficit is contributing to the problems in manufacturing that are hindering a robust, investment-led recovery in the United States. There are two ways in which the trade deficit has hindered recovery. First, the deficit drains spending out of the U.S. economy, so that jobs are lost or are created offshore instead of at home. Using a methodology that estimates the labor content embodied in the deficit, economist Robert Scott of the Economic Policy Institute estimates that the U.S. trade deficit with China in 2003 represented 1,339,300 lost job opportunities. Using Scott's job calculations and assuming the composition of trade remained unchanged in 2004, the 2004 trade deficit with China of $162 billion represents 1,808,055 lost job opportunities.

Second, China's policies hurt U.S. investment spending through a range of channels. The draining of demand via the trade deficit creates excess capacity, which reduces demand for new capital. The undervaluation of China's currency makes production in China cheaper, and this encourages firms to both shift existing facilities to China and build new facilities there. Undervaluation also reduces the profitability of U.S. manufacturing and this reduces investment spending.

The U.S. economy is of course a huge economy and these China effects are small in terms of total investment. However, China is likely exerting a chilling effect at the margin of manufacturing investment, and it is at this margin where the recessionary impacts of investment decline have been and continue to be felt.

Together, these employment and investment effects risk tipping the U.S. economy back into recession after what has already been a weak expansion. If this happens, there will be significant adverse consequences for the Chinese economy, and for the global economy as a whole, since the U.S. economy is the main engine of demand growth that has been keeping the world economy flying. (Much is made of China as itself an engine of demand growth, particularly benefiting Japan. China *is* buying capital goods and production inputs from Japan. However, China's internal demand growth depends on the prosperity generated by exporting

to the U.S. economy. In this sense, the U.S. economy is the ultimate source of demand growth; this demand growth is then multiplied in the global economy, where China plays an important role in the multiplier process.)

That's why China must replace its export-led growth strategy with one based on expanding domestic demand. China's people need to have the incomes and the institutions that will enable them to consume a far larger share of what they produce.

For the moment, thanks to continued debt-financed spending by U.S. households, China's adverse impact has not derailed the U.S. economy. China has therefore continued to grow despite the weak U.S. recovery from recession. But there are reasons to believe the U.S. economy is increasingly fragile—a Wily Coyote economy running on thinner and thinner air. The recovery has been financed by asset price appreciation, especially in real estate, which has provided collateral for the home-equity loans and other borrowing consumers have used to keep spending. This means the U.S. economy is increasingly burdened by debt which could soon drive the economy into recession. Once in recession, with private sector balance sheets clogged with debt taken on at current low interest rates and not open to refinancing, the U.S. would not have recourse to another recovery based on consumer borrowing and housing price inflation.

Policymakers, including those in China, tend to have a hard time grasping complex scenarios such as this one, where the damage to China is indirect, operating via recession in the United States. Now that it has become a global manufacturing powerhouse, China's export-led manufacturing growth model is exerting huge strains on the global economy. Until now, China has been able to free-ride on global aggregate demand. The strategy worked when Chinese manufacturing was small, but it cannot continue working now that it is so large. The difficulty is to persuade China's policymakers of the need for change now, when the model still seems to be working and the crash has not come.

DEVELOPING THE DEMAND SIDE OF THE CHINESE ECONOMY

In place of export-led growth, China must adopt a model of domestic demand-led growth. Such a model requires developing structures, institutions, and economic relations that

CHINA: RAPID ECONOMIC GROWTH, RAPID EXPORT GROWTH	
Average annual GDP growth 1980-2002:	9.5%
Average annual export growth 1980-2002:	15.5%
Trade as a share of GDP in 1980:	13%
Trade as a share of GDP in 2002:	50%
Market share in the United States in 1980:	0.5%
Market share in the United States in 2002:	11.1%

Source: Internal Monetary Fund, www. imf.org/external/np/apd/seminars/2003/ newdelhi/wang.pdf. Box prepared by *Dollars & Sense.*

generate sustained, stable internal demand growth. This is an enormous task and one that is key to achieving developed-country status, yet it is a task that has received little attention.

Economic theory and policy have traditionally focused on expansion of the supply side in developing countries. This is the core of the export-led growth paradigm, which emphasizes becoming internationally competitive and relying on export markets to provide demand and absorb increases in production. The demand side is generally ignored in the main body of development economics because economists assume that supply generates its own demand, a proposition known as Say's Law.

Nor are traditional Keynesian policies the right answer. Though Keynesian economics does emphasize demand considerations, it operates in the context of mature market economies in which the institutions that generate stable, broad-based demand are well established. For Keynesians, demand shortages can be remedied by policies that stimulate private sector demand (e.g., lowering interest rates or cutting taxes) or by direct government spending. These policies address temporary failures in an established demand generation process.

Developing countries, however, face a different problem: they need to build the demand generation process in the first place. Application of standard Keynesian policies in developing countries tends to create excessive government deficits and promote an oversized government sector. Increased government spending adds to demand but it increases deficits, and it also does little to generate "market" incomes that are the basis of sustainable growth in demand. What is needed is a new analytic approach, one focused on establishing an economic order that ensures income gets into the hands of those who will spend it and encourages production of needed goods that have high domestic employment and expenditure multipliers. This can be termed "structural Keynesianism," in contrast with conventional "demand-side Keynesianism."

In China, then, the challenge is to develop sustainable, growing sources of noninflationary domestic purchasing power. This means attending to both the investment allocation process and the income allocation process. The former is critical to ensure that resources are efficiently allocated, earn an adequate rate of return, and add to needed productive capacity. The latter is critical to ensure that domestic demand grows to absorb increased output. Income must be placed in the hands of Chinese consumers if robust consumer markets are to develop. But this income must be delivered in an efficient, equitable manner that maintains economic incentives.

While banking reform is critical to improving China's capital allocation process, the greater challenge is to develop an appropriate system of household income distribution that supports domestic consumer markets. Investment spending is an important source of demand, but the output generated by investments must find buyers or investment will cease. Likewise, public sector investment can be an important source of demand, but private sector income must grow over time or else the government sector will come to dominate, with negative consequences.

With a population of 1.3 billion people, China has an enormous potential domestic market. The challenge is to distribute its rapidly growing income in a decentralized, equitable fashion that leaves work and production incentives intact. The conventional view is that markets automatically take care of the problem by paying workers what they are worth and that all income is spent, thereby generating the demand for output produced. In effect, the problem is assumed away. Indeed, to intervene and raise wages to increase demand would be to cause unemployment by making labor too expensive.

This conventional logic contrasts with Keynesian economics, which identifies the core economic problem as one of ensuring a level of aggregate demand consistent with full utilization of a nation's production capacity. Moreover, the level of aggregate demand is affected by the distribution of income, with worsened income distribution lowering aggregate demand because of the higher propensity to save among higher-income households. From a Keynesian perspective, market forces do not automatically generate an appropriate level of aggregate demand. Demand can be too low because of lack of confidence among economic agents that lowers investment and consumption spending. It can also be too low because the distribution of income is skewed excessively toward upper income groups.

In sum, for neoclassical economists, labor markets set wages such that there is full employment, and income distribution is a by-product that in itself has no effect on employment. For

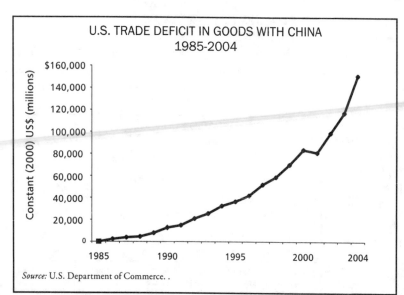

U.S. TRADE DEFICIT IN GOODS WITH CHINA
1985-2004

Constant (2000) US$ (millions)

Source: U.S. Department of Commerce. .

Keynesians, full employment requires an appropriate level of aggregate demand, which is strongly affected by the distribution of income.

The importance of income distribution for demand means that labor markets are of critical significance. Labor markets determine wages, and wages affect income distribution. The problem is that bargaining power can be highly skewed in favor of owners, leading to wages that are too low. This problem is particularly acute in developing countries. Trade unions are a vital mechanism for rectifying imbalances of bargaining power and achieving an appropriate distribution of income. Evidence shows that improved freedom of association in labor markets is associated with improved income distribution and higher wages.

Rather than representing a market distortion, as described in conventional economics, trade unions may correct market failure associated with imbalanced bargaining power. Viewed in this light, trade unions are the market-friendly approach to correcting labor market failure because unions set wages in a decentralized fashion. Though set by collective bargaining, wages can differ across firms with unions in more efficient firms bargaining higher wages than those at less efficient firms. This contrasts with a government-edict approach to wage setting.

This suggests that a key priority for China is to develop democratic trade unions that freely bargain wages. Just as China is reforming its corporate governance and financial system, so too it must embrace labor market reform and allow free democratic trade unions. This is the market-centered way of establishing an income distribution that can support a consumer society. Outside of Western Europe, only the United States, Canada, Japan, South Korea, Australia and New Zealand have successfully made the transformation to mature developed market economies. In all cases this transformation coincided with the development of effective domestic trade unions.

Free trade unions should also be supported by effectively enforced minimum wage legislation that can also promote demand-led growth. China is a continental economy in which regions differ dramatically by level of development. This suggests the need for a system in which minimum wages are set on a regional basis and take account of regional differences in living costs. Over time, as development spreads and backward regions catch up, these settings can be adjusted with the ultimate goal being a uniform national minimum wage.

Lastly, these wage-targeted labor market reforms should be paired with the development of a social safety net that provides insurance to households. This will increase households' sense of confidence and security; with less need for precautionary saving, households can spend more on consumption.

These reforms raise the issue of wage costs. As long as China follows an export-led growth strategy, production costs will be paramount. This is because export-led growth forces countries to try to ever lower costs to gain international competitive advantage, thereby creating systemic downward pressure on wages.

A domestic demand-led growth paradigm reverses this dynamic. Now, higher wages become a source of demand that strengthens the viability of employment. Capital must still earn an adequate return to pay for itself and entice new investment, but moderately higher wages strengthen the system rather than undercutting it.

Independent democratic trade unions are key to a demand-led growth model, as they are the efficient decentralized way of raising wages. However, independent unions are unacceptable to the current Chinese political leadership. That means China must also solve this political problem as part of moving to a domestic demand-led growth regime.

This paper is a shortened and revised version of "External Contradictions of the Chinese Development Model: Export-led Growth and the Dangers of Global Economic Contraction," *Journal of Contemporary China*, 15:46 (2006), forthcoming.

Sources: Blecker, R.A. (2000) "The Diminishing Returns to Export-Led Growth," paper prepared for the Council of Foreign Relations Working Group on Development, New York; Palley, T.I. (2003) "Export-led Growth: Is There Any Evidence of Crowding-Out?" in Arestis et al. (eds.), *Globalization, Regionalism, and Economic Activity*, Cheltenham: Edward Elgar; Palley, T.I. (2002) "A New Development Paradigm: Domestic Demand-Led Growth," *Foreign Policy in Focus*, www.fpif.org, also published in *After Neoliberalism: Economic Policies That Work for the Poor*, Jacobs, Weaver and Baker (eds.), New Rules for Global Finance, Washington, DC, 2002; Palley, T.I. (2005) "Labor Standards, Democracy and Wages: Some Cross-country Evidence," *Journal of International Development* 17:1–16; Hong Kong Trade & Development Council, www.tdctrade.com/main/china.htm.

SWEATSHOPS 101

BY DARA O'ROURKE

Navy blue sweatshirts bearing a single foreign word, Michigan, and a well-known logo, the Nike swoosh, were piled high in a small room off the main factory floor. After cutting, stitching, and embroidering by the 1,100 workers outside, the sweatshirts landed in the spot-cleaning room, where six young Indonesian women prepared the garments for shipment to student stores and NikeTowns across America. The women spent hour after hour using chemical solvents to rid the sweatshirts of smudges and stains. With poor ventilation, ill-fitting respiratory protection, no gloves, and no chemical hazard training, the women sprayed solvents and aerosol cleaners containing benzene, methylene chloride, and perchloroethylene, all known carcinogens, on the garments.

It used to be that the only thing people wondered when you wore a Harvard or Michigan sweatshirt was whether you had actually gone there. More and more, though, people are wondering out loud where that sweatshirt was made, and whether any workers were exploited in making it. Students, labor activists, and human-rights groups have spearheaded a movement demanding to know what really lies beneath the university logos, and whether our public universities and private colleges are profiting from global sweatshop production.

WHERE WAS THAT SWEATSHIRT MADE?

So far, few universities have been able to answer these questions. Universities generally don't even know where their products are produced, let alone whether workers were endangered to produce them. Indeed, many apparel manufacturers cannot trace the supply chains which lead to the student store, and are blissfully ignorant of conditions in these factories.

As part of a collaborative research project funded by Harvard University, the University of Notre Dame, Ohio State University, the University of California, and the University of Michigan, I joined a team investigating where and under what conditions university garments were being made. Under pressure from student activists across the country, a small group of university administrators had decided it was time to find out more about the garments bearing their schools' names and logos.

The research team was asked to evaluate garment manufacturing for the top apparel companies licensing the logos of these five universities. We looked at factories subcontracted by nine companies, including Adidas, Champion, and Nike. The nine alone outsource university apparel to over 180 factories in 26 countries. That may sound like a lot,

but it is the tip of the global production iceberg. Americans bought about $2.5 billion worth of university-logo garments in 1999. Overall, however, U.S. apparel sales accounted for over $180 billion. There are an estimated 80,000 factories around the world producing garments for the U.S. market. The university garment industry is particularly important not for its size, but for the critical opening it provides onto the larger industry.

The university research team visited factories in each of the top seven apparel-producing countries, China, El Salvador, Korea, Mexico, Pakistan, Thailand, and the United States. We inspected 13 work sites in all. I personally inspected factories for the project in China and Korea, and then inspected factories in Indonesia on my own to see what things looked like outside the official process. It was a learning experience I call "Sweatshops 101."

LESSON #1—GLOBAL OUTSOURCING

The garment industry is extremely complicated and highly disaggregated. The industry has multiple layers of licensees, brokers, jobbers, importer-exporters, component suppliers, and subcontractors on top of subcontractors.

The University of Michigan does not manufacture any of the products bearing its name. Nor does Notre Dame nor Harvard nor any other university. These schools simply license their names to apparel makers and other companies for a percentage of the sale—generally around 7% of the retail price for each T-shirt, sweatshirt, or key chain. Until recently, the universities had little interest in even knowing who produced their goods. If they tracked this at all, it was to catch companies using their logos without paying the licensing fee. →Royalty Fee

Sometimes the companies that license university names and logos own the factories where the apparel is produced. But more often the licensees simply contract production out to factories in developing countries. Nike owns none of the hundreds of factories that produce its garments and athletic shoes.

A sweatshirt factory itself may have multiple subcontractors who produce the fabric, embroider the logo, or stitch subcomponents. This global supply chain stretches from the university administration building, to the corporate office of the licensee companies, to large-scale factories in China and Mexico, to small-scale subcontractor factories everywhere in between, and in some cases, all the way to women stitching garments in their living rooms.

LESSON #2—THE GLOBAL SHELL GAME

The global garment industry is highly mobile, with contracts continuously shifting from subcontractor to subcontractor within and between countries. Licensees can move production between subcontractors after one year, one month, or even as little as one week.

It took the university research team three months to get from the licensee companies a list of the factories producing university-logo garments. However, because the actual factories producing university goods at any one time change so fast, by the time I had planned a trip to China and Korea to visit factories, the lists were essentially obsolete. One licensee in Korea had replaced eight of its eleven factories with new factories by the time I arrived in town. Over a four-month period, the company had contracted with 21 different factories.

Even after double-checking with a licensee, in almost every country the project team would arrive at the factory gates only to be told that the factories we planned to inspect were no longer producing university goods. Of course, some of this may have been the licensees playing games. Faced with inspections, some may have decided to shift production out of the chosen factory, or at least to tell us that it had been shifted.

Some of the largest, most profitable apparel firms in the world, known for their management prowess, however, simply did not know where their products were being produced. When asked how many factories Disney had around the world, company execs guessed there were 1,500 to 1,800 factories producing their garments, toys, videos, and other goods. As it turns out, they were only off by an order of magnitude. So far the company has counted over 20,000 factories around the world producing Disney-branded goods. Only recent exposés by labor, human rights, and environmental activists have convinced these companies that they need better control over their supply chains.

LESSON #3—NORMAL OPERATING CONDITIONS

The day an inspector visits a factory is not a normal day. Any factory that has prior knowledge of an inspection is very likely to make changes on the day of the visit.

In a Nike-contracted shoe factory in Indonesia I visited in June 2000, all of the workers in the hot press section of the plant (a particularly dangerous area) were wearing brand new black dress shoes on the day of our inspection. One of the workers explained they had been given the shoes that morning and were expected to return them at the end of the shift. Managers often give workers new protective equipment—such as gloves, respirators, and even shoes—on the day of an inspection. However, as the workers have no training in how to even use this equipment, it is common to see brand-new respirators being worn below workers' noses, around their necks, or even upside down.

At one factory the university team visited in Mexico, the factory manager wanted to guarantee that the inspectors would find his factory spotless. So he locked all of the bathrooms on the day of the inspection. Workers were not allowed to use the bathrooms until the project team showed up, hours into the work day.

Licensees and subcontractors often try to subvert monitoring. They block auditors from inspecting on certain days or from visiting certain parts of a plant, claim production has moved, feign ignorance of factory locations, keep multiple sets of books on wages and hours, coach workers on responses to interviews, and threaten workers against complaining to inspectors.

LESSON #4—CONDITIONS IN UNIVERSITY FACTORIES

Factories producing university apparel often violate local laws and university codes of conduct on maximum hours of work, minimum and overtime wages, freedom of association, and health and safety protections.

In a 300-worker apparel plant in Shanghai, the university team found that many of the workers were working far in excess of maximum overtime laws. A quick review of timecards found women working over 315 hours in a month and 20 consecutive days without a day off. The legal maximum in China is only 204 hours per month, with one day off in seven. A sample of 25 workers showed that the average overtime worked was 101 hours, while the legal limit is 36 hours per month. One manager explained these gross violations with a shrug, saying, "Timecards are just used to make sure workers show up on time. Workers are actually paid based on a piece rate system."

The factory also had a wide range of health and safety problems, including a lack of machine guarding on sewing and cutting machines, high levels of cotton dust in one section of the plant, several blocked aisles and fire exits, no running water in certain toilets, no information for workers on the hazardous chemicals they were using, and a lack of protective equipment for the workers.

Living conditions for the workers who lived in a dormitory on site were also poor. The dormitory had 12 women packed into each room on six bunk beds. Each floor had four rooms (48 women) and only one bathroom. These bathrooms had only two shower heads and four toilet stalls each, and no dividers between them.

And what of workers' rights to complain or demand better conditions? The union in this factory was openly being run by the management. While 70% of workers were "members" of the union, one manager explained, "We don't have U.S.-style unions here." No workers had ever tried to take control of this group or to form an independent union.

LESSON #5—THE CHALLENGES OF MONITORING

Finding a dozen factories is relatively easy compared to the job of tracking the thousands of rapidly changing factories that produce university goods each year. Systematically monitoring and evaluating their practices on wages, hours, discrimination, and health and safety issues is an even bigger challenge.

Most universities don't have the capacity to individually monitor the conditions in "their" factories, so some are joining together to create cooperative monitoring programs. The concept behind "independent monitoring" is to have a consulting firm or non-governmental organization inspect and evaluate a factory's compliance with a code of conduct. Two major monitoring systems, and a number of less influential initiatives, have recently been developed to meet the need for university monitoring. The Fair Labor Association (FLA) now has over 140 universities as members, and the Worker Rights Consortium (WRC) has over 55 member universities.

The FLA emerged from the Clinton-convened "White House Apparel Industry Partnership" in 1998. It is supported by a small group of apparel companies including Nike, Reebok, Adidas, Levi-Strauss, Liz Claiborne, and Philips Van Heusen. Students and labor-rights advocates have criticized the group for being an industry-dominated organization that allows companies to monitor only 10% of their factories, to use monitors that the companies pay directly, to control when and where monitors inspect, and to significantly restrict the information released to the public after the audits.

United Students Against Sweatshops (USAS) and UNITE (the largest garment-workers' union in the United States) founded the WRC in 1999 as an alternative to the FLA. The WRC promotes systems for verifying factory conditions after workers have complained or after inspections have occurred, as well as greater public disclosure of conditions. The WRC differs from the FLA in that it refuses to certify that any company meets some code of conduct. The group argues that because of the problems of monitoring, it is simply not possible to systematically monitor or certify a company's compliance. The WRC has been criticized by some universities and companies as being a haphazard "gotcha" monitoring system whose governing body excludes the very companies that must be part of solving these problems.

Both groups profess to support the International Labour Organization's core labor standards, including upholding workers' rights to freedom of association and collective bargaining, and prohibiting forced labor, child labor, and discrimination in the workplace. The WRC, however, goes further in requiring that workers be paid a "living wage," and that women's rights receive particular attention. Both programs assert a strong role for local NGOs, unions, and workers. However, the two have widely varying levels of transparency and public disclosure, and very different systems of sanctions and penalties.

LESSON #6—HOW NOT TO MONITOR

Corporate-sponsored monitoring systems seem almost designed to miss the most critical issues in the factories they inspect. Auditors often act as if they are on the side of management rather than the workers.

PricewaterhouseCoopers (PwC) is the largest private monitor of codes of conduct and corporate labor practices in the world. The company claims to have performed over 6,000 factory audits in 1999, including monitoring for Nike, Disney, Walmart, and the Gap. PwC monitors for many of the top university licensees, and was hired as the monitor for the university project.

PwC's monitoring systems are representative of current corporate monitoring efforts. The firm sends two auditors—who are actually financial accountants with minimal training on labor issues—into each factory for eight hours. The auditors use a checklist and a standard interview form to evaluate legal compliance, wages and benefits, working hours, freedom of association and collective bargaining, child labor, forced labor, disciplinary practices, and health and safety.

On the university project, PwC auditors failed to adequately examine any major issue in the factories I saw them inspect. In factories in Korea and Indonesia, PwC auditors completely missed exposure to toxic chemicals, something which could eventually cost workers their lives from cancer. In Korea, the auditors saw no problem in managers violating overtime wage laws. In China, the auditors went so far as to recommend ways for the managers to circumvent local laws on overtime hours, essentially providing advice on how to break university codes of conduct. And the auditors in Korea simply skipped the questions on workers' right to organize in their worker interviews, explaining, "They don't have a union in this factory, so those questions aren't relevant."

The PwC auditing method is biased towards managers. Before an inspection, PwC auditors send managers a questionnaire explaining what will be inspected. They prep managers at an opening meeting before each inspection. In the Chinese factory, they asked managers to enter wages and hours data into the PwC spreadsheet. Even the worker interviews were biased towards the managers. PwC auditors asked the managers to help them select workers to be interviewed, had the managers bring their personnel files, and then had the managers bring the workers into the office used for the interviews. The managers knew who was being interviewed, for how long, and on what issues. Workers knew this as well, and answered questions accordingly.

The final reports that PwC delivered to its clients gave a totally sanitized picture of the factories inspected. This is unsurprising, considering PwC stands to make huge amounts of money by providing companies with safe and comfortable audits.

WHERE TO BEGIN?

Universities face increasing public pressure to guarantee that workers are not being injured or exploited to produce their insignia products. They have no system, however, to track apparel production around the world, and often no idea where their production is occurring. Monitoring systems are still in their fledgling stages, so the universities are starting from a difficult position, albeit one they have profited from for years.

What can universities do about this? They should do what

they are best at: produce information. They should take the lead in demanding that corporations—beginning with those they do business with—open themselves up to public inspection and evaluation. Universities have done this before, such as during the anti-apartheid campaign for South Africa. By doing this on the sweatshop issue, universities could spur a critical dialogue on labor issues around the world.

To start, the universities could establish a central coordinating office to collect and compare information on factory performance for member universities' licensees. (The WRC has proposed such a model.) This new office would be responsible for keeping records on licensee compliance, for making this information available over the Internet, for registering local NGOs and worker organizations to conduct independent verifications of factory conditions, and for assessing sanctions.

Such a program would allow universities to evaluate different strategies for improving conditions in different parts of the world. This would avoid the danger of locking in one code of conduct or one certification system. In place of sporadic media exposés embarrassing one company at a time, we would have an international system of disclosure and learning—benchmarking good performers, identifying and targeting the worst performers, and motivating improvements.

It is clearly no longer enough to expose one company at a time, or to count on industry-paid consulting firms. The building blocks of a new system depend on information. This fits the mission of universities. Universities should focus on information gathering and dissemination, and most importantly, on learning. If the universities learn nothing else from "Sweatshops 101," they should learn that they still have a lot of homework do to—and that their next test will be coming soon.

May/June 2003

IS IT OIL?

BY ARTHUR MacEWAN

Before U.S. forces invaded Iraq, the United Nations inspection team that had been searching the country for weapons of mass destruction was unable to find either such weapons or a capacity to produce them in the near future. As of mid-April, while the U.S. military is apparently wrapping up its invasion, it too has not found the alleged weapons. The U.S. government continues to claim that weapons of mass destruction exist in Iraq but provides scant evidence to substantiate its claim.

While weapons of mass destruction are hard to find in Iraq, there is one thing that is relatively easy to find: oil. Lots of oil. With 112.5 billion barrels of proven reserves, Iraq has greater stores of oil than any country except Saudi Arabia. This combination—lots of oil and no weapons of mass destruction—begs the question: Is it oil and not weapons of mass destruction that motivates the U.S. government's aggressive policy towards Iraq?

THE U.S. "NEED" FOR OIL?

Much of the discussion of the United States, oil, and Iraq focuses on the U.S. economy's overall dependence on oil. We are a country highly dependent on oil, consuming far more than we produce. We have a small share, about 3%, of the world's total proven oil reserves. By depleting our reserves at a much higher rate than most other countries, the United States accounts for about 10% of world production. But, by importing from the rest of the world, we can consume oil at

a still higher rate: U.S. oil consumption is over 25% of the world's total. Thus, the United States relies on the rest of the world's oil in order to keep its economy running—or at least running in its present oil-dependent form. Moreover, for the United States to operate as it does and maintain current standards of living, we need access to oil at low prices. Otherwise we would have to turn over a large share of U.S. GDP as payment to those who supply us with oil.

Iraq could present the United States with supply problems. With a hostile government in Baghdad, the likelihood that the United States would be subject to some sort of boycott as in the early 1970s is greater than otherwise. Likewise, a government in Baghdad that does not cooperate with Washington could be a catalyst to a reinvigoration of the Organization of Petroleum Exporting Countries (OPEC) and the result could be higher oil prices.

Such threats, however, while real, are not as great as they might first appear. Boycotts are hard to maintain. The sellers of oil need to sell as much as the buyers need to buy; oil exporters depend on the U.S. market, just as U.S. consumers depend on those exporters. (An illustration of this mutual dependence is provided by the continuing oil trade between Iraq and the United States in recent years. During 2001, while the two countries were in a virtual state of war, the United States bought 284 million barrels of oil from Iraq, about 7% of U.S. imports and almost a third of Iraq's exports.) Also, U.S. oil imports come from diverse sources, with less than half from OPEC countries and less than one-quarter from Persian Gulf nations.

Most important, ever since the initial surge of OPEC in the 1970s, the organization has followed a policy of price restraint. While price restraint may in part be a strategy of political cooperation, resulting from the close U.S.-Saudi relationship in particular, it is also a policy adopted because high prices are counter-productive for OPEC itself; high prices lead consumers to switch sources of supply and conserve energy, undercutting the longer term profits for the oil suppliers. Furthermore, a sudden rise in prices can lead to general economic disruption, which is no more desirable for the oil exporters than for the oil importers. To be sure, the United States would prefer to have cooperative governments in oil producing countries, but the specter of another boycott as in the 1970s or somewhat higher prices for oil hardly provides a rationale, let alone a justification, for war.

> IRAQI OIL COULD COST AS LITTLE AS 97 CENTS A BARREL TO PRODUCE. AS ONE OIL EXECUTIVE PUT IT, "NINETY CENTS A BARREL FOR OIL THAT SELLS FOR $30—THAT'S THE KIND OF BUSINESS ANYONE WOULD WANT TO BE IN."

THE PROFITS PROBLEM

There is, however, also the importance of oil in the profits of large U.S. firms: the oil companies themselves (with ExxonMobil at the head of the list) but also the numerous drilling, shipping, refining, and marketing firms that make up the rest of the oil industry. Perhaps the most famous of this latter group, because former CEO Dick Cheney is now vice president, is the Halliburton Company, which supplies a wide range of equipment and engineering services to the industry. Even while many governments—Saudi Arabia, Kuwait, and Venezuela, for example—have taken ownership of their countries' oil reserves, these companies have been able to maintain their profits because of their decisive roles at each stage in the long sequence from exploration through drilling to refining and marketing. Ultimately, however, as with any resource-based industry, the monopolistic position—and thus the large profits—of the firms that dominate the oil industry depends on their access to the supply of the resource. Their access, in turn, depends on the relations they are able to establish with the governments of oil-producing countries.

From the perspective of the major U.S. oil companies, a hostile Iraqi government presents a clear set of problems. To begin with, there is the obvious: because Iraq has a lot of oil, access to that oil would represent an important profit-making opportunity. What's more, Iraqi oil can be easily extracted and thus produced at very low cost. With all oil selling at the same price on the world market, Iraqi oil thus presents opportunities for especially large profits per unit of production. According to the *Guardian* newspaper (London), Iraqi oil could cost as little as 97 cents a barrel to produce, compared to the UK's North Sea oil produced at $3 to $4 per barrel. As one oil executive told the *Guardian* last November, "Ninety cents a barrel for oil that sells for $30—that's the kind of business anyone would want to be in. A 97% profit margin—you can live with that." The *Guardian* continues: "The stakes are high. Iraq could be producing 8 million barrels a day within the decade. The math is impressive—8 million times 365 at $30 per barrel or $87.5 billion a year. Any share would be worth fighting for." The question for the oil companies is: what share will they be able to claim and what share will be claimed by the Iraqi government? The split would undoubtedly be more favorable for the oil companies with a compliant U.S.-installed government in Baghdad.

Furthermore, the conflict is not simply one between the private oil companies and the government of Iraq. The U.S.-based firms and their British (and British-Dutch) allies are vying with French, Russian, and Chinese firms for access to Iraqi oil. During recent years, firms from these other nations signed oil exploration and development contracts with the Hussein government in Iraq, and, if there were no "regime change," they would preempt the operations of the U.S. and British firms in that country. If, however, the U.S. government succeeds in replacing the government of Saddam Hussein with its preferred allies in the Iraqi opposition, the outlook will change dramatically. According to Ahmed Chalabi, head of the Iraqi National Congress and a figure in the Iraqi opposition who seems to be currently favored by Washington, "The future democratic government in Iraq will be grateful to the United States for helping the Iraqi people liberate themselves and getting rid of Saddam.... American companies, we expect, will play an important and leading role in the future oil situation." (In recent years, U.S. firms have not been fully frozen out of the oil business in Iraq. For example, according to a June 2001 report in the *Washington Post*, while Vice President Cheney was CEO at Halliburton Company during the late 1990s, the firm operated through subsidiaries to sell some $73 million of oil production equipment and spare parts to Iraq.)

The rivalry with French, Russian and Chinese oil companies is in part driven by the direct prize of the profits to be obtained from Iraqi operations. In addition, in order to maintain their dominant positions in the world oil industry, it is important for the U.S. and British-based firms to deprive their rivals of the growth potential that access to Iraq would afford. In any monopolistic industry, leading firms need to deny their potential competitors market position and control of new sources of supply; otherwise, those competitors will be in a better position to challenge the leaders. The British Guardian reports that the Hussein government is "believed to have offered the French company TotalFinaElf exclusive rights to the largest of Iraq's oil fields, the Majoon, which would more than double the company's entire output at a single stroke." Such a development would catapult Total-FinaElf from the second ranks into the first ranks of the major oil firms. The basic structure of the world oil industry would not change, but the sharing of power and profits among the leaders would be altered. Thus for ExxonMobil, Chevron, Shell and the other traditional "majors" in the industry, access to Iraq is a defensive as well as an offensive goal. ("Regime change" in Iraq will not necessarily provide the legal basis for cancellation of contracts signed between the Hussein regime and various oil companies. International law would not allow a new regime simply to turn things over to the U.S. oil companies. "Should 'regime change' happen, one thing is guaranteed," according to the *Guardian*, "shortly afterwards there will be the mother of all legal battles.")

Oil companies are big and powerful. The biggest, ExxonMobil, had 2002 profits of $15 billion, more than any other corporation, in the United States or in the world. Chevron-Texaco came in with $3.3 billion in 2002 profits, and Phillips-Tosco garnered $1.7 billion. British Petroleum-Amoco-Arco pulled in $8 billion, while Royal Dutch/Shell Group registered almost $11 billion. Firms of this magnitude have a large role affecting the policies of their governments, and, for that matter, the governments of many other countries.

With the ascendancy of the Bush-Cheney team to the White House in 2000, perhaps the relationship between oil and the government became more personal, but it was not new. Big oil has been important in shaping U.S. foreign policy since the end of the 19th century (to say nothing of its role in shaping other policy realms, particularly environmental regulation). From 1914, when the Marines landed at Mexico's Tampico Bay to protect U.S. oil interests, to the CIA-engineered overthrow of the Mosadegh government in Iran in 1953, to the close relationship with the oppressive Saudi monarchy through the past 70 years, oil and the interests of the oil companies have been central factors in U.S. foreign policy. Iraq today is one more chapter in a long story.

THE LARGER ISSUE

Yet in Iraq today, as in many other instances of the U.S. government's international actions, oil is not the whole story. The international policies of the U.S. government are certainly shaped in significant part by the interests of U.S.-based firms, but not only the oil companies. ExxonMobil may have had the largest 2002 profits, but there are many additional large U.S. firms with international interests: Citbank and the other huge financial firms; IBM, Microsoft, and other information technology companies; General Motors and Ford; Merck, Pfizer and the other pharmaceutical corporations; large retailers like MacDonald's and Wal-Mart (and many more) depend on access to foreign markets and foreign sources of supply for large shares of their sales and profits.

The U.S. government (like other governments) has long defined its role in international affairs as protecting the interests of its nationals, and by far the largest interests of U.S. nationals abroad are the interests of these large U.S.

companies. The day-to-day activities of U.S. embassies and consular offices around the world are dominated by efforts to further the interests of particular U.S. firms—for example, helping the firms establish local markets, negotiate a country's regulations, or develop relations with local businesses. When the issue is large, such as when governments in low-income countries have attempted to assure the availability of HIV-AIDS drugs in spite of patents held by U.S. firms, Washington steps directly into the fray. On the broadest level, the U.S. government tries to shape the rules and institutions of the world economy in ways that work well for U.S. firms. These rules are summed up under the heading of "free trade," which in practice means free access of U.S. firms to the markets and resources of the rest of the world.

In normal times, Washington uses diplomacy and institutions like the International Monetary Fund, the World Bank, and the World Trade Organization to shape the rules of the world economy. But times are not always "normal." When governments have attempted to remove their economies from the open system and break with the "rules of the game," the U.S. government has responded with overt or covert military interventions. Latin America has had a long history of such interventions, where Guatemala (1954), Cuba (1961), Chile (1973) and Nicaragua (1980s) provide fairly recent examples. The Middle East also provides several illustrations of this approach to foreign affairs, with U.S. interventions in Iran (1953), Lebanon (1958), Libya (1981), and now Iraq. These interventions are generally presented as efforts to preserve freedom and democracy, but, if freedom and democracy were actually the goals of U.S. interventions the record would be very different; both the Saudi monarchy and the Shah of Iran, in an earlier era, would then have been high on the U.S. hit list. (Also, as with maintaining the source of supply of oil, the U.S. government did not intervene in Guatemala in 1954 to maintain our supply of bananas; the profits of the United Fruit Company, however, did provide a powerful causal factor.)

> IF FREEDOM AND DEMOCRACY WERE ACTUALLY THE GOALS OF U.S. INTERVENTIONS, THE RECORD WOULD BE VERY DIFFERENT.

The rhetorical rationale of U.S. foreign policy has seen many alterations and adjustments over the last century: at the end of the 19th century, U.S. officials spoke of the need to spread Christianity; Woodrow Wilson defined the mission as keeping the world safe for democracy; for most of the latter half of the 20th century, the fight against Communism was the paramount rationale; for a fleeting moment during the Carter administration, the protection of human rights entered the government's vocabulary; in recent years we have seen the war against drugs; and now we have the current administration's war against terrorism.

What distinguishes the current administration in Washington is neither its approach toward foreign affairs and U.S. business interests in general nor its policy in the Middle East and oil interests in particular. Even its rhetoric builds on well established traditions, albeit with new twists. What does distinguish the Bush administration is the clarity and aggressiveness with which it has put forth its goal of maintaining U.S. domination internationally. The "Bush Doctrine" that the administration has articulated claims legitimacy for preemptive action against those who might threaten U.S. interests, and it is clear from the statement of that doctrine in last September's issuance of The National Security Strategy of the United States of America that "U.S. interests" includes economic interests.

The economic story is never the whole story, and oil is never the whole economic story. In the particular application of U.S. power, numerous strategic and political considerations come into play. With the application of the Bush Doctrine in the case of Iraq, the especially heinous character of the Hussein regime is certainly a factor, as is the regime's history of conflict with other nations of the region (at times with U.S. support) and its apparent efforts at developing nuclear, chemical, and biological weapons; certainly the weakness of the Iraqi military also affects the U.S. government's willingness to go to war. Yet, as September's Security Strategy document makes clear, the U.S. government is concerned with domination and a major factor driving that goal of domination is economic. In the Middle East, Iraq and elsewhere, oil—or, more precisely, the profit from oil—looms large in the picture.

An earlier version of this article was prepared for the newsletter of the Joiner Center for War and Social Consequences at the University of Massachusetts-Boston.

ARTICLE 8.12

May/June 2003

FAIR TRADE AND FARM SUBSIDIES: HOW BIG A DEAL?

TWO VIEWS

In September 2003, the global free-trade express was derailed—at least temporarily—when the World Trade Organization talks in Cancún, Mexico, collapsed. At the time, the inconsistency of the United States and other rich countries—pressing poor countries to adopt free trade while continuing to subsidize and protect selected domestic sectors, especially agriculture—received wide attention for the first time. Where does ending agricultural subsidies and trade barriers in the rich countries rank as a strategy for achieving global economic justice? Dollars & Sense *asked progressive researchers on different sides of this question to make their case.*

MAKE TRADE FAIR

BY GAWAIN KRIPKE

Trade can be a powerful engine for economic growth in developing countries and can help pull millions of people out of poverty. Trade also offers an avenue of growth that relies less than other development strategies on the fickle charity of wealthy countries or the self-interest of multinational corporations. However, current trade rules create enormous obstacles that prevent people in developing countries from realizing the benefits of trade. A growing number of advocacy organizations are now tackling this fundamental problem, hoping to open a route out of poverty for tens of millions of people who have few other prospects.

FALSE PROMISES ON TRADE

BY DEAN BAKER AND MARK WEISBROT

Farmers throughout the Third World are suffering not from too much free trade, but from not enough. That's the impression you get from most media coverage of the recent World Trade Organization (WTO) meetings in Cancún. The *New York Times*, *Washington Post*, and other major news outlets devoted huge amounts of space to news pieces and editorials arguing that agricultural subsidies in rich countries are a major cause of poverty in the developing world. If only these subsidies were eliminated, and the doors to imports from developing countries opened, the argument goes, then the playing field would be level and genuinely free trade

continued on page 157

continued on page 158

MAKE TRADE FAIR
continued from page 156

continued from page 156

WHY TRADE?

Poor countries have few options for improving the welfare of their people and generating economic growth. Large debt burdens limit the ability of governments in the developing world to make investments and provide education, clean water, and other critical services. Despite some recent progress on the crushing problem of debt, only about 15% of the global South's $300 billion in unpayable debt has been eliminated.

Poor countries have traditionally looked to foreign aid and private investment to drive economic development. Both of these are proving inadequate. To reach the goals of the United Nations' current Millenium Development campaign, including reducing hunger and providing universal primary education, wealthy countries would have to increase their foreign aid from a paltry 0.23% of GDP to 0.7%. Instead, foreign aid flows are stagnant and are losing value against inflation and population growth. In 2001, the United States spent just 0.11% of GDP on foreign aid.

Likewise, although global foreign direct investment soared to unprecedented levels in the late 1990s, most developing countries are not attractive to foreign investors. The bulk of foreign private investment in the developing world, more than 76%, goes to ten large countries including China, Brazil, and Mexico. For the majority of developing countries, particularly the poorest, foreign investment remains a modest contributor to economic growth, on a par with official foreign aid. Sub-Saharan Africa, with the highest concentration of the world's poor, attracted only $14 billion in 2001.

In this environment, trade offers an important potential source of economic growth for developing countries. Relatively modest gains in their share of global trade could yield large benefits for developing countries. Gaining an additional 1% share of the $8 trillion global export market, for example, would generate more revenue than all current foreign aid spending.

But today, poor countries are bit players in the global trade game. More than 40% of the world's population lives in low-income countries, but these countries generate only 3% of global exports. Despite exhortations from the United States and other wealthy countries to export, many of the poorest countries are actually losing share in export markets. Africa generated a mere 2.4% of world exports of goods in 2001, down from 3.1% in 1990.

Many factors contribute to the poorest countries' inability to gain a foothold in export trade, but the core problem is that the playing field is heavily tilted against them. This is particularly true in the farm sector. The majority of the global South population lives in rural areas and depends on agriculture for survival. Moreover, poverty is concentrated in the countryside: more than three-quarters of the world's poorest people, the 1.1 billion who live on less than one dollar a day, live in rural areas. This means that agriculture must be at the center of trade, development, and poverty-reduction strategies throughout the developing world.

Two examples demonstrate the unfair rules of the global trading system in agriculture.

"IT'S NOT WHITE GOLD ANYMORE"

Cotton is an important crop in Central and West Africa. More than two million households depend directly on the crop for their livelihoods, with millions more indirectly involved. Despite serious social and environmental problems that have accompanied the expansion of cotton cultivation, cotton provides families with desperately needed cash for health care, education, and even food. The cotton crop can make a big difference in reducing poverty. For example, a 2002 World Bank study found a strong link between cotton prices and rural welfare in Benin, a poor West African country.

Cotton is important at a macroeconomic level as well; in 11 African countries, it accounts for more than one-quarter of export revenue. But since the mid-1990s, the cotton market has experienced chronic price depression. Though prices have rebounded in recent months, they remain below the long-term average of $0.72 a pound. Lower prices mean less export revenue for African countries and lower incomes for African cotton farmers.

But not for U.S. cotton farmers. Thanks to farm subsidies, U.S. cotton producers are insulated from the market and have produced bumper crops that depress prices worldwide. The global price of cotton is 20% lower than it would be without U.S. subsidies, according to an analysis by the International Cotton Advisory Committee. Oxfam estimates that in 2001, as a result of U.S. cotton subsidies, eight countries in Africa lost approximately $300 million—about one-quarter of the total amount the U.S. Agency for International Development will spend in Africa next year.

DUMPING ON OUR NEIGHBOR

Mexico has been growing corn (or maize) for 10,000 years. Today, nearly three million Mexican farmers grow corn, but they are facing a crisis due to sharply declining prices. Real prices for corn have fallen 70% since 1994. Poverty is widespread in corn-growing areas like Chiapas, Oaxaca, and Guerrero. Every year, large numbers of rural Mexicans leave the land and migrate to the cities or to the United States to try to earn a living.

The price drops are due to increased U.S. corn exports to Mexico, which have more than tripled since 1994. These exports result in large part from U.S. government policies that encourage overproduction. While Mexican farmers struggle to keep their farms and support their families, the United States pours up to $10 billion annually into subsidies for U.S. corn producers. By comparison, the entire Mexican government budget for agriculture is $1 billion. Between 2000 and 2002, a metric ton of American corn sold on export markets for $20 less than the average cost to produce it. The United States controls nearly 70% of the global corn market, so this dumping has a huge impact on prices and on small-scale corn farmers in Mexico.

To be fair, the Mexican government shares some of the responsibility for the crisis facing corn farmers. Although the North American Free Trade Agreement (NAFTA) opened trade between the United States and Mexico, the Mexican government voluntarily lowered tariffs on corn beyond what was required by NAFTA. As NAFTA is fully phased in, though, Mexico will lose the option of raising tariffs to safeguard poor farmers from a flood of subsidized corn.

WHAT DO POOR COUNTRIES WANT?

Cotton and corn illustrate the problems that current trade regimes pose for developing countries and particularly for the world's poorest people. African countries want to engage in global trade but are crowded out by subsidized cotton from the United States. The livelihood of Mexican corn farmers is undermined by dumped U.S. corn. In both of these cases, and many more, it's all perfectly legal. WTO and NAFTA rules provide near impunity to rich countries that subsidize agriculture, and increasingly restrict developing countries' ability to safeguard their farmers and promote development.

How much do subsidies and trade barriers in the rich countries really cost the developing world? One study estimates that developing countries lose $24 billion annually in agricultural income—not a trivial amount. In today's political climate, it's hard to see where else these countries are going to find $24 billion to promote their economic development.

The benefits of higher prices for farmers in the developing world have to be balanced against the potential cost to consumers, both North and South. However, it's important to remember that many Northern consumers actually pay more for food *because of* subsidies. In fact, they often pay twice: first in higher food costs, and then in taxes to pay for the subsidies. Consumers in poor countries will pay more for food if farm commodity prices rise, but the majority of people who work in agriculture will benefit. Since poverty is concentrated in rural areas, the gains to agricultural producers are particularly important.

However, some low-income countries are net food importers and could face difficulties if prices rise. Assuring affordable food is critical, but this goal can be achieved much more cheaply and efficiently than by spending $100 billion on farm subsidies in the rich countries. The World Bank says that low-income countries that depend on food imports faced a net agricultural trade deficit of $2.8 billion in 2000-2001. The savings realized from reducing agricultural subsidies could easily cover this shortfall.

Each country faces different challenges. Developing countries, in particular, need flexibility to develop appropriate solutions to address their economic, humanitarian, and development situations. Broad-stroke solutions inevitably fail to address specific circumstances. But the complexity of the issues must not be used as an excuse for inaction by policy-makers. Failure to act to lift trade barriers and agricultural subsidies will only mean growing inequity, continuing poverty, and endless injustice.

Sources: Xinshen Diao, Eugenio Diaz-Bonilla, and Sherman Robinson, "How Much Does It Hurt? The Impact of Agricultural Trade Policies on Developing Countries," (International Food Policy Research Institute, Washington, D.C., 2003); "Global Development Finance: Striving for Stability in Development Finance," (World Bank, 2003); Lyuba Zarksy and Kevin Gallagher, "Searching for the Holy Grail? Making FDI Work for Sustainable Development,"(Tufts Global Development and Environment Institute/WWF, March 2003); Oxfam's website on trade issues <www.maketradefair. com>.

FALSE PROMISES ON TRADE

continued from page 156

would work its magic on poverty in the Third World. The media decided that agricultural subsidies were the major theme of the trade talks even if evidence indicated that other issues—for example, patent and copyright protection, rules on investment, or developing countries' right to regulate imports—would have more impact on the well-being of people in those countries.

There is certainly some element of truth in the argument that agricultural subsidies and barriers to imports can hurt farmers in developing countries. There are unquestionably farmers in a number of developing countries who have been undersold and even put out of business by imports whose prices are artificially low thanks to subsidies the rich countries pay their farmers. It is also true that many of these subsidy programs are poorly targeted, benefiting primarily large farmers and often encouraging environmentally harmful farming practices.

However, the media have massively overstated the potential gains that poor countries might get from the elimination of farm subsidies and import barriers. The risk of this exaggeration is that it encourages policy-makers and concerned nongovernmental organizations (NGOs) to focus their energies on an issue that is largely peripheral to economic development and to ignore much more important matters.

To put the issue in perspective: the World Bank, one of the most powerful advocates of removing most trade barriers, has estimated the gains from removing all the rich countries' remaining barriers to trade in manufactured and farm products *and* ending agricultural subsidies. The total estimated gain to low- and middle-income countries, when the changes are phased in by 2015, is an extra 0.6% of GDP. In other words, an African country with an annual income of $500 per person would see that figure rise to $503 as a result of removing these barriers and subsidies.

SIMPLISTIC TALK ON SUBSIDIES

The media often claim that the rich countries give $300 billion annually in agricultural subsidies to their farmers. In fact, this is not the amount of money paid by governments to farmers, which is actually less than $100 billion. The $300 billion figure is an estimate of the excess cost to consumers in rich nations that results from all market barriers in agriculture. Most of this cost is attributable to higher food prices that result from planting restrictions, import tariffs, and quotas.

The distinction is important, because not all of the $300 billion ends up in the pockets of farmers in rich nations. Some of it goes to exporters in developing nations, as when sugar producers in Brazil or Nicaragua are able to sell their sugar in the United States for an amount that is close to three times the world price. The higher price that U.S. consumers pay for this sugar is part of the $300 billion that many accounts mistakenly describe as subsidies to farmers in rich countries.

Another significant misrepresentation is the idea that cheap imports from the rich nations are always bad for developing countries. When subsides from rich countries lower the price of agricultural imports to developing countries, consumers in those countries benefit. This is one reason why a recent World Bank study found that the removal of *all* trade barriers and subsidies in the United States would have no net effect on growth in sub-Saharan Africa.

In addition, removing the rich countries' subsidies or barriers will not level the playing field—since there will still often be large differences in productivity—and thus will not save developing countries from the economic and social upheavals that such "free trade" agreements as the WTO have in store for them. These agreements envision a massive displacement of people employed in agriculture, as farmers in developing countries are pushed out by international competition. It took the United States 100 years, from 1870 to 1970, to reduce agricultural employment from 53% to under 5% of the labor force, and the transition nonetheless caused considerable social unrest. To compress such a process into a period of a few years or even a decade, by removing remaining agricultural trade barriers in poor countries, is a recipe for social explosion.

It is important to realize that in terms of the effect on developing countries, low agricultural prices due to subsidies for rich-country farmers have the exact same impact as low agricultural prices that stem from productivity gains. If the opponents of agricultural subsidies consider the former to be harmful to the developing countries, then they should be equally concerned about the impact of productivity gains

in the agricultural sectors of rich countries.

Insofar as cheap food imports might have a negative impact on a developing country's economy, the problem can be easily remedied by an import tariff. In this situation, the developing world would gain the most if those countries that benefit from cheap imported food have access to it, while those that are better served by protecting their domestic agricultural sector are allowed to impose tariffs without fear of retaliation from rich nations. This would make much more sense, and cause much less harm, than simply removing all trade barriers and subsidies on both sides of the North-South economic divide. The concept of a "level playing field" is a false one. Mexican corn farmers, for example, are not going to be able to compete with U.S. agribusiness, subsidies or no subsidies, nor should they have to.

It is of course good that such institutions as the *New York Times* are pointing out the hypocrisy of governments in the United States, Europe, and Japan in insisting that developing countries remove trade barriers and subsidies while keeping some of their own. And the subsidy issue was exploited very skillfully by developing-country governments and NGOs at the recent Cancún talks. The end result—the collapse of the talks—was a great thing for the developing world. So were the ties that were forged among countries such as those in the group of 22, enabling them to stand up to the rich countries. But the WTO remedy of eliminating subsidies and trade barriers across the board will not save developing countries from most of the harm caused by current policies. Just the opposite: the removal of import restrictions in the developing world could wipe out tens of millions of farmers and cause enormous economic damage.

AVOIDING THE KEY ISSUES

While reducing agricultural protection and subsidies just in the rich countries might in general be a good thing for developing countries, the gross exaggeration of its importance has real consequences, because it can divert attention from issues of far more pressing concern. One such issue is the role that the IMF continues to play as enforcer of a creditors' cartel in the developing world, threatening any country that defies its edicts with a cutoff of access to international credit. One of the most devastated recent victims of the IMF's measures has been Argentina, which saw its economy thrown into a depression after the failure of a decade of neoliberal economic policies. The IMF's harsh treatment of Argentina last year, while it was suffering from the worst depression in its history, is widely viewed in the developing world as a warning to other countries that might deviate from the IMF's recommendations. One result is that Brazil's new president, elected with an overwhelming mandate for change, must struggle to promote growth in the face of 22% interest rates demanded by the IMF's monetary experts.

Similarly, most of sub-Saharan Africa is suffering from an unpayable debt burden. While there has been some limited relief offered in recent years, the remaining debt service burden is still more than the debtor countries in that region spend on health care or education. The list of problems that the current world economic order imposes on developing countries is long: bans on the industrial policies that led to successful development in the West, the imposition of patents on drugs and copyrights on computer software and recorded material, inappropriate macroeconomic policies imposed by the IMF and the World Bank. All of these factors are likely to have far more severe consequences for the development prospects of poor countries than the agricultural policies of rich countries.

Sources: Elena Ianchovichina, Aaditya Mattoo, and Marcelo Olareaga, "Unrestricted Market Access for Sub-Saharan Africa: How much is it worth and who pays," (World Bank, April 2001); Mark Weisbrot and Dean Baker, "The Relative Impact of Trade Liberalization on Developing Countries," (Center for Economic and Policy Research, June 2002).

CONTRIBUTORS

Randy Albelda, a *Dollars & Sense* Associate, teaches economics at the University of Massachusetts-Boston.

Dean Baker is co-director of the Center for Economic and Policy Research.

Aldo Caliari is coordinator of the Rethinking Bretton Woods Project at the Center of Concern.

Angel Chen is a former *Dollars & Sense* intern.

Attieno Davis is the Racial Wealth Divide Education Coordinator at United for a Fair Economy.

Daniel Fireside is co-editor of *Dollars & Sense.*

Ellen Frank, a *Dollars & Sense* collective member, teaches economics at Emmanuel College in Boston.

James K. Galbraith is professor at the Lyndon B. Johnson School of Public Affairs, University of Texas at Austin, and Senior Scholar of the Levy Economics Institute.

Amy Gluckman is a co-editor of *Dollars & Sense.*

Elise Gould is an economist at the Economic Policy Institute, where she specializes in health and labor issues.

Lena Graber is a former *Dollars & Sense* intern.

William Greider has been a political journalist for more than 35 years. He is currently the National Affairs Correspondent for the *Nation* magazine.

Deborah James is the Global Economy Director of Global Exchange.

Paul Krugman teaches economics at Princeton and is a columnist for the *New York Times.*

Gawain Kripke is a senior policy advisor at Oxfam America.

Arthur MacEwan, a *Dollars & Sense* Associate, teaches economics at the University of Massachusetts-Boston.

Ann Markusen is a former Senior Fellow at the Council on Foreign Relations and Professor of Public Policy and Planning at the Humphrey Institute of Public Affairs, University of Minnesota.

Gretchen McClain, a former member of the *Dollars & Sense* -collective, is an economic consultant.

John Miller, a *Dollars & Sense* collective member, teaches economics at Wheaton College.

Gina Neff is the associate director of Economists Allied for Arms Reduction.

Dara O'Rourke is an assistant professor in the Department of Environmental Science, Policy, and Management at the University of California, Berkeley.

Doug Orr teaches economics at Eastern Washington University.

Thomas Palley is an economist who has held positions at the AFL-CIO, Open Society Institute, and the U.S./China Economic and Security Review Commission.

Robert Pollin teaches economics and is co-director of the Political Economy Research Institute at the University of Massachusetts-Amherst. He is also a *Dollars & Sense* Associate.

Alejandro Reuss is former co-editor of *Dollars & Sense.*

William M. Rodgers III teaches economics at Rutgers University and is the chief economist at the John J. Heldrich Center for Workforce Development. He was the chief economist at the U.S. Department of Labor from 2000-2001.

Jonathan Rowe is a contributing editor at the *Washington Monthly.*

Adria Scharf is co-editor of *Dollars & Sense.*

Michelle Sheehan is a member of the *Dollars & Sense* collective.

Bryan Snyder teaches economics at Kansas State University-Manhattan.

William E. Spriggs is a senior fellow with the Economic Policy Institute and was formerly the executive director of the National Urban League Institute for Opportunity and Equality.

Eoghan Stafford is a former *Dollars & Sense* intern.

Bob Sutcliffe is an economist at the University of the Basque Country in Bilbao, Spain.

Chris Tilly, a former *Dollars & Sense* collective member, teaches at the University of Massachusetts-Lowell.

Mark Weisbrot is co-director of the Center for Economic and Policy Research in Washington, D.C.

Rick Wolff teaches economics at the University of Massachusetts-Amherst.

Keith Yearman is assistant professor of geography at the College of DuPage.